# First In Line

One Woman's Groundbreaking Path to
Ordination in the Church of England

## Judith Rose

First Published in 2025 by Kevin Mayhew Ltd

Fengate Farm, Rattlesden, Bury St Edmunds, Suffolk, IP30 0SZ

Copyright © 2025 Judith Rose

ISBN (paperback): 9781838582210
ISBN ( eBook): 9781838582227
Paperback product code: 1501748
eBook product code: 1501749

All rights reserved.

No part of this book may be reproduced in any form or by any electronic or mechanical means, including information storage and retrieval systems, without written permission from the author, except for the use of brief quotations in a book review.

## Contents

| | |
|---|---|
| Foreword | v |
| Introduction | vii |
| 1. My First Career | 1 |
| 2. The Beginning of my Faith Journey | 6 |
| 3. The Call of God | 9 |
| 4. A Parish Worker | 17 |
| 5. What Next? | 22 |
| 6. Becoming a Deaconess | 26 |
| 7. Should Women be Ordained? | 35 |
| 8. Moving On | 40 |
| 9. Cathedral Ministry | 43 |
| 10. Acting Team Vicar | 52 |
| 11. The Diaconate | 57 |
| 12. Conducting Weddings | 62 |
| 13. Deacons Now | 66 |
| 14. The Debate Continues | 69 |
| 15. Rural Dean | 73 |
| 16. Multitasking | 78 |
| 17. Bishop's Chaplain | 82 |
| 18. David | 86 |
| 19. The Decision | 93 |
| 20. Ordination to the Priesthood | 98 |
| 21. Archdeacon | 104 |
| 22. The Implications of Change | 112 |
| 23. Women Bishops | 118 |
| Post Script: Titles | 121 |
| Time Lines | 123 |
| Acknowledgments | 125 |

# Foreword

The early 1990s were the culmination of many years of debate and controversy within the Church of England about the ordination of women to the priesthood. As Bishop of Rochester, I was embarrassed that we had no female on the senior staff meeting. From a human point of view this was a great weakness in the leadership dynamic of the diocese. From a political angle it meant that we didn't hear directly from a woman minister when we were making decisions which might easily affect the way our minds were informed. From a theological viewpoint this gap in our work together was a serious flaw.

The problem was solved by appointing Judith Rose as my chaplain. Judith was already a highly respected senior Deaconess in the diocese, was a member of General Synod and a competent administrator and understood the theological questions which currently faced the church. I was so relieved when Judith said yes to my invitation. As my chaplain she had a place at senior staff meetings.

The General Synod had also seen her value and she became

FOREWORD

a member of the panel of chairmen. In that work, Judith played a vital role in seeing through the motions which eventually opened the doors to women's priesthood. It was a memorable day in 1994 when I ordained Judith amongst the first women priests. My successor at Rochester later appointed Judith as the first woman Archdeacon in the country.

There is, therefore, no one better than Judith Rose to tell the inside story of those tumultuous years, when the character of the Church of England was changed forever. Mixing the national narrative with her very personal story, she has given us a unique insight which will become a crucial contribution to the whole story of the Church of England.

- Michael Turnbull
  *Bishop of Rochester 1988-1994*
  *Bishop of Durham 1994-2003*

# Introduction

I never set out to be a pioneer or a trail blazer, but things just sort of happened to me as the second half of my life progressed. On looking back, I realise that on several occasions I have found myself in a job or with a responsibility before I was officially given the appropriate title or authority. I am certainly not alone in that. Many people get on with doing a job, and doing it well, without the powers that be giving that person the recognition that their competence and dedication to duty deserves. Perhaps this is a situation that particularly affects women. So my experience, as a woman, is certainly not unique. What makes my experience unusual is that it has happened in the context of the Church of England during the past 50 years.

It was in 1966 that I began my full time paid ministry as what was then called a Parish Worker. Back then, and even before then, there were questions being asked about the role of women in the leadership of the Anglican Church; but the issue was not to the fore, and certainly not in the circles in which I moved. It was not an issue that particularly interested or bothered me. It

## Introduction

did not enter my thinking when I was wrestling with my call to ministry in the church. I don't even remember the subject being discussed when I was at theological college in 1964/66, even though it was a college that only trained women.

Those with any basic knowledge of the church will realise that for the nearly 60 years since 1966, the issue of women's roles in leadership in the Church of England has been a contentious one - and those years have coincided with the years I spent in ministry. So my ministry has been coterminous with that development.

The expression 'a glass ceiling' has often been applied to situations in which women, because they are women, are unable to progress in their career, however well qualified. It usually applies in situations in which there is no legal prohibition to their progress, but nevertheless there are unwritten rules or prejudices which prevent women reaching their potential. Hence a glass ceiling.

Prior to 1994 there was an actual legal ceiling which prevented women from being considered for the priesthood or episcopate, but my experience showed that there were cracks beginning to appear in that ceiling. Some of us believe that the Spirit of God was challenging the situation that had persisted in the Church for many centuries, and I happened to be around while that was happening.

Although I did not seek to break through boundaries, I found myself on several occasions ahead of the church. I found myself, in effect, doing a job for which the church was not yet ready to give me the appropriate title. The title did not particularly matter to me, so long as I was able to use my gifts and the

## INTRODUCTION

experience that I gained in the service of the church in the places in which I found myself. How did I end up as the first woman Archdeacon in the Church of England, and indeed the only woman Archdeacon in that capacity for about 3 years? This account tells how that came about.

# Chapter 1

# My First Career

I was born in 1937 in London, the eldest of 4 children. When war broke out in 1939, it was decided that my mother and I should go to stay in Somerset with relations. My father had been born in that part of the country and had sisters living there. By the end of the war my parents had bought a house near the village of Wedmore in Somerset, and we never went back to live in London.

My father was an electrical engineer by profession, and worked in various parts of the country. My parents, however, decided to bring up the family in Somerset, which meant that for years dad would leave home on Sunday evening, travel by train to wherever he was working, stay in digs during the week (or sometimes for a month) and then come home at weekends. This continued until he finally moved to Bristol to work in the aircraft industry, which was within commuting distance from home. Dad's profession supported the family until he retired, but his real passion was farming. As children we were brought up with chickens, geese, a pony and pet lambs.

*With Daisybell. 1949*

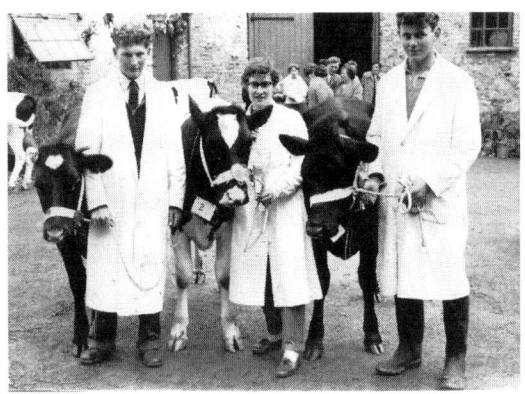

*Wedmore Young Farmers Club, Show and Sale. 1956*

I belonged to the Brownies and Guides in the village and learnt lots of useful skills, not least a love of camping. It was with the Guides that I went to Northern Ireland and to Holland. I also joined the local Young Farmers Club, and in due course became the secretary. The Young Farmers Club was an opportunity to meet with other young people, and included various activities. Some of us reared calves and prepared them for showing at the annual YFC village Show and Sale. This involved not only looking after the animal but also teaching it to be led on a halter and then grooming it for the show. On several occasions I was awarded a first or second prize for my animal. The YFC also encouraged us in public speaking, which was probably where I first learnt something of that skill which was to prove very useful in later life.

From five years of age I attended the local school, which was a half mile walk from home. At the time, the school catered for primary aged children, who at the age of eleven took what was then called the 11+ exam. If they passed, they left for the Grammar school. If they failed that exam, they stayed at that school until leaving age. I passed this exam and went to the local grammar school. For me that meant a three mile cycle ride each way to school and back, through the lanes, in all weathers, every school day for the next five years. Of course in those days there were fewer cars on the road, so safety was not an issue. I don't think cycle helmets had been invented!

I enjoyed school, but I knew what I wanted to do on leaving, and that was to farm. I saw no point in staying on into the sixth form so, against the advice of both the school and my parents, I left school at 16 with eight O levels to start my career. I later regretted having no A levels, but can blame no one but myself.

On leaving school, I spent a year getting experience on a dairy farm about 10 miles from home and then went to the Somerset Farm Institute. The Institute offered four one-year courses in Horticulture, Poultry Management, Dairying, and General Agriculture. Most of the girls took one of the first three options; I chose the course in General Agriculture. There were

30 students on my course: 28 men, me and one other girl. I was entering a man's world, but took it in my stride. In fact, in the test at the end of the first term I surprised everyone by coming out on top!

Then followed three years back at home trying to turn my father's smallholding into a viable dairy farm. My father did not own much land, so he rented various fields in differing locations. But we didn't have the capital to finance this properly. I started with one cow and after three years had increased the herd to 10. I milked the cows by hand, as there was no money for a milking machine or even a tractor. My means of transport to these fields was a horse and cart, so early every morning I first had to catch the horse, who was not very keen on work, and harness her up to the cart. I then had to put the milking bucket, stool and churn in the back and trot to the field where the cows were grazing. The cows stood to be milked, the milk was strained into the churn, and I then trotted back to our small dairy where I cooled the milk, finally trundling the churn to the nearby milk stand for collection. This was primitive dairy farming and it was very hard physical work. After three years I realised there was little prospect of much improvement, so I decided that a change of direction was necessary.

I had to wait until I was 21, when in the eyes of the local authority I was an independent adult, in order to apply for a grant to do further studies.

This took me to an agricultural college in Devon. I would have liked to continue my studies in General Agriculture, with a view of possibly becoming a farm manager. However, I was advised that as a woman I would have limited success in finding such an appointment. A woman farm manager in those days! So I was advised to take the two year course leading to a diploma in dairying.

On leaving college, I applied for a Civil Service post with the Ministry of Agriculture (as it was then called). My application form allowed me to indicate any preference for the location in the country. I noted that I was free to go anywhere, but would prefer that it not be in the far North or in Cornwall. Both seemed remote for someone brought up in Somerset. I was interviewed and appointed to be a Milk Officer - based in Cornwall! For three years I was based in Liskeard and loved visiting the small dairy farms on Bodmin Moor. I regularly passed Jamaica Inn. I was then moved to the office in Truro and so got to know another part of that lovely county and had the opportunity to visit many of the beauty spots.

All farms that sold milk for public consumption had to be registered, and my role was to inspect such farms for cleanliness and to give advice if the milk was not fresh. They also had to have a clean water supply. Many farms in Cornwall did not have mains water, so their supply had to be tested. If they were fortunate they had a borehole, which was usually a good source of water, but many relied on the well in the yard or spring on the farm, in which case I had to take a sample which would be tested in our laboratory. If I reported poor bacteriological content the farmer could be very indignant, as their family had drunk that water for generations without realising they had built up immunity to whatever bugs were present. My job was then to advise how the water supply could be made safe.

I had started on my second career in agriculture, and now had a secure job and a decent income. I assumed that my course was set for the foreseeable future.

What I did not realise was that even though the experiences I had gained would stand me in good stead, God had other plans which would take me in a different direction.

## Chapter 2

## The Beginning of my Faith Journey

'David, why at the end of our prayers do we always say, "through Jesus Christ, our Lord?"'

It was 1958, in the Christian Union of the agricultural college. I was sitting next to my boyfriend, and although we were both Christians, David seemed to have more answers than I did when it came to basic questions about the Christian faith. He considered this one carefully.

'Well, I think it's because we can only come to God through Christ. Jesus is like a bridge between a holy God and us fallible human beings.'

As David replied, the penny finally dropped. I'm sure I had been told that before, but now, somehow, I understood.

It wasn't exactly a conversion experience: the church had always been part of my life. As children we were taken to church, and in due course to Sunday school. We lived a mile from the village church, and I remember cycling to Sunday school on a Sunday afternoon. We used to help my mother decorate the church for the festivals: she was responsible for decorating a small ledge around the pillars in the choir stalls.

Red apples and moss for harvest, and for Easter small fish paste jars of primroses, again with moss to hide the jars. Polishing the apples and picking primroses was all part of this ritual.

In preparation for confirmation, we had to learn the Catechism by rote from the Book of Common Prayer. I was thirteen when I was confirmed in Cheddar Church, three miles from my home. I think I have always believed in God, and had no crisis of faith as I went through my teenage years. As I got older I used to cycle to the 8.00am communion service. These were the years before the Parish Communion Movement, so most morning services took the form of Matins from the 1662 Prayer Book. Despite finding these services a bit tedious, with what seemed like endless chanting of psalms and the Te Deum, if for any reason I did not go, I felt that something was missing. So I did have a faith, but I doubt if I could have told you exactly what I believed.

In deciding to join the Christian Union at agricultural college, I suppose I just wanted to understand more of what Christians believe and to think it through as an adult. Over the next two years I heard talks by mature Christian leaders and was involved in discussions and Bible studies - we all used the Authorised Version of the Bible in those days. It wasn't that I had serious doubts, but I needed to ask some of the basic questions about the Christian Faith, like the one I asked David. As he replied, it all began to make sense. The effect was that my faith was now in technicolour rather than black and white.

I began to learn the importance of my own personal Bible reading, prayer and praising God. But if we are to praise God in our own devotions, what words should we use? I remember underlining verses from the Psalms and from the Book of Revelation with which I could start my prayers. Verses like, 'Thou art worthy, O Lord, to receive glory and honour and power: for thou hast created all things and for thy pleasure they are and were created.' (Rev 4:11)

I also came to understand that the Christian faith is not just about believing, it also has to be put into practice and that is about how we live our lives. Further, if we believe that God is 'The Boss' and has our best interests at heart, then we have to do what we believe he is telling us to do, even if that does not seem very attractive at the time. So I had no dramatic conversion experience: rather, it was a gradual realisation that my faith, and the implications of it, would become my philosophy of life. My conversation with David that day was only the next step in my spiritual journey, even though it was an important one. It is a journey that lasts a lifetime.

## Chapter 3

## The Call of God

'Selected for training'. I stared at the words in dismay. This was not what I had expected - was it really God's plan for me to make such a drastic change?

Now in my mid twenties, I had once again begun to question what I should be doing with my life. With my practical and theoretical training in agriculture, but also a committed Christian faith, I thought that perhaps becoming an Agricultural Missionary would tick all the boxes. I had heard of such ventures as 'Faith and Farm', which were small Bible colleges set in some of the underdeveloped parts of the world which also taught basic agricultural skills. This seemed like an appropriate adventure for which I might be suited. After taking advice I approached a Mission Society and met a representative who was encouraging. He explained that currently they did not have an opening for an agricultural missionary, but that anyway I would first need to undertake missionary training. I left that meeting sensing that God was saying either 'No' or 'Not yet'. I don't know how I knew. I didn't hear a voice or see writing in the sky, but for the moment that door closed.

Although I was living in Cornwall, which is not exactly the centre of the universe, I had begun to hear or to read in the church press about women 'parish workers'. This was a nationally recognised full time role for theologically trained women to assist in parish ministry in the Anglican Church. I had never met a parish worker. There were none working in the Diocese of Truro at the time. I was not attracted to this role. I assumed that such parish workers were all 'old' - at least 40! - and wore felt hats, tweed skirts and brogue lace up shoes to do their good works. It was not exactly the concept of an exciting career for someone my age. But as the idea would not go away, I had decided that I would apply, get turned down and then think about the next thing.

In 1964 Truro Diocese had no structures in place for dealing with potential parish workers, so there was no one to help me discern my possible vocation. Eventually I was sponsored personally by the bishop. I then had to attend a two day residential selection panel which was parallel to the one for potential ordinands. A few days later, the letter I now held in my hand had arrived. It was decision time. I could have written back to say, 'Thank you but no thanks,' but I was beginning to think that this was God's call.

And yet, it would mean giving up my job. For the first time in my life I was earning decent money - £1,192 a year and was beginning to think about renting my own flat. Until then I had lived with various families who took in paying guests. I had also saved up and bought my first car, not actually a car but a second hand mini van, which I would have to sell if I went to college. Oh, why couldn't they have just rejected my application?!

It was a Sunday evening when, with the church youth group, I was at the local old people's home where we went once a month to sing their favourite hymns. One resident chose a hymn with the chorus, 'I'm standing on the promises of God'. As I sang, those words challenged me. Could I trust God enough to follow what I then believed to be his calling? I reflected long and hard and told myself that if I really believed that Christ was my Lord then I had to trust him and follow his direction. I agreed to start training in September 1964.

But where to train? In those days the women trained separately from the male ordinands. There were three colleges approved for the training of Parish Workers: Gilmore House in London, Dalton House in Bristol and St Michael's House in Oxford. I then learned that one's church tradition could influence one's choice of college. I had never thought whether I was high, low or middle, I was just a Christian! Looking back, I suspect that the local churches I had attended were probably middle to low; but while trying to sort this out in my mind, I felt drawn to the more Anglo-Catholic tradition. I visited Gilmore House, which probably had a higher ethos than the other two colleges. On the other hand, I thought, perhaps my high church leanings should be moderated by attending a college of a lower tradition.

Having lived in Somerset, Bristol was a relatively local large city, although we didn't go there very often. Transport was not so easy in those days and the family didn't have a car. Oxford on the other hand sounded much more romantic, the city of spires and famous for its university. In future I would be able to say I had studied in Oxford, although our college was not part of the university. I was accepted for training at St Michael's House and spent the next two years in Oxford. I never regretted the choice.

The majority of the women were training for overseas missionary work, either in South America or among God's own people the Jews: in the 1960s the high calling for women, particularly in the evangelical wing of the church, was to be an overseas missionary. A one year course was also available for qualified school teachers who wished to specialise in Religious Education, leading to a Certificate in Religious Knowledge (CRK). I joined the two year course for those of us training to be parish workers in the Church of England. In my year there were just three of us on that course.

The principal was the remarkable but rather formidable Miss Barter Snow. The college was run a bit like a girls' boarding school, with house rules more appropriate to teenagers even though most of us were mature students who had previously been looking after ourselves. In our first year, students had to share rooms. Rumour had it that Miss Snow paired the most unlikely students together on the principle that it was GMT - good missionary training! There was a rota for having a bath. We were not allowed to use public transport on Sundays, and not allowed to go to the cinema but could go to the theatre if the production was deemed suitable. I'm not sure that all make-up was forbidden, but I do remember one student being reprimanded for wearing lipstick.

We were allowed to attend the University Christian Union, and for me that was a highlight of the week. Not necessarily because of the quality of debate or excellence of the speaker, but being in mixed company was quite a relief after spending most of the week in an all female institution. We were also encouraged to attend a local church on Sundays. On occasions I went to one of the large student churches in Oxford, either St Ebbe's or St Aldate's, but more regularly attended St Clement's, which felt more like a local church.

In the summer vacation we were expected to get involved with a mission activity: either a Christian summer camp or an organised parish mission. In the summer of 1965 I joined a parish mission team to Christ Church, Orpington, in Kent, led by the vicar of St Clement's. One of the other team members was a university medical student who came from South Wales. He and I became good friends, a friendship that lasted for several years.

In 1965 Miss Snow retired, but before she did so she appointed me as senior student for the following year. As senior student I had the privilege of a small single room with a wash basin and even an adjacent toilet for my sole use, so I lived in comparative luxury.

The new principal was Miss Jean Cooke. I suggested to her that the house rules be updated to reflect the maturity of the students, pointing out that the current rules included, 'Thou shalt not use a fountain pen in bed'. Miss Cooke promised to look at them, but the revised version was no better so I gave up the unequal struggle. There were more important things on which to concentrate.

Alongside our schedule of lectures, assignments and essays, every student had to get involved in the college's Bible reading course. This involved reading at least one whole book of the Bible each week, starting with Genesis. On a Wednesday morning there was a test on the contents of that book. If a student failed that test, it was noted and they would have to repeat it the following year. Imagine having to read the whole of Leviticus or Isaiah in one week and then being tested on how much you had taken in! For some students this was a real challenge, but it did mean that we had read the whole Bible before we left college. I found it a great privilege to have two whole years to study the Bible.

We had excellent lecturers. I especially appreciated the teaching of Peggy Knight, who lectured in Old Testament studies. She gave a profound insight into that often neglected part of the Bible, and the way she taught was not dry theology, but enriched with deep spirituality. We were also given good training for pastoral ministry and mission outreach. There were no sermon classes as such: we had training in how to give devotional talks to women's meetings. I don't think there was any realisation that this training could be equipping potential priests of the future.

My training led to the basic qualification for parish work, which was an Inter Diocesan Certificate (IDC), the equivalent of the clergy General Ordination Exam (GOE). I decided that, given this opportunity, I would also study for the London University Diploma in Theology (Dip Th). This involved more theology, and even some knowledge of New Testament Greek. For the latter it was arranged for me to attend lectures at the University College of St Peter's. Languages are not my strong point, so I struggled to reach the necessary standard, but I got there and achieved those two qualifications. I found the study of theology both stimulating and challenging . It awakened in me a love for teasing out theological issues, and in due course would lead to the desire to share some of this knowledge in teaching the faith.

About four months before I finished my studies I had an unexpected visit from The Reverend Herbert Watkins, who was the vicar of a parish in Swindon. He had been visiting Oxford, and decided to call at St Michael's House to see if there was a student who could replace the deaconess[1] that was leaving his parish. Without any prior warning, I was called for interview. The interview went well and I subsequently received a letter inviting me to visit the parish. He told me that the work would be essentially pastoral but with plenty of opportunities for working with children, young people and women.

He also said that he would have more information about stipend, holidays and the accommodation available. I visited a couple of weeks later and decided to accept the job of parish worker at St Mary's Church, Rodbourne Cheney.

The final term ended in June 1966 with a garden party in

the college grounds to which families and friends were invited. My parents came. My mother had encouraged me in my change of career, noting that my father had spent his working life in a career which supported the family, although he would have loved to have been doing something different. During the garden party there was a service at which those of us who were leaving were commissioned for our future ministries. As senior student, I had to give a short address.

So after two years of hard study I had gained a basic grounding of theology and qualified for Parish Ministry. I now had the right to put the following letters after my name: NDD (National Diploma in Dairying), DipTh. (Diploma in Theology), and IDC (Inter Diocesan Certificate).

I was to take up my new appointment in September, so spent the next month or so at my parents' home in Somerset. My sister Margaret, two and half years younger than me, was by then a domestic science teacher but still living at home with my parents. She was due to get married later in the year, so we were both preparing to set up home for the first time. Neither of us had much money, so we had to do the best we could. Together we bought a dining room table and four chairs. I had the table and Margaret had the chairs. Mine was the better deal, as that drop-leaf gate legged table served me well for the next forty years. Margaret's chairs had a relatively short life span! During that summer we also made ourselves several feather pillows from an old feather mattress. The pillowcases were made from a closely woven material called ticking, which was feather proof. We then chose a hot, dry day when there was no breeze. We put the feather mattress on the lawn, cut it open and then stuffed the pillowcases. Even though there was no wind, feathers are not easily managed and we both ended up looking as if we had been plucking chickens. Those pillows served us well for a few years. It was quite exciting as each of us was starting a new phase of our lives.

---

1. At the time women who were trained and qualified began their ministry in the Church of England with the title 'Parish Worker'. After two years they could then apply to enter the lay order of Deaconesses. This was not the same as being ordained deacon (see chapter 6)

## Chapter 4

## A Parish Worker

'Cor, Miss! An't you got a lot of books!'

I looked over to the little white-wood bookcase my young visitor was admiring. I had just finished staining it, and the small handful of books I owned didn't even fill its shelves. This lad from the village probably had no books at home: my small collection must have looked like a library to him.

It was September 1966, and, with the official title of 'Accredited Lay Worker' I had just started work at St Mary's Church, Rodbourne Cheney, in the Diocese of Bristol. The parish included the village of Haydon Wick.

My accommodation was The Vicarage Cottage which was an extension of the old and rambling vicarage, but with its own entrance. I had moved in with what limited furniture I possessed. I bought a single bed, a Parker Knoll armchair with wooden arms and some second hand dining chairs. I bought a small kitchen table which was reduced in price because it had a chip on the surface of one corner. There were no carpets, but I bought a few rugs for the floors. The cottage was very damp, and most mornings the first job was to brush up the live and dead woodlice before I stepped on them. The dampness didn't help my arthritis to which I had been vulnerable for several years. However, for the first time in my life, I had my own home - my own front door - and the lad who had come from the village to investigate the newcomer seemed suitably impressed.

I was also offered the use of part of the large garden. The garden had been neglected so it took time to clear the weeds and cultivate the ground so that I could grow a few vegetables.

I started on a stipend of £700 a year, about half of what I would have been earning if I had stayed with the civil service. However, I did have free accommodation and was thrilled to be beginning my new way of life. There was not a lot of money to spare, but I had grown up in the war and the years afterwards when food was in short supply, and had learnt from my mother how to eat healthily with cheap joints of meat and plenty of vegetables and fruit.

On leaving college, curates were expected to attend 'post ordination training'. This was not expected of parish workers. (There had been no pre-'ordination' retreat for me, either - I just started on the appointed date. In fact the diocese did not even get around to licensing me until after I had been in post for over a year, and that was a private affair in the bishop's chapel.)

My male contemporaries, on the other hand, attended regular seminars on theological issues. On hearing about this, I asked if I could join them, and was given permission by the Diocesan Director of Ordinands (DDO), Canon Geoffrey Paul, who had become Canon of Bristol Cathedral in the same year that I moved to the diocese. He was a man of considerable theological scholarship and a great expositor of Christian theology, who had been a missionary in India for 15 years. I was to be grateful to him in more ways than one, and although I never learned exactly what he thought theologically about women's ordination, he was always very encouraging to me in my ministry as a parish worker. Perhaps he was influenced by the fact that he had five daughters! (His daughter Jane married Rowan Williams, who became Archbishop of Canterbury.)

The church staff at St Mary's included the Reverend Herbert Watkins, two curates, and me: the parish worker. My role was mainly pastoral, which included much visiting of church members in their homes - or when necessary, in hospital - and door to door visiting in the streets to which we were allocated. The Reverend Watkins expected me to do at least 30 visits a week. I was also responsible for training Sunday school teachers, who had to attend a training session on a Tuesday evening if they were to teach on the following Sunday. I attended the women's fellowship, which was led by the vicar's wife. I also worked with the Girls' Brigade, for which I was given the uniform that had belonged to my predecessor. She was tall, and as I am only five feet it had to be cut down to size.

Parish workers had a limited liturgical role, and so on Sundays I normally sat in the congregation. We did, however, have recognised liturgical attire which in my case was borrowed from the diocese. It was a maroon coloured gown with a matching hat: a Canterbury cap, which was a bit like a mortar board without the tassel. Of course all women wore hats in church in those days, but nobody else's hat earned them the nickname 'Cardinal Wolsey'.

After I had been in the parish for about a year, the vicar asked me to speak at the Family service. My preaching ministry had begun in a very low key way.

I enjoyed my ministry, although it was not always easy. In the first year or so, one problem was loneliness. Reverend Watkins insisted that our Christian names were not to be used in the parish, so I was known as Miss Rose, although the youth club members compromised by calling me 'Rosie'. Nor were we to have close friends in the parish, as he thought that would show partiality. My day off was during the week when my contemporaries would be at work. I could take time off during the day, but worked in the evenings when most working people were free. So it was difficult to find time to build friendships beyond the parish. Perhaps this was easier for the clergy who were married, but parish workers were single, almost by definition. If one decided to marry, resignation was expected.

I realised that we need trusted friends or family with whom to share some of our inner thoughts and feelings in order to express our personality. Being, in a measure, deprived of this felt like being less of a person. I reflected on that from a theological perspective. As Christians we use personal pronouns when speaking of God. God is not just a great power who controls everything; rather, we speak of the Fatherhood of God. This is not about God being male but rather about a God who cares like the perfect father. So it is not inappropriate to speak of God as 'he' rather than 'it'. As Christians we also believe that God is Trinity: Father, Son and Holy Spirit, the mystery of, 'three persons, one God'. Is it appropriate to speak of God in personal terms also because of the relationships within the Trinity, the divine community of love?

The parish had a thriving youth group which was run by one of the curates. When he left, the remaining curate did not want to take over the leadership, so that responsibility fell to me. At the time, new Christian hymns, songs and choruses were being published, including 'Youth Praise'. These hymns had singable tunes, good Christian teaching and words which were more meaningful for young people. One activity that proved popular was showing 'Fact and Faith' films which were designed with young people in mind. We also organised youth weekends away. I thoroughly enjoyed it and found it very stimulating working with young people with all their questions and helping them to grow in their faith.

There was one evening when the group was meeting in the church hall and things got a bit out of hand. A prank went wrong, voices were raised and several of the girls were in tears. The two sons of the vicar were in the youth club, so perhaps that was how word got back to the vicarage. Whatever the means, the result was that the Reverend Herbert Watkins came storming in, absolutely enraged. Those who seemed to be the culprits were ordered to leave, and he stormed out again. Tears were mopped up, an uneasy peace was restored and the club closed for the evening.

The next day, Reverend Watkins sheepishly admitted to me that his initials, H.E., could stand for, 'Highly Explosive'. He therefore asked me to visit the family concerned in order to sort things out. It was passing the buck, but he knew his limitations. In any case I was the youth leader, so had responsibility for the behaviour of those in the group. I visited the family of the main trouble maker to speak to the parents and to the young people concerned. Apologies were offered and accepted, and promises made that it would not happen again. I took it as a sort of compliment that the vicar thought I was capable of handling the situation.

No one has ever suggested that working with young people would always be plain sailing, but thank God for the enthusiasm and high spirits of the young, even though those characteristics sometimes need channelling in the right direction. They were a great group of young people. I know that at least one of them went on to be ordained and another became the manager of a Christian bookshop. I like to think that those times helped some of them to grow up in their faith, and so live enriched lives.

## Chapter 5

## What Next?

'What are you expecting in terms of your future ministry?' Canon Geoffrey Paul looked at me kindly as I considered his question. I had just been telling him all about my work with the youth group and my increasing involvement at the mission church in leading services and preaching - the church had opened a mission hall in Haydon Wick, and I was finally getting a chance to speak and lead more often.

Canon Paul was visiting the parish to speak to the curates about their futures, and had made sure to include me. What could my answer be, though? After a curate had been in post for about three years, he expected to move to either a more senior curacy or to become a vicar or take up a job with more responsibility. Curates had already come and gone in my four years in post. Yet none of those options would be available to me. I was a woman, and could not be ordained even if I had wanted to.

'I'll always be happy working as an assistant in a parish,' I told Canon Paul with confidence. He nodded, smiled and with more insight than I had at the time, replied, 'You wait, my girl.'

'I would like to do more theological study, all the same,' I admitted. It was the right thing to say to a man who had spent most of his adult life studying and teaching Christian theology. 'Well, do it!' he said enthusiastically.

But that was easier said than done. To study for a theological degree I would need at least two A levels; I had none. I could not afford the fees and would be unable to get a local authority grant as I had already had one for my agricultural studies. Besides, I was not sure I could face another three years of study. I told God that if a degree course had his blessing, then I would give two years to this, would need to be accepted without any A levels, and the fees would have to be provided.

I applied to the special entrance Board of London University for exemption of the two A levels and was accepted. My Diploma in Theology, which had been validated by London University, counted as the equivalent of one A level and also exempted me the first year of the course. So a two year course was possible, I still had no A levels, and the money for the fees arrived from various sources - including a generous grant from Bristol Diocese, no doubt initiated by Canon Paul. It seemed that this course of action had God's approval!

In October 1971 I began studying for a London BD at the London Bible College (as it was then called) based in Northwood on the edge of London. The College took students from several denominations. A significant number were Baptists, some of whom were training for Baptist ministry. Alongside the academic studies, which I found very stimulating, students were allocated in teams for practical pastoral or mission activities at the weekends. Each team at the time was led by one of the male students. I was in a team linked to the local Anglican Church and led by a man who, though very capable, was younger than me and much less experienced in Christian ministry. This did not particularly concern me, as my reason for being at the college was my theological studies; however, in my second year I did question why the most suitable person was not chosen to be the team leader regardless of gender.

The question of women in leadership in the church was now being discussed much more frequently, and was beginning to exercise my mind. On one occasion, I was in the common room minding my own business when a fellow student, whose name was Mark, joined me and we got into conversation. He was a young man who had come to the college after taking his A levels at school and was studying theology with a view to the possibility of ordination at some time in the future. He told me something of his background, and asked what I had been doing since leaving school. I told him that I had been a farmer but then was called by God to parish ministry.

I explained what I had been doing in the recent past, and of my growing involvement with leading services and preaching. This provoked a quite heated discussion on the role of women in the church. With the great conviction of an eighteen year old, he said, 'God would not call a woman to any form of leadership in the Church. Having women in leadership is against the teaching of scripture.'

'But Mark,' I replied, 'I believe God has called me - and I have been exercising this ministry for five years.'

To try to square the circle, he explained to me very carefully that God could indeed have *used* me, for God can use anyone or anything. After all, in the Old Testament story of Samson, God used the jawbone of an ass, in the hand of Samson, to kill a thousand Philistines!

At the time - taken aback by being compared to a donkey's jawbone - I had no answer, but it made me think. Had I been called, or just used by God? I began to realise that I would need to do much more theological thinking about this whole subject.

Over-confident 18 year olds aside, I greatly enjoyed the stimulus of debate with other students. Being in a college with Christians from various denominations was also enriching, and helped to broaden my understanding of the differing traditions, even though these were mainly from the evangelical wing of the church. Again I was pleased to sit at the feet of the Old Testament lecturer, the same Peggy Knight who had been on the staff of St Michael's House and had now moved to lecture at The London Bible College. In 1973 I graduated with a London honours degree in theology BD (2:2), 20 years after leaving school. I am not an academic, so I was pleased with the grade. But as the course finished, once again the question of my future arose. Could this degree take me any further than I had already been?

## Chapter 6

## Becoming a Deaconess

As my time at the London Bible College was drawing to a close, I had to decide what next - or rather where next, as I was expecting to go back into parish ministry. A fellow student drew my attention to an advertisement for a parish worker at St George's Church in Leeds. Having been brought up in the West Country, I hadn't thought of going so far north. (Actually Leeds is about in the middle of the country being equal distance from London and Edinburgh and an equal distance from the East and West coast.) However, I applied and was invited for an interview. I drove to Leeds and found the church.

St George's is a large city church in the centre of Leeds adjacent to the Leeds General Infirmary, near the Town Hall and with the University just up the road. I found my way into the church and was met by a man with almost white hair, wearing purple trousers, purple shirt, a purple corduroy jacket and purple suede shoes. This was the vicar, the Reverend Michael Botting.

Michael was an impressive figure and always well dressed;

somehow he even looked smart when he wore jeans. Twelve years older than me, he was a maths graduate and had taught for some years before training for ordination at Ridley Hall in Cambridge. He had been a vicar in Fulham before moving to Leeds the year before I met him. He showed me around the church and told me about their style of ministry and how he expected me to fit into the team, if appointed.

I stayed the night with Michael and his wife Mary at the Vicarage in Headingley which was some two miles from the church. I warmed to Mary immediately: she was not the smart dresser like her husband but made up for it by such a lovely personality. I also met their two children, Ruth and David. Michael was a well organised person and quite a strategic thinker. I knew I would be able to work with him.

So my next appointment was as a parish worker at St George's Church, Leeds. I joined the staff consisting of the vicar, two curates and me. It had a small parish which was fairly 'downtown' and a quite large, eclectic congregation which included families, but also medical personnel and university staff and students. St George's is also famous for their work in the crypt with the more deprived members of society: St George's crypt was opened in the depression years of the 1930's by the then vicar, Don Robbins. Although I was to work in the church (rather than the crypt) we worked very closely together and supported one another.

My accommodation was in a house owned by the church and within walking distance of the church and near the University. I lived in the ground floor flat and the curate and his wife lived on the first floor. I had a large bedroom and large sitting/dining room with a kitchen, bathroom and toilet on a lower level. The kitchen door opened onto a small yard and back gate. The yard was just about big enough for the washing line, and I soon added two large pots in which I grew runner beans. On the window sill of the sitting room I fixed a window box and grew some flowers. I rented a garage a few blocks away. I had no complaints. For me this was the beginning of more than seven years of exciting, stimulating and enriching ministry.

On arrival I discovered that I was better qualified in theology than my fellow clergy. They all had degrees, but I was the only theological graduate. One of my first responsibilities was to develop better lay training facilities for the congregation. I was treated as a full member of staff and on the preaching rota alongside my clergy colleagues. I began to discover that I had some abilities in preaching and teaching the faith. Many in the congregation were very articulate so it was not unusual to be questioned about the content of one's sermon, which was in itself encouraging and stimulating.

Some time after my appointment Michael said to me: 'When thinking about appointing you, I did have hesitations. A previous parish worker disagreed with me on the importance of the resurrection. If your appointment had not proved to be satisfactory, I would never appoint another woman minister. I'm glad that you and I are on the same page theologically!' I reflected that if he had made a bad appointment of a (male) curate, he would have determined to do better next time, rather than never appointing another curate. It was another reminder that there was not a level playing field.

Over the following years I was involved in many aspects of the church's life. I worked with young people and was a leader of our Pathfinder Group. As we were a student church I had a ministry among the students, especially the women students. I was involved in setting up a telephone ministry. This involved asking members of the congregation and the clergy to write a short sort of, 'Thought for the day', which I would then edit if necessary before it was recorded. The telephone company gave us an easily remembered number which people could ring to hear a brief Christian message. We publicised it by producing small leaflets which could be kept in the pocket or handbag. Something similar had been done previously by Nora Coggan, the sister of Donald Coggan, the one time Archbishop of Canterbury.

In 1974 I had been appointed as the Ripon Diocesan Lay Minister Advisor (DLMA). This role in effect made me the 'shop steward' for the parish workers of the diocese and gave me access to senior members of the clergy. It also gave the opportunity to meet up with others in a similar role in other dioceses. One of the concerns at the time was that parish workers, unlike clergy, had no career structure. With a few specialist exceptions, parish workers were unable to take further responsibilities in parish ministry, because no matter how experienced they were in other respects, they did not have the basic qualification of ordination. I tried to open discussions about further responsibilities for those of us that were qualified lay ministers, but got nowhere. Perhaps there were no answers.

The Revd Michael Botting was largely responsible for the growth of the Family Service Movement. He had begun experimenting with family services in the late 1960s in his previous parish of St Matthew's Fulham. These were less formal, non-eucharistic services using visual aids with the aim of making the Gospel clear to families who were unfamiliar with attending church. He had written up his thinking and the principles behind this development in a book entitled 'Reaching the Families', which was first published in 1969. He later published at least five books giving outlines of suitable talks/sermons with suggested visual aids for such family services, including ideas for the various seasons of the year and biblical stories. These family services became a feature of the pattern of services at St George's. I learnt from Michael, sometimes spoke at these services and in due course submitted my own such talks for inclusion in some of his books.

In 1978, Michael and I were invited to the USA under the auspices of Evangelism Explosion, a lay training programme in evangelism. After an initial period in Fort Lauderdale, we were sent in different directions to various parts of the States to study evangelism in the context of some of the large and growing churches of different denominations. What particularly impressed both Michael and me were the Sunday schools linked with these churches. Those Sunday schools were for all the congregation, not just for the children. Church members attended a study group either prior to or after the service of worship; this alongside groups for children and well organised creches. When we met up after our allocated visits we asked each other whether this pattern would be effective and accepted back home.

Some twelve months later we launched The Christian Education Programme at St George's, which included study groups followed by worship. I was involved alongside the vicar in the planning, discussion with the PCC and others, modifying and not least training lay leadership for the study groups. I wrote up the experience in a Grove Booklet (now out of print) entitled *Sunday Learning for All Ages*.

Among other things, what I learnt from the whole exercise was the importance of careful planning, listening and helping a congregation to embrace quite a radical change. After all the discussions, changes and consultations with the congregation, Michael discovered that there were about four people or couples who declared that if we went ahead they would leave the church. Michael visited all of them and made arrangements for them to be welcomed into another church if they felt this was not for them. Of course we were working in a large city where there were other churches nearby and not in a remote rural community where this would not be so easy.

At St George's I made some good friends, many of whom I have kept in touch with over the years. Christine was our excellent administrator. Like me, she was single although also like me, married some years later. We both enjoyed camping and as she owned a tent we would, from time to time, take ourselves off for a couple of days camping at one of the beauty spots in that part of the country. We also took camping holidays together in the summer. One year we drove across Europe to what was then Yugoslavia. The campsite was somewhat basic and we were woken each morning by an announcement over the loudspeaker. As it was in the local language we did not know what we were being told but it sounded a bit like a political message. I was in danger of being arrested for wearing a two piece bathing costume which I did not realise was forbidden - and in any case it was modest and not a bikini! After two days we decided to move on to the northern coast of Italy, where we found a lovely campsite near the beach from which we were able to take a boat trip to Venice, and walk to the famous St Mark's Square.

Other good friends were Marjorie and Ruth. Marjorie worked in the Crypt Office, so I saw her most days. Her friend Ruth was a school teacher. On several occasions the three of us went on holiday together. One year we drove to Scotland and stayed in Edinburgh for a couple of days, then drove across to the West coast and took the car on the ferry to the Outer Hebrides. We stayed for a week in a caravan on the Isle of Harris. The sea was a wonderful blue green colour but icy cold. A day trip took us to Stornaway on Lewis. On another occasion, taking two tents, we drove to Penzance and took the car on 'The Scillonian' for a very rough crossing to the Isles of Scilly. We camped on St Mary's. The tents must have been

## Judith Rose

pitched close together. I was in a single tent, but one night when it was very windy I could hear a constant rattling. It turned out to be my friend's false teeth which she had put in the pocket of their tent. Life was good.

I remember a conversation during a social occasion. Someone asked, 'Why do you help lead services and preach, although you are not ordained?' I understood the confusion. Although I was treated as a full member of the staff of the church, I was not clergy because I did not wear a dog collar or clerical attire; yet it seemed to most people that I fulfilled a role very similar to the curates.

I explained that as a woman I could not be ordained, but that I was as fully trained as the clergy, I was authorised for my ministry by the bishop and that women in my position were called parish workers. My questioner's confused look remained, so I added that I was a sort of deaconess. That seemed to help. Perhaps people could more easily fit me in a box if I had an ecclesiastical title. It made me think. I knew that becoming a deaconess would not make much difference to what I was allowed to do, but if it helped others to understand my role then perhaps it was the right thing to do? I also discovered that the title deaconess had more credibility within clerical circles and the national church seemed to notice that women like me existed! I decided to explore the possibility of becoming a deaconess.

The Church has had differing views on women's ministry for centuries, but there were women deacons/deaconesses in the early church. Phoebe in the letter to the Romans is described as a deacon, but as the word means 'servant', it doesn't help to define the role. The Order of Deaconesses was revived in the Church of England in the 1860s. It was defined by the Lambeth Conference in 1920 and reaffirmed in 1930, noting, 'The office is primarily a ministry of succour, bodily and spiritual, especially to women and should follow the lines of the primitive, rather than the modern diaconate of men...distinct from and complimentary to the historic Orders of the Church'.

At the time, one had to have been in parish ministry for at least two years before being considered for the ministry of a deaconess. This was not a problem for me, as it was 10 years since I was first authorised as a licensed lay worker. Then there was a selection process and in my case a two week training course. I was made a deaconess in St George's Church by the Bishop of Knaresborough in May 1976. My title was then Deaconess Judith Rose rather than Miss Judith Rose. This would be a title I could hold for life, unlike that of parish worker. The service was called an ordination service, and rightly so, as I was entering the Order of Deaconesses - or rather, the Lay Order of Deaconesses. When explaining that a deaconess was not in holy orders, I might quip that that presumably meant we were in unholy orders!

Another advantage of having the title Deaconess was that officially the national church now seemed to recognise my ministry. If I check my entry in Crockford's Clerical Directory, it looks as though my ministry started in 1976 when I was made a (lay) deaconess. This ignores the previous 10 years of stipendiary ministry after I had completed my ministerial training and received my qualification as a parish worker. I am pleased to report that at least the Pensions Board recognises that my stipendiary ministry started in 1966.

As I explained earlier, the liturgical dress for parish workers was a maroon robe and hat. The outfit that I wore in my first parish had been on loan from the diocese, so was returned when I left. At St. George's, when taking part in a service or preaching, I had worn my black undergraduates gown. The liturgical dress for deaconesses was a blue cassock, which I eventually acquired when I moved to Bradford Diocese in 1981.

One of the advantages of living in Leeds was that it is in the beautiful county of Yorkshire. It did not take very long in the car to get to the Yorkshire Dales and even the Lake District was accessible. There were many enjoyable days of walking with the young people and with friends during my time based in Leeds. Scargill House, which is a retreat centre similar to Lee Abbey in Devon, is in the Yorkshire Dales and became a favourite place of retreat and parish weekends, with its inspiring chapel and wonderful views and walks.

Another advantage of living in that part of the country at that time was that the cost of housing was relatively low. The church gave me permission to move into my own house, although I waived an accommodation allowance. In 1978 I was on a stipend of £2,280 a year. The West Yorkshire Building Society was prepared to loan me a mortgage of £6,950 which enabled me to purchase a small 3 bedroom terraced house in the parish for £7,950. I had managed to save the £1,000 deposit, although I was only just able to afford the mortgage repayments each month.

I redecorated my new home throughout. It had a small front garden and a slightly larger back garden where I planted a lawn and had a vegetable patch. I had a garage erected at the end of the back garden where there was vehicular access. I had become a proud homeowner for the first time.

## Chapter 7

# Should Women be Ordained?

After a service, somebody stopped me at the door. 'Have you seen this news from General Synod? What do you think - should women be ordained?'

In 1975 the issue of the ordination of women had been before the General Synod. That Synod had agreed that, 'there were no fundamental objections to the ordination of women to the priesthood'.

Although this motion was passed it did so by a narrow majority, particularly in the House of Clergy, and because there was such divided opinion on the matter it was decided to put the matter on hold. In fact it stayed on hold for nearly 20 years. From then on, church members and others began discussing the issue much more frequently. Because I was part of the leadership team of the church, it was natural that people would ask me what I thought. My initial reaction was to say that I did not think that women should be ordained. Didn't the Bible say women should not be in leadership? However I began to think this through more carefully, grappling with both scripture and my own experience.

In the circles in which I moved at the time the arguments against this included, 'Women should be under the authority of men'. In thinking this through I questioned, 'Which men?' A husband? Perhaps, but I was not married. My father? But I was in my thirties and my father lived 250 miles away. My church elders? Yes, in matters concerning the church, but was I to consult my minister about where I went on holiday or how I managed my finances? So the question was to which men was I under authority, and on what issues?

Others said that women could hold positions of responsibility in secular society but not in the church. This argument suggested, for example, that it was acceptable for a woman to teach Religious Studies in a school or college but not in a church; or an able Christian woman may have oversight responsibilities at her place of work but should not do so in church. This line of reasoning would mean that a talented and experienced woman would have to leave her gifts and training at the church door, or perhaps that she should not have been educated in the first place.

Some believed that it would be acceptable for such gifts to be used among other women and children but not in a mixed congregation. If this line of argument were followed it would mean that our lay training programme, which I headed up, would only be available to the women of the church. Most of our church activities were for the whole church and not specific gender groups. So in some circles, the particular gifts that were not acceptable to be exercised by women were the gifts of leadership and teaching. Yet these were two of the gifts that I believed God had given me and had been developing slowly over the years.

Then there were those who said that the women were only looking for status, and wasn't ministry about service? This argument was not used about men who sought ordination but it did lead me to a discussion about the place of ambition in the life of a Christian. We concluded that ambition is wrong if it is a selfish means of acquiring a position at the expense of others, but if it is a desire to offer one's gifts and experience in the service of God, then this is not necessarily wrong.

These and other issues made me search the scriptures for answers. My searches took me to the oft quoted verses, but these needed to be read in their context and alongside other biblical teaching. I came to realise that the presenting issue needed to be seen in the light of some of the great themes of Scripture including the doctrines of creation, salvation, vocation and the gifts of the Spirit. I noted that the gifts of the Spirit as listed in Corinthians and Romans are not gender specific, rather it is the Spirit who decides on their allocation.

So it was that over the months, as I thought through these and other related issues, I changed my views and became convinced that it was right to support the cause of women's ordination. I believed the Spirit of God was moving the church to make this change in the Church of England in my generation. My decision was based on my study of the scriptures. There were of course other theological, ecclesiastical and ecumenical issues about which I became very aware over the next few years; this was a subject about which many felt deeply and sincerely on both sides of the argument.

'Have you ever considered standing for General Synod?' I was somewhat surprised at this question from a member of our church. My immediate answer was, 'No'. 'Well, I think you should - you would do well in that role,' she replied. It was 1975 and the person asking the question was retiring as a lay representative for the diocese of Ripon.

Every diocese in the Church of England has the right to elect a specific number of clerical and lay people to represent the diocese on General Synod, which is the Church's governing body. Elections take place every five years. The Synod is made up of three houses: the House of Bishops, to which every diocesan bishop is automatically a member, the House of Clergy and the House of Laity. As a lay person in the diocese, I had the right to stand for election to the House of Laity.

I had never considered getting involved in church politics, but having been asked I began to think about it seriously. I talked to those who had served in this way in the past to get some idea of what was involved. It would mean attending the sessions which were held three times a year. Each session lasted two to four days, and they were held twice a year in London and once a year at York. I obviously had to discuss this with my vicar, but as Michael had himself been a member of Synod, he supported me. I decided to throw my hat into the ring.

To get elected one had to get the support of sufficient voters, so I wrote an election address which was circulated to the electorate by the diocese. I included a photograph - this indicated my approximate age without having to give specific dates. Ripon Diocese includes the City of Leeds and smaller towns such as Harrogate, but also many villages and rural areas. I was able to refer to the facts that I was brought up in a village, involved in farming, worked with young people and in a suburban parish as well as my current post in the centre of a city.

I attended hustings, and in October 1975 was informed that I had been elected. I attended the inaugural session the following month which began with a grand service in Westminster Abbey attended by Her Majesty Queen Elizabeth. On the same day I was an invited guest of the Bishop of Ripon to a meal in the House of Lords. Most sessions started in a much less dramatic way!

As a member of General Synod I became much more aware of some of the significant issues relevant to the national church.

Much of the business was, for me, a bit mundane; but what I especially appreciated were some of the excellent reports published by working parties made up of people with expertise in their field and with differing insights into the subject in hand. When these reports were discussed on the floor of Synod we were privileged to hear some first rate speeches on the subject, along with some not so good! My own particular interest was in matters concerning ministry in the church, and within the year I became a member of The Committee for Theological Education.

One day, being a member of General Synod would give me the opportunity to contribute to the debate on women's ordination at national level. All of that was still to come.

## Chapter 8

## Moving On

By 1980 I had been at St George's for seven years. Some fine young men had joined the staff team as curates, stayed for about three years and then moved on to become vicars, or on to other responsible positions. Most of those opportunities were not open to me as I was not a priest, so I stayed largely because the openings were not there for women with my experience. I had learnt much from my vicar and held him in great respect, but I sometimes found myself critical, thinking, 'If he had done things differently, the outcome would have been better'. I began to want, not only to be responsible for my own decisions, but also for the things that went wrong. It was time for me to move on. I had served a long apprenticeship.

I began to look for other opportunities in parish ministry, and started applying for vacant posts for a deaconess. In fact most of the posts I applied for were that of team vicar. I knew that technically I was not qualified for such a post as I was not ordained, but if the sacramental ministry could be covered, I would be able to fulfil other aspects of such a position. My search led me to apply for posts in the Dioceses of Lichfield,

Wakefield, Oxford, Hereford, Liverpool and Chelmsford. In some cases I was not shortlisted or not appointed, and when I was offered a post it was either less demanding and varied than my role at St George's, or the incumbent that I would be working with was either younger or less experienced than I was. In these cases I instinctively felt that within a short time I would be wanting to tell him what to do! I knew it would not be a good working relationship if number two really felt that they should be number one.

I also applied for a post in the pastoral studies department of a theological college. After the interview, the principal took me aside and although he had invited me to apply for the post said, 'I'm very sorry, but we have decided not to offer you this position.' Although I knew that was the right decision, it was another avenue closed to me. This search took me about a year and was probably one of the most frustrating times of my ministry.

Towards the end of 1980 I had a visit from The Very Reverend Brandon Jackson. Brandon was the Provost (Dean) of Bradford Cathedral. Bradford and Leeds are only a few miles apart; they are both in West Yorkshire, but at the time were in different dioceses. (Bradford and Ripon together with Wakefield are now in the enlarged diocese of Leeds.) Brandon knew St George's, as he had served a curacy there before becoming the much loved incumbent of St Peter's Shipley, on the outskirts of Bradford. He was appointed provost in 1977 and was also Religious Advisor to Yorkshire Television.

Brandon was a dynamic character. As provost he had the opportunity to be involved in civic affairs, which he took in his stride. The cathedral was the obvious venue for many civic events. The cathedral was also the mother church of the diocese, and so hosted some of the significant diocesan occasions such as ordination services. In addition, Bradford

Cathedral was the spiritual home of many who lived in the city, so in that respect functioned as a large city centre church.

'Would you be prepared to consider joining the staff of Bradford Cathedral?' Brandon said. 'As the provost, a lot of my time is taken up with civic and diocesan responsibilities and I feel I'm not able to give enough time to the pastoral needs of the regular congregation. I know from my own experience how important this is. I'm thinking of appointing a chaplain.'

'What would that entail?' I asked.

'It would in fact be the equivalent role of their vicar - you would have pastoral responsibility for the regular worshippers, and be part of the preaching team. I've heard rumours from St George's that you're a competent preacher.'

I wondered how the cathedral team and worshippers would react to a woman as chaplain. It wasn't until I arrived at the cathedral that I realised that Brandon had not mentioned that the new chaplain might be a woman.

I considered his offer seriously and in due course visited Bradford Cathedral, met some of the staff, had discussions about the role and was shown the accommodation on offer. I was excited about this new opportunity, and only time would tell whether I was making the right decision.

## Chapter 9

## Cathedral Ministry

In March 1981 I moved about nine miles up the road from the centre of Leeds to the centre of Bradford. It made me think that the good Lord has a sense of humour! I found myself, with my farming background and a diploma in dairying, again living and working in an urban environment; but it was the right place for me at the time.

I was not a member of the Cathedral Chapter, but in many ways was treated as part of the ministry team at the cathedral, and I appreciated working with some very able colleagues. I adjusted to the regular pattern of cathedral worship, played my part in leading the worship during both mid week and Sunday services and was included on the Sunday preaching rota. For this I finally acquired the blue cassock of a deaconess. It was not an off-the peg cassock but rather more shapely, being a long blue dress with long sleeves and a stand up collar. I made it myself. My mother had been a professional dressmaker before she married and had taught her three daughters something of the craft.

On 24th April, just a few weeks after I had arrived, we woke to deep snow. The daffodils, which were in full bloom, were buried or bent double. It was the day when the new Bishop of Bradford was to be enthroned in the cathedral. Due to the snow many guests were unable to get there, but the local press issued an open invitation and the cathedral was packed. The new bishop was none other than Bishop Geoffrey Paul, who had been so helpful to me when I began my ministry in Swindon. After leaving Bristol Diocese, Geoffrey Paul had become Warden of Lee Abbey in Devon before becoming Bishop of Hull in 1977. He was now my bishop, but his time in Bradford was limited: I visited him in hospital in Leeds just a few weeks before he died in 1983.

Soon after my appointment, the local newspaper interviewed me and printed an article about my vocation and new role at the Cathedral. In response, a woman travelled from the outskirts of the city to meet me: she promised to pray for me, and often came to help with routine jobs. We have kept in touch ever since. I was particularly moved by this as she was a member of a Plymouth Brethren Church (not known for their encouragement of women in leadership) although she was also an occasional worshipper at the cathedral.

The following day I received a letter from a Christian woman who believed that I had missed my vocation, which was surely to be a wife and mother, rather than have a leadership position in the Church of God which she felt was against the teaching of the Bible. In my reply to her, I resisted the temptation to explain that, to date, God had failed to provide me with a husband - but I did invite her to meet with me to discuss the matter. She did not reply. These two responses indicated the strongly differing views held at the time, by both women and men, on the role of women in Christian ministry.

As I settled into my new ministry, I came to appreciate the role of the cathedral in the life of the diocese and of the city, and the importance of good liturgical worship, especially for the big occasions like ordination and civic services. A tragic event happened a few years later which made me realise that the cathedral could play a part in the lives of those who lived in the city even if they were not church goers.

On the afternoon of Saturday May 11th 1985, Bradford City Football Club was playing against Lincoln City at their home ground, The Valley Parade Stadium. The game was near half time when a fire broke out and spread very quickly. There was panic as spectators rushed to the exits. 56 people died, most of whom were Bradford City supporters. Of those, 11 were under 18. A further 265 were injured. The disaster touched the lives of thousands who lived in the city and surrounding areas.

The match was being televised on Yorkshire television, so word quickly spread. At the time, some of us were in the hall preparing for a missionary supper that was to be held that evening. On hearing the news, Provost Jackson put on his coat and headed towards the stadium to see if he could help in any way. He also made contact with the television studio where he had the role of being the Religious Advisor. Before the end of the day plans were in place for a service in the cathedral at 3.00pm the following afternoon. The media let people know that this was happening. The bishop preached and the cathedral was packed.

For the rest of the week it was made known that the cathedral would be open for any who wanted to grieve or just to sit quietly. The club's scarves and shirts were laid on the altar. Many came, including some of the young people who had lost friends or family members in the fire. The cathedral building and the staff had a role to play in the immediate aftermath of this tragedy. It was somewhere distressed people could go: something they could do even if what had happened could not be undone. A multi-denominational memorial service was held at the Football Stadium a couple of months later, which 6,000 people attended.

All this was taking place while I did my best to settle into my new home. The provost insisted that I live on site in the accommodation provided; this was a first floor flat in a large house opposite the Cathedral Close. The curate had the flat above me. The flat itself was adequate enough, and I soon made it into a comfortable home. There was a driveway at the back with an open shed for the car and open access to a garden with lawn, flower beds and a small walled garden, much neglected, which ran parallel to the main road leading into town. I enjoyed the garden and was soon growing my own vegetables.

Situated near the city centre and the cathedral, like all those who lived in the Close, I had regular visits from the homeless. I was happy to make endless mugs of tea and sandwiches. I was often asked for money, usually with the expressed need for a bus fare. I never gave money but offered to take my visitor to the bus stop and buy his ticket, which usually resulted in a change of plan. Only once did I actually walk with my 'friend' to the bus stop, but even then, after a few minutes, I was left standing on my own. I was never attacked, but sometimes one of these gentlemen would sleep in my garage: a bit unnerving when I got back late in the dark. On one occasion I opened the back door to discover a man urinating near the door. One of these men, who we called Paddy, had mental issues and would often pace around my lawn at night, just below my window, moaning and screaming. I became especially nervous if I was in the house on my own. On one occasion vandals climbed over the garden wall and trashed my plants. I am not of a nervous disposition, but I began to dread going back to the flat at night.

As my request to move to my own rented accommodation was refused, I began to consider looking for a new job. I also decided that I might feel safer if I had a guard dog. With this in mind I acquired a puppy. She was a very small Manchester terrier, black and tan and smooth haired, and I called her Tuppence. She proved to be useless as a guard dog but remained a faithful companion for the next 10 years.

Eventually, after I had been in post for about 20 months, I was allowed to move out of the accommodation provided and into a rented flat a mile or so from the city centre. I was given a study in the cathedral and travelled in every day. This led to a much happier domestic situation. As Bradford is only a few miles from Leeds, I was able to keep in touch with many of the friends that I had made while working at St George's.

I soon became very involved in lay training. Building on the experience I had gained at St George's Church in Leeds, we initiated an outreach programme which we called 'Teach and Reach'. This was based on Evangelism Explosion principles whereby we trained and then accompanied the lay people involved on visits to our contacts to talk through the meaning of the Gospel and its implications.

After lengthy discussions with the cathedral clergy, we also started a series of study groups on Sunday evenings at the cathedral. This was an adaptation of the Christian Education Programme that had been running in St George's Leeds. We called it 'Exploring the Faith'. It was a series of study groups, usually about six or seven different subjects, with each course lasting six weeks and for three terms in the year. (In Leeds it was part of the Sunday morning worship, but that timing was not appropriate for the cathedral.) We trained lay people in adult education principles to act as leaders of the groups, as well as using cathedral clergy and other local clergy.

Initially this was for the cathedral congregation, but we soon opened it to Christians and others from the area. The pattern evolved to the study groups meeting in the early evening on Sundays followed by worship in the cathedral. It was an exciting and enriching project and I was very involved in setting it up, training leaders and organising the publicity. We also initiated and appointed area pastors to care for the needs of our regular congregation.

While I was in Bradford I was not a member of General Synod, but I continued to have links with the national church which took me to Church House, Westminster and elsewhere from time to time. I continued my links with the Church Army, The Church Pastoral Aid Society and as a member of the Board of Ministry's Committee for Theological Education which met a couple of times a year. In 1983 I was invited to be a bishops' selector. This involved being on a selection panel that sought to discern the vocation of potential ordinands on behalf of the bishops.

So in many ways I was exercising a very full ministry in terms of pastoral care, lay training, and liturgical involvement and I sensed that for the most part my ministry was appreciated by the cathedral congregation. Yet there were frustrations. I remember one incident which illustrates the point. Working with the congregational committee, we had thought about how we could encourage members of the regular congregation to be more involved in the life and ministry of the cathedral. We decided to launch a project which some churches called 'Time and Talents' but which we called 'Skills and Service'. It would involve inviting our members to complete a questionnaire indicating in what ways they would like to serve in cathedral activities. The questionnaire would include things such as music, involvement with children or young people, flower arrangement, catering, coffee rotas, finance, cleaning, administration, visiting, leading groups and many other issues.

We had thought through how to respond to offers of help, any training that we might need to offer and other implications of what we were intending. So we had put a great deal of time and thought into this and had kept Provost Jackson fully informed, for which he gave us his enthusiastic support. We had also considered the best time to initiate the project, and how to help the congregation understand what was involved and why we thought this was important. I asked the provost if I could have a sermon slot prior to the launch date, to which he agreed. Near the time of our preferred launch date, the new preaching rota appeared but my name was not included. When I asked the provost why not, he said he had forgotten. I asked if the rota could be amended, the answer was no; it had already gone to print. Our scheme was not cancelled, but it was delayed and we had to think again about a start date.

To have responsibility without the appropriate authority can be difficult. As I was not a member of the cathedral chapter, I was not present when the provost and canons met to discuss and make decisions about the ministry of the cathedral, even though I had significant responsibility for one aspect of that ministry. Sometimes a staff meeting would be replaced by a chapter meeting without letting me know. This was particularly frustrating if I had a concern that I needed to discuss with the whole team.

The ministry team of the cathedral were all men apart from myself. They were all very able men with much experience under their belts, and individually they were wonderful people. However tensions arose from time to time either because of a clash of priorities or personalities. It was not always a comfortable place to be. The style of leadership was different from my style, and from time to time I was made aware of my unordained status.

Not being ordained also meant that my future was uncertain, and I seriously considered two alternatives. First, I wondered if I should leave the ministry and seek secular employment. I made an appointment to see a careers advisor at the university which was not very helpful, partly because I had no idea what else I wanted to do; and partly, as he implied, I was a bit too old to start a new career!

The other alternative I considered was to transfer to the Methodist Church, where women ministers were fully accepted. Without making an appointment, I walked to the nearby manse intending to discuss this with the local Methodist minister. There was no reply when I knocked. On thinking about it, I was glad that this line of inquiry was fruitless. It was not a good basis for changing denomination. Having had time to reflect on both these alternatives I came to the conclusion that God, who had given me my vocation, had not revoked that call. I had to stick with it.

The question of the ordination of women was not a hot topic at the cathedral. I think the canons supported my position, although at that time I suspect the provost still had reservations. In many ways Provost Brandon Jackson was not an easy man to work with, although I came to have a great respect for him. I was told that, when my appointment was announced, a leading man in the city who knew Brandon very well, predicted that a woman in that position would not last more than six months! I stayed for nearly five years and have kept in touch with Brandon and his lovely wife Mary ever since. Sadly Brandon died in 2023.

After about three years in post, however, the difficulties and frustrations led me to discuss my future with my colleagues and with the bishop and to begin looking for other jobs. For the next year I considered over 20 different jobs in various parts of the country. I was hoping to move further south as my parents were getting elderly and it would be easier to help from time to time if I lived nearer, but my options were limited. I enquired about posts in theological colleges, retreat houses, diocesan appointments in five different dioceses, and for numerous team vicar jobs. I faced the same frustrations that I had faced some five years previously: not being ordained was a significant barrier. Of course there were probably other reasons why I was not qualified for some of these posts. In some cases I was shortlisted and interviewed, but nothing proved suitable.

I also had an interview with the National Clergy Appointments Advisor who advertised my details. These were available to bishops and others looking to recruit staff. It was through this latter contact, that six months after that interview I received an invitation to consider a team vicar's post in the Diocese of Rochester. After visiting twice and meeting the incumbent and others in the parish, I was offered the job and accepted. I left Bradford and moved to the Parish of South Gillingham at the end of 1985. I could not have known it at the time, but this proved to be probably the most important decision of my ministry.

## Chapter 10

## Acting Team Vicar

It wasn't exactly an ecclesiastical looking building: the scout hut had a brownish wooden interior, and the extra chairs borrowed by the scout masters accommodated the 150 people who had come to my first Sunday on duty in South Gillingham. As I looked out over my new congregation, I was delighted to spot Brandon and Mary Jackson from Bradford and a previous curate and his wife who had travelled from York. It was a great occasion and very affirming as I began a new phase in my ministry.

The Parish of South Gillingham is in the Medway Towns in the Diocese of Rochester. At the time I moved there the population of the parish was said to be about 22,000. It consisted of four distinct areas, each with its own place of worship. At the centre was Wigmore where there was a modern church with a parish hall, ancillary rooms and the rectory adjacent. There was the community of Hempstead with a relatively new church and accommodation for one of the curates. The third area was the village of Bredhurst with its ancient, fairly small but beautiful church which proved very popular for weddings. Bredhurst Church was situated at the end of a lane, a little apart from the rest of the village. It was said that the cottages surrounding the church were destroyed after the Black Death and new properties built.

The fourth area of the parish was the modern housing estate of Parkwood, said at the time to be the largest private housing estate in Europe. Population wise it was also the largest area within the parish. At the centre of the estate was a large car park surrounded by an area of shops, a petrol station, pub, community centre and a modern Baptist church. There was also a fairly large green space with mature trees. The Anglican presence consisted of two adjacent town houses in a terrace just off the centre. One of these houses was to be my home for the next 5 years. The ground floor of the other house had been converted into a chapel, a rectangular room which ran the depth of the house and seated up to 30 people. This was St Paul's Parkwood, for which I was given pastoral responsibility. My brief was to build the church on Parkwood - not in terms of a building, although that happened later, but in terms of building up the church of people from the estate.

The Rector, The Reverend Peter Bird, had served a curacy in a team ministry and understood the value of such a ministry. His vision was that South Gillingham should become a team ministry, and he had set in place the structures to enable that to happen in due course. Hence each of the four churches had their own district church council and the curate and I were treated as if we were team vicars. As I was not ordained and could not have been an actual team vicar (for which ordination to the priesthood is a legal necessity), Peter's policy was that the three of us should be ministers of all four churches, although we each had specific responsibility for one of them. Peter and his wife were keen supporters of the ordination of women, and he was a man secure in himself and his ministry. I could not have had a more supportive and encouraging incumbent. We came from slightly differing church traditions but had mutual respect for each other.

Initially Peter expected me to be at St Paul's for the main Sunday service on two Sundays a month and at one of the other churches on the other two Sundays. I persuaded him that I needed to be at St Paul's on three Sundays a month if I was to build relationships and grow the church on Parkwood. My ministry consisted of normal parish responsibilities. This included funerals and baptisms. A deaconess was allowed to take baptisms, and at the time there were many. It was not unusual to baptise children from at least 3 families on the same occasion, and often on consecutive Sunday afternoons. I was not allowed to take weddings, however, as without being ordained I was not qualified as a registrar of marriages.

Together with the rector and curate, we revised our baptism policy. The aim was to offer an initial welcome to every family that approached us about baptism, but then to help them to understand both that we took baptism very seriously and that they would be making significant promises to bring their child up in the Christian faith. We began by inviting every family that asked for the baptism of their child, to first come to church for a thanksgiving service. This met the needs of some families without the demands that baptism implied. For those who wished to proceed to baptism, the first visit was by trained lay people to talk through what baptism means; this was followed by a visit from the rector, curate or me with a more in-depth baptism preparation session.

The biggest frustration to my ministry was being unable to preside at the services of Holy Communion. We overcame this by regular use of 'Communion by extension'. This meant that when I was taking a Communion service, I had first to take the bread and wine to an earlier service for the elements to be consecrated by one of the clergy. On a typical Sunday, this meant attending an 8am service for the elements to be consecrated, leaving before the end of that service to get to a 9.30am service in my own church. This was certainly not ideal, not to mention theologically doubtful - but it was the only way that I could effectively fulfil my responsibilities and provide Communion for my congregation. We did not embarrass the bishop or archdeacon by asking permission. They may have felt obliged to refuse; but I suspect they knew what was happening and turned a blind eye.

I chaired St Paul's District church council, which was a much more informal occasion than I had been used to, but we were at that time a small church. I was also given responsibility for adult christian education across the whole parish.

In due course I was able to initiate various study courses for the whole parish, often working with the local Baptist lay minister to plan the studies.

*As a deaconess. Home Communion using the reserved sacrament. 1987*

During my first year the congregation at St Paul's remained fairly static, but I was getting to know the church members and slowly things were developing. By the end of the year we had moved the monthly family service from the small chapel to the scout hut where we could accommodate a larger congregation and include some of the uniformed organisations.

Life was not so pressured during the week, and within six months I was invited by the diocese to be Director of Reader Training in addition to my parish responsibilities. This gave me an interest beyond the parish and an insight into the life of the diocese. This was an honorary post working alongside the Warden of Readers, who was one of the residential canons at the cathedral. I also continued my commitments to the national church as an assessor for the Church Army candidates in training and as a bishop's selector for ordination candidates. These duties took me out of the parish a few times each year. For this I had the support of my incumbent and it kept me abreast of issues beyond the coal face: a dimension I have always appreciated.

Now that I was living in Kent, I had a new part of the country to explore and began the process of making new friends. My father's parents had lived for some time in Kent and I had an aunt and cousin living in the Rochester area. I was now slightly nearer my parents, who still lived in Somerset, and as I had easy access to the M2 I was able to visit more frequently. I kept up with friends from Yorkshire and returned to the north of England for holidays, often stopping in Bradford on the way.

CHAPTER 11

# THE DIACONATE

On one level, it was an important day when I received a letter from the Bishop of Rochester inviting me to become a deacon. This would become legally possible once the relevant canon was promulgated by the General Synod in February 1987. On the other hand, as I stood reading the letter, I thought that this was only an official way to recognise what I had in effect been doing for many years. In his letter the bishop explained that as a deacon I would cease to be a member of the House of Laity and become a member of the House of Clergy and thus able to use the title 'The Reverend'. Although I had never used that title, many of my regular congregation already thought of me as their parish priest.

The plan was for the ordinations to take place in March 1987. As I was a deaconess no further training was expected. It was a big step for the church, but a very small step for me.

A significant issue at the time concerned what we would wear as deacons. In his initial letter to me the bishop included these words, 'The Archbishops of Canterbury and York have suggested that as deaconesses possess blue cassocks, they should continue to wear these and not feel obliged to purchase a black cassock. After ordination as deacon they may, like their male colleagues, also wear a surplice with black scarf and an academic hood (where appropriate), or a coloured stole worn across the shoulder...As for male clergy, this will not apply to clerical collars and stocks, because the wearing of these is entirely optional. Indeed, it is much to be hoped that eventually a suitable feminine alternative will be evolved! A 'dog collar' is not an essential article of clothing and is, of course, of comparatively recent origin! It will be in order for a deaconess's silver cross to continue to be worn with a cassock or ordinary clothes, until such time as it is replaced by a lapel badge.'

A few weeks later, when I received a further letter from the bishop accepting my application and giving more details of plans for the ordinations, his letter concluded thus: 'I am leaving the Head Deaconess to consult with all those concerned about the vexed question of dress. I ask only for as much agreement and as little public discussion as possible! May we rejoice over the great event of the admission of women to Holy Orders, but be careful to avoid encouraging those who would trivialise the occasion by fashion gossip!'

In my own case it was several months before I eventually purchased some clerical shirts and a dog collar; in the meantime I tried to find a suitable white blouse with a roll neck. We were all feeling our way as we came to terms with this significant change in the life of our church. I suppose it was a symbolic attempt to tease out in what ways women clergy would make their distinctive contribution, rather than just ape the male role. By the nature of things we had no female role models within the Church of England, and despite the bishop's frustration, of course the 'vexed question' continued. At an informal meeting of women deacons some time later I made the rather flippant suggestion that perhaps we should wear hot pants in the appropriate liturgical colours. Fortunately, as women clergy come in many shapes and sizes, as do men clergy, no one took my suggestion seriously!

The date for the ordination of Parish Deacons in the Diocese of Rochester was Sunday, March 15th 1987. In a pastoral letter to cathedral and parish clergy, dated March 9th 1987, the bishop started his letter by writing that on March 15th he 'expected to ordain 23 deaconesses and two licensed lay workers to the Order of Deacon in the Church of God in the presence of a congregation of more than 1400 people from all parts of the diocese...Later this summer the 700 or more women who will have been ordained as deacons throughout the country will elect their own representatives to General Synod until 1990, when both men and women will stand for election in each diocese in the usual way'.

Regarding authority to conduct marriage services, the bishop wrote that the House of Bishops had decided 'that where a deacon solemnises a marriage...he or she may pronounce the blessing of the couple, for which the authorised rites provide...deacons should not normally solemnise marriages in the first year following ordination. The normal practice of the Church continues to be that a priest, if present, should solemnise a marriage. But when a deacon officiates it is right, as an exception...for the deacon, having solemnised the marriage, to pronounce the nuptial blessing. But in respect of the final blessing...the deacon should follow the normal practice of using the "us" form.'

On Saturday March 14th, those of us to be ordained were invited to lunch as guests of the bishop. Lunch was followed by a rehearsal in the cathedral, the necessary legal business, cathedral evensong and then the Bishop's Ordination Charge, given to the ordinands in private. It is usual practice that before any ordination service those to be ordained will gather in the presence of the ordaining bishop, who will address them with words of support and encouragement. This is called the Bishop's Charge.

The Bishop of Rochester at the time was David Say. He was much respected and had served in the church for many years. In his ordination charge he laid out his theological and biblical reasons for being a supporter of the full inclusion of women in the ministry of the church, and hinted that he had held that conviction for more than 20 years. For a man of his generation, his views were ahead of their time. He noted that during his more than 25 years in Rochester the number of women in full-time ministry had grown from three to 25 as well as many women readers and women in other forms of lay ministry. He recognised that what he called the 'modest step' of admitting women to the Holy Order of Deacon would in fact make very little difference to the actual ministry of these women; but he added, 'the first hand experience of ordained men and women ministering alongside each other will do more than a thousand debates or pamphlets to help people understand the wholeness of ministry.'

The bishop continued by recognising the distinctive contribution that women make and expressed the desire that they should not seek to be pseudo-men. He paid tribute to Deaconess Muriel Pargeter who would become the Diocesan Deacon, and hoped to live to see the day when she could be an archdeacon. That honour did not come to Muriel, although in due course, she was one of the first women to be made an honorary cathedral canon. Little did the bishop know that one of the women he was to ordain deacon on that occasion, would in fact be the first woman to be appointed as archdeacon in the Church of England, and that in Rochester Diocese.

This charge was very affirming of women in ministry but David Say, even though in many respects forward thinking, was still a man of his time. The one part of his charge that I found upsetting was his fear that ordained women should assume an unnatural male veneer. He added, 'We all want you to remain women and to be revered and honoured as such.' I appreciated his sentiment, but what did it mean? Were we expected to conform to the male image of a woman? I also wondered if I was feminine enough, whatever that means. Why couldn't I be accepted as me, unashamed to be a woman created as such by God? I have wondered since, if when giving a charge to male ordinands he exhorted them to be masculine! However, we were on the eve of a momentous and significant event; and for a man of his time Bishop David Say was 100% supportive.

The ordination service the next day was a significant occasion for all involved. The atmosphere was one of celebration. Yet, as I walked in the procession into the cathedral on that Sunday morning, tears of humiliation welled up. I had in effect been exercising the ministry of a deacon for at least 20 years; in fact for more than 10 years I had been serving in a way more akin to that of a parish priest. Now I was expected to be grateful to the church for allowing me to be part of the third order of ministry. However, my personal feelings were unimportant compared with the significance of the step made by the Church of England.

## Chapter 12

## Conducting Weddings

The following day I was back in the parish and life continued as before. The liturgical act of making me a deacon only had one practical effect. I had been conducting baptisms and funerals for many years, but now I was legally able to conduct weddings.

A Church of England cleric is recognised as a registrar of marriages. I was serving in a large parish where in the 1980s there was a high demand for church marriages. It was not unusual for there to be five or more services on a Saturday in the marriage season. My incumbent valued some help. On one particular Saturday I took four marriage services on the same day, although I did complain that it was too many if I was to give each one the careful attention that they deserved. At the time the situation regarding deacons taking marriage services was regarded as legal but irregular. I was to conduct nearly 100 such services during the next three years while I remained in that parish.

Our marriage preparation policy was not very comprehensive. I would meet with the couple in advance and talk through the content of the service with them, stressing the significance of the vows they would be taking and explaining that I would not be marrying them: rather, they were marrying each other, and I was there to conduct the service, to pray for them and to ensure that they would leave as a legally married couple. This interview would be followed by a rehearsal in the church a day or so before the service.

As happens in all walks of life, sometimes things don't go according to plan. There was an occasion when my incumbent was due to fly back from holiday on a Saturday in time to take two marriage services the same afternoon. On reflection he realised it had not been a very sensible decision. I received an overseas phone call from him at 6.45am to say that his flight was delayed, and would I stand in for him? My plans for the day were immediately cancelled and I made a quick dash to the parish office to retrieve as much information as possible concerning the details of both weddings. Then, in turn I visited the home of the brides concerned. As you can imagine each family was very involved in all the preparations that take place on the day of a wedding. I explained what had happened and that I would be conducting the service. I assured them that as far as they were concerned their day could go ahead as already arranged, they had nothing to worry about and I would make sure that the service went ahead as had been planned. For me, the next few hours meant hasty preparations to conduct two marriage services. In the event both weddings went off without a hitch. When Peter got back later in the day he was full of apologies, but was at least back in time for the Sunday services the following day.

When the Church of England had deacons who were women taking more of the occasional offices such as weddings and funerals, there were occasionally objections on the basis of gender. Some church people genuinely believed this to be contrary to scripture and tradition, and that view had to be respected. There were others for whom it 'just did not feel right'. This view was also held by some who had limited experience of Christian worship and who felt that it was more appropriate for a clergyman to conduct such services. For these and other reasons, women clergy were occasionally the subject of discrimination. When this happened the situation had to be handled with some sensitivity.

There was one occasion when I was asked to take the wedding of a young couple. I arranged to meet them. They came to see me, I got to know them a little, we talked through the significance of their vows and what would be included in the service. They were looking forward to the big day. Presumably they went back to tell their family about our meeting. The next thing I knew was that Peter had had a complaint from the bride's mother. She said she was a Roman Catholic and objected to a woman taking her daughter's marriage service.

It was obvious that her daughter had not been brought up as a Roman Catholic because if she had been, she would have asked and expected to be married in a Roman Catholic Church by a Catholic priest. The couple had asked to be married in an Anglican church, and presumably the mother knew that. In view of these circumstances Peter would not, on principle, countenance a change of officiant. I took the service as planned and it was a very happy occasion.

There was another occasion which was during the vacancy when we were short staffed. I received a request to take the funeral of a man in the parish. I visited the widow, and when she realised that I was to take the funeral she was very upset and said to me, 'He had a hard life, he had the second best in life and now he is having the second best in death'. However, I stayed and talked with her about her late husband and what she would like included in the funeral service. I promised to do the very best I could to give her husband all the respect he deserved at his funeral.

Situations like that happened occasionally, and not just in the early days after women were ordained. It was still happening some ten or more years later. A friend of mine who was then a curate had a request from the undertaker to conduct a funeral. This was the first one she had ever taken. She visited the bereaved, and talked through the plans for the funeral. When the woman realised that my friend was to take the funeral, she said, 'Troubles always come in threes: my husband died, the washing machine broke down and now you are taking the funeral!' It was sometimes hard to bite one's tongue, but occasions like that were not the time for debates about the role of women; rather these were situations where sympathy and kindness were called for, and as ministers we had to do the best we could for those we were called to serve.

## Chapter 13

## Deacons Now

When women were made Deacons in 1987, they were in effect disenfranchised from representation on General Synod. They were no longer eligible for the House of Laity, and had not been eligible for the House of Clergy when the elections were held in 1985. So it was agreed that there should be a special constituency of women deacons for the remainder of the current Synod. Women deacons were to be elected on a provincial basis in October 1987. I was elected as one of seven women deacons representing the Province of Canterbury, and so in November of that year I returned to serve on General Synod after a gap of six years.

The Church of England does not have a very clear theology of the diaconate. Although recognising the three orders of ministry - bishop, priest and deacon - and that bishops and Priests also remain Deacons for the whole of their ordained ministry, the diaconate had become, in effect, an apprenticeship for priesthood, with the majority of clergy serving for about a year before being priested. A few men opted to remain deacons and so the church did have a very small permanent diaconate.

With the ordination of women to the diaconate in 1987 the situation changed. By 1989 there were about 1,000 permanent deacons in the church at a time when the possibility of women being priested was still unresolved. The majority of the women who were deacons would have liked to have had their vocation to priesthood tested, but at the time, that was not possible.

For at least the previous ten years I had been asking hard questions about a career structure for women in accredited ministry. There will be those who say that ministry is not about career development, rather it is about service. That is true, and yet there were expectations that clergy would move to positions of more responsibility as they gained experience. Most curates became vicars or chaplains in various contexts. Some later moved on to be team rectors, or joined the staff of a cathedral, moved into theological education or into specialist ministries with increased responsibility. A few became archdeacons and even fewer were consecrated as bishops. None of these opportunities were open to women, however experienced they were, because they did not have the basic qualification of ordination.

Although I had been asking the question, it was not taken seriously until women became clergy. In 1987 with the prospect of there being many women clergy, i.e. deacons, the church began to realise that this was an issue. Thus it was that in 1989, the Advisory Council for the Church's Ministry (ACCM), as it was then called, set up a working party to address this matter. Among the terms of reference of that working party was, 'To assess the potential for development in the areas of ministry that women deacons in the Church of England might undertake, and to examine the theological, legal and practical reasons for placing them in senior posts.' I was asked to chair the working party, which met and worked on recommendations for the following 12 months.

There were two major issues to address. Firstly, how could the church benefit from the body of experienced women who were now deacons? Most of these women were, on average, much older than their male counterparts and had considerable life experience: about 15% had over ten years experience in ministry and 5% had over 20 years of such experience. I was among that 5%.

The second issue was about moving deacons on from their training posts in order for training posts to be available for those women leaving theological college. Most of the recommendations were addressed to the Dioceses asking that these matters be given serious consideration at diocesan level. The report contained recommendations of how eucharistic ministry was to be covered when deacons who were women were given sole pastoral charge of parishes. The question basically was, 'Now that we have a permanent diaconate, how do we best use this resource?' Our report, entitled 'Deacons Now', was published in 1990.

## Chapter 14

# The Debate Continues

With the ordination of women to the diaconate in 1987, the debate about their priesting intensified. This was an issue that had been under debate for the whole of my ministry and for many years before that. Long before I was actively involved, there had been women and men raising the issue and presenting theological and other arguments urging the church to take the matter forward. When I joined General Synod in 1975 notable speakers in the debate included Christian Howard of Castle Howard fame, Deaconess Diana McClatchey, Jean Mayland and Canon Colin Craston.

'The Movement for the Ordination of Women' was the main campaigning organisation in favour of this development, and kept the issue in the headlines. It produced good quality publicity, arranged meetings for discussion and debate and enlisted speakers who were knowledgeable on all aspects of the matter in hand. Sometimes it felt as if they were raising insignificant matters, and they sometimes caused antagonism rather than support; but that was almost inevitable for a campaigning organisation that was motivated by a sense of injustice, frustration, discrimination and increasing impatience at the slow progress of change.

The Movement was also concerned for the good of the church. Although there was plenty of publicity about the numbers who might leave the church if women were ordained, there was no way of knowing how many had already left the Church of England because of its attitude to women in ministry. The Movement alerted us to that fact.

I became a member and sent them my subscription to show my support, but rarely attended their meetings. As one of many who were in the job and lived with the frustrations and limitations on a daily basis, I did not find it helpful to go to a meeting which raised emotions concerning the issues; and sometimes actions were suggested which I did not think would be helpful. Such meetings left me feeling angry, more frustrated and depressed and less able to get on with the job in hand. Yet I did not want to discourage those who were putting so much energy into something that they and I believed in passionately.

I decided that my contribution to the cause was to do my job as well as I could. There had been those, especially in the early days of the debate, who did not think women were capable of being priests, so initially we had to show that some women could in fact do the job, although the only model was the male one. Later the emphasis changed and there were those who did not want us to be pseudo male priests, although no one quite knew what distinctive contribution women priests could make. We were all on a steep learning curve.

I was a regular speaker in debates on the issue at local and national level, at theological colleges and at evangelical fellowships. I was particularly interested in debates concerning the scriptural basis for my position. I was sometimes involved in discussions with those of a more Anglo-Catholic persuasion and felt it important to understand the theological views of those from that tradition, who held a differing view from my own. I was quite shocked to learn that some people actually thought God was male, confusing the title of God as 'Father' with the maleness of a human father.

There were times when the level of debate was appalling. On one occasion I was in Church House, Westminster for the meeting of General Synod. During breaks in the Synod sessions there were opportunities for fringe meetings organised by special interest groups. I attended such a fringe meeting led by 'Forward in Faith', who were, and still are, an organisation of mainly Anglo-Catholic members who sincerely believe that it is wrong to ordain women. As far as I remember the speaker did not spend much time on the theological reasons for the views that he held; rather he seemed to be trying to show that women were not suitable for ordination.

He used as an illustration the case of illegal ordinations that had happened in the Episcopal Church in America some years previously. During the delays in that church before it was finally agreed that women could be ordained, a retired bishop had ordained several women - illegally. The speaker made a point of explaining that in his view none of those so ordained were suitable candidates for the priesthood. He reminded us that among those ordained on that occasion, one was divorced, one had had a mental breakdown, and one or two were retired and so too old.

The implication was that any woman who aspired to ordination was either morally, mentally or educationally unfit, or just too old for ordination. I was so shocked at what he was saying that I admit I may have missed other points that he made in his speech. What I heard was that women like me, who sincerely believed that they had a vocation to ordination, were just not good enough. It was humiliating and showed a complete lack of respect for those who held different views to that of the speaker.

That attitude was certainly not true of all who disagreed with women's ordination. In Rochester Diocese I knew several clergy within the Anglo-Catholic tradition who were also opposed. It was interesting that among those who held that position there were some who would not make eye contact when I was in conversation with them, while with others I could have an open and good hearted discussion which showed mutual respect. That latter attitude was true of Archbishop David Hope. On one occasion we were both at a residential conference and got into conversation over breakfast. He did not believe women should be ordained, and he knew my views, but we talked about it without any embarrassment and agreed to differ.

At the time of that unfortunate fringe meeting, feelings about the issue were running high. There was a genuine fear that if things did not move in a positive direction there could be illegal ordinations in this country. Fortunately that did not happen. In November 1989, General Synod referred 'The Legislation for the Ordination of Women to the Priesthood' to the dioceses for a response, so the debate continued.

CHAPTER 15

# RURAL DEAN

'But I don't understand how you could be about to become my rural dean. Surely a woman can't be in authority over men?' Thomas Collett White, the much-loved vicar of a large evangelical church, leaned back in his armchair and waited for my reply.

At the end of 1987 the rural dean of our Deanery of Gillingham had stood down.

Gillingham Deanery, which covered some of the Medway Towns, was not very large but included a range of differing churches. They differed in both size and churchmanship, from the extremes of high Anglo-Catholic to low evangelical and charismatic. The bishop invited the incumbents of the deanery to offer him suggestions as to who should be appointed. Not being an incumbent I was not, of course, consulted and only learnt later of the names that were suggested.

In January 1988 I was surprised to receive a letter from Bishop David Say asking me to consider accepting this role. I wondered how the clergy of the deanery would react, especially those who had not put my name forward. This would be breaking new ground, both to have a deacon as rural dean and for that deacon to be a woman. I am told that at the time the ecclesiastical lawyers were divided as to whether a deacon could hold the office of rural dean, and can only assume that our bishop consulted one who was positive about such an appointment.

I had been told by the bishop that the incumbent of St Mark's Church in Gillingham, the Revd Thomas Collett White, had reservations about my appointment because I was a woman. St Mark's was, and still is, a large thriving evangelical church and one of the first to be influenced by the charismatic movement. I was later to become a member of that church. Thomas held the view, shared by others within the evangelical tradition, that a woman should not have authority over a man. Before my appointment as rural dean was confirmed I had decided to go to discuss the matter with Thomas.

'As rural dean, I will not have any authority over the incumbents in the deanery,' I replied. 'I will be coordinating deanery affairs, chairing meetings of the deanery chapter and synod and representing your views to the archdeacon and bishop.'

A gracious discussion followed, and Thomas conceded the point.

I obviously discussed the possibility of this appointment with my incumbent, who was enthusiastically supportive. I suspect it was because my incumbent was secure in himself and in his ministry that this worked. We respected each other's role, which had nothing to do with gender or seniority. Within the parish I was under his authority, and in the deanery he respected my position.

I was commissioned as Rural Dean of Gillingham in February, the first woman in the Church of England to hold such a position. My appointment caused a flurry of media interest in the local press and a telephone interview with Teesside local radio, but there was also national interest with an article in the Daily Telegraph and even an interview with BBC television. The report in the Church Times was followed by letters to the editor both critical and supportive.

The legality of a deacon being a rural dean was confirmed by General Synod in 1989. There was also a debate in General Synod in 1989 about deacons being appointed as archdeacons. That motion was lost.

One of my first responsibilities as rural dean was to find a new deanery secretary, as the previous one was about to retire for personal reasons. The outgoing rural dean suggested that I approach David Gwyer. David had previously held that position but had given it up to nurse his wife. I was told his wife had since died, leaving him with two teenage daughters; but he had been very efficient and might now be prepared to return to the role.

I knocked on his door, and it was opened by a rather large gentleman with a big smile. He invited me in and we talked about his previous role as secretary to the deanery synod. I asked if he would be prepared to take on the role again, to which he agreed.

The other significant event for me in 1988 (and of course for many others) was the retirement of Bishop David Say as Bishop of Rochester. Bishop David had been very supportive and indeed appointed me as rural dean. Fortunately for me, his successor was my archdeacon, Michael Turnbull. Michael knew me and my situation and had been part of the bishop's staff and therefore part of the discussions when this appointment was made. I continued to get full episcopal support.

Sundays were particularly busy days. It was not unusual for me to be officiating or at least present at five services on a Sunday. If my responsibilities included a Communion service, I would first have to take bread and wine to be consecrated at an early service. Then I would take the service at St Paul's at 9.30 and sometimes go from there to take a service in one of our other churches at 11.00am. There were often Baptism services on a Sunday afternoon, and sometimes an evensong. On one particular Sunday I was not only present at five services but had an afternoon meeting with young people and then a later evening meeting with my church wardens. Seven commitments in one day is not to be recommended! These are the sort of pressures that many parish priests face from time to time, so I was not complaining (except, of course, I was not a parish priest).

If life was busy then, it was to get more so when my incumbent decided it was time for him to move on. The other ordained member of staff held a position similar to my own, in that he was in effect the team vicar of one of the churches in the parish. He was an older man approaching his sixties who had been a non-stipendiary minister and probably did not fully understand the demands of full time parish ministry, especially in a large and busy parish. Also his health was not good. With a vacancy looming he was not able to take on extra responsibilities - indeed his doctor had advised him not to undertake any stressful duties - and he decided to retire.

During a vacancy the churchwardens have the care of the parish, and other clergy can be called on to help with Sunday services; but in practice the pastoral work and occasional offices fell mostly on my shoulders. The number of funerals for which I was responsible increased as the curate said he could only manage at most one a week. It was not unusual for me to take two funerals on the same day. Life was very busy and somewhat pressured.

On the positive side, the congregation at St Paul's, Parkwood which was my base, was becoming too large for the chapel which we occupied on the ground floor of the terraced house next to my home. We needed bigger premises, and having discussed this with the diocese we were delighted to learn that a site for a new church building had been purchased. The site was a disused petrol station right in the heart of the estate, and although it would be several years before the new church would be built, we had a great service of dedication of the site by Bishop Colin Buchanan who was living in the diocese.

## Chapter 16

## Multitasking

Planning deanery events often meant meeting with my friend David Gwyer, the one with the big smile whose ready laugh I was coming to appreciate.

'Thank you for the minutes of the last meeting, David. Your knowledge of the deanery is such a great help when I'm so often away with my other responsibilities.'

'Well, the information you bring back from General and Diocesan Synod are very helpful to us here in the deanery,' he said. 'But you must be very busy as rural dean with the vacancies and having to meet with potential incumbents.' Having been secretary for the previous rural dean, David always understood my role and it was a relief to discuss it with him.

'Yes, and I've had meetings with the archdeacon and bishop as well - and although I'm no longer the director of reader training, I'm now training tutors for the new Lay training scheme. I can't seem to stop!' I replied. He responded with his signature laugh.

The diocese worked relatively swiftly in seeking a new incumbent for our parish, and I soon became involved with the parish representatives in discussing the needs of the parish and sometimes meeting potential new incumbents. Within a month of the outgoing incumbent leaving, a new appointment had been made, although it was several months before he took up his responsibilities. Towards the end of 1989 I had the privilege, as rural dean, of planning and partaking in the licensing of the next vicar of my own parish.

It was while I was feeling the pressure of parish life during the vacancy that in October 1989, I had an invitation from the suffragan bishop to attend an in-service Clergy Short Course of 10 days at St George's House, Windsor Castle. I tried to refuse on the basis that I was under too much pressure but was told I had to attend.

It was indeed a privilege to have been invited to be a participant of this rather prestigious training course, which I was told was for clergy with the potential for more senior appointments. Of the 22 participants, I was the only woman, and all the staff were white, male clerics. The subjects under discussion were interesting and challenging, but at no point was there any recognition that the future of our church might include women priests, or any discussion regarding the implications of either the inclusion or rejection of such a move. The atmosphere was male and hierarchical in orientation, with in-jokes about mothers-in-law and washing up. Even the housekeeper, who was very efficient, ran the establishment with military precision and I sensed she did not really approve of my presence.

We had a conducted tour of Windsor Castle and it was a great experience to worship in St George's Chapel, but the worship was male dominated and it seemed that it would not be 'proper' to include women. While I recognised the significance of even being invited to participate, I did not find it the most helpful form of in-service training.

## Judith Rose

I was continuing to enjoy parish ministry, and it was good to have a new colleague as vicar. I had been in the parish for just over four years and intended to continue there for the next few years at least. Then, in February 1990, Bishop Michael Turnbull asked to see me. I went to Rochester not knowing the reason for the meeting. After some preliminary conversation the bishop said, 'Would you consider moving to Rochester to become my personal chaplain? I think you have the experience that I need and you know the diocese fairly well. It would also be good to have a woman on the staff alongside the archdeacons, dean and diocesan secretary, all of whom are men.' We talked further about what the job would entail and I was asked to think about this seriously.

I reflected that prior to my previous two moves it had taken me over a year of applications, interviews and frustrations before I found the right move. Now when I wasn't thinking of moving I had been asked to take on a new responsibility. If I accepted the post it would be within the same diocese, and I already knew something of Michael as he had been my archdeacon before being made bishop.

I thought about it very carefully and took advice from my present and previous incumbents. Both were sympathetic to my situation. I was a deacon, and because the question of the ordination of women to the priesthood was still unresolved and I may never be able to become a vicar, my options for a different responsibility in the next few years were limited. I would be sad to leave the parish, but in the end decided that the offer on the table was too good an opportunity to be missed, and so accepted the post.

I moved to Bishopscourt in Rochester in August 1990. I was provided with a self-contained flat on the top floor of the bishop's residence and was given an area of the garden for my hobby of growing vegetables.

Although I began my new role as bishop's chaplain in September of that year, for the next few months I returned to the parish at weekends (a distance of only a few miles) to help with weddings on Saturdays - on a couple of occasions, three weddings on the same day - and services on the Sundays, with up to four services in the churches across the parish. I also went back to take the occasional funeral. This was because the parish, which usually had a complement of three full time clergy, already had one vacancy: my move had left them with only the newly appointed vicar. I think my help was appreciated, but it meant a rather disjointed move to my new position.

## Chapter 17

# Bishop's Chaplain

The role of bishop's chaplain varies from bishop to bishop. I was not to be a liturgical chaplain. The Bishop of Rochester at that time had the services of a retired cleric for that role. I was grateful for this, not least because Bishop Michael was tall and I am short! My role included dealing with much of the correspondence that came into the bishop's office. After the secretary had opened the post, I was often able to draft a reply which would be typed up and back on the bishop's desk by later in the same day. If he was content with the response, he could sign or amend, and in this way we could get prompt replies sent back. Sometimes this involved me making phone calls to clarify the situation before drafting a reply. Obviously some matters could only be dealt with by the bishop personally. When the bishop and his wife held dinner parties for clergy from the diocese I would help with the hospitality.

As bishop's chaplain, I was present at staff meetings when the bishop met with his archdeacons, the dean of the cathedral and diocesan secretary. I was thus abreast of the issues in the diocese and when appropriate could put in a word for the ordained women. Occasionally I would represent the bishop if he was unable to attend a particular event. The role also included that of the bishop's press officer. I did not have any expertise in press matters, so had to take advice from the diocesan press officer, and consulted him regularly.

In addition I had the further role as assistant diocesan director of ordinands working alongside the director of ordination for the diocese, primarily with women exploring a vocation of ordination. My appointment to this new role coincided with the retirement of the diocesan deacon, so that responsibility was added to my brief. This role was in effect the 'shop steward' for the women in the diocese who were deacons. I had a pastoral role for the ordained women; I endeavoured to meet with each of them regularly, and we met together as a group a few times a year. From time to time I invited a half dozen or so for a meal. I would also meet with women who held a similar role in other dioceses, so we were aware of national developments in this particular field.

As this was 1990, the ongoing debate about the priesthood of women in the Church of England was high on the agenda and I was frequently called on to speak to the issue both in the diocese and nationally. At the time there was much publicity about the issue. A book entitled *Women in Ministry*, edited by Susan Penfold, outlined many of the issues by telling the stories of women in ministry. I was invited to contribute a chapter under the heading of 'Growing in Ministry', which told my story up to that date. The book was published in 1991.

In that year, General Synod referred the issue to the dioceses for a response. Rochester Diocese in turn referred the matter to the deaneries for debate and a vote. I was called on to speak in favour of the ordination of women to the priesthood at five of our deanery synods. In each case the motion was passed, usually with a significant majority but on at least one occasion by a very narrow majority. The opinion of church members on the matter was far from unanimous.

On my appointment, the bishop had agreed that I could continue my membership of General Synod. A new Synod was due to be elected in 1990. As a deacon, I was now eligible to stand to represent the clergy of Rochester Diocese and was the only woman among those candidates. In my election manifesto I again included a photograph instead of giving my exact age. I explained my past experience in ministry and my views on the ordination of women. At least one of the candidates standing was an experienced clergyman who had served on General Synod and many of its committees for many years. I was up against tough opposition. The election was by single transferrable vote (STV), and perhaps to everyone's surprise, I was elected. I was thus a member of General Synod as the debate concerning the ordination of women to the priesthood continued on its way.

After about a year of being returned to General Synod, I was invited to join the Panel of Chairmen. I took this responsibility very seriously. When invited to chair a debate in Synod, it was the chairman's responsibility to manage the debate. For this, one needed a working knowledge of the standing orders. I learnt these by recording them onto a tape and playing the tape to myself when travelling alone in the car. During a debate it was important to call speakers representing the whole constituency: from among bishops, clergy and laity, from a range of dioceses, those holding differing theological perspectives, those both for and against any motion that was on the table and especially any members of synod who had a specialist knowledge of the subject under debate. It was also important to call for any amendments at an appropriate time, so that the debate could be concluded as far as possible in the time allocated. The chairman had the advice of the general secretary and of a legal advisor, who sat on either side of the chairman.

The power lay in the ability to switch off the microphone of any speaker who spoke inappropriately or beyond their allocated time. On one occasion I had to order a very good natured but somewhat garrulous bishop to 'sit down'. For this I got a round of applause from Synod members. Thankfully, I have remained friends with the bishop concerned.

I found being the chairman of General Synod very demanding. I spent hours preparing for the debates I was to chair, and was grateful for the advice of the general secretary and legal adviser. I must have fulfilled the role reasonably well, as after I had gained some experience I was asked to chair a few debates on quite sensitive issues.

## Chapter 18

## David

'Would you like some help when you move from Parkwood to Rochester?' David Gwyer asked. 'Yes please', was my reply. He came one day in August 1991 and we packed boxes ready for the move. As he was leaving, without anything relevant having been mentioned, I said to myself, 'One day I will marry that man'. I did not write this down or ever tell anyone but I knew it would happen. I then had to wait until David felt the same.

David had been born and brought up with his older sister Edna, in Ramsgate, which is at the far eastern end of Kent. Their parents ran a fish and chip shop. He had met his wife at the youth club of the church they attended. As a young married couple they moved to Gillingham where their two daughters were born. They joined St Mark's Church in Gillingham and made many friends with other young couples and their children, who also attended that church.

David and I met primarily concerning deanery business, but also from time to time on other occasions. As a single woman I sometimes found it awkward if invited to a formal occasion, as the invitation usually included a guest. When I was rural dean I was invited by the Commandant and Officers of the Royal School of Military Engineering, who were based at the Brompton Barracks in Chatham, to a cocktail party, followed by Beating the Retreat. The invitation was to Reverend Judith Rose and Guest, so, with some trepidation, I rang David: 'Would you be prepared to accompany me to Brompton Barracks for a rather special do?' I explained what was involved and was delighted when David agreed. We had a most enjoyable evening.

On New Year's Eve in 1990 I invited him for a meal at my flat. We had a good evening together and he left at about 11.45. I was a bit surprised he did not stay to see the New Year in, but later discovered that he had had a previous invitation to celebrate the New Year with other friends and must have arrived just a few minutes before midnight. I wondered if his friends questioned why he was so late arriving - and did he tell them where he had had supper?

About four weeks later, I was invited, as one of the deanery clergy, to the institution of Bishop Colin Buchanan as the new vicar of St Mark's Church in Gillingham. This was the church of which David was a member and had previously been a churchwarden. I travelled for the service from Rochester with Bishop Michael and was duly ushered into the room where the clergy were robing to find that David was responsible for marshalling the clergy prior to the service. After the service we went to the Church Hall for refreshments and the usual social gathering. I was constantly turning to find David at my elbow, and at the end was invited back to coffee with a group from the church. As Bishop Michael had by now returned to Rochester, David offered to take me home.

Two days later I had a phone call from him inviting me to the theatre the following Saturday. He duly turned up to collect me bearing a bunch of flowers. When we got back from the theatre in Canterbury, I invited him in for coffee. We discussed the evening and David said to me, 'I was very moved when you put your head on my shoulder during the performance'. He then added, 'I don't want this relationship to go any further unless you are serious.' I assured him that I was.

We then began talking about the possibility of getting married. David's situation was more sensitive than mine because he had two teenage daughters, who had lost their mother less than four years previously and may not understand if their father was considering remarrying. The same could have been true of his mother-in-law who had lost her beloved daughter, although as an older woman she was more likely to understand.

I don't remember David actually proposing to me, but somehow before he went home we had agreed to get married. So we became informally engaged after our first date! David then had to choose his moment to tell his girls.

Early the next morning I had a prearranged appointment in the studio of the local radio station. I can't remember the subject about which I was to be interviewed but it was a great temptation, which fortunately I resisted, to tell the whole of Kent that I was engaged to be married. If I was surprised at what had happened, the same was true for our families and friends. The engagement ring arrived after about three weeks and we got married six months later in July 1991. I was 54 and David 47 years old.

*With David*

We were married in St Mark's Church by the vicar, Bishop Colin Buchanan. Bishop Michael Turnbull gave the address and the organ was played by Norman Warren, who at the time was Archdeacon of Rochester. So a truly ecclesiastical affair! The service was in the early afternoon followed by the reception which took the form of a strawberry tea, generously prepared by the members of the church who had great affection for David.

My family travelled up from Somerset in a minibus. I had told my father that I did not want to be 'given away' like a piece of property, and in any case I was not leaving home for the first time. I preferred the symbolism of walking into church on my own and walking out with David as a married couple. Although my father did not give me away, he did give a splendid speech at the reception. David's daughters entered into the spirit of the occasion and had decorated the car in which we drove away for our honeymoon. Thus began eight and half years of happy married life.

And Tuppence came too. Tuppence, the dog, had been my faithful companion since Bradford days and was welcomed into the Gwyer household; but she was getting old, and when she became ill she had to be put down. It was David's daughter Sarah who begged her father to get another dog. (Her mother had not been too keen on pets and only allowed the girls to each have a tortoise.) David agreed, and they located a rescue dog from local kennels. The evening before they went to collect him, Sarah searched the Bible for a suitable name. She reasoned that all the family had biblical names so the same should be true for the dog. She and David chose the name Barnabas. Barny, a black labrador, arrived and joined the family.

Like all marriages, ours had its ups and downs. I think it was particularly hard at the beginning for David's daughters, Rachel and Sarah. They had been in their early teens when their mother died. Although I never met Helen, I understand she was a wonderful wife and mother, full of life, a trained nurse and an active member, with the whole family, of their church. So it was a great bereavement to all concerned when she died of cancer aged 39. The girls, particularly Sarah, found it hard to understand why her father should want to marry again, and on one occasion explained that although her father could have a new wife she could never have a new mother. These were understandable reactions from a bereaved teenager, so it took time, care and patience especially in the early days of our marriage.

By the time David and I married the girls were 18 and 19 and I never tried to become a replacement mother, but I was to live with David in the family home. My role was to support him in his continued care for his daughters. In fact, the date of our marriage was determined by Sarah's A level results. We had to be back from our honeymoon when the results came out.

On leaving school, Sarah went on to train as a nurse. In due course she met and married Tim, who was from New Zealand. They moved to live in New Zealand where they have two children. Rachel, the elder of the two, was at university in 1991 and after working in Europe and America, married Jonathan, an American, and is now settled in America with two adopted boys. I am sure their parents would be very proud of them both.

At the time of our marriage David's mother-in-law was still alive and living in Thanet, the eastern tip of Kent. She was quite a formidable woman with strong views on most things. She had of course been devastated at the death of her daughter and had come to rely on David's regular visits, but she accepted me and we got on well. At the time she expected us to visit her every other weekend. I put my foot down about that as it was a regular commitment and limited other things that we could do at weekends. However I made it clear that if there was an emergency we would go immediately and in any case continued to visit on a fairly regular basis. In the past the family had always gone to Thanet for Christmas, but the first Christmas we were married I wanted to celebrate it in our own home as it was the first time I had had my own family. We invited Grandma and Granddad to join us and had a good time together.

The other issue was that David suffered from depression, of which I had little experience. He frequently felt 'down' especially if things got difficult. He had spent his working life in the Civil Service, and when I met him worked in the Contributions Agency of the Social Services in Chatham. My speculation is that this was due to his promotion - not above his level of competence, for he was a very good administrator - but he took the responsibility for his staff too personally, and tried to carry their burdens. Whatever the reason, his mental health suffered. There were numerous appointments with the doctor, long periods of sick leave, various recommended medications and a period of counselling sessions. Within two years of our marriage, he was granted early retirement on health grounds.

## Chapter 19

## The Decision

As 1992 dawned I found myself in a very interesting and fulfilling job and with a husband and family. In addition to the responsibilities I have mentioned, which included attending numerous diocesan committees, meetings of rural deans and arranging ordination retreats, I continued with involvement in various national church interests, which took me out of the diocese probably at least one day a month.

The time had come for the church to make the big decision. After years of debate the Church of England was about to decide whether or not women could be ordained to the priesthood. Even after all the debates and discussions, opinions were still undecided.

This was brought home to me after I had taken my father's funeral. My parents had lived in the village of Wedmore in Somerset since 1940. After he retired my father became increasingly involved in the life of the village. He was a Freemason, was on the parish and then district council, had belonged to the village church with the family, was a school governor and took part in many village activities. So he was well known in the area. He died in 1992 aged 86 and I agreed to take the funeral in the village church. It was quite emotional, but I prepared well and the service went as well as could be expected. Many people came to the funeral from the village and from our extended family. I was later told by my cousin that after the service, a distant relative had said: 'If a woman can take a service like that, then I see no reason why women should not be ordained'. This was not a theological response, but a positive experience had changed someone's mind.

Many people at the time, who were less aware of the theological arguments, just had the feeling that this was not right. They could not conceive of a woman 'vicar'. There were no role models in the Church of England. I realised the significance of this by the opposite reaction of a long standing church member who had been brought up in the Baptist Church. As a younger woman she had known of women Baptist ministers and took it for granted that some women could quite well exercise this role. Yet others thought differently. I remember one elderly woman who was concerned that I should even be asked to take a funeral. Was that not too much to ask of a woman?

It was not uncommon for some to think that women were not capable or competent to exercise an ordained ministry. An extreme example of this was the speech of an elderly clergyman at a diocesan synod I attended in the late 1970's, who declared that women could not possibly be vicars, for how could you expect a woman to stoke the church boiler, which he did every Saturday evening? On another occasion, when the matter was under discussion, a gentleman told the synod that he had asked his wife and she declared that she definitely didn't want to be ordained, which clinched the matter as far as he was concerned.

There were also lay people who had never experienced a woman taking a service. Perhaps this was particularly true in rural areas where the vicar had always been a man and where they were much less likely to have a woman deacon or parish worker as part of the team. It was the vicar (a man) who had taken all the baptisms, weddings and funerals, who took the Sunday services and preached, who was seen in the school and fulfilled all the other duties expected of the vicar. That was how it was and always had been. Why change things which seemed to have worked well enough? For some it just did not feel right for the vicar to be female. Would she command respect? Would she have the status and be able to do the job well? Would her voice be strong enough to be heard in church? Much of this may not have been articulated but was influencing people's instinct.

The debate continued during the early part of 1992 and I was often involved, including a debate with an opponent on the local radio. When General Synod met in July, the issue was debated and voted on in the five constituent Houses, namely, the House of Bishops, the Convocations of both Canterbury and York and the Houses of Laity in both provinces. In all five houses the result was in favour of the motion but did not obtain the 2/3 majority among the laity that would be necessary when the definitive vote was to be taken at the meeting of the General Synod in November. There was no certainty that the issue was settled. The debate continued at local level for the next few months.

It was during the November 1992 group of sessions of General Synod, held at Church House Westminster, that the decision as to whether women could be ordained as priests was to be made. The Synod met from 10th - 12th. I chaired two debates on the 10th, but the significant debate was scheduled for Wednesday 11th. Living in Kent meant that I could travel to London each day.

On the day of the debate several of us living in or near the

Medway Towns met at 6.30am in a local church to pray and then adjourned to the pub for breakfast together. Among our number were those in favour and some opposed to the issue. I remember in particular a very able young priest in the Anglo-Catholic tradition who felt strongly that to admit women to the priesthood would be wrong, but who was confident that he and those who thought like him would be vindicated by the end of the day. Sadly that was the last time I saw him. Some time later, he and members of his church left the Church of England. Others of us who had a different conviction were less sure of the outcome of the day's debate, but we had prayed, so had to trust the outcome to God and would have to live with the consequences.

The debate in Synod lasted all day. Both the floor of the debating chamber and the public gallery were packed, as was the press room. The debate was of a high standard and was broadcast live on the radio. I understand that many people who were not necessarily church people tuned in, fascinated by the arguments on both sides of the issue. Finally the vote was taken. To be passed, a 2/3 majority was needed in all the three houses of Bishops, Clergy and Laity. We were told that the result, when announced, had to be received in silence both on the floor of the chamber and in the public gallery. This was obviously because it was such a sensitive issue and some would be bitterly disappointed. As the records show, the motion was carried by the necessary majority although only by very few votes in the house of Laity. The silence was observed in the debating chamber, but there was no such restraint among those gathered outside Church House, who broke into spontaneous applause.

I was told that many of the bishops had cleared their diaries for the week following the debate as they were expecting to have to give pastoral support to many of their women clergy who would be questioning their future ministry if the motion failed.

How much of that diary space was used to support the clergy who were shattered by the decision going the other way, I do not know. I do know that Bishop Michael Turnbull wrote to all his clergy on the day following the debate.

Although the General Synod had given approval, the proposed legislation still had to go before the Ecclesiastical Committee of Parliament. It passed this hurdle in July 1993. During the following year Bishop Michael attended most of the deanery synods in the diocese to discuss the implications of the decision, and I often accompanied him.

There was no official discernment process for the women who were already deacons and wished to be ordained priests, but the bishop interviewed each one of us to be confident of our calling. It was during the year following the decision that plans began to be put in place for the ordination services scheduled for 1994.

As a member of General Synod, I was present in November 1993 when the 'Act of Synod' was presented. This made provision for those opposed, by giving the PCCs of any parish the right to pass 'Resolution B'. This gave them the legal right to only consider male candidates for an incumbency. I think this was the only occasion when I abstained from voting. Although I had sympathy for those who in conscience could not accept this development, neither could I support explicit discrimination against women within the Christian Church.

## Chapter 20

## Ordination to the Priesthood

It was not until the meeting of General Synod in February 1994 that the final legal hurdle to the Ordination of Women to the Priesthood was crossed, but in anticipation of this, plans were afoot in the dioceses for such ordinations to take place. As is well known, the first such ordinations took place in Bristol Cathedral on March 12th. History was made. In my diocese of Rochester it was decided that these services would be held in May, when for the first time in history the ordination of women would take place in Rochester Cathedral. As bishop's chaplain and diocesan deacon, I was very involved in these plans. How many ordination candidates take part in planning their own ordination?! As there were 31 candidates to be ordained it was decided that there would be two services in the cathedral, on Saturday 28th and Sunday 29th May.

We all met together in the cathedral on the Thursday afternoon for the rehearsal and the legal preliminaries. We then travelled for the ordination retreat, which was held at the Roman Catholic Emmaus Retreat Centre at West Wickham and was led by our own Bishop Michael Turnbull. Much of the time was spent in silence interspersed with acts of worship. I am not a person who shows emotion easily but even I burst into tears after one of the sessions. This was an event that had been a long time coming.

Our retreat ended on the Saturday afternoon, and I travelled back to Rochester with the bishop. The first of our two services was to take place at 7.00pm that evening. This was the service at which I was to be ordained along with 13 others. The women ordained in that first service were those of us who had been in stipendiary ministry the longest (in my case, for 28 years). It was a great occasion and the cathedral was packed. The sermon was preached by the suffragan Bishop of Tonbridge, Bishop Brian Smith. At the end of the service those of us who had been ordained were each given a posy of yellow and white flowers.

I know the bishop was nervous that there might be demonstrations outside the cathedral by those opposed to such ordinations. In fact, there was a small group of protesters. They caused no trouble and surprisingly were in favour of what was happening. So why were they protesting? They were a group of Roman Catholic women, requesting that their church should consider the possibility of ordaining women.

My two sisters, my brother and other members of the family travelled up from Somerset for the occasion, as did David's sister-in-law and her husband. The bishop and his wife hosted a reception for me at Bishopscourt after the service, to which we were able to invite other friends. It had been an emotional few days.

The following morning, when no doubt many of the women who had been ordained alongside me were presiding at Communion for the first time in their own churches, I was

## Judith Rose

back in the cathedral. At 10.00am David and I attended the second ordination service to support the further 17 women who were ordained to the priesthood. Again it was a great occasion. On the evening of that day we were at St Mark's Church in Gillingham when Jean Kerr, the curate who had been ordained that morning, presided at a Communion service for the first time.

As I was not in parish ministry at the time, my ordination to the priesthood was perhaps less significant in practice than it was for others. In many ways I felt that I had been exercising a priestly ministry for many years, although of course my sacramental ministry had had to be limited. I first presided at a Holy Communion service two weeks after my ordination in St Mark's Gillingham, the church where David and I worshipped regularly. I also had the privilege of being the first woman to celebrate the Eucharist in Rochester Cathedral on June 25th. From time to time I was invited to take services at other churches in the diocese, often when there was a vacancy, and found it a privilege to be able to take Communion services for them. On many occasions for the next few years I was the first woman to have celebrated Communion in the church to which I had been invited.

For those of us women who had been ordained and for all who believed this was the right development within the Church of England, these ordinations were a cause of great celebration, but for others they were devastating. A significant minority still sincerely believed that this was contrary to the will of God and the tradition of the church. So our ordinations were a cause of sadness, pain and anger to some. This occasionally resulted in outbursts of discriminatory words and actions. After I had been the first woman to preside in the Cathedral there were rumours circulating that, because I as a woman had celebrated, the Cathedral altar was now contaminated.

More seriously there were some clergy who now felt they could no longer remain within the Church of England. Provision had been made for clergy who had been ordained prior to the decision of 1992 to receive financial compensation should they choose to resign over this issue. This was based on the principle that they had been ordained into a church that did not allow women to be ordained and that church had now decided otherwise. Some clergy did resign, probably after a lot of heart searching, and were compensated as promised.

I don't know the number involved, but some years later a report was published giving numbers and the amount of compensation that had been paid out. What saddened me was how that report was headlined in The Church of England Newspaper. The headline ran something like, 'Women priests cost the Church (the specified amount of money).' I didn't question the figures, but a more accurate headline would have read, 'Those opposed to the ordination of Women, cost the Church...'. The blame was laid at the feet of the women, who had not received any of the money involved.

It is understandable that significant changes such as this provoke strong reactions. Women clergy have continued to experience discrimination to a greater or lesser extent ever since, although I have not been greatly troubled by it myself - or perhaps I just take it for granted that it will happen from time to time.

Of course the ordination of women to the priesthood was hugely significant for the individuals concerned and for the Church, but life goes on and my work as bishop's chaplain continued. The other important event for us that year was a change in bishop. Early in the year it was announced that my bishop, Michael Turnbull, was to be the next Bishop of Durham. (David and I were delighted to be able to attend his enthronement in Durham Cathedral in October 1994.) Soon after the announcement of the Bishop's 'translation' the process for appointing the next Bishop of Rochester began. I was elected to represent the Diocese on the Crown Appointments Commission, so this issue was on my agenda.

Towards the end of June it was announced that our next bishop was to be Bishop Michael Nazir-Ali, who would take up the post at the beginning of the following year. As bishop's chaplain based at Bishopscourt I was very involved in the comings and goings associated with a change of diocesan bishop, with the bishop's staff and of course with the suffragan bishop before and during the vacancy. All this was in addition to my ongoing responsibilities as associate DDO, bishop's press officer, representative of the ordained women in the diocese and my involvement with General Synod which now included chairing some of the sessions. I was also invited to join the patronage board of the Simeon Trustees which involved meeting, usually in Birmingham, a few times a year. I was elected as chairman of the Rochester House of Clergy in October. In September 1994 I attended a conference at St George's Windsor which explored the early experiences of women in the priesthood. This innovation was being monitored.

So life was very busy, often finding me at work at 7am and sometimes with evening meetings as well. Family life was good despite these pressures, although David's health was not 100%. His daughters were beginning their adult lives, so were with us sometimes and often needing a lift to the station or to London or wherever! All part of family life.

I did enjoy being married after so many years as a single person. Holidays were special. David owned a family tent so camping holidays were on the agenda, usually to somewhere in France, sometimes on our own and sometimes meeting up with friends of David. It was fun loading up all the camping gear into the small trailer behind the car and driving into the sunset - well, not always the sunset! The last few years for both of us had seen so many changes, and it was good to relax and reflect on all that had happened.

## Chapter 21

## Archdeacon

Our new bishop, Michael Nazir Ali, was of course a very different person to our outgoing bishop. He was from Pakistan, was fluent in several languages and had specialist knowledge of Persian poetry. He had been head of the Church Mission Society, so had extensive international knowledge of the Anglican Communion, and was an academic theologian. Whether a diocesan in the Church of England was the best use of his remarkable talents could be debated, but it was certainly not for me to question.

Bishop's chaplains have differing roles from diocese to diocese and from bishop to bishop. In addition a bishop's character and style of working is a personal matter. It is also reasonable that a bishop should want to appoint his own chaplain. I had been chaplain to Bishop Turnbull for five years and in 1995 was aged 58, so for reasons also associated with the above it became obvious that I needed to think seriously about a new position so that I could give at least seven years of ministry to my final appointment before retirement. It was now legally possible, for the first time in nearly 30 years of ministry, for me to apply for an incumbency because I was now a priest. Within the next 12 months I was likely to be in a new job.

Like any new diocesan, Bishop Michael needed time to get to know his diocese and his staff. One of his fairly early responsibilities was the appointment of an archdeacon. Rochester Diocese had three archdeaconries. The Archdeaconry of Bromley covered parishes bordering on S.E. London. The Archdeaconry of Rochester included the Medway towns and parishes on the south of the Thames Estuary and was linked with a residential canonry at the cathedral. The Archdeaconry of Tonbridge included Sevenoaks, Tonbridge and Tunbridge Wells and much of the Weald of Kent, so the more rural part of the diocese and the largest geographical area. It also bordered on the dioceses of Canterbury and Chichester. At the time the current archdeacon of Tonbridge was due to retire within six months of the new bishop's appointment. Discussions about a successor were on the table in his early weeks. Quite early on the possibility of appointing a woman to this post was hinted at. (This was in the days before such posts were advertised. The appointment was the bishop's gift.) The outgoing archdeacon was also the incumbent of a parish, and initially it was assumed that the next appointee would also have parish responsibilities. There was no written job description.

For months the issue was unresolved, although David and I were encouraged to visit parsonage houses in various parishes that might be linked with the post even though I had had no clear invitation to consider the appointment. I found this very unsatisfactory and unsettling, as if I was not to be offered the post I would need to consider other options. Finally, the suffragan bishop helped to resolve the issue and drafted a job description. I made the case for not linking it to a parish as I felt both the parish and archdeaconry would suffer from divided loyalties, especially as a small parish is less likely to have other clergy or lay ministers available. Rather it would be more satisfactory for the archdeaconry to be linked with other diocesan responsibilities. Finally, in June 1995, the bishop offered me the post of Acting Archdeacon of Tonbridge, but not linked with a parish. Even then this appointment was not made public for another month, when the bishop finally wrote to the clergy of the archdeaconry and a press release was issued two weeks later.

This was the first time in the Church of England that a woman was invited to be an archdeacon, so another first for me. Initially it had to be 'Acting Archdeacon' because at the time it was not legally possible for a woman to be appointed as archdeacon. Canon law stipulated that an archdeacon had to have been in priests' orders for at least six years. I had of course only been in priests' orders for a year! However a decision had already been made by General Synod for this to be changed to six years in Holy Orders, so the eight years since I was made deacon meant that I would qualify as soon as the ecclesiastical law changed. The necessary legislation was before parliament awaiting ratification, which was expected within the coming year. Once again I was to be doing a job before I was legally qualified to do so. That seems to be the story of my life.

There were practical matters to settle associated with my appointment, not least where we would live, as this was no longer to be in a parsonage house. It was decided that it would be good to have a senior member of the bishop's staff living in the southern part of the diocese, so a search began for a suitable house within the archdeaconry. David and I looked at several properties, and eventually a house in Tunbridge Wells was purchased by the diocese. This needed a small extension to enlarge the dining room and make provision for a secretaries' office. It proved to be a lovely home and suitable for the entertaining that we intended.

In the meantime, David and I had to decide on the future of our own properties. We were currently living in a house owned by David, and I owned a small cottage in Somerset that I had purchased from my aunt in 1980, when I had had to sell my house in Leeds. We decided to sell both properties and invest the money in a joint account, to be available to purchase a retirement house when I retired. Taking up a new appointment in a different location was easier for us than for many couples, largely because my husband had taken early retirement so only one of us was in employment. Also, David's daughters had left school and begun their own careers so were no longer living at home, although they visited regularly.

The other issue we had addressed when we got married was the name I was to use. My married name was Judith Gwyer but professionally I was the Rev Judith Rose (my maiden name). David was more than happy for me to continue to use 'Rose' for professional purposes, and this was particularly important when I stood for election to General Synod, as that was the name by which I was known to many of the electorate. So from then on I have continued to use both names: Gwyer for personal matters and Rose professionally. I just have to remember who I am, depending on the situation! As a mark of David's support in this matter, when it came to opening a joint bank account I was quite happy for it to be in the names of David and Judith Gwyer but it was David who insisted it be David Gwyer and Judith Rose. We also agreed that I should retain my own 'Rose' bank account without changing the name.

Another personal matter that David and I had to resolve was to which church we should belong. At first, David often came with me on a Sunday to whichever church in the archdeaconry I was visiting; but although that was part of my job it meant that David did not belong anywhere, and that was not good for him. We decided to become members of a church in Tunbridge Wells where David would attend regularly and I went when I had a free Sunday. That church understood that I would not be there very often, but we both belonged to a home group and so had a spiritual home and began to build friends in that context.

I took up my new appointment as acting archdeacon of Tonbridge at the beginning of September 1995, although the house was not ready to move into for a further six weeks. As in many new jobs there was a steep learning curve, although having worked for five years as bishop's chaplain, at least I knew the diocese quite well. The first thing I did was to write to the clergy of the archdeaconry introducing myself. At the end of that letter I wrote, 'I am pleased that my new job title includes the word "deacon" which is a reminder that I am to be a minister/servant of the church, and in particular to the clergy and lay leaders of the archdeaconry, and to the bishop'. I always saw the role of archdeacon as that of facilitating the church to work well, a bit like the oil in a machine.

One of the additional responsibilities in my portfolio was that of chair of the Diocesan Committee for the Deaf. This was a new field of ministry for me and one from which I learnt much and have continued to have a great respect for the church of the deaf and the chaplains that work among the deaf. I have never learnt sign language but am fascinated to watch those who do sign, especially deaf choirs. I would love to see more churches welcome those without hearing, and provide a sign language interpreter for the services. On one occasion I was asked to take the funeral of someone from this constituency. I spoke the words, but of course all eyes were on the interpreter who stood a few yards to my right. I am used to having eye contact with the congregation when I lead a service or preach, but that was not appropriate on that occasion, which I found a little strange.

As my appointment was within the first year of women in the Church of England being ordained priest, and since I was the first woman to hold such a post, there was considerable press interest. I also understand that there was a meeting of some conservative evangelicals to consider whether it was appropriate for a woman to hold such a post. Was an archdeacon a leadership position for which women were not qualified, on the basis of the so called 'headship' argument? I was not present at that meeting, so I don't know how the discussion went. In practice I found that I was welcome at conservative evangelical parishes, where they were happy for me to preside at their Communion service but I was not invited to preach; whereas at the conservative Anglo-Catholic Churches I would be invited to preach but not to celebrate at their Eucharist.

This did not concern me greatly: for my whole ministry I have been aware of deeply held views on the role of women in the church. I have appreciated the opportunities I have had to minister rather than fretting over what I was not allowed to do. In any case, when I was in post as archdeacon, I would often contact a parish and ask if I could join them for worship on a Sunday - but I would only exercise any particular ministry if invited to do so.

It was in February 1996, the necessary legislation being in place, that I was installed and commissioned as archdeacon of Tonbridge in Rochester Cathedral, and history was made. The press statement noted that I had been the first woman to hold the post of rural dean in the Church of England and was now the first to be appointed archdeacon. For the next three years I was the only woman to hold such a post, which meant that at any meeting of archdeacons I would be the only woman present.

There was a very light hearted debate as to whether I was then the most senior woman in the Church of England: opinions were divided as to whether a cathedral dean or an archdeacon were the more senior. In any case as I pointed out, the constitution of the Church of England recognises the sovereign as the head of the Church of England, who at that time was the queen. (As an archdeacon I was invited to a Buckingham Palace Garden Party. The invitation included my husband, so we dressed up appropriately and enjoyed a trip to London and the opportunity to be entertained in the palace gardens. Unfortunately we were not among those who were personally introduced to Her Majesty - despite being one of the most senior women in the Church of England!)

As far as was appropriate, David shared my ministry. We would endeavour to go together to visit clergy families who were new to a parish, especially if they were also new to the diocese; if possible we visited after they had moved into the parsonage house but before they were inducted or licensed. David would often accompany me for the induction service, sitting in the congregation as I took part in the ceremony. Thus David got to know many of the clergy in the archdeaconry, which was helpful when it came to entertaining. Fairly regularly we invited a few clergy couples and single clergy for supper which meant getting to know them in a less formal setting. David enjoyed entertaining and often cooked the meal for these occasions.

Another advantage that I had being married to a retired husband was that David looked after many of our domestic responsibilities. He was good at and enjoyed shopping so was a frequent visitor to the supermarket; he bought appropriate birthday cards and birthday presents for family and friends, dealt with domestic finances, did all the practical arrangements for holidays and did such things as getting the cars serviced. I think we were a good team and I greatly appreciated David's support.

## Chapter 22

## The Implications of Change

In the early years after the decision to ordain women to the priesthood, as they began to be appointed to incumbencies and other appropriate posts, there were various meetings to discuss the issue and its implications. On at least two occasions I was invited to take part in such a discussion at St George's House Windsor, as well as at more local venues such as deanery synods and on local radio. We were also very aware that due respect had to be given to those clergy and parishes for whom this development was not welcome.

An Act of Synod gave parishes the right to veto the appointment of a woman as their vicar. There was one situation in my archdeaconry where, in my opinion, that right was abused. The parish concerned had on their staff a woman curate who was much loved and respected, and so they passed the necessary resolution in order that a man should be their next vicar to give them a gender balanced leadership team. I sympathised with their motive but this was not the reason for the passing of that particular Act of Synod!

Another parish that needed a new vicar did not formally

veto the appointment of a woman, but made it clear to me that they would much prefer a man to be appointed. The vacancy was advertised and three candidates shortlisted, including one woman. The candidates were to be interviewed on three separate occasions with a decision made at the end of the interviews. The second interview was with the woman, after which the parish representatives informed me that she was the one and asked me to cancel the third applicant. It proved to be the right choice and the parish never expressed any regrets.

In order to ensure that those who opposed the ordination of women continued to have a respected presence and role in the church, episcopal visitors (sometimes called flying bishops) were appointed and every diocese was allocated such a bishop to support that constituency. In Rochester Diocese, our episcopal visitor attended the bishop's staff meeting, of which as archdeacon I was a part, and he contributed helpfully to discussions and the appointments to parishes. I felt that he and I had a mutual respect for one another.

This bishop was at the time the chairman of 'Forward in Faith'. Forward in Faith is an organisation that sincerely believes that only men should be ordained, and has worked hard to ensure that those who hold such a position remain a respected constituency within the Church of England. It was some six years after the first women had been ordained priest that I was particularly upset by a report in the Church Press of a comment made at the annual assembly of Forward in Faith. In his address, the chairman included these words, 'No real woman wants to be a priest because real women know that women are not priests'.

I found this statement offensive, not just on my account but on behalf of those women who sincerely believed they had been called by God to this ministry. I conveyed my distress to my own bishop and sent a copy of that letter to the bishop concerned, who as explained was a colleague at our staff meetings. As far as I know my own bishop did nothing. The chairman of Forward in Faith sent me a copy of his letter to the Church press complaining about the press coverage of the meeting and explaining that the comments that I had found offensive were, 'unscripted and hopefully a humorous aside'. I was not impressed. In my letter to my own bishop I had written, 'I suppose it is the sort of insult and verbal abuse that women have to accept in the interests of unity...I had hoped that this sort of language was a thing of the past. It is not what I would expect from a bishop in the Church of England and certainly not from a colleague.' Nothing more was done and I never received any apology.

I suppose it was inevitable that in these early years after the ordination of women as priests there were bound to be hiccups as we all felt our way forward. For the most part I was able to accommodate these sensitivities and continued to enjoy my ministry. I found my role as archdeacon a fulfilling one. I realise not every clergy person would be comfortable in that job, but for me it enabled me to use the experience that I had gathered over the many years that I had been in ministry.

I particularly enjoyed the privilege of doing ministerial reviews with the clergy in my archdeaconry. In advance of each of these reviews, I would ask if I might join the congregation of the clergy concerned. I was quite happy to sit in the pew, but inevitably was often asked to preach. These visits gave me an opportunity to get the feel of the clergyperson's church and meet some of the people. I would also meet with the churchwardens so they could give me their perspective on the strengths and weaknesses of their vicar and let me know of any way that they thought that I or the diocese could give him/her more support. It was particularly good to have time to listen to each parish priest and appreciate the good and sometimes the problems that they faced. As an archdeacon I found that it was often the clergy who were the 'high flyers' or the ones with problems that took up much of the time, so it was good to know that the majority were just getting on with the job and serving the Lord faithfully day in and day out.

Another aspect of this ministry that I enjoyed was the part I played in the appointment of incumbents (or priests in charge) to parishes. It involved meeting with PCCs in advance, exploring their vision for the future of their parish and so helping them think of the qualities they were looking for in their new vicar in order to begin to fulfil that vision. Then it came to encouraging applicants, shortlisting and interviewing and working with the patron and parish representatives in order to, as far as possible, appoint 'round pegs in round holes'. There were disappointments along the way but as was frequently said, 'It is better to get it right than get it quick'.

An archdeacon inevitably gets involved in numerous meetings and committees, some long and tedious, but the theory is to work towards policies that support parish ministry and the spread of the Gospel. I had always been interested in parish policy that supported these aims so I was now involved in that at diocesan level. A significant aspect of an archdeacon's role is to advise parishes wanting to alter or modernise their church building. In this respect I worked with the diocesan committee, which gave advice and explained to the parishes limitations and opportunities available to them. The three areas in which I did not have personal expertise were that of finance, ecclesiastical law and buildings, all three many would think essential for an archdeacon. But I did know to whom to go for wise advice on these matters.

David and I marked the turn of the century by joining the congregation for a meal in our local church, and then early in 2000 we went to Somerset to celebrate my sister's 60th birthday.

## Judith Rose

We were planning a holiday cruising down the Nile in Egypt for the end of January. David's younger daughter had done this previously and said, 'Dad, you must do it, it was fantastic'. Wednesday, January 26th was memorable. David had put the final plans for the holiday in place, and leapt around the bedroom in great excitement. We were entertaining the following evening, and as I knew I had a day of meetings that day we laid the table on the Wednesday evening. We had planned the menu and David was to cook the meal. We put together a list and, after David had agreed to do the shopping on the Thursday morning, we went to bed having made all the plans for the next day and in anticipation of our holiday in a few days time.

The following day, January 27th, I went into Rochester for a meeting in the morning and then a pub lunch with the other archdeacons. When I went into the diocesan office after lunch for a meeting of the DAC, I was told that my husband had telephoned, but on ringing back there was no reply. I sensed this was important so asked that I be called out of the meeting if he rang again. In due course I was called to the phone. It was our doctor, who asked me if I was sitting down. The doctor told me David had died. He had evidently gone shopping, felt ill and called the doctor on his return. He had a massive heart attack at home and although the ambulance was called they could not revive him.

The doctor, who was a friend, member of our church and sometimes played golf with David, then asked me which funeral director I wished to use! I hadn't a clue, but he gave me his advice and I agreed that they should be asked to collect David's body. A friend from Rochester offered to take me home, where I found the table laid for our guests.

On returning home the first thing I did was to arrange to see David at the undertakers. I spent most of the rest of the day telephoning family and friends letting them know what had happened. Friends who had known David and his girls for many years, offered to go to London to tell Sarah, and I telephoned Rachel, who was working abroad at the time. These two young women had now lost both parents. In due course the holiday was cancelled and all the other necessary arrangements put in place. David and I had been married for eight and half years.

Of course this was not a unique experience, and adjustment is nearly always necessary after a bereavement. I was offered time off work, but as times off work were times that I shared with David, that was the one thing I did not want: so I carried on, initially coping with the routine matters as I slowly came to terms with what had happened. I had lived most of my life as a single person, so I knew how to do that alongside a full-time job; nevertheless it took a while to manage the domestic responsibilities that David had assumed, as well as my job. I reflected that if I had died David would not have had to take on my responsibilities, but on his death I had to take on his. I am sure others who have lost a marriage partner while still in work will have had a similar experience.

I found my role as archdeacon very fulfilling and would probably have been happy to continue in that role for a couple of years beyond my 65th birthday. However, with the loss of David I felt the need for a new start in a different location. I had promised to serve in this role for seven years, so I wrote my letter of resignation to the bishop and retired to Somerset in September 2002.

## Chapter 23

## Women Bishops

In 1995 I had been re-elected to General Synod, continuing to represent the clergy of Rochester Diocese, a position that I held for the five year term until 2000. From 2000 until I retired in 2002 I remained a member of the Synod, but then as the archdeacon representative for the diocese. As a Synod member, one has the opportunity to table a private members motion on any issue about which you are concerned. Other members are then invited to add their names if they wish to see the issue debated. Motions with the highest number of signatures have a chance of being debated by the whole synod.

Like many others I was aware that as women were now able to be ordained as deacons and priests, the issue of the consecration of women as bishops would inevitably need to be on the agenda before too long, so I tabled a private motion on the issue. My motion asked the House of Bishops to initiate further theological study on the episcopate, focusing on the issues that needed to be addressed in preparation for the debate on women in the episcopate and for a progress report within two years. In due course this motion attracted a high number of signatures and reached the Synod agenda for debate in July 2000, and I had the privilege of speaking to the motion and moving it for debate.

I started my speech by misquoting the beginning of the poem by Jenny Joseph, 'When I am an old woman I will NOT wear purple', explaining that I was near retirement age so had no personal interest in becoming a bishop. My motion was not about whether or not women should be eligible to be bishops, but rather that when the Synod had that debate it should be an informed debate with a carefully thought out theological report setting out the issues to be addressed and the implications of any decision to admit women to the episcopate.

There were amendments proposed to my motion, notably one which asked that legislation be prepared to admit women to the episcopate, which would have brought the substantive debate forward, which was not my intention at the time. Another wanted to draw special attention to, 'any ecumenical and ecclesiological difficulties'. These were not unimportant and would need to be addressed but I did not wish to specify particular issues. I resisted all amendments and my motion was eventually passed without any amendments.

I had hoped that the outcome would promote discussion on the matter at local level. I think it probably had the opposite effect, as some waited for the publication of the report. By 2000 the Church of England had had the experience of women as priests for six years, and it was only a matter of time before the next step would be taken. I like to think I made a small contribution to that development.

A working party was set up under the chairmanship of the Bishop Michael Nazir-Ali who was at the time the Bishop of Rochester. An interim report was produced in 2002 and the final report, entitled 'Women Bishops in the Church of

England?' (note the question mark!) was published in November 2004.

I retired in 2002, but the issue was now on the agenda and on several occasions during the next few years I was invited to speak in debate at various meetings and conferences up and down the country, in favour of women in the episcopate.

It was not until 2014 that it was legally possible for women to be consecrated as bishops. The first such consecration was of Libby Lane in 2015.

# Post Script: Titles

The ecclesiastical title for an archdeacon is The Venerable (The Ven) but an archdeacon only holds the title while in office. However, the diocesan bishop may offer to a retiring archdeacon the role of Archdeacon Emeritus of the Diocese. Titles don't bother me much, although they are of some limited use as a way of identifying the role held by the entitled person. In view of the historical significance of being the first female archdeacon in the Church of England, and that in Rochester Diocese, I accepted the bishop's offer of Archdeacon Emeritus and so am still legitimately able to call myself the Venerable Judith Rose, although I don't use the title very often.

On retiring to Somerset, in due course I applied to the Bishop of Bath and Wells for Permission to Officiate (PTO) which gave me authority to lead services in the diocese at the invitation of the parish priest. (When I was farming many years ago, the term PTO meant 'power take off' with reference to agricultural machinery!) A few years ago I was asked to take a marriage service. I met the bride and her mother to discuss the order of service, which the mother was to get printed, so she

## Post Script: Titles

asked me how I should be named. I told her that officially I was the Venerable Judith Rose, to which she replied, 'I think the Reverend Judith Rose sounds much nicer'. And so I was entitled on that occasion. I did not tell her that at about the time her daughter was born I would not have been able legitimately to even use that title.

My title has changed since 1966 from Parish Worker to Deaconess, then as a deacon and priest to Revd Judith Rose and finally to the Venerable Judith Rose. I doubt if God is interested in titles, but in spite of that it has been a very challenging and interesting journey.

*Judith Rose*

# Time Lines

**1964 - 66 St Michael's House, Oxford**
*Training for Parish Ministry*

**1966 - 71 St Mary's Church, Rodbourne Cheney, Swindon**
*Parish Worker*
Title, Miss Judith Rose

**1971 - 73 London Bible College, Northwood**
*Studying for a Degree in Theology*

**1973 - 80 St George's Church, Leeds**
73 - 76 *Parish Worker* - Title, Miss Judith Rose
75 - 80 *House of Laity of General Synod representing Ripon Diocese*
76 *Ordained Deaconess in St George's*
76 - 80 *Deaconess* - Title, Deaconess Judith Rose

**1980 - 85 Bradford Cathedral**
*Cathedral Chaplain*

## 1986 - 90 Parish of South Gillingham, Rochester Diocese

*Acting Team Vicar, based at Parkwood*
*87 Ordained Deacon in Rochester Cathedral*
Title, The Reverend Judith Rose
*87 - 90 General Synod, special constituency of women deacons representing the Province of Canterbury.*
*88 - 90 Rural Dean of Gillingham*

## 1990 - 2002 Bishopscourt, Rochester

*Chaplain to the Bishop of Rochester*
*House of Clergy of General Synod representing Rochester Diocese*
*91 Married David Gwyer* - Title, Mrs Judith Gwyer
*93 Made an Honorary Canon of Rochester Cathedral*
Title, Canon Judith Rose
*94 Ordained Priest in Rochester Cathedral*
*1995 - 96 Acting Archdeacon of Tonbridge, Rochester Diocese*
*95 -02 House of Clergy of General Synod representing Rochester Diocese*
*1996 - 2002 Archdeacon of Tonbridge, Rochester Diocese.*
Title, The Venerable Judith Rose
*2000 David died*
2002 *Archdeacon Emeritus of Rochester Diocese and Retired.*
Title, The Venerable Judith Rose

# Acknowledgments

My story is only unique in so far as we all have our own individual life experiences. I have written this as just one example of the issues faced by many women who felt called to leadership in the Church of England in the second half of the 20th century. The question of the ordination of women had been raised much earlier than this and there were many women who worked faithfully in parish ministry for years, in various parts of this country, before my time. Some of these parish workers were either too old or had died before their ordination was possible. There have been others with different gifts and opportunities who made a positive contribution leading to the ordination of women.

I was very fortunate to work with clergy and lay people who encouraged and supported me and gave me the opportunities to develop my gifts and my ministry. To them I am very grateful. Many other women ministers were not so fortunate.

I am also grateful to Amy Scott Robinson of Kevin Mayhew for her editorial skills, which have made this a much more readable account.

I recognise that the ministry of women in the Church of England has developed significantly in the past 20 years, but felt that something of the history should be recorded. I have sought to do that through the eyes of someone who was personally involved during part of that history. It was not always easy, but I look back with gratitude to what has been a very fulfilling ministry and life experience.

STEVE NALLON is a writer, voice artist, actor and occasional academic and lecturer. Steve's acting and voice artist work ranges from theatre, film and television, to video games, puppetry and audio books. As a playwright and comedy writer, Steve has a considerable body of credits to his name, including plays and series for BBC radio, three one-man theatre shows, plus the satirical book *I, Margaret*, which he co-wrote with the novelist Tom Holt. *The Time That Never Was*, the first in Steve's Time Adventure book series THE SWIDGERS, was published by Luath Press in 2022. For most of the 1990s Steve was a Visiting Lecturer at the University of Birmingham, where his specialist areas of study were story theory, comedy and Greek theatre, and he continues to teach and offer workshops on a freelance basis. Over the years, Steve has contributed to numerous periodicals such as *The New Statesman* and *Musical Stages*, and is a much sought after speaker on the lecture circuit for his insightful and amusing talks.
@SteveNallon

DICK FIDDY has researched into, and written extensively about, archive television for many years. He is the author of *Missing Believed Wiped: Searching for the Lost Heritage of British Television* and is the coordinator of the British Film Institute's Missing Believed Wiped initiative, which seeks to uncover items absent from the official TV archives. Dick is employed at the BFI as their Archive Television Programmer.
@DickFiddy

# Destination Time Travel

STEVE NALLON & DICK FIDDY

**Luath** Press Limited
EDINBURGH
www.luath.co.uk

First published 2023

ISBN: 978-1-80425-101-0

The paper used in this book is recyclable. It is made from low chlorine pulps produced in a low energy, low emission manner from renewable forests.

Printed and bound by CPI Group (UK) Ltd, Croydon, CR0 4YY

Typeset in 10.5pt Sabon by Lapiz

The authors' right to be identified as author of this book under the Copyright, Designs and Patents Acts 1988 has been asserted.

© Steve Nallon & Dick Fiddy 2023

*To all fans of the time travel story world,
past, present and future.*

# Contents

| | | |
|---|---|---|
| Acknowledgements | | 9 |
| Recommended Reading | | 10 |
| Introduction | | 11 |
| CHAPTER 5 | It's Story Time! | 15 |
| CHAPTER 7 | Who Tells the Time Tale? | 42 |
| CHAPTER 8 | Who Knows What, When and Why? | 57 |
| CHAPTER 10 | The Time Machines | 67 |
| CHAPTER 12 | Portals, Passageways, Gateways and Vortexes | 78 |
| CHAPTER 14 | Potions, Magic, Genii, Artefacts and Other Tickets for the Time Terminal | 86 |
| CHAPTER 11 | Time Windows and Time Threads | 95 |
| CHAPTER 15 | Time Beings, Time Villains and Time Guardians | 102 |
| CHAPTER 13 | Time Loops and Causal Loops in Time Tales | 114 |
| CHAPTER 4 | The Paradoxes of Time and Time Travel | 134 |
| CHAPTER 6 | The Stories and Plots of Time Tales | 152 |
| CHAPTER 9 | The Dramatic Devices of the Time Tale | 177 |
| CHAPTER 3 | The Rules of Time and Time Codes | 190 |
| CHAPTER 17 | Dreams, Foretellings and Memory | 197 |
| CHAPTER 18 | Ageing, Immortals and Ghosts | 211 |
| CHAPTER 16 | Utopias/Dystopias, Counterfactuals, Time Sleep and Time Stopped | 221 |

| CHAPTER 19 | Time Tales and Genre Crossovers | 231 |
| CHAPTER 1 | The Science of Time | 240 |
| CHAPTER 2 | The Philosophy of Time | 263 |
| CHAPTER 20 | The Appeal of The Time Tale | 273 |

| | |
|---|---|
| Steven Moffat Interview | 307 |
| Index | 311 |

# Acknowledgements

GRATEFUL THANKS TO Karen Baldwin, Matthew Barnbrook, Jack Bowman, Steve Bridle, Ed Clarke, Martin Coxhead, Barry Gurney, Ryan McGivern, Moray Laing, Mark Mander, Brian Sledzico, Paul Smith, Sam Supple and Adam Trembath for their suggestions and encouragement. Thanks too to Victor Surí for his translation of the lines from *Aura*, Julie Scattergood for her forensic proofreading of the manuscript, Kira Dowie for her detailed edit and excellent suggestions, and to Justin Johnson and Marcus Prince at the British Film Institute for their input and support. Special thanks to writer Steven Moffat for sharing with us his thoughts on writing the time travel tale.

Back cover photo credit: Richard Pickard at the British Film Institute. With thanks to the BFI for allowing us into the projection room of NFT1.

# Recommended Reading

TIME MACHINE TALES: *The Science Fiction Adventure and Philosophical Puzzles of Time Travel* by Paul J. Nahin (published by Springer 2017) is a remarkable and very accessible book covering in detail both the practical science of time travel (Nahin is an emeritus professor of electrical engineering) and the many paradoxical and philosophical questions it raises. James Gleick's *Time Travel: A History* (published by 4th Estate in 2016) is a fascinating and insightful look at the concept of time and time travel across history. *Paradoxes of Time Travel* by Ryan Wasseram (published by Oxford University Press) is an intriguing and in depth mathematical analysis of the near innumerable paradoxes that time travel throws up, accompanied by useful and easily understood graphic illustrations. Colin M. Barron's *Travels in Time: The Story of Time Travel Cinema* (published by Extremis Publishing 2019) offers a comprehensive and meticulous journey through movie history and its fascination with the time travel story. Elizabeth Howell's *The Science of Time Travel: The Science Behind Time Machines, Time Loops, Alternate Realities and More!* covers literature, television and the movies, and many chapters offer a thoughtful analysis of the psychological and emotional aspects of the story being told. *The Scientific Secrets of Doctor Who* by Simon Guerrier and Dr Marek Kukula (published in 2015 by BBC Books, part of the Penguin Random House group of companies) looks at the real and theoretical science behind the concepts explored in *Doctor Who*. We would like to gratefully acknowledge our indebtedness to the scholarship and research of all these authors whose books have been invaluable help in the preparation of our own examination of the Time Tale.

# Introduction

THIS IS A book about time travel which you can, like a time traveller, approach in whatever order you see fit. Leap straight into those chapters which sound the most fun and then go back in the future to the ones with big words. Skip some altogether as time travellers might skip those historical events that hold no interest to them, such as general elections in Belgium, the War of Jenkin's Ear or the invention of the shoe umbrella. But to help with your choices, here's a brief summary (now predetermined in a 'fixed' universe because this book has now been printed) as to what to expect...

Our opening chapter, if that is where you really wish to begin, is called **It's Story Time!** and it asks why we even bother to tell stories about time travel and how writers go about crafting their tales. To illustrate all this we've chosen two contrasting Time Tales: Bob Gale and Robert Zemeckis' *Back to the Future* and Charles Dickens' *A Christmas Carol*. **Who Tells the Time Tale?** asks who is the storyteller and how should the tale be told and the following chapter, **Who Knows What, When and Why?** considers the importance of story information in building a Time Tale. The next chapter, **The Time Machines,** looks at the technology, science and design of some well known and a few lesser known mechanisms of temporal transport. **Portals, Passageways, Gateways and Vortexes** considers what you might call 'Time Doorways' to the past, future or alternate timeline universes. **Potions, Magic, Genii, Artefacts and Other Tickets for the Time Terminal** explores the many and various clever ways you can time travel, especially if you know a friendly wizard or two. **Time Windows and Time Threads** examines the need sometimes in a Time Tale to connect one time world with another. After all that it's time to celebrate some of the main players in a Time Tale in **Time Beings, Time Villains and Time Guardians**. The next two chapters, **Time Loops and Causal Loops in Time Tales** and **The Paradoxes of Time and Time Travel**, reflect on the many tricky conceits of time travel that often require you to have a corkscrew mind that can think backwards. **The Stories and Plots of the Time Tale** looks at reoccurring scenarios such as endangered futures, being stranded in the wrong time and encountering multiverses. **The Dramatic Devices of the Time Tale** considers some of the tricks of the trade, so to speak, and **The Rules of Time and Time Codes** examines the various rules and strictures that are required, depending on the type of Time Tale. **Dreams, Foretellings, Prophecy and Memory** does what it says on the tin in that it reflects on dreams, foretellings, prophecy and memory. **Ageing, Immortals and Ghosts** looks at those who are immune to the ravages of time (or strive to be) and reflects on that vexing question: Are ghosts time travellers? **Utopias/Dystopias, Counterfactuals, Social Commentary, Time Sleep, and Time Stopped** takes a side-step into certain aspects of Time Tales which aren't strictly speaking about time travel but do involve a fundamental alteration of time or our understanding of it. **Time Tales and Genre Crossovers** asks whether there is such a thing as the time travel genre and examines the way the time travel plot has now found its way into the rom-com, horror movies and even westerns. The aim of **The Science of Time** and **The Philosophy of Time** is to explore in layman's terms some of the scientific principles underlying the possibility of time travel and the philosophical ideas around time itself. We, however, are not scientists or philosophers and in these chapters we are greatly indebted to Paul J. Nahin's indispensable book *Time Machine Tales: The Science Fiction Adventure and Philosophical Puzzles of Time Travel* and James Gleick's remarkable history of the thinking around the very idea of time in his book *Time Travel*. We conclude with **The Appeal of the Time Tale** which reflects on the enduring popularity of time travel stories.

In *Destination Time Travel* our purpose is not to reveal, as it were, the man behind the curtain, but rather to enhance the appreciation of the magic of the time travel tale by offering an insight into the storytelling craft and the decisions which go with it. The book is aimed primarily at the children of the streaming era who prefer to find their stories on multiple platforms. Although reference is made to the works of classic SF authors such as Philip K. Dick and Robert Silverberg and, of course, the great H.G. Wells, the majority of examples in *Destination Time Travel* come from movies and television shows.

In putting this book together we have done our best to credit as many writers as possible, as no story can be written without them. We acknowledge that there are quite a few 'spoilers', but, wherever possible, we have tried to avoid giving too much away as to the actual endings. That said, we have assumed anyone interested in time travel stories has seen *Back to The Future* (many times) and probably *Dark* and *Looper* as well. We hope in our plot summaries we have offered just enough of the story to encourage readers and viewers to seek out those Time Tales with which they are unfamiliar.

The idea for the book came as I (Steve Nallon) was putting together THE SWIDGERS, my own time adventure book series. I found it curious just how many options there were in creating a time travel story world, plus, of course, the various narrative choices concerning how the tale could be told. Many decisions would have to be made before starting to plan or write. And those option choices became the inspiration for this book. Our examples are far from exhaustive but we hope they will be enough to prompt readers to recognise some of the same story principles and tropes in their own favourite Time Tales.

The history and analysis that follows is by no means complete, nor is it meant to be an assessment of the merit of one Time Tale over another, though inevitably some observations are made on what works well and what does not. The aim is simply to offer a flavour of the many creative and dramatic choices available to the writer, plus the many scientific and philosophical ideas that can be explored when telling the tales of time.

# It's Story Time!

*We all have our time machines, don't we.*
*Those that take us back are memories...*
*And those that carry us forward, are dreams.*
H.G. Wells

STORIES ARE AN essential part of our human survival kit. When we're very young, our need for story is like an unquenchable thirst and that's because it's stories that help us to understand ourselves and the world around us.

Story is the playground of the mind where we can imagine a place beyond the one we live in, but it's also in a way an emotional gym, for it's in the world of story that we can explore and develop feelings and passions. And related to this is the idea that story offers a safe environment for human beings to examine and reflect on emotional conflicts and complex moral dilemmas.

One of the key reasons then why human beings tell stories is that they give us the ability, as it were, to 'walk in another's shoes' and so see how people who aren't like us perceive the world. And for that we don't just need imagination, we need empathy (from *em-pathos*, meaning 'in feeling'), that is the ability to understand and share the feelings of others. Story then encompasses the entire spectrum of human experience, from the cerebral and the intellectual to the psychological and the emotional. But let's now examine some specific purposes of story in more detail and see how they play out within the framework of a Time Tale.

In his series of lectures on the novel, E.M. Forster defined a story as 'a narrative of events in their time-sequence.' Forster then went on to say that 'The king died and then the queen died' could be said to be a story, but that 'The king died, and then the queen died of grief' was/is a plot. His point was that the phrase 'and then' added what he called a 'sense of causality'. The time-sequence was still there but 'and then' added reason and consequence, for when you say 'The king died, and then the queen died of grief' you are constructing a connecting relationship between one event and another. Causality and learning how life events connect could then be said to be another key reason why human beings tell stories.

And the point here is that causality is often the most crucial element of a time travel story. In fact, no other genre or type of story draws attention to the nature of causality more than a Time Tale. Why? Because a Time Tale often by its nature has knowledge of the future and so has already seen how events of the past have played out. There are many Time Tales that depend on the concept of consequence and causality for their plotting to work. Think here of TV series and movies such as *Travelers* (2016–18), *Dark* (2017–20), *Star Trek IV: The Voyage Home* (1986) and *Groundhog Day* (1993). Some here might want to add *12 Monkeys*, except that in *12 Monkeys* (1995) the main character assumes a causality which turns out to be incorrect. No problem with that because going right back to the philosopher David Hume, there have been those whose thinking has always been suspicious of making too many assumptions about the nature of causality and consequence. The point is that there is no right or wrong answer. Some have the philosophy of life that everything connects and has purpose, others that the universe is random, amoral and meaningless. And the Time Tale you tell is likely to reflect which end of that philosophical axis you stand.

It should be said that the power of story doesn't end on the last page or the final reel. After we have read a book or seen a movie we may think about it, mull it over, consider it, question it – and in so doing the tale it has told stays with us and becomes part of how we think. In other words, we assimilate its meaning in such a way that story becomes part of how we perceive the world and feel about life. Just follow the debates on any fan website, or go to any science fiction convention and listen to the legion of enthusiasts of such series as *Doctor Who* or *Star Trek* discuss and argue the meanings, purposes and intentions of the episodes they love.

Another reason we like reading or watching stories is that they allow us to escape into another world – and don't mock escapism if you've never lived a life where you needed to escape. People have difficult domestic situations and so a book or movie with a captivating tale to tell offers a few hours in another world, where the reader or cinemagoer can forget the cruelty of their own. And it's often such people who become the storytellers of the future, who, psychologically, develop a need to share their vision of the world. So what might we say about the philosophy and psychology of the teller of Time Tales? Well, many time travel stories offer would-be fixers and dreamers the opportunity to change the past by altering timepaths – and usually this is done in the hope of making the world a happier place. Foolish to generalise, of course, but might 'optimistic idealists' be a fair summary of the thinking of many time travel writers? Perhaps. Yet Time Tale writers often assume a dystopian world worse even than our own, so maybe 'realistic idealists' might be a better tag. And here we'd offer Ray Bradbury's 1984 short story *The Toynbee Convector* as the archetypal time travel story. Why? Because the time traveller is revealed to be a liar, there's no such thing as time travel and there never will be, but the idea of time travel as it is presented in the story is to 'weave dreams'. As the fraudulent time traveller says, 'What seems a lie is a ramshackle need, wishing to be born.' And perhaps no one has ever summed up the nature of the time travel tale better than that.

If the psychological purpose behind the concept of plot can be summed up as change through conflict, then one of the reasons stories exist could be said to be to recognise the personal developments that that dramatic conflict brings about. In other words, story becomes, at least in part, a way of understanding the importance of change in our lives. Transition. Maturation.

Evolution. And witnessing and reading stories about what we might call 'becomings' in others can prepare us for potential transitions in our own lives. And this is where certain types of Time Tales have something unique to offer, for not only can the time era change for the time traveller, so can the physical body they find themselves in. Just ask Dr Sam Beckett.

Stories offer us as well moral codes by which to live. In simple terms, stories act as morality tales, guiding us to understand what is right and what is wrong. Morals need a habitat and stories are a perfect home. The Bible is full of such tales, as is *One Thousand and One Nights*, *Mahabbarata*, and the works of Homer. But of course morality depends on the ideology of a particular society. Some stories affirm moral codes and conventions, others question them or even undermine them in an attempt to have them altered. Here again, the Time Tale offers something no other genre can because alternate histories, utopias and dystopias, and befores and afters – that can often exist within the same story – give you the opportunity to compare and contrast.

But in all this talk about the writer's psychology, moral codes and transformational becomings, let's not forget the more vibrant and colourful end of the story spectrum – and that's the idea of what we might call the 'Story Funfair'. Here is where story's primary purpose is to divert, entertain, make us laugh, arouse sensations and even sometimes, with horror and ghost tales, scare us to death! And it's interesting that so many writers of different genres have recently embraced the Time Tale and developed its appeal way beyond science fiction. Think here of the comedy *Palm Springs* or the slasher horror movie *Triangle*. Both time loop tales, but so, so different in intention and purpose.

*****

So those are some of the purposes of story, but when writers make up a tale, what 'building blocks' do they use to construct it?

Well, one way of exploring that question is to ask: *What are the main elements of a story that you couldn't do without if it is to be a story?* In reply you might say a protagonist and an antagonist; a sudden change in the status of things; an event from the past which still haunts the main character; a puzzle or question that needs answering; a goal or quest of some sort; an action or strategy to alter the way things are or have become, plus maybe a problem within the main character that needs to be rectified before that final goal can be reached and achieved. All of these will probably lead to conflicts of various types, a crisis, a battle or confrontation and ultimately a climax and resolution. And we might add three aspects of story that are not strictly speaking building blocks of plot but which are integral to story construction and they are the setting, the theme and the image system.

But of course no storyteller treats any of these elements of story as if they are some sort of blueprint that must be strictly adhered to, for it's the variations, deviations and exceptions that make a tale truly original, engaging and entertaining. Yet these fundamental story building blocks are essential in understanding how a tale works, so let's now consider each in turn, plus other important story elements that can often be added to enhance a tale. And as we go along, we'll look at two classic but contrasting Time Tales: Charles Dickens' *A Christmas Carol* and Bob Gale and Robert Zemeckis' *Back to the Future*. And as we go through our story building blocks, let's ask how the writers of each took these principles and made from them unique and perfect Time Tales.

**Protagonist and Antagonist** – the writer John le Carré once said that 'The cat sat on the mat' is not the beginning of a story, but 'The cat sat on the dog's mat' is. What he was perhaps hinting at was that as soon as the dog comes along and sees his mat occupied by the cat, there's bound to be trouble. Most stories then have a central character (the protagonist) who is trying to do something and another character (the antagonist) whose aim is to stop them doing it – and it's usually that conflict which is the main dynamic of the tale. There are other terms it is possible to use in this context, including 'hero' and 'villain' (or sometimes 'nemesis' or 'shadow'), but strictly speaking the instigator of the plan is technically the protagonist and that character is not always the same as the 'hero'. It's also worth noting that protagonist and antagonist are gender neutral terms and so often preferred in contemporary story theory.

So how does the plot of *Back to the Future* fit in with the protagonist–antagonist dynamic? We would say that Marty and Doc Brown are essentially joint protagonists for the simple reason that they share the action and the tasks. Biff could be said to be the main antagonist for Marty, whereas it is the circumstances and the environment, what some story theorists such as Robert McKee call 'forces of antagonism', that primarily work against the Doc. Psychologically you might call Marty the 'hero' of the story, because that's who we, the audience, are rooting for. However, without the plan and task action of the Doc, Marty would never get back to 1985, which is the key action drive of the story.

What about protagonist–antagonist dynamic in *A Christmas Carol*? The main character is clearly Scrooge, but he isn't the one who comes up with the plan, and the ones who do – the Spirits – are on his side. So where's that protagonist–antagonist conflict? Scrooge is initially reluctant to go along with the plan or indeed go with the phantoms, but this unwillingness soon changes. Hmm. Little quarrel or argument there. No, most of the conflict in *A Christmas Carol* is internal in the sense that it's Scrooge's belief that he is unable to change that is the main struggle of the tale. Inner struggle then can make you your own antagonist.

**Back-Story** – this is what has happened before the story began but which is still relevant to what is going on right now. The back-story is also sometimes called 'The Ghost', because what happened in the past is still 'haunting' people in the present.

Often there is a literal scar, as with Henry in Audrey Niffenegger's *The Time Traveler's Wife*. And Time Tales are unique in the respect that back-story, unlike in any other genre, can be visited and witnessed first-hand, as is the case with Henry and Scrooge. And in some cases the back-story can even be changed.

*Back to the Future* has a plot where Marty's family back-story is altered in such a way that puts his very existence in jeopardy and so Marty has to put right what he himself put wrong in order to keep himself and his family in 1985 alive. What we have here is back-story being used to create a literal existential crisis. Other Time Tales have done the same, but arguably none better than Bob Gale and Robert Zemeckis with Marty McFly.

In *A Christmas Carol*, the Ghost of Christmas Past takes Scrooge back to his back-story and this is possible because we have entered the world of the supernatural. And the creation of such a happening in an era when time travel tales were almost unknown shows us Dickens' remarkable powers of imagination and inventiveness.

**The Day of Change** – when something occurs that creates an imbalance in the life of a character. The day of change is often referred to by writers as the 'catalyst event' because it's what upsets the apple cart and the status quo but isn't necessarily integral or directly connected with the action that follows. The crucial point is that the day of change is not enough on its own, it must incite a need to alter things or return them to what they were.

There are various elements to the day of change in *Back to the Future*, all of which are integral to the plot. There is the discovery that the flux capacitor works and time travel is possible, but that is then immediately followed by the arrival of the Libyans and their attack, which results in the shooting of Doc Brown. However, the key event which alters everything dramatically for Marty, is him accidentally travelling back in time to 5 November 1955. Of course Marty could just stay in the past and live out his days there, as many time travellers do when they by chance find themselves in their past. But on the same day as he arrives, there is another accident, a collision, which alters his own family history in such a manner that it puts his future life at risk – and if the time track he has lived up until now disappears, so will he.

*Back to the Future* then has multiple imbalances and alterations in the status quo, all of which need to be fixed in some way. It's worth mentioning here that one of the golden rules of storytelling is that a coincidence or an accident can be the catalyst event which starts off a chain of events, but it's never a coincidence or accident that should bring those events to an end. In good storytelling that is always down to the protagonists alone.

The day of change in *A Christmas Carol* is simply the arrival of Marley. Marley first manifests himself in the knocker, but his appearance is foreshadowed in the opening line. Marley is essentially the herald of the tale and as such has three main functions. The first is to tell us what will happen – three Spirits will visit Scrooge. Second, Marley acts as a call-to-action to Scrooge to change his ways and to this end shows Scrooge what would happen if he does not. Third, Marley offers the reader an early glimpse into the unknown supernatural world into which they are about to journey.

**The Trigger for Action** – an incident in the tale that incites the desire in a character to change things or correct something that has gone wrong. And that's why this event is often referred to by writers as the 'inciting incident'. It is the action that follows this trigger that drives the story forward, where action can be defined as the purposeful intent of the character to achieve their goal. That's why the 'action' of any tale is always a verb such as *to win, to find, to make, to sell, to escape, to discover...*

The title *Back to the Future* isn't a verb as such but one of the key actions of the tale is *to get back to the future*. But crucially that isn't the only action of the tale, for Marty's parents must kiss for the first time at the dance, which will eventually lead to Marty being born. And making this happen is Marty's main purposeful intent or action. But the time travelling DeLorean is Doc Brown's problem and so his action is to work out how to utilise the energy from the electrical strike on the clock tower and get it into the DeLorean. Essentially there are two separate actions and that's why Marty and the Doc should really be seen as joint protagonists. But there's a subplot action too and that's to somehow save the Doc's life in 1985 when he is shot and apparently killed by the Libyan terrorists.

**The Puzzle** – in any story, especially a mystery, there is usually a secret to be uncovered or revealed. The mystery element of a tale raises curiosity and this is important because one of the reasons why people keep on reading a story is that they want to know what happens next. As Lee Child has said, 'You ask or imply a question at the beginning of the book and you absolutely self-consciously withhold the answer. It does feel cheap and meretricious but it absolutely works.'

However, neither *Back to the Future* nor *A Christmas Carol* are mystery stories as such. There is a puzzle of sorts in *Back to the Future* – where to get 1.21 gigawatts of power – but that is soon solved by the knowledge that in a few days' time there is to be a lightning strike on the clock tower. There is the question in *A Christmas Carol* as to who the dead man is in Stave Four, but the reader surely knows it is Ebenezer Scrooge himself, even if he doesn't. Scrooge is 'in denial', is how perhaps a psychiatrist might put it. But there are of course many well-plotted Time Tales that are mysteries, notably the Spanish murder whodunit *Mirage* (*Durante la tormenta* 2018) and indeed most of the *Doctor Who* plots.

**The Inner Flaw or Problem** – what is lacking or missing in a character that requires putting right in order to make that character a more complete and better person. The Greek word for this, which Aristotle uses in his *Poetics*, is *hamartia*. It's a term incidentally which in Greek times was used in archery and meant 'just missing'. The story guru John Truby usefully divides the idea of the flaw or problem into psychological need – those aspects of a character's nature that are lacking within her or him, for example, a need to be more self-confident – and moral need – how a character must learn to act differently towards others, for example, be kinder or less bossy. And often in a story what a character learns about themselves and why they must change becomes part of how they ultimately achieve their goal.

Scrooge's problem in *A Christmas Carol* is pretty obvious: he's cut himself off from the world like an oyster in its shell ('It's enough for a man to understand his own business, and not to interfere with other people's'). Scrooge's moral need is that he must reconnect with that world and the people in it. His psychological need is that he must believe that it is possible for him to change.

But where's the character defect in Marty McFly? Well, there's the don't-call-me-chicken issue and Marty's weakness in succumbing to dare challenges, but that does not come up until the sequels. You could say then that in the first of the series Marty doesn't have a character issue that needs fixing. However, there is someone who does, for the problem-need in *Back to the Future* belongs to his father George, who needs to become more self-confident. And it's Marty's task action to make sure that happens.

**Motivation and Desire** – there is always a reason behind a character's actions and this usually comes from a want or desire in that character. However, what someone wants at the start of a tale isn't always the same as what they want by the end – and this is because the story journey can alter how a character sees themselves and the world.

There is plenty of motivation in *Back to the Future*, but as it's primarily an action movie, what you might call 'the desire line' doesn't change that much. *A Christmas Carol* is very different, for it begins with little motivation on Scrooge's part – quite the opposite in fact because he really doesn't want to be bothered by the Spirits – but his story ends with a passionate desire for life and a new beginning.

**The Character Arc** – this is what writers call the internal change that occurs in the character as the story progresses. An arc in geometry is a curve between two points, and storytellers use the term 'character arc' because as the character moves through a story there is a transition between what they were like at the beginning point and what they are like by the end point. The 'arc' can be many shapes – smooth and gradual or rapid and acute – depending on the story you're telling.

The character arc in *A Christmas Carol* is arguably one of the biggest and most spiritual in literature. And it's this arc of redemption that is key to the story's enduring appeal. But why is this so? Well, perhaps we all need to believe in the possibility that we can change for the better and, of course, the concept of redemption runs through Judaeo-Christian philosophy and much of Western thought and culture.

The character arc in *Back to the Future* is nowhere near as big as that in *A Christmas Carol*, and, as said, it doesn't belong to the protagonist but rather to young George, Marty's father. He is the one who grows in confidence across the story and it's George who ultimately saves Lorraine from Biff. But it's a character arc that is long-lasting, for what is achieved in 1955 alters what George becomes by 1985.

**The Task and the Strategy** – in a story the main character is sometimes given a task to complete or they have to come up with some sort of action plan in order to achieve their goal. Either way, the character needs to find the right strategy and tactics to attain what they want.

The tasks and strategies in *Back to the Future* are very clear and practical. Marty has to create a situation where George has the confidence to ask Lorraine to the dance and then kiss her on the dance floor, which will lead to their romance and marriage. At the same time, Doc Brown has the challenge of finding a way to transfer the power of the lightning strike into the car.

In *A Christmas Carol*, Marley is the one who tells Scrooge that he must change his ways and, to help bring this about, he informs Scrooge that he will be visited by three Spirits. Later, the Ghost of Christmas Past is more specific about his task when he says that his aim is Scrooge's welfare and 'reclamation'. And to help make this happen the Ghost of Christmas Past shows Scrooge his past, including his lonely school days and the happy time he had working for Mister Fezziwig. The strategy then in *A Christmas Carol* is also clear, but it's in the hands of the three Spirits. If this is so, what is Scrooge's own action task?

Scrooge is what you might call a passive character in that he does not initiate the actual plan. However, that doesn't mean that Scrooge hasn't got things going on inside him. The key to Scrooge's internal action can be found all through the tale, but particularly in the scene at his nephew's Christmas party where Dickens writes,

> When this strain of music sounded, all the things that Ghost had shown him, came upon his mind; he softened more and more; and thought that if he could have listened to it often, years ago, he might have cultivated the kindnesses of life for his own happiness with his own hands, without resorting to the sexton's spade that buried Jacob Marley.

Scrooge is made *to think* and *to feel* (both verbs) and so it's *thought* and *feeling* brought together that become Scrooge's action. You might here make a comparison with Phil in *Groundhog Day*. Ultimately Scrooge's task action is to change and it's these acts of contemplation as he observes each scene that accumulatively leads to his reclamation or redemption.

**Helping Hands and Opposing Forces** – usually in a story there are numerous forces and obstacles which work against the main character and their plan. Apart from the antagonist (sometimes called villain), these opposing forces can include the weather, objects that go wrong and gateways or thresholds that the character can't get past. But usually as well there are allies, helpers and gifts that can assist the protagonist on their way.

Doc Brown in *Back to the Future* is more than a helping hand as one of the key actions is his and his alone. But Doc Brown does have opposing forces to the action. In fact, the sequence on the clock tower, as Doc Brown tries to make a connecting circuit direct to the DeLorean, is a masterpiece of the action/counteraction dynamic. So many things go wrong and Doc Brown has to be incredibly inventive in how he puts them right.

As said, in *A Christmas Carol*, the central 'action plan' is in the hands of Marley and the Phantoms, and so technically this makes them collectively the protagonists, with Scrooge the one resisting their offer of help (compare here perhaps the angel Clarence and George Bailey in the movie *It's a Wonderful Life*). However, as *A Christmas Carol* is essentially a redemption story, the central conflict and toil is mainly within Scrooge himself. And in a way it's this aspect of the tale which makes it still so relevant to today, as we live with our own internal struggles to do the best we can in this world.

**Time Limit** – often a story will have a deadline to be met which means that the main character must complete the task within a fixed period of time. This increases the jeopardy and the story stakes. In storytelling this is usually referred to as 'The Clock'.

On this point, *Back to the Future* has one of the best 'clocks' in movie history. And a literal one at that! 10.04 pm is when the lightning strikes and everything has to be in place at precisely that moment. So iconic did this exact moment become that it is referenced in the movie *Mirage* (2018) which also has a tower struck by lightning when the clock was at 10.04.

But what of *A Christmas Carol*? There doesn't seem to be a 'clock' at all, and in some ways the opposite. In this magical tale, time in its most literal sense collapses, for the hours that Scrooge is away with the Spirits is not one long night measurable by a clock. For a start, the Fezziwig Christmas Eve party takes up an entire evening in itself and on top of that Dickens makes it clear that Scrooge's visitation by the Ghost of Christmas Present lasts the whole Christmas season of 12 days. His time with the Spirits cannot be measured simply by the turning of a dial, but that's exactly how Scrooge does think of time – as something that should and can only be quantified by the ticking of timepieces and the clanging of bells. Yet Fred, Scrooge's nephew, offers Scrooge a different perspective. He sees Christmas Time 'as a good time: a kind, forgiving, charitable, pleasant time: the only time I know of, in the long calendar of the year, when men and women seem by one consent to open their shut-up hearts freely.' And that's the whole point of *A Christmas Carol* – Scrooge must learn to see time not as something measurable but as something to be part of. And by the end of the story, Scrooge understands that to be a complete human being, he must live in the past, the present and the future. What his journey in time teaches him is that to live in the past is *to be alive to memory*, to live in the present is *to know your fellow Man*, and to live in the future is *to be open to hope*. So when Scrooge says, 'The Spirits of all Three shall strive within me' what he is really expressing is the importance of connecting with all aspects of ourselves, plus, as Fred puts it, our 'fellow-passengers to the grave.' Achieve this and 'time' will be always be measured by love and not by the turning of dials of a clock on the wall.

**The Unexpected Outcome** – this is when a character thinks something will go one way but instead it goes another and sometimes even in a diametrically opposed direction. The Greek word for this kind of change to the opposite, which Aristotle uses in his *Poetics*, is *peripeteia*. The general point here is that stories aren't just built on '*What happens next?*' but also '*What could happen next!*' – for it's those unpredictable or unforeseen happenings and surprises that keep people turning the pages.

*Back to the Future* uses the plot device of the unexpected outcome to its opposite in the scene where Marty saves his father from an on-coming car but in this process not only prevents his father from meeting his mother but ends up being hit by the car himself, taken into the house and looked after by his mother who then begins to fall for him. And it's this bizarre and extreme change in the family history which Marty must then reverse. *A Christmas Carol* has its own unexpected outcome to the opposite – a sudden and dramatic change from Life to Death – in the crisis moment when Scrooge seeks to discover the identity of the dead man in the cemetery, only to be shown the name on the grave and realise that it is himself. But, as said, surely by then Scrooge must know deep down that the man who lay abandoned under that sheet and now lies beneath that 'unkept grave' is one 'Ebenezer Scrooge'?

**From Ignorance to Knowledge** – the moment of realisation when a character discovers, for example, that someone they thought they knew well is not what they seemed or said they were. The Master in *Doctor Who*, for example, has had several incarnations where The Doctor only discovered his/her true identity after already knowing them as someone else. The Greek word for this, which Aristotle again uses in his *Poetics*, is *anagnorisis*. It's worth saying here that in story terms the idea of ignorance to knowledge doesn't just involve people, for it can apply to objects and places too. And that includes another time world.

Sometimes one of the frustrations of a Time Tale is how long the accidental time traveller takes to realise they are now in a completely different time era. In *Back to the Future* Marty McFly does take a while to realise he's no longer in 1985 but rather 1955. It's the date on the newspaper Marty finds in the trash which finally swings it. But let's cut the writers some slack here, for in a Time Tale, movie or otherwise, creatives need to properly establish the new time world, and as this is usually done through the point of view of the time traveller, that character needs to keep up their bewilderment for as long as possible. And what this means is that expositional necessity sometimes triumphs over character credibility. To borrow an old movie expression, it sometimes takes a while to realise that 'we ain't in Kansas anymore'.

The key ignorance-to-knowledge moment is much clearer and more crucial to character development in the plot of *A Christmas Carol*. And it's that the true identity of the man Scrooge saw earlier laid out dead is in fact himself and it's he who now lies under the gravestone that reads 'Ebenezer Scrooge'. It is this knowledge or recognition which leads to Scrooge's existential crisis.

**The Hour of Despair** – this is the lowest point that the character faces in the story. The rock bottom, you might say. This part of a story is sometimes referred to by writers as the 'nadir' (the word nadir comes from the Arabic *naḍhīr* meaning 'opposite'— the opposite, that is, of the 'zenith', the highest point of the celestial sphere). The nadir is the moment in the tale where the character is at maximum remove from their goal. A plot can have several low spots, but the one where all seems lost and unwinnable is the most important. Writers also use the term 'crisis point' for this part of the tale – and importantly it nearly always comes just before the climax.

In both *A Christmas Carol* and *Back to the Future* the hour of despair is an existential crisis where Marty and Ebenezer are confronted by their own non-existence. With Marty it's literally a fading hand that is disappearing right in front of him to the tune of *Earth Angel (Will You Be Mine)* and for Scrooge it's the Ghost of Christmas Yet to Come indicating Scrooge's own grave. And, as said, it's here in the graveyard that Scrooge comes to realise that he was the abandoned body he saw earlier, wanted only by rats gnawing at the door. Oddly enough, the scene with the laid-out corpse is rarely included in movie versions, which as a result means Scrooge never sees his own corpse. Perhaps the grave is enough, but the abandoned dead body scene offers a powerful moment in the lead-up to the cemetery. This is what Dickens writes as Scrooge stares at the body under the sheet,

> Scrooge glanced towards the Phantom. Its steady hand was pointed to the head. The cover was so carelessly adjusted that the slightest raising of it, the

motion of a finger upon Scrooge's part, would have disclosed the face. He thought of it, felt how easy it would be to do, and longed to do it; but had no more power to withdraw the veil than to dismiss the spectre at his side.

**The Impossible Choice** – nothing in a story is ever easy for a character. Often a drama is based on a situation where there is a difficult dilemma that must be faced and a choice made. Scrooge is seen in his back-story choosing the security of money over his love for Belle, yet, though it's a decision he comes bitterly to regret, it's a choice he makes freely without too much of a struggle. George perhaps knows that standing up to Biff could make his life worse, so there's an internal conflict there, but frankly neither *A Christmas Carol* nor *Back to the Future* are stories where the impossible choice is central. This is a good excuse to briefly mention *Yesterday's Enterprise* (1990), a greatly admired episode of *Star Trek: The Next Generation*, written by Trent Christopher Ganina and Eric A. Stillwell. The Enterprise encounters a 'temporal rift' in space and from it emerges the USS Enterprise-C from its past, 22 years ago to be precise, and as soon as this happens the present-day Enterprise changes its timeline. Only Guinan, played by Whoopi Goldberg, notices this and Data theorises that this might be because her species (she's an El-Aurian) has a perception that goes beyond linear time. Anyway, in the alternate timeline the Enterprise is at war, but sending the Enterprise-C back where it came from would mean it would face destruction. It's one of those classic 'for the greater good' dilemmas where the certain death of a few might (or indeed might not) save the lives of thousands, if not millions. It's a well-regarded episode not only because of the finely balanced choices it presents but also because of the way it explores, in the case of Lieutenant Natasha Yar, the idea of an 'empty death' as opposed to one with purpose. Impossible choice digression over.

**The Confrontation or Battle** – this is the final encounter between the protagonist and the antagonist. The outcome of this meeting decides how the story action will end.

From this point of view Marty's father George McFly is in charge of his own destiny, for it is George, without any direct intervention from Marty, who belts Biff in the face and knocks him out. Likewise George reclaims with some force his dance with Lorraine when some oik briefly takes her from him. As for the clock tower scene, Doc's battle is primarily with the elements, which, at the very last moment, he overcomes and so achieves his task of getting the power of the lightning strike to the time travelling DeLorean. As said, there isn't really a protagonist–antagonist relationship in *A Christmas Carol*, but Scrooge's final confrontation with the Ghost of Christmas Future is crucial in how Scrooge changes. As Ebenezer says, pleadingly, 'Men's courses will foreshadow certain ends, to which, if persevered in, they must lead. But if the courses be departed from, the ends will change. Say it is thus with what you show me.'

**The Reversal of Fortune** – the change of fortune in story can be slow and gradual but more often it goes from the worst situation to the best situation in a matter of moments and this is simply because that sort of dynamic is exciting to read or watch. This is certainly the case in *A Christmas Carol*, where Scrooge believes he is dead but suddenly finds himself very much alive and in his own bed. Likewise, Marty goes from fading into near nothingness to being a dazzling rock'n'roll virtuoso. Yet how that reversal of fortune is achieved shouldn't be too obvious. The key to all story endings, according to screenwriter William Goldman, 'is to give the audience what it wants, but not in the way it expects.'

**The Climax** – this is when the protagonist reaches their goal. It may or may not be that they achieve or complete the task, but whatever happens, the important point of the climax is that there is no turning back and things can never be the same again.

The climax is often described as the apex/top/pinnacle/zenith of your tale.

The climax in *A Christmas Carol* is a reversal of fortune, for Scrooge is no longer a corpse in a forgotten grave but a man alive and bursting with energy. In *Back to the Future* there are two actions and therefore there are two climaxes. The first is when George kisses Lorraine on the dance floor and so changes the future and the second is when the power of the lightning enters the car and as a result Marty is successfully returned to 1985.

**The Rebirth** – this is when the protagonist changes inside and becomes different in some way and grows as a person. This often relates back to the inner flaw or what was missing or lacking in the character at the beginning of the tale but has now been fixed as a result of what has happened in the story. And often here there is what appears to be a physical rebirth of some kind. In *A Christmas Carol*, Scrooge becomes a changed man from what he was, and furthermore, on waking up, he's born anew – 'I don't know how long I've been among the Spirits. I don't know anything. I'm quite a baby. Never mind. I don't care. I'd rather be a baby. Hallo! Whoop! Hallo here!' There's no real internal change within Marty, there rarely is in an action hero, but he does have a symbolic rebirth when he goes from fading and fainting on the college stage to becoming immediately revitalised to the extent that he gives a performance that might even have been the spark that created rock'n'roll. And that is one heck of a rebirth.

**The Resolution** – this is the final element of a story or narrative in which the strands of the plot are drawn together, loose ends are reconnected, and matters that need to be explained are cleared up. The resolution could be said to be the aftermath or breathing space following the climax, and in theatre plays this part of the story is traditionally called the *dénouement* (from the French word *dénouer* meaning 'unknot'). It's that part of the tale that gives you a sense of what may come next for the characters and the world they live in. If the opening of a story starts with '*Once upon a time...*', then it's the resolution that says '*And they all lived happily ever after.*'

Scrooge, Dickens tells us in the final Stave, 'had no further intercourse with Spirits, in that respect, but lived upon the Total Abstinence Principle, ever afterwards; and it was always said of him, that he knew how to keep Christmas well, if any man alive possessed the knowledge.'

*Back to the Future* has a more complex resolution in that after the return to 1985 it is revealed that Doc Brown's death by shooting at the hands of the Libyan terrorists has been reversed as a result of the Doc taking note of the letter Marty gave the Doc in 1955. This subplot involves another rebirth in that Doc is seen apparently lying dead on the ground but then his eyes open and he sits up. We also see in the resolution the change in the dynamics of Marty's family in 1985 that Marty's intervention in 1955 has now brought about. George and Lorraine are happier and more successful, and the bullying Biff didn't crash the car but is now in fact waxing it. There is also the beginning of what seems to be a new story involving Marty and Jennifer's children.

*****

Every analogy or comparison breaks down eventually but, we might say, if what we've looked at so far are the building blocks of story, then setting, the image system and theme could be said to be the cement which helps bind the 'story bricks' together into a coherent whole.

**Setting** – this is the world of your story and includes not only the physical space and that world's moral and political culture, but also the time period or era. World building is the phrase that writers use for creating an environment and world laws that are believable and credible, even if it is a fantasy, a dystopia or has a supernatural setting. A key issue for time travel stories is how time travel rules operate in that universe. Is the time traveller able to interact with those in the past or future? Can there be dual existence? Is time travel one way? Is the past changeable? All these questions must be thought through and decided upon before the writer can begin.

*Back to the Future* brilliantly creates two time settings, the one contemporaneous to the film's creation, 1985, and a stylised version of 1955, but the key to their construction is to show how they contrast in terms not only of their physical spaces, but also the cultural, political and moral values of their respective eras. Think here of Mayor Goldie Wilson, rock'n'roll music, President Ronald Reagan and Lorraine's attitude to sex. The film's Oscar nominated script was written by Bob Gale and the film's director Robert Zemeckis, two men born in the early 1950s, who logically set the film in a nostalgic version of the era they grew up in, as well as present-day 1985. And in his new world of 1955 Marty can not only interact with those he finds there but do so in such a way that alters the past and his family history.

In *A Christmas Carol* there are very different time rules for the Spirits impose a key stricture which is adhered to and that is that Scrooge cannot interact with the worlds in which he finds himself, he can only observe. Yet this is a supernatural story and so the locations in these worlds can change and be replaced by another in an instant. One location in Dickens' era stood out to readers above all others and that was the home of the Cratchitts on Christmas Day, for the description of their Christmas dinner is said to have set a blueprint for all urban families in Victorian England and to a degree that pattern can still be seen in homes today. In contrast, the Christmas Eve celebration of the Fezziwigs was Dickens' way of recreating the 18th century rural tradition of having a village party in one of the barns of the lord of the manor. Ultimately, of course, it's the mental juxtaposition of the merry Christmas dinner scene with the Cratchitt's home in mourning in a Christmas of the future which packs the big emotional punch. Scrooge sees that the world of joy and laughter has now become a world of sorrow and black ribbons.

**Image System** – essentially a strategy of symbols and images, physical or metaphorical, that are used to explore themes, create aesthetic emotional responses and increase intellectual awareness. The term itself originates with Robert McKee but other story gurus have come up with other expressions. For example, John Truby calls it the symbol web and Caroline Spurgeon's 1935 pioneering study on the use of images in William Shakespeare's plays, *Shakespeare's Imagery and What it Tells Us*, is worth a particular mention here. An image system can incorporate physical objects, but equally it can include the use of language and names. Another term that is often used in this area is *motif*, where the *motif* is a recurring element within the story, the ultimate aim and purpose of the storyteller being to create a certain atmosphere or to convey, sometimes subliminally, a particular thematic idea or even moral. Another expression is *mise-en-scène*, which literally means 'what is put into the scene'. Although the term is used mainly in film criticism, its principles can also apply to narrative descriptions of place and setting in a novel.

The idea that the world, and the life one lives in it, can be a prison is a repeating metaphor in the work of Dickens. John Dickens, Charles Dickens' father, spent several months in 1824 in the Marshalsea Debtors Prison and during part of this time Charles, then aged only 12, was sent to work in a shoe-blacking factory. The literal imprisonment of his father combined with Charles' own sense of entrapment in the factory left huge psychological scars that never truly healed and the prison metaphor is a reoccurring image throughout his writing. In *A Christmas Carol* Scrooge lives an isolated and lonely existence and the language and metaphors of the story constantly reiterate the sense of enclosed entrapment. According to the narrator, Scrooge is as 'solitary as an oyster' and even Scrooge's final resting place is a kind of prison – 'it was a worthy place. Walled in by houses;

overrun by grass and weeds, the growth of vegetation's death, not life; choked up with too much burying.' But the most famous image of entrapment in *A Christmas Carol* is the chains of Jacob Marley – 'Oh! captive, bound, and double-ironed!' But Dickens' imagery often works in counter-point and antithesis, and the descriptions of entrapment are alternated and balanced by images of freedom, especially in the description of the appearance and clothes of the Ghost of Christmas Present. Words and phrases such as 'loose', 'free', 'disdaining to be warded or concealed', 'ample folds', 'open hand', 'unconstrained' are all the very opposite of confinement. What these prison/freedom *motifs* do is set a tone that helps in our understanding and feeling for the characters. They're subtle and not always that obvious, but perhaps all the better and more powerful for it.

In time travel stories an obvious *motif* would be a clock or watch. In *Back to the Future*, the film's opening credits involve a tracking shot showing various clocks, and one even includes a figure of the silent movie actor Harold Lloyd hanging off the big hand pointing to 11 o'clock, which anticipates what actually happens to Doc Brown himself on the clock tower towards the end of the movie. A bit of foreshadowing seems appropriate enough in a movie about a past with a known future. There are other timepiece references associated with *Back to the Future*. Doc Brown is usually seen wearing two watches and Marty staring at his watch from the movie poster became one of the iconic images of 1985. And clocks especially are of course important to the narrative of *Back to the Future* itself. For example, there's the obvious plot point of the Hill Valley Courthouse clock being struck by lightning and its importance in getting Marty home, but a clock also features in Doc Brown's back-story where hitting his head after falling when trying to hang a clock in his toilet back in November 1955 was the pivotal moment in his devising the concept of the flux capacitor. The timepieces, watches and clocks then emphasise the Doc's obsession with time and time travel. The screenwriters found as many ways as possible to introduce time *motifs* into their story. Pretty obvious you might think, but few other time travel movies had previously done that. Repeated viewing reveals a true sense of artistry in every aspect of the movie's composition.

**Theme** – 'Literature must rest always on a principle, and temporal considerations are no principle at all. For, to the poet, all times and places are one; the stuff he deals with is eternal and eternally the same: no theme is inept, no past or present preferable.' The words of Oscar Wilde. What Oscar perhaps means here is that there should always be some sort of point to the tale you tell. But in life there are many truths, and when a writer tells their story, what they are expressing is essentially their philosophy of life. And it's the way they see the world that is what we'd loosely call the theme (or the 'controlling value' as some story gurus put it). It is usually personal for the simple reason that no writer wants to create something they don't believe in.

*A Christmas Carol* has several themes, including, as we've seen, Time. But there's another and more subtle idea running through the story and that is the need for a fancy of the mind. Just before Scrooge sees the door knocker become the face of Jacob Marley, the narrator tells us that 'Scrooge had as little of what is called fancy about him as any man in the city of London, even including – which is a bold word – the corporation, aldermen, and livery.' What Dickens calls 'fancy' is what we would now probably call 'creative imagination'. And yet, once upon a time, he did. In his lonely hours at school Scrooge had friends with whom he shared his long winter days and when the Ghost of Christmas Past takes Scrooge to his old school room, he sees them once again:

> 'Why, it's Ali Baba!' Scrooge exclaimed in ecstasy. 'It's dear old honest Ali Baba. Yes, yes, I know. One Christmas time, when yonder solitary child was left here all alone, he did come, for the first time, just like that.'

# IT'S STORY TIME!

What Scrooge did was create his 'friends' from his reading. Dickens contrasts this Scrooge with the man the men of the city know:

> to hear Scrooge expending all the earnestness of his nature on such subjects, in a most extraordinary voice between laughing and crying; and to see his heightened and excited face; would have been a surprise to his business friends in the city, indeed.

Fancy is a theme that runs through much of Dickens' work. Writing in the first issue of his magazine *Household Words* (30 March 1850) Dickens set out in *A Preliminary Word* his views on the importance of imagination for his readers:

> we would tenderly cherish that light of Fancy which is inherent in the human breast; which, according to its nurture, burns with an inspiring flame, or sinks into a sullen glare, but which (or woe betide the day!) can never be extinguished.

Yet as Scrooge grew older, his fancy and imagination simply waned and the security of money took its place. One way then of looking at *A Christmas Carol* is to see how the human value of imagination can be rekindled, albeit by supernatural means beginning with the appearance of Marley's face in the knocker: 'To say that he was not startled, or that his blood was not conscious of a terrible sensation to which it had been a stranger from infancy, would be untrue.' It's a slow re-awakening of fancy but grow it does. Even if the Ghosts were all a dream, what a dream it was. It brought alive again Scrooge's inventive mind. And it is our 'fancy' that when Dickens says Scrooge became a 'second father' to Tiny Tim, what he was perhaps saying was that good old uncle Ebby spent many an evening reading to Tim all his favourite Ali Baba stories that he himself loved as a boy.

*Back to the Future* is in part an action movie with car chases and the rest, but there is a beating heart at its centre as well, for it is a family tale of reclamation. Marty's task is to put right his own accidental intervention so that his father does kiss his mother on the dance floor. But Marty's exploits do more than intended and George, now with more self-confidence, punches and knocks out Biff. And it's this event which changes the whole ongoing relationship between Biff and George in the future, for when Marty returns to 1985 the power dynamic between the two men has been completely altered. But can one punch in the face 30 years ago make that much difference? Well, er, yes. According to this Hollywood movie. You must stand up for yourself in life seems to be, if not exactly the theme, then at least the message you take away from the action of *Back to the Future*.

Another way of looking at the theme of a tale is when the character values of the hero/protagonist clash with the beliefs of the shadow/antagonist and how that personal battle is then played out, as it were, at an ethical level. Some story gurus call this 'the axis of conflict'. The axis of conflict in a story can often represent/stand in for more than the individual players/protagonist/antagonist themselves. And you can find that dynamic in *Back to the Future II*, where the greed of Biff is contrasted with the family values of Marty. The two futures offered in *Back to the Future II* compare, perhaps, with the two contrasting worlds of Pottersville and Bedford Falls in *It's a Wonderful Life*.

*****

What we've set out in this chapter is a brief summation of the purpose of story, how story works and how the key components of story can be put together in terms of plot construction, setting, imagery and theme. But as we can see from the different ways *A Christmas Carol* and *Back to the Future* adapt, develop and indeed deviate from these story building blocks, no storyteller is obliged to keep to these 'story rules' as if they are some sort of strict formula. What matters is how writers modify and reinvent these story steps in order to create an engaging, entertaining, imaginative and ultimately original work. But why choose *A Christmas Carol* and *Back to the Future*? Samuel Taylor Coleridge argued that Henry Fielding's *Tom Jones* was one of the 'three most perfect plots ever planned' (the others were *Oedipus Rex* and Ben Johnson's *The Alchemist*). To nail our own colours to the mast, we would contend that *A Christmas Carol* and *Back to the Future* are the two most near-perfect Time Tale plots ever constructed. And much can be learnt from both.

# Who Tells the Time Tale?

*If you want your children to be intelligent, read them
fairy tales. If you want them to be more intelligent, read
them more fairy tales.*
Albert Einstein

IN HIS LECTURES E.M. Forster essentially argued that the difference between 'story' and 'plot' was that story is all the events that happened in chronological order, but that plot involves the rearrangement of those events in a different time order (in the sense either of how the story is told or when it is that we discover what happened and why), and that those events are presented as happening in a causal 'this-occurred-because-of-that' manner. So what we are talking about here is essentially plotting and structuring. But there's another factor to take into account in the presentation of a story, and that is its narrative design.

Let's go back to E.M. Forster's observation that 'the king died and then the queen died' is a story, but 'the king died and then the queen died of grief' is a plot. Well, that's fine, but Forster didn't say from what point of view that story should be told. From the perspective of the queen or standpoint of their son or daughter? Or even perhaps from the sidelines through the eyes of the court jester? Think of it like this: if story is everything that occurred, and plot is the discovery of the when and the why those things happened, then narrative design is the way that tale is communicated.

The aspect of the time tale we are looking at here then is who tells it, the way they tell it, plus the perspective from which they tell it, meaning, is it told with hindsight (retrospective narration) or is it, as it were, happening right now?

And beyond these options there are other narrative choices to be made. For instance, what sort of narrative voice should the story have? Will the narrative be told as an objective narration, a subject narration or even stream of consciousness? Is the tale to be communicated in first person or third person? Will it be written in present tense or past tense or a mixture of both? Are events to be imparted exclusively through narrative description or might some aspects be told through letters, diaries or emails (the epistolary form) or exclusively through direct speech (as in a play or drama)? And these are important questions, not least because all these decisions have to be made well ahead of any actual composition or writing.

You might think here that we're talking only about the narrative fiction in novels or short stories, but movie and television have their parallels, even if some of the terms are slightly different.

**Objective Narration** – the standard narrative form of most novels, and indeed the Hollywood movie, is what is usually known as objective narration (or, in fiction only, the 'implied author'). In other words, it can be assumed when reading a book or watching a film that someone has put the narrative all together and so controls how, what and when the reader or viewer sees and hears what there is. *Back to the Future*, *Edge of Tomorrow* and *The Terminator* are classic examples of this. Of course, the story's creator or creators, want the story to be told in the best possible way. No good story maker would ever, for example, tell you what the twist is at the start of the narrative. And nor would you as a viewer or reader want them to. So you assume that whoever has put the story together has done so for strategic reasons. Put simply, those presenting the story, plotted it out in order to achieve the greatest possible effect on the reader or viewer, be that emotional, comedic or dramatic.

A further point to make about objective narration is that it's exactly that – *objective*. Objective narration keeps its distance. It's all about showing and presenting as impartially as possible, rather than putting forward a moral judgement or pointing out with a voice from above where one of the characters made a terrible mistake. Objective narration can still be expressive in how it conveys its story, it's just that it chooses, on the whole, to keep its distance when it comes to passing on its opinion.

Another important point to make here about objective narration is that it rarely keeps to the perspective of one character. Usually in objective narration there is equal access to a fair range of characters across the whole narrative. That's why objective narration is an obvious choice for historical fiction and drama. However, most time travel stories have a time traveller protagonist at their heart who is usually the main focus of the story, so an objective narrative isn't always the best option. But there is a type of narrative that does keep itself to a very limited number of characters, or even just one character, and this way of presenting story is usually known as 'restricted narration'.

**Restricted or Reflector Narration** – perhaps a better phrase to use rather than restricted narration is 'reflector narration', for what we're really talking about here is keeping the range of knowledge to one or maybe two people in the narrative who act as a kind of 'reflector' through which the story is presented. Put simply, it's from their point of view alone that the reader or viewer will experience the tale and all that happened in it. And that's why restricted narration is a bit of a misnomer, for what it often means in practice is actually seeing more but only from one point of view. A narrower perspective, yes, but usually one that's far deeper and more penetrating in that in certain cases we are told what the reflector character is actually thinking.

Many Time Tales involve a lone time traveller and so are reflector stories to a greater or lesser extent. Not surprisingly, restricted/reflector narration is popular as well in mystery stories and a typical combination of the two can be found in Philip K. Dick's 1952 short story *The Skull*, where our time traveller, Conger, is set the task of going back into the past to assassinate someone, but the only clue he has to the man's identity is a skull.

A puzzle indeed. The reader follows Conger, which means that we discover whose skull it was at the same time he does. The reflector narrative is there as well in Philip K. Dick's 1952 novelette *Paycheck*, a mystery centring on Jennings, a man whose memories have been wiped after a secret mission. In the story, in place of the money he was expecting as payment, Jennings discovers only a pocketful of trinkets. Like the breadcrumbs left by Hansel in the Grimm Brothers' fairy story, these trinkets lead Jennings to the discovery of a 'time scoop'. And in *Paycheck*, not only do we follow Jennings, Dick even takes us into his internal world, revealing his thoughts and deliberations.

Of course not all reflector narrations are as clear cut as the classic investigation tale. Take the movie *Primer* (2004). It's true that *Primer* is presented pretty much exclusively from the perspective of Aaron and Abe. However, there are so many missing pieces in this multi-dimensional jigsaw puzzle of a tale that even at the end, coming to any sort of full understanding of this elliptical time travelling narrative is neigh on impossible. Detractors on IMDb mock this but those who are admirers of the movie see it as one of its greatest strengths.

Another point to make about the restricted/reflector narration is that the character being followed can, as it were, be switched as the story develops. Jonas, for example, is the main reflector in the television series *Dark*, but not exclusively so. But again *Dark* is a mystery crime tale, and ultimately it is Jonas who must discover a clear path – his own *Holzweg* you might say – through the forest-like complexity of the plot. And it's only when Jonas succeeds in this, and so finally comes to an understanding of the whole mystery, that he is able to make the decision that will change everything. And that of course is why Jonas is the central reflector, because that moment is the pivot on which the whole Time Tale rests.

**Unrestricted Narration and Subjective Narration** – unrestricted narration goes a lot further than either objective narration or reflector narration in that unrestricted narration does what it says on the tin: it's a narration that is unlimited in knowledge and truly ubiquitous. An unrestricted narration can go anywhere, including sometimes even inside the minds of the various characters. An example of an unrestricted narration in a movie might be said to be the movie *The Jacket*, where the narration takes the audience into the mind/memories/dreams/hallucinations of Jack Starks (Adrien Brody). But what's real and what's imagined is not always that easy to tell. At least not until the very end of the movie.

Subjective narration is similar to unrestricted narration, except with subjective narration one character alone is the 'centre of consciousness', as Henry James once put it. But pure subjective narration is very rare in movies simply because, by definition, pure subjective narration would also mean subjective camera or POV (point of view) throughout the film. Subjective camera can occasionally be found in objective narrations, for example, when we see the red images from the red-eyed Model 101 in *The Terminator*. However, this technique is only used in a few scenes.

**Stream of Consciousness** – the ultimate subjective narration is stream of consciousness or 'mindscreen', as it's sometimes referred to in cinema, and this subjective narration can include dreams, memories and interior monologues. In subjective narration internal thoughts are often a central part of the narrative, plus any subjective sound that only that one character is hearing. Or believe they are hearing.

'Stream of consciousness' was actually a phrase coined by William James, psychologist brother of the novelist Henry James. It describes in a psychological sense the continuous flow of thought and feeling in the human mind. Literary critics then picked up the phrase and started to use it to sum up a particular type of narrative which tries to imitate this process in literary form. Think here of some of the works of Virginia Woolf or Samuel Beckett. A movie example worth mentioning in this context is *Jacob's Ladder*. It's similar to *The Jacket*, except in

*Jacob's Ladder* there is little consistency, for both time and reality are fractured. However, it is possible to think of it as pure subjective narration because it can ultimately be understood – apart from the scene where the protagonist is pronounced dead – as a narrative existing only in the mindscape of a confused and dying soldier. His memories are dream-like in that time and characters have all become mixed up in his thoughts in his dying moments. And which were true and which were invented as a result of his state of delirium is never made clear. This, in a way, now takes us on to what is commonly known as unreliable narration.

**Unreliable Narration** – some people think of unreliable narration as a relatively modern form of narrative, but this isn't necessarily the case. You can find the unreliable narrator in Homer's *The Odyssey*, where Odysseus is a 'Trickster' figure who can't always be relied upon to tell the whole truth – especially if being economical with the truth is to his advantage. You could even argue that the tale Odysseus tells of his life adventures at the court of the Phaeacians comes entirely from his own vivid imagination. Anyway, an unreliable narration is usually defined as a narration that is not being entirely honest in what is being told or presented. And, as in *Jacob's Ladder*, this can include tales of dreams that are not at first revealed to be dreams and memories that are later discovered to be false.

A famous example of an unreliable narration is found in Kurt Vonnegut's 1969 novel *Slaughterhouse-Five*. Billy Pilgrim is suffering from what used to be called 'shell-shock' or 'battle-fatigue' but is now classified as PTSD or Post-Traumatic Stress Disorder. Patients with this condition lose the capacity to differentiate between past and present and so become, as it were, unhinged from the realities of time. Are the Tralfamadororians in the story actual beings? Who truly knows? And perhaps such questions can't even be answered by Billy Pilgrim himself.

It is also possible to have an unreliable narrator telling a story within the story. What is told by Prairie Johnson in *The*

*OA* and also by Eduard in *If I Hadn't Met You* could be said to be examples of this, or at least it is suggested that the stories they tell aren't exactly truthful. And all this makes the narrative more interesting, for seeding doubt in an internal narrative can be, if used guardedly, a very useful dramatic technique.

**Intrusive Narrative** – is basically a narration with some sort of outsider commentary, for example an educational film, travelogue or newsreel. Intrusive narration can also include intruding subtitles or inter-titles. A basic example of this would be the words *British Makeshift Headquarters* suddenly appearing at the bottom of the screen in *Austin Powers*. Such intrusive subtitles are mainly put there for expositional and explanatory reasons, usually what year it is, or where we are geographically in a story, but sometimes they are added for humorous or even didactic purposes. And let's not forget their dramatic potential, as in the over-text on the screen of *Henry is 8 and 22 and 17 and 31 and 40 and 37 and 24 and 25 and 34 and 32 and 12 and 15 and 23 and 39 and 10 and 23 and 29 and 28 and 38 and 41* after the scene of his mother's death in Steven Moffat's adaptation of *The Time Traveler's Wife*. Many Henrys gravitate there and the one by one appearance of each age on the screen is a powerfully dramatic series of reveals.

Subtitles are sometimes referred to by academics as 'non-diegetic intrusions' because they come, as it were, from outside the world of the story (what they would call the *diegesis*). Music that accompanies the movie can be included as a non-diegetic intrusion, but not of course any music in a scene that comes from a radio on the table or that is heard through car speakers or whatever, for the radio and the car are both part of the *diegesis*. Those intercut musical 'stings' in *Austin Powers* are most definitely not part of the *diegesis*.

Not that you'd ever want to cut them.
*Oh, behave!*

Many of the narrative forms or narrative voices discussed so far are not mutually exclusive. There's no reason why a restrictive narration might not include some intrusive narration in the form of subtitles, as *Dark* sometimes does in explaining where and when we are on the timeline. And there's no reason why a subjective narration might not also be an unreliable narration, as we've seen with *Jacob's Ladder*. That said, a pure subjective narration shouldn't be able to relate first-hand those events or scenes where the character narrating the tale wasn't present as happens in a typical objective narration.

**Meta-fiction** – the storyteller, writer or film director is just one side of the equation – let's not forget the reader or the spectator too. Theatre, of course, can break what actors call 'the fourth wall' and so draw attention to the fictional nature of what is being presented. This is traditionally found in pantomime but actually it's a convention that goes back to the days of Aristophanes and early Greek comedy. It's rarer in movies but breaking from the fictionality to remind the watching audience that the movie is a fiction can be found in *Wayne's World* (1992) and *Hellzapoppin'* (1941).

Arguably the most famous example of meta-fiction in English literature is Laurence Sterne's *The Life and Opinions of Tristram Shandy, Gentleman* (first published in 1759). The book isn't a Time Tale as such but it comes very close in that little if anything happens in linear order. You could even say that Shandy's mind and his memory is in constant time travel mode. Perhaps that would be stretching the point but one of the themes of the book is the dislocation of time.

Actually, it's rare to find meta-fiction and time travel mixed together for the simple reason that accepting time travel depends on a leap of faith into the incredible and so undermining by breaking the fourth wall isn't probably such a good idea. That said, there are exceptions and one Time Tale that does occasionally hint at its own fakery is *Austin Powers*, but that's comedy and a parody to boot.

*Oh, smashing, groovy, yay!*

**First Person Narration** – is a narrative, putting it as simply as possible, that uses the word 'I' a lot. If a novel begins 'I journeyed back in time and I am now going to tell you what I saw...' then it would be a first person narration. And so what we have in first person narration is a character narrator basically telling you, the reader, the story.

The main advantage of first person narration (sometimes also called the 'autobiographical voice') is its accessibility, in that you get to know the character doing the telling. As a result, the decisions the narrator makes throughout the story are usually clearly understood by you the reader, for the narrator and reader develop a sort of bond. First person narration then allows for a form of storytelling that is very direct, intimate and immersive – you're always right there inside the narrator's mind, after all. The style of speech or writing can also be very conversational and relaxed. First person narration needn't have the formality of third person narration (or the 'assumed narrator' as writing theorists sometimes call that type of author).

It is true that first person narration is by definition restricted narration – the narrator cannot know what is going on in someone else's mind or how they are feeling – but, as we all do in real life, the teller of the tale can interpret looks and tone of voice. Interestingly, *The Time Traveler's Wife* by Audrey Niffenegger uses dual first person narratives, the time travelling husband and the non-time travelling wife. But neither are linear and so it's up to the reader to put together the jigsaw puzzle of these two very personal narratives.

The overall arc of THE SWIDGERS book series is that of a developing child who is on a quest of discovery about himself and the universe around him – and for that reason it makes sense that he should tell his story himself. And *The Time That Never Was*, the first in the series, is essentially a mystery story, which certainly suits first person narration. However, as William says in his narration, 'Better to tell my tale as it happened and not as it came to be understood. And I do this as much for myself as for you. For isn't it sometimes in the very telling of our story that we come to understand it?' In a way then, the reason William is writing his story is, at least in part, to fully understand it himself, for sometimes in life, it's as we are describing to a friend a strange happening that we suddenly understand its significance. William wants to tell you exactly what happened and he occasionally struggles to do so because he's not always certain himself. Take the description of what William calls the 'cable-snakes', where suddenly everything inexplicably becomes frozen in time, only to come alive again a moment later:

> What was happening? Had the minutes and seconds somehow – I don't know – stopped? Or was I in some sort of Circle of Time? …The only way I can describe all this is that it was as if The Now, the moment we live in, was ever changing. As if Time itself was somehow shifting between What Is and What Could Be. At least that's what I thought. I wish I could explain it better, but I can't. What I can tell you is it felt like the beginning of madness.

William isn't being an unreliable narrator, as such. In a way he's the opposite, for he's honestly telling you that he didn't know what was going on and being forthright too in saying he finds it difficult to get across in words what he was witnessing and how he felt. And that perhaps makes it even more real as don't we all struggle sometimes in relating complex and confusing events?

In mystery adventures such as THE SWIDGERS, the reader essentially sees what the protagonist sees and discovers the tale's many secrets at the same time as they do. It's possible the reader might even work things out before the protagonist if all the clues are there. In telling the tale retrospectively, the first person narrator can move back and forth in the story's plotline or, indeed, cleverly use foreshadowing to hint at what is to come without actually giving the whole game way. And the emotional stakes are always likely to be much higher for readers who have got to know the narrator as a friend as a result of living inside their head for hours at a time. Yes, there is the disadvantage that the narrator protagonist can't describe himself or herself objectively, but on the other hand the first person narrator is constantly revealing who they are through their thoughts, and anyway they can ultimately be judged by their actions.

There are couple of other points worth mentioning about first person narration. One is that the first person narrator can be an outsider who is, as it were, looking in on the central action. Think here of *To Kill a Mockingbird* or, in a way, *The Great Gatsby*. The second point is that the narrator doesn't actually have to be a person. There are numerous books narrated by animals, famously Anna Sewell's *Black Beauty*. Is there perhaps a Time Tale still to be told of the family pet who accidentally wandered into a time machine or through a time portal gateway? Disney, Amazon, Apple or Netflix, would any of you be up for it?

## So, Which Viewpoint or Narrator is Best?

Are there multiverses out there where the same Time Tale is told both from the main character's perspective and that of an outsider? Hmm. Probably not, for writers are usually smart enough to choose the best reflector or narrator for their story. However, there is one tale by Robert Silverberg which does exist, as it were, in two different narrative worlds. Silverberg's *Gianni* was written for *Playboy* magazine in 1982 and concerns a composer who is taken from the 1700s and brought to contemporary California. The tale is narrated in the first person by the man in charge of the project, Dave Leavis, but the editor at *Playboy*, Alice K. Turner, wanted Silverberg to switch the narrative voice to the publicity agent, Sam Hoaglund. Silverberg resisted the idea at first but Turner showed how it could be done and this version was published in *Playboy* (and later in *The Playboy Book of Science Fiction*) with Hoaglund as the narrative 'eye'. However, as Robert Silverberg says in his book *Time and Time Again* (collection 2018), whenever the opportunity has arisen to put *Gianni* in an anthology he has always chosen the Leavis narrator version. That said, the outcome of the tale doesn't change. The early 18th century Gianni Battista Pergolesi discovers rock music with the band Shining Orgasm Revival – the wonderfully imaginative names that Silverberg comes up make his prose sparkle – and as a result the hedonist Gianni begins to share the lifestyle that goes with being in a rock band. Well, perhaps you can guess the rest for yourself.

## The Narration and Narrators of H.G. Wells' *The Time Machine*

First person narration is sometimes like one of those Russian dolls, for it's possible to have a first person narration within first person narration. That's the case with *The Time Machine* by H.G. Wells. The dinner guest is the narrator of the story (he is never named) who tells us what happened at the evening dinners with the time traveller (also unnamed). However, it's the time traveller himself who narrates in first person the story of his adventure. In effect it becomes a story-within-the story. Of course you could get into an argument about how accurate the dinner guest is in relating every precise detail of the time traveller's tale – I mean, how could he possibly remember it word for word? – but, on the whole, readers accept the convention of this type of story-within-a-story in the novel form.

Actually some critics believe the dinner guest narrator to be the character called Hillyer, who is mentioned briefly by the Time Traveller, but others assume that Hillyer is more probably a servant and nothing to do with the narration itself. Anyway, whatever our narrator's name is or isn't, like most of the other guests, we are told very little about him. We do know that he goes to the Linnaean Society, so he might have a scientific background, but our narrator also talks about having a meeting with his publisher, so he might be a writer. Or, of course, he could be both.

Whatever his occupation, the important point is that our narrator, before he wrote the story, clearly thought about its implications a great deal. And he's still thinking about them as he composes the Epilogue, which is written for the most part in present tense:

> I say, for my own part. He, I know – or the question had been discussed among us long before the Time Machine was made – thought but cheerlessly of the Advancement of Mankind, and saw in the growing pile of civilization only a foolish heaping that must inevitably fall back upon and destroy its makers in the end. If that is so, it remains for us to live as though it were not so. But to me the future is still black and blank – is a vast ignorance, lit at a few casual places by the memory of his story. And I have by me, for my comfort, two strange white flowers – shrivelled now, and brown and flat and brittle – to witness that even when mind and strength had gone, gratitude and a mutual tenderness still lived on in the heart of man.

Our narrator is open to the possibility of time travel and, in part at least, believes the story the Time Traveller has told. A narrator who was sceptical, as some dinner guests are, would naturally have given the novel an entirely different feel. It should be said, however, that our narrator doesn't share the philosophical pessimism of the Time Traveller, but, compared to some of the guests, our narrator is, thankfully, a thoughtful and deep thinker. And an optimistic one, for the narrator offers the hope that even now the Time Traveller, as he writes these words, may be 'wandering on some plesiosaurus-haunted Oolitic coral reef, or beside the lonely saline lakes of the Triassic Age.' Plus the narrator has by him a symbol of hope, namely those strange flowers.

**Third Person Narration** – sometimes also called the 'assumed narrator' or 'implied narrator'. The main advantages of third person narration are that it allows for omniscience across the whole story and potentially for insights into a range of characters. It also gives the writer the opportunity to impart information unknown to the characters and move around in time and space. But with third person narration there are greys. A narration that is objective yet keeps its central perspective to just one character, which is to say the story is essentially being told from their point of view, is called 'third person limited' or 'third person restrictive'. It has the obvious advantages of objectivity and, to a degree, omniscience, yet since you are following one particular person it is also a way of telling that remains very personal. There is also what is known as 'free indirect speech' or 'free indirect discourse', where the narration moves, often imperceptibly, into a character's consciousness while still maintaining the form of the third person narrator. You'll find this technique used in many Philip K. Dick stories, for example Jennings' internal questioning in *Paycheck* – 'An impulse came to throw the code key away. What good has it been? But surely *he* had known what he was doing. *He* had already seen all this.'

**The Narratee and Second Person Narration** – 'you' is a second person pronoun and it can occasionally be used by the narrator to address the 'narratee', that is the one to whom the story is being told. Put more simply, the 'Reader'. Some academics call this 'dialogic conscription', others 'intrapolation', and there's even a special term for the second person in this context and that is 'the intra-diegetic Reader', though some might think that sounds more like an invasive instrument used in diagnostics of complaints of the colon or bowels.

But are any of these strictly speaking what you could call 'second person narrations'? Well, the answer to that is not really, because in true 'second person narration', the 'You', the 'Reader', is a specific and actual character in the story. Indeed, 'You' is – or, to be grammatical, 'you' *are* – the protagonist. Not surprisingly perhaps, second person narration, where the second person pronoun 'You' is an actual character in the narrative, is incredibly rare in fiction. Jay McInerney's 1984 novel *Bright Lights, Big City* is written entirely in second person, but that's not a Time Tale.

Of course, it's possible to argue that second person narration brings you even closer to the story than first person narration because you *are* the story, because the 'you' of the narrative is the protagonist of the tale. It's possible to argue as well that second person narration avoids the so-called unreliability of the first person narration in that the second person narration tells 'you' the reader what you are or aren't feeling and thinking and so why would you doubt, as it were, 'yourself'.

But there are problems with second person narrations. Suppose the reader simply isn't the type of person who, like the shy and retiring aunt at Christmas, particularly enjoys playing charades or dressing up as a pirate of the late 17th century. And it's the nature of second person narration – '*You did this*', '*You did that*' – that it inevitably becomes accusatory, with the 'you' of the story becoming complicit in whatever nefarious activities go on. Still, it's an experimental narrative form that may be worth exploring for the writers of a time travel tale. Who after all wouldn't mind being told they are Doctor Who? What a wish-fulfilment novel that would be! Copyright permitting, of course.

# Who Knows What, When and Why?

> *'This suspense is terrible. I hope it will last'.*
> Gwendolen in *The Importance of Being Earnest*
> by Oscar Wilde

THE MOST POWERFUL card the creator of any tale holds in their hand is story information. What we are talking about here is the knowledge and facts the audience, viewer or reader, is given or presented with as the story progresses. When to reveal the secret that's hidden in the box? What would be the most dramatic moment? It's an old adage but one worth repeating: *Make 'em cry, make 'em laugh and then... make 'em wait.* A useful rule but with it comes a warning: don't withhold information too long or you may end up frustrating your reader or audience.

**Suspense** – in a typical 'suspense story' neither the characters nor the audience should know too much about what is happening, or what is about to happen, for a reader or audience to be gripped in suspense depends on a feeling of trepidation – *'What's behind the door at the end of that dark passage?'* – and so tension and anticipation are what the suspense story aims to create. And, as Tom Clancy has observed, 'Suspense is achieved by information control: What you know. What the reader knows. What the characters know.' And when that balance of knowledge works well it can be very dramatic.

A key feature of a suspense story worth noting is that from the first reel or chapter to the very last, the main character is rarely out of danger. The name given to these types of 'lowbrow' suspense story in the United States was 'Dime Novels', whereas in Britain they were known as 'Shockers'. The time loop movie *Triangle* could be said to be a suspense thriller in this mould.

**Dramatic Irony** – this is when the audience or reader knows far more story information than the characters in the story, or at least more than some of the characters. The result of this is that the full significance of what someone says in a scene is understood by the audience to have a different meaning to the one intended. The effect is sometimes comic, notably in the movie *Groundhog Day*, which is pretty much pure dramatic (and comic) irony from the first repeated day onwards, but at other times it can lead to pathos, for example, the end moments of *Looper*.

Certain time travel stories by their nature offer perfect opportunities for dramatic irony and comic irony. *Back to the Future* establishes both the personal world of the McFlys and the political world of 1985 before going back in time to 1955. And that knowledge of 1985 is playfully used in 1955. There is, for example, that scene in the dining room when Lorraine's mother asks Marty why he looks so familiar. Is it perhaps that she knows his mother? Marty looks in Lorraine's direction and says that yes, he thinks she does know her. Lorraine's father later says of Marty that he's an idiot and blames his upbringing. Well if that's the case the joke's on you, granddad! Then there is Goldie Wilson, the busboy clearing tables in the 1955 diner who believes that he will make something of himself. Marty says that indeed he will, for Marty knows he will become mayor well before 1985 because he's seen it for himself. The owner of the soda shop where Goldie works shakes his head in disbelief, but Marty and we, the audience, know better. Another point is that maybe it's Marty's remark about being mayor that gives Goldie the belief in himself to indeed become mayor, though Steven Moffat in our interview spotted a potential inconsistency here in the story's time rules.

In *Travelers* (2016–18, created by Brad Wright), much of the comedy comes from the travellers lack of knowledge or awareness of food. Or at least 21st century fast food. Grace, Traveler 0027, is given some French Fries while awaiting the outcome of her trial. She loves them and says that no matter what happens she can say that she had '21st century French cuisine'. But there are more serious moments too. Grant MacLaren (the time traveller) and his wife Kathryn (not a time traveller) are discussing children and Kathryn suggests setting up a trust fund for college. Grant puts her off by saying that that's years hence. His wife replies that they need to think about the future. Grant from the future says that he has given that some thought.

**Mystery** – the word 'mystery' comes from the Latin word *mysterium*, meaning 'a secret thing'. The American mystery writer Mary Roberts Rinehart put it well when she said that the 'mystery story is two stories in one: the story of what happened and the story of what appeared to happen.' Mystery yarns are usually told from a reflector perspective and the appeal is not so much suspense as curiosity. As the writer Elizabeth Gaskell noted, 'There is always a pleasure in unravelling a mystery, in catching at the gossamer clue which will guide to certainty.'

Mystery is the key narrative drive in both book one (*The Time That Never Was*) and book two (*The Time They Saved Tomorrow*) of THE SWIDGERS Time Adventure series. The story begins with a mysterious attack on a seemingly normal Saturday morning in a north London high street. William, it seems, is the focus of the attack, yet when the strike comes it is not directed towards William but instead towards the man he was meant to save. William is a curious Swidger and wants to know exactly what is going on and so does his best to find out the truth behind this time mystery and his own special place in it. To that end William does a lot of uncovering – literally uncovering when in Echo's railway carriage – and he discovers much about himself and the Swidger world. During William's lodging at the Old Coach Inn there is the new mystery as to how it is that Aloysius has control over those who live there, plus what is the secret of the house and why has Granny brought William to it? But there's something else too, for during this period at the Old Coach Inn, William gains an insight into himself (what story gurus call a 'self revelation') and the nature of what it is to be a Swidger. And this knowledge, it seems, may offer him a way out of the situation he has found himself in – which leads into the action of the second book in the series, *The Time They Saved Tomorrow*.

**Anticipation** – one of the key dramatic devices in the toolbox of the writer. Knowing what is coming but not when it will come can be edge of the seat stuff. But too much waiting or anticipation has its drawbacks. Remember the old joke: A man in a guest house is a woken up in the middle of the night by the noise of someone in the room above returning from the pub. The man upstairs throws one of his boots to the floor. One minute goes by. Then ten, then twenty. Finally the man in the room below can bear it no longer and shouts, 'For God's sake, throw down the second boot so I can get back to sleep.' Waiting for that other boot to drop is anticipation gone wrong and can be very frustrating indeed.

Not surprisingly anticipation can be a key narrative device in Time Tales, because, if you know a bit about history, when a time traveller arrives on a ship in the Atlantic called the RMS *Titanic*, or on the island of Krakatoa hours before its eruption, or in the Japanese consulate in Honolulu a day ahead of the attack on Pearl Harbour (all settings in the 1960s series *The Time Tunnel*), then you will soon begin to anticipate the big event that will change these worlds. The point here is that anticipation in a Time Tale is never about if but when.

## Story Information and the Television Adaptation of *The Time Traveler's Wife*

Time travel romances such as *Somewhere in Time*, *Berkeley Square* and *The Time Traveler's Wife* often work within a Rigid Universe or Block Universe, meaning that events in time are essentially fixed. There is even a brief discussion in *The Time Traveler's Wife* around the concept of a Block Universe versus chaos and the free will/God world view of Thomas Aquinas. Henry says that Clare's life is not running on a track and it's her decisions that will make the future, even though he knows what that future is. However, for now let's leave the question of predeterminism, God and free will aside and concentrate on the storytelling.

Essentially *The Time Traveler's Wife* is a romantic drama with the very human theme of grief being the price we pay for love. Steven Moffat in our interview expressed his huge admiration for the book, especially the beautiful prose of Audrey Niffenegger, but he made the point that a dramatised adaptation was all about finding and developing the right scenes. And dramatic scenes need action and a dramatic climax, sometimes with revelations. A key piece of information in the story is the marriage of Henry to Clare, yet there is no scene as such in the book where the time travelling Henry tells Clare that one day they will be man and wife. Moffat in his dramatisation had it that the action of Clare in many scenes is to discover whether or not she is right in her assumption that Henry will become her husband. However, when pressed on this Henry either resists, deflects the questioning or even seemingly lies. But that dynamic conflict had to come to a head at some stage and so Moffat used a subplot concerning Jason, a young man who took sexual advantage of Clare and is later captured by Henry. Moffat built a scene where Henry confronts Jason and in it what Jason says about Clare riles Henry so much that in anger he blurts out the truth – 'Because I'm her fucking husband!' In making the revelation the climax of the Henry/Jason confrontation Moffat found the most powerful and dramatic moment to reveal to Clare what she had always wanted to know. And there's another scene Moffat added which again shows how even when you as an audience have foreknowledge it is still possible to create a powerful dramatic moment. There's an exchange where the Older Henry is telling the Younger Henry, aged only 8, exactly what he will do next. The Younger Henry will, says the Older Henry, get up in 30 seconds and run across the room. The Younger Henry defiantly says he won't and grips hold of his chair and refuses to let go. Only then he turns round and sees his mother alive (in the time period they are currently in the mother was killed several months later), and instinctively lets go of his grip and does, as predicted, run across the room. Yes, philosophically *The Time Traveler's Wife* is a Rigid Universe, but that does not mean it cannot be a dramatic one.

\*\*\*\*\*

## It's All Getting Very Tense

So much for story narrative information, but we're not yet finished with narrative technique. There's another key choice to be made – and that is the verbal tense in which your story is/was/will be told. If this sounds a bit dull and too much like school then it's worth considering that there is one highly regarded and commercially successful Time Tale that has verb tense at its very centre.

> *Imperative mood, present tense: Do not thou go home, let him not go home, let us not go home, do not ye or you go home, let not them go home. Then, potentially: I may not and I cannot go home; and I might not, could not, would not, and should not go home; until I felt that I was going distracted, and rolled over on the pillow, and looked at the staring rounds upon the wall again.*
> Charles Dickens' *Great Expectations*

**Past Tense** – when telling any story concerning the past, the events of the past are usually over and done with. That's a pretty obvious thing to say but you could argue that time travel tales on this point are not so clear cut, for the past and the time traveller's present are essentially one and the same thing. And what this means is that for many travellers in time the people they meet are already dead. But that way of thinking can get a time traveller into trouble. For example, there's a scene in *Berkeley*

*Square* (play 1926, movie 1933) where Peter, from the future, meets a famous 18th century duchess. He praises her qualities but she takes offence at his phraseology. He speaks of her, she says, 'as if thinking of me in the past tense.' Not so, he replies, he did not use the past tense, yet the tone was certainly that of an obituary and now the damage has been done. And it's such subtleties and intricacies of language that can be the big give away for our time traveller.

**Praesens Historicum (or the Historical Present)** – when telling a story concerning the past we sometimes slip quite naturally into what is known as the 'historical present' (also sometimes referred to as the 'dramatic present', the 'narrative present' and the 'vernacular present'). Whatever you want to call it, it simply means the employment of the present tense when narrating past events (it was widely used in writing about history in Latin, hence its Latin name, *praesens historicum*.)

The historical present is a rhetorical style that heightens the dramatic force by describing events as if they were still unfolding and so gives any narrative a sense of immediacy. By way of illustration here's this old joke: 'Yesterday, I was at the doctor's. There I am, sitting in the chair, and I says to him, "Doctor, doctor. I think I'm a time traveller." And he says, "When did this begin?" And I says, "Next Thursday!"' You could argue that a past tense narration that occasionally drops into the historical present at the most exciting moments takes advantage of the best of both worlds. And that's why William in *The Time That Never Was* does slip quite naturally into the historical present in the exciting bits of his tale such as the escape from the fire.

**Present Tense** – where whatever is happening is happening right now. The standard mode of the novel has traditionally been the past tense, but there has been a trend in recent years towards the use of the present tense. For example, the narratives of both Henry and Clare in *The Time Traveler's Wife* are largely in the present tense but for obvious reasons the Older Henry uses past tense when describing 'his' experiences as Henry when Henry was five in 1968. There are some obvious advantages to the use of the present tense, for one, it gives a sense of pace and continuous forward motion and immediacy. Present tense particularly in a first person narration can also offer a sense of intimacy, where the reader believes and trusts their narrator. But there can be problems as well, the main being that you're pretty much stuck with it. The present tense narration has no ability to move through time in the same way a narrative told in the past tense, when all is usually known, is able to do. Then there is the issue that if you're only living (and writing) in the moment, from a consistency point of view, you should really include every single moment, even the most banal and insignificant.

So how can the present tense be useful for time travel tales? Well, it's interesting to note that Robert Silverberg uses it in several short stories in his collection *Time and Time Again*. In *Trips* Silverberg sends his protagonist to a dozen or so alternate Californias (one includes a visit to President Kennedy in 1973 from Fuehrer Goering). *Many Mansions* explores the idea that a single act of transit through time can generate a host of parallel time tracks and Silverberg's tale offers us brief glances into these time worlds. They may only be fragmentary, but each brilliantly presents to the reader a range of the seemingly infinite possibilities concerning the relationship (or rather relationships) between the main characters of the tale Martin, Ted and Alice. The point is that by writing both of these stories in the present tense rather than the past tense, which by its nature is more fixed, Silverberg creates an ever-changing precarious 'now' that never quite feels either permanent or stable. Which perhaps is the right tone for such multiverse tales.

**Future Tense** – an alternative to past tense or present tense is future tense, but narratives in the future tense are exceptionally rare. Not surprisingly that great rationalist Aristotle in book three of his *Rhetoric* says, speaking of political oratory, that no one can narrate what has not yet happened. Perhaps he was thinking mainly of those politicians who endlessly talked about what they 'will do for Athens'. However, *Aura* (published in 1962) by the Mexican writer Carlos Fuentes is an example of the use of the future tense and to a degree it's a time travel story. *Aura* concerns Felipe, who answers an advertisement in the paper to do a translation – 'You will live that day, just like all the others, and you will not remember it again until the next day, when you sit down again at the coffee table, order breakfast and open the newspaper.' It turns out that a lady called Consuelo wants Felipe to translate the journal of her dead husband, General Llorente. As Felipe goes through this document he discovers some intimate details about both the now elderly Consuelo and the late General. As Felipe reads the journal, he begins more and more to identify with the dead husband. Equally, Aura, the niece of Consuelo, though young, begins to appear older and wiser. Felipe with the encouragement of Consuelo, seduces Aura, only to find when he does that she, Aura, has become Consuelo, and he, Felipe, has transformed into General Llorente. Well, perhaps not officially time travel, more mind transference across time, which in a way makes it an even odder tale, and odder still is that some of the tale is presented in the future tense. The effect of all this is to create a dream-like state in an unclassifiable temporal world.

But what of that highly regarded and commercially successful Time Tale hinted at earlier? Well, think about the plot of *Arrival* (2016) with screenplay by Eric Heisserer and based on *Story of Your Life* by Ted Chiang. Isn't the key twist in the tale centred around language and the special nature of the future tense as understood and perceived by the aliens?

## Time Tale Tenses and the Future Semi-conditionally Modified Subinverted Plagal Past Subjunctive Intentional

When in doubt about anything – including what verbal tense to use – always consult *The Hitchhiker's Guide to the Galaxy* by Douglas Adams. This invaluable book tells you that one of the main problems of time travel is not becoming your own father or mother but grammar and use of tenses. And it suggests that the best book to consult is Dr Dan Streetmentioner's *Time Traveller's Handbook of 1001 Tense Formations*. All time travellers should buy a copy as it covers such grammatical conundrums as the correct tense to use to describe what would have happened had you not done a time leap and its variations in reference to your time standpoint in terms of 'further future' or 'further past'. Oh, but it's that tricky Future Semi-conditionally Modified Subinverted Plagal Past Subjunctive Intentional where even the most intrepid time travellers finally jump in the old wormhole and give up.

# The Time Machines

*'There are really four dimensions, three which we call the three planes of Space, and a fourth, Time.'*
The Time Traveller in H.G. Wells' *The Time Machine*

IN 1934, H.G. WELLS wrote in the preface to a collection of his 'Scientific Romances', which included *The Time Machine*,

> These stories of mine collected here do not pretend to deal with possible things; they are exercises of the imagination ... they are all fantasies; they do not aim to project a serious possibility; they aim indeed only at the same amount of conviction as one gets in a good gripping dream.

Maybe so, but what a dream and what a fantasy.

It should be explained that 'scientific romance' was the term first given to what we now call science fiction. Romance as used here comes from the type of story that centres on quest and adventure. A typical romance would also include some sort of spiritual development, often resulting from misfortune, plus an element of magic and possibly a love component, but not necessarily so. The blueprint of the classic romance would be Homer's *Odyssey*, but you'll also find it in some of the later plays of Shakespeare such as *Pericles*.

To bring us up to date it's worth mentioning here Philip K. Dick's definition of science fiction (or SF as he calls it) as set out in a letter written in 1981 which became the Preface of *Paycheck and Other Stories* (1987). Dick offers a useful distinction between science fiction and fantasy in saying that fantasy involves what people would always regard as impossible, whereas SF involves that which people might believe possible given the right circumstances. For Dick, an essential ingredient of SF is a 'distinct new idea' which should lead in the reader's mind to 'the shock of dysrecognition'. 'Conceptual dislocation' is how he sums up this reading experience. Dick goes on to say, referencing Dr Willis McNelly at the California State University, that the true protagonist of a science fiction tale is the idea not the hero. Certainly Wells' tale ticks all those boxes. Other terms incidentally in play at the beginning of the 20th century were the 'scientific novel', 'scientifification' and the 'hypothetical novel'.

But going back to Wells' story in the development of SF, it was the addition of that word 'science' that changed the genre into something completely new and even revolutionary. H.G. Wells published his seminal novel *The Time Machine* in 1895 and it has since set the bar high for everyone who followed. Of course, it wasn't the first time travel story in literature. The early Victorian period already had its fair share of time travel fiction, notably Washington Irving's *Rip Van Winkle* (1819) and Edgar Allan Poe's *The Tale of the Ragged Mountains* (1844), though these are more 'Time Sleep' tales. *Memories of the Twentieth Century* (1733) by Samuel Madden is an 18th century Swiftian satire centring on diplomatic letters supposedly sent back in time from the 1990s that was published over 250 years before H.G. Wells' tale. And then there is a play called *Anno 7603* (1781) by the Norwegian playwright Johan Herman Wessel in which Julie and Leander are taken into the future by a fairy to see how gender roles have changed (it's only women now who fight in wars). But letters aren't people, falling asleep isn't time travel and a fairy isn't science.

It is true that in Wells' own lifetime there had been a story published that featured a mechanical device of sorts (namely a clock, in *The Clock That Went Backward* by Edward Page Mitchell published in 1881), yet that was not a time machine as such, for it wasn't a specially designed contraption that you could sit in or had levers. Yes, the first tale to have a machine was arguably the satirical farce *El Anacronópete* a three-act zarzuela (operetta) by the Spanish writer Enrique Gaspar y Rimban in 1887, but that's just a metal box. Besides, it's the scientific theory behind the design that makes Wells' *The Time Machine* so important in the history of science fiction.

But there are other aspects of the story too. Its unique combination of the explained over the inexplicable, social commentary instead of cheap thrills, and, of course, reasoned science rather than magic. And it's these in combination which make *The Time Machine* the seminal Time Tale.

Wells was living in the industrial age, an era of unbelievable technological advancement. Trains were running at speeds never witnessed before and electric-powered airships were taking to the skies. Perhaps it was these great advances that helped to make the possibility of time travel more credible. It was an era as well when Darwinian selection was still being discussed, and questions were being asked about social equality. Not surprisingly then *The Time Machine* became a talking point not only for its ability to fascinate and entertain but also its capacity to raise issues around an industrial sub-class in late Victorian England, who, like the Morlocks of the tale, lived most of their lives underground or in enclosed and oppressive factories. It is perhaps for these reasons that it is Wells' *The Time Machine* which is remembered rather than the novel *The British Barbarians* by Canadian writer Grant Allen, a romantic melodrama about a 25th century anthropologist who travels back to the past to study the British barbarians of the 19th century. Both were published in 1895, but only one has remained in print to the present day. *The Time Machine* has indeed stood the test of time.

## Time Machine Technology

Most time travel stories use a specific machine or device to achieve temporal transportation. Some you sit on, as with the Time Traveller's chair; with some you go inside, as with the TARDIS; others are manufactured portals, as with *The Terminator* films.

Whichever method is used these are pure science fiction stories in the sense that they are using science, in that a machine or portal is specially built to achieve time travel.

A pioneering work is the aforementioned *El Anacronópete* (the title is a neologism meaning roughly 'One Who Flies Against Time'). The machine in the story is a large cast iron box propelled by electricity. Conveniently, the mechanics in this box also produce a fluid that stops travellers becoming their child selves as they move backwards through time. Preventing people looking younger would hardly be commercial in today's world, but it's an interesting aspect of time travel that is now rarely considered. The point here is that it is a machine. But here's the difference with Wells' time machine, for in *The Time Machine*, not only is the chair a specially designed mechanical device, a technological apparatus with levers and so on, but the means of travel is based on a specific scientific theory. Exactly how Wells' time machine mechanism goes about its purpose is left vague (quartz crystals are mentioned on a few occasions), but it is most definitely a machine and one that is based on detailed mathematical and scientific theory. In fact, much of the first chapter is taken up with a discussion of the errors in classical geometry and the recent development of the concept of the 'Fourth Dimension', including this thought from the Time Traveller:

> 'Scientific people', proceeded the Time Traveller, after the pause required for the proper assimilation of this, 'know very well that Time is only a kind of Space. Here is a popular scientific diagram, a weather record. This line I trace with my finger shows the movement of the barometer. Yesterday it was so high, yesterday night it fell, then this morning it rose again, and so gently upward to here. Surely the mercury did not trace this line in any of the dimensions of Space generally recognized? But certainly it traced such a line, and that line, therefore, we must conclude was along the Time-Dimension.'

It's worth mentioning too that Wells' prose describing what the Time Traveller sees though not flowery is nevertheless literally wonderful to read:

> 'I saw the moon spinning swiftly through her quarters from new to full, and had a faint glimpse of the circling stars. Presently, as I went on, still gaining velocity, the palpitation of night and day merged into one continuous greyness; the sky took on a wonderful deepness of blue, a splendid luminous colour like that of early twilight; the jerking sun became a streak of fire, a brilliant arch, in space; the moon a fainter fluctuating band; and I could see nothing of the stars, save now and then a brighter circle flickering in the blue.'

You might suppose an obvious means of travelling in time would be some sort of magical clock and that was in fact the device used in *The Clock That Went Backward*, the short story published in 1881, 15 years before H.G. Wells' *The Time Machine*. In this story, it is a Dutch clock from 1572 which takes the person standing near it back in time to 1574 and the Siege of Leiden. A more up-to-date time travel timepiece is The Watchmaker's apparatus in *Dark* (2017–20, a complex German TV series about a sinister time travel conspiracy). This apparatus uses Caesium-137, a radioactive isotope that when combined with a Higgs field (the so-called God Particle) creates the black hole that makes time travel possible. *Dark* (created by Baran bo Odar and Jantje Friese, with other writing credits for Jantje Friese, Ronny Schalk, Marc O. Seng, Martin Behnke and Daphne Ferraroalso) makes use of doors hidden in underground caves beneath the Winden nuclear power plant to take characters into alternate time worlds.

The first time machine in the movies is thought to be in *Szíriusz* (Hungary 1942) directed by Dezsõ Ákos Hamza and based on the novel written in 1894 by the Hungarian writer Ferenc Herczeg. In the film, Professor Sergius claims he has built a machine that can fly faster than the speed of the Earth's rotation and so is able to fly into the past. Britain had its first home-grown movie time machine in *Time Flies*, a film made by Gainsborough Pictures in 1944, directed by Walter Forde and featuring famous comic of the time, Tommy Handley. The machine was a spherical metal ball. A sphere, albeit one with what looks like big metal tyres that spin inordinately fast, later also became the shape of the time travelling 'Lifeboat' and 'Mothership' in the television series *Timeless* (US NBC TV 2016–18).

The aesthetic designs of time machines range from the steampunk look in Terry Gilliam's *12 Monkeys* (1995) and the iconic DeLorean car in *Back to the Future* (1985) to the homemade box of *Primer* (2004) and the bubbling hot tub in *Hot Tub Time Machine* (2010). However, how time machines are *dramatically* designed is far more crucial. Yes, of course they are designed to travel in time – and how this is to be achieved may be lovingly detailed – but from a plot point of view, time machines are often written to go wrong in some way: losing a power source, having a vital component fail, becoming a victim of sabotage, or simply materialising in an unexpected place and time. Which brings us, not surprisingly to *Doctor Who*.

The most famous time machine in Time Tales is arguably that bizarre-looking police box in the world's longest running sci-fi TV show *Doctor Who*. And what a brilliant 'character' it is in the drama. The implication in the show is that this time machine is an organic sentient entity, and as such can 'regenerate' its interior design to suit the personality of the Doctor's current incarnation, resulting (especially in the latter stories) in a regular reboot of the show's only recurring set. And it comes in the form of that iconic (and now BBC trademarked) blue Police Box. The intention is that the TARDIS is supposed to alter its outside shape to fit in best with its surroundings, but the Doctor's one has a faulty 'chameleon circuit' rendering its exterior permanently as a dark blue Metropolitan Police call box. And it often breaks down at the worst possible moment (or best possible moment in dramatic terms). Not only is the chameleon circuit broken, but the guidance system also seems faulty, resulting in some unpredictable journeys. In the Neil Gaiman scripted adventure *The Doctor's Wife* (2011), it is revealed that some of this misrouting was intentional on the part of the TARDIS, deciding to take the Doctor to where he needed to be rather than where he wanted to go. A different malfunction, the doors of the TARDIS opening in mid-flight, results in the ship's occupants being miniaturised in the 1964 adventure *Planet of the Giants*; in the 2010 adventure *The Lodger*, localised time loop disturbances cause the Doctor to be ejected from the TARDIS and the ship itself cast into a time vortex; in 1964's *The Edge of Destruction* a small explosion on the ship (caused by the Doctor's attempt to fix the guidance circuit) knocks out the travellers and when they come to they seem to be at each other's throats. In the end their aggressive behaviour is revealed to be the TARDIS' way of warning them of imminent destruction. Their dilemma is resolved when the Doctor discovers the malfunction, a broken spring(!)

In a neat nod to *Doctor Who*, the time travelling machine in *Bill and Ted's Excellent Adventure* (1989 – written by Ed Solomon and Chris Matheson) is also a telephone box, albeit a modern one made of metal and glass. The phone booth itself is steered to its destination by The Circuits of Time Directory. Sounds complicated, but it's easy-peasy really: just punch your 14 digits into the keypad and these will take you to specific destinations and times. Of course, it works very well, better than most, but it ain't the TARDIS.

As everyone is aware, the TARDIS (or T.A.R.D.I.S) stands for – *and all together now!* – 'Time and Relative Dimensions in Space'. Some sources cite this as a backronym, that is, an acronym deliberately formed to create a memorable name or as a fanciful explanation. The Doctor did once claim it stood for 'Totally And Radically Driving In Space', which is about as backronym as you can get.

In essence, the TARDIS is a tesseract, that is, a four-dimensional cube. The universe is now seen thanks to Einstein and others as, scientifically speaking, four-dimensional. Space has up/down, left/right, back/forth and then there's time. Humans, of course, can only control three of those dimensions but the Doctor isn't human, he's a Time Lord and so it makes logical sense that if they could build an object that had four dimensions, that extra dimension could control more than just space.

The Doctor's Time and Relative Dimensions in Space machine is famously bigger on the inside than it is on the outside. The Fourth Doctor, Tom Baker, explained this once. He said that if you took a very small box and brought it up close, it would obviously look much bigger. And if that box could exist in the simultaneous dimension as a larger box further away, then indeed it would be bigger on the inside. If all this sounds too complicated, simply put a small matchbox in front of your eye and then look with the other eye at a skyscraper a mile away and so see, from that particular perspective, how a very tall building could easily fit inside the tiny matchbox. In fact, the TARDIS goes even further than that for, according to Doctor Who, the interior is in its own infinite dimension, with an infinite number of rooms. The Doctor refers to all this as Transdimensional Engineering, the key discovery of the Time Lords. And the TARDIS has other tricks up its sleeves in that it can also move between atoms and in doing so it is moving outside of space and time and so is able to circumnavigate along both. Essentially, the TARDIS leaves one dimension of space-time and enters another at a different point in space-time. And when it does, well, that's when the adventures really begin.

The TARDIS is not the first TV time machine, that would be the ZX-99, from *Captain Z-ro* a US TV series that ran locally in San Francisco and Los Angeles from 1951 to 1953 (in 10 minute segments) and was later nationally syndicated (1955–56) in 25 minute episodes. The premise: in a secret laboratory, scientist Captain Z-Ro (pronounced 'Zero') and his teenage assistant Jet, review anomalies in time and then use the time machine to send Jet back in time to correct the errors in history and ensure that the past (and the consequent future) plays out correctly. As with

*Doctor Who*, it was partly designed as presenting entertaining history lessons for children, using the device of a time machine. However, how the time machine in *Captain Z-ro* actually works is never properly explained.

Most Time Tales do offer some sort of reasoning for the possibility of time travel. The iconic DeLorean time machine in *Back To The Future* sports a teleporting 'flux capacitor'. Calling it a flux capacitor sort of makes sense in that a capacitor is an electronic device that stores energy and flux means anything that flows. Scientists have even conjectured that what it is doing is storing and then releasing the flow of time. A Time Battery, if you like. But hey, who cares, it works – well, if it's going at the right speed and serviced by the right amount of energy – and that's all that matters.

If you're one of those readers who has been hopping about all over this book in a non-linear exploratory mode then it could be you've already read the chapter **The Science of Time**. No worries if you haven't but if you've been intrigued by the scientific possibilities of time travel for real, then now might be a good time to give it a look. We predict that page 260 would be the place to look. (Actually, it was until the arrival of the Slozzerborgs who with their temporal adjustment technology moved it retrospectively in all copies and so it now begins on page 240. Ed).

Ever since Einstein, Minkowski and Gödel there has been much discussion about whether time travel is theoretically possible or could even be achieved. Well, let's just say everything is provable with the right kind of universe, the tick-box mathematical equations and enough pen and paper, plus, if you have them handy, some cosmic string, a few anti-gravity fields and a bit of negative energy (all items actually discussed in the construction of theoretical time machines by physicists working in universities). The physicists Ben Tippett and Dave Tsang went even further and wrote a paper called *Traversable Achronal Retrograde Domains in Space-time*, (oh yes, can you see what they've done there – it spells T.A.R.D.I.S) that uses Einstein's theories to show how breaching the boundaries of space-time is mathematically possible. And you thought it was all just a BBC prop built in Cardiff Bay.

## Most Memorable On-Screen Time Machines

### 1/ The TARDIS

First seen in the opening episode of the long-running time travel adventure *Doctor Who* (BBC from 1963). Although equipped with a device to change the outer shell of the time machine to reflect its current whereabouts, the Doctor's version is stuck as a British Metropolitan Emergency Police Box from the early 1960s, a plot device that ensured a relatively cheap prop but also inadvertently created an iconographic object. As time has passed this police box has acquired a further sheen of interest as a nostalgic, arcane object in its own right. The real thing is an obsolete and redundant concept now, except in 1996, a police box based on the Mackenzie Trench design was stationed on Earls Court Road and equipped with CCTV cameras. Apparently funding later lapsed, but the Metropolitan Police has since taken up the costs again for its upkeep, recognising its role as a community icon.

### 2/ H.G. Wells' Time Machine (1960)

The sublime prop from George Pal's classic movie adaptation of Wells' novel was designed by MGM's Bill Ferrari, in close collaboration with director Pal and with a nod to the sparse description of the machine in the original book. The design recalled the sledges of a bygone era and featured a barber's chair for the traveller. The prop itself was built by Wah Ming Chang who would later go on to work on *Star Trek*, creating, among others, the cute (but troublesome) aliens the Tribbles.

### 3/ The DeLorean

First seen in *Back to the Future* (Robert Zemeckis 1985), this machine follows the TARDIS idea of having a recognisable object (a DMC DeLorean) as the outer shell of the time travel device. Like the Wells machine, the time travelling element of the DeLorean is created by a brilliant inventor (Doc Brown) though this genius sports the more comical attributes of a classic 'absent-minded professor'. The controversy surrounding the real life story of John DeLorean and his ill-fated company, may have helped keep the car's name in the public psyche but its appearances in the *Back to the Future* franchise have ensured its timeless fame. Incidentally, in an early draft the time machine was a fridge, but then the writers Robert Zemeckis and Bob Gale realised they needed to move it around and so a car took over as the most obvious and practical means of temporal transport.

## 4/ The Waverider

The stolen time-ship (designation: WR-2059) used by the Legends of Tomorrow from the TV series of the same name (CW 2016–22 – created by Greg Berlanti, Marc Guggenheim and Andrew Kreisberg) has the look and style of an interstellar starship, though its interior control system does bear a passing resemblance to the classic console of the TARDIS. The large ship consists of 36 separate compartments with crew quarters, dining areas, a library, a large captain's office ('parlour') and a state-of-the-art medical bay. Time travel with an Enterprise-like five star level of comfort and accommodation. And since the Waverider travels in time, it comes with its own cloak shield, a holographic camouflage projection that allows it to remain hidden while in a different time period.

## 5/ Backpacks

Two genius high school students invent time travelling backpacks in *See You Yesterday* (Netflix 2019) a film written by Stefan Bristol and Fredrica Bailey and produced by Spike Lee. The unreliable, high-tech-looking backpacks can only send our heroes back 24 hours as they desperately try to prevent the brother of one of them from being shot by a police officer in a case of mistaken identity.

# Portals, Passageways, Gateways and Vortexes

*The rabbit-hole went straight on like a tunnel for some way, and then dipped suddenly down, so suddenly that Alice had not a moment to think about stopping herself before she found herself falling down a very deep well.*
From Lewis Carroll's *Alice's Adventures in Wonderland*

MANY TIME TALES feature what you might call 'Time Doorways' or 'Time Vortexes' that people just stumble across or are specially created in the scientific laboratory. The latter was the case in the 1960s classic series *The Time Tunnel* (ABC 1966–67) which concerns a top-secret US government time travel initiative. In 1968, deep beneath the Arizona desert is a vastly expensive, experimental laboratory working on Project Tic-Toc: creating a 'time tunnel' which can project humans into the future or the past. When government officials threaten to pull the plug on the funding for the project, two scientists activate the device and – though they prove it works – get stranded in the labyrinth of time, as the means to bring them safely back home have yet to be worked out. The travellers are transported from different places and times – a great premise for an episodic adventure series – able to be seen (and sometimes communicated with) through the Time Tunnel by their colleagues at the base camp. The Time Tunnel was a rare purpose-built set (producer Irwin Allen consistently borrowed sets, costumes and props from his other films and TV shows), and operated not only as a portal but also as a window allowing the crew at base camp to keep track of their colleagues lost in time. Though only running a single season the show certainly left its mark and the disappearing black and white swirls of that time tunnel has now become one of the iconic images of time travel and there's even a homage to it in the *Austin Powers* series of films.

The lost-in-the-maze-of-time concept was also the premise of *Quantum Leap* (NBC 1989–93) which similarly has the threat of government funding being pulled from a colossally expensive project, causing our hero (Dr Sam Beckett) to use his invention prematurely and become stranded in the vortex of time, unable to 'leap home'. And this time travel drama has a neat twist. By means of the 'Quantum Accelerator' invented by Sam, he can travel backwards through time by 'leaping' into the bodies of people from the past – but only within the timeline of his own life span. Lee Harvey Oswald yes, John Wilkes Booth no. As with the *Time Tunnel* (and indeed *Doctor Who*) the time traveller concept has allowed for an anthology-like continuing series where each episode could be very different in style and tone and of course be set in different time periods. *Quantum Leap* occasionally apes famous movies, for example, when time travelling back to the '50s there is a distinctly *Good Morning, Vietnam* vibe in the episode *Good Morning, Peroia* about a radio station playing rock'n'roll. And travelling specifically to 1955 in *The Color of Truth* the episode had a definite *Driving Miss Daisy* feel. Actually, the film *Driving Miss Daisy* came out later that year but the play was already well known. *Quantum Leap* is a prime example of how the time travel concept can be used imaginatively to tell vastly different stories which still have contemporary resonance. The series (which was never resolved) was revived as a 30-years-later sequel in 2022 (NBC).

It's useful dramatically to make your time portal unreliable in some way. Perhaps it's unstable or is only available at certain times. The word 'midnight' is a big clue to the time the hotel room becomes a portal in *Midnight at the Pera Palace* and it's worth mentioning as well that in this series there are hints that time travelling can cause mental and physical illness. In *Sijipeuseu: The Myth (Sisyphus)*, the 2021 South Korean TV time adventure series, the development of the time portal comes about after the invention of a quantum transmission. Han Tae-sul is a genius Mark Zuckerberg-like figure who has written the computer code that allows for teleportation. Initially his coding cannot cope with the immense amount of data it would need to transport humans but eventually the Han Tae-sul of the future does come up with coding that is able to transmit huge amounts of data across both space and time and it is this device that leads to people being 'copied' and 'sent to the other side' via the 'Uploader'. But the 'Uploader' has its problems. Or at least its apparent problems. It seems the chances of getting through are put at less than ten percent and many time travellers arrive misshaped and malformed. This is the reason, it is explained, that people arrive in their underwear. They believe that being semi-naked will create little static and so it will be safer for them when they are transmitted. However, all is not what it seems. At 'the other side', that is the past, there exists the Control Bureau, a kind of unofficial unit that polices illegal time migrants, and the head of the group explains to the captured Gang Seo-hae that a person's actual biological body clock can be tampered with and in truth it's this that alters the feasibility and safety of travelling in time. Conspiracy theories are never far away from time travel adventure stories.

There are many tales, of course, where time travel is achieved simply by walking down alleyways (*Goodnight Sweetheart* BBC TV 1993–99) or going through the backs of wardrobes (*Time Bandits* UK 1981) or via unusual houses (*From Time to Time* UK 2009) or falling out of a hayloft (*Split Infinity* 1992), or jumping off the Brooklyn Bridge (*Kate & Leopold* 2001) or a hole in the floor of a motel (*41* 2007) or even a visit to a Gents toilet (*Frequently Asked Questions About Time Travel* UK 2009). The children's series *Class* (BBC 2016), from the BBC *Doctor Who* stable, uses the fairly standard 'tear in space and time' scenario which, in the story, allows aliens to cross over inside the Coal Hill Academy. The Doctor explains it by saying that there's been so much Artron energy around Coal Hill that Time itself has worn thin. This tear leads to the presence of the Shadow Kin, shadows that can kill, and all this results in some creepy and frightening scenes in and around the school.

There are two important points to make about time portals and passageways. The first is that dramatically they act as a sort of decompression chamber that transitions the time traveller – and in a way the reader or viewer – when moving from one world to another. A narrative bridge, if you like, from the real to the fantastical. The master of this narrative device was Lewis Carroll, not of course a writer of Time Tales, but his transitional portals, especially the rabbit-hole, are often referenced in modern Time Tales, for example in Stephen King's *11.22.63* where Al says of his diner pantry portal, 'The first time, I actually *fell* down those stairs, like Alice into the rabbit-hole. I thought I'd gone insane.' In book one of THE SWIDGERS, *The Time That Never Was*, there is a passageway from our world to another time through an old disused railway tunnel (in fact, it is not the railway tunnel itself that allows for this, but rather the wood of the sleepers, but this is not revealed until later in the series). William, as he steps along the railway tunnel, draws attention to the strange sense of dark and cold he feels as he steps towards the world of the Old Coach Inn:

> As I walked, I didn't just notice light disappear, I somehow felt it go out inside me. Fading away in my very being. I wanted to turn round to see Granny. But I did as she had told me and looked only ahead.
>
> I had to trust the dark. One step, then another until I felt a sudden death-like chill. The day had been warm and sunny but now my world was oh so very cold.

It is later revealed that Time in Swidger philosophy is not just an energy such as heat or light, but almost a conscious sentient entity. For a Swidger then Time is the Soul of Nature and for

William to travel in or, as he says himself, 'with Time', he must find that Soul.

And an important dramatic point about portals is that they usually get closed down or blocked in some way, trapping our heroes in whatever new time world they have found themselves in. A classic example of this is *The City on the Edge of Forever* from the original series of *Star Trek*, season one, episode 28. Plus, of course, the actions of the Morlocks in *The Time Machine* in moving the Time Traveller's contraption into the White Sphinx.

A word here about hotels. In *Midnight at the Pera Palace* Esra, a young journalist in contemporary Istanbul is writing an article on the 130th anniversary of the Pera Palace Hotel. On her visit there she meets its manager, Ahmet, who gives her a brief history lesson of the hotel and its famous guests, including the real life Peride, who saved the Turkish hero Mustafa Kemal from an assassination plot orchestrated by the British in 1919. Esra is given a key and then stays overnight in one of hotel's rooms which becomes a time travelling portal back to 1919, where she is soon mistaken for her doppelganger, Peride. The real Peride is killed and so Esra takes her place, as it were, in the task of stopping the assassination attempt on Mustafa Kemal, thus preserving the timeline of Turkey's independence.

As the plot develops Esra/Peride discovers that the hotel has many rooms that act as a portal and different keys take you to a variety of time periods past and present within the lifetime of the hotel. The back-story of the hotel is that it was built on a graveyard and the numerous keys which are necessary for time portation came from metal found in the cemetery. But of course keys can get lost or stolen, and there is the problem that you have to return to your time (or the base time you have found yourself in as is the case with Esra) by midnight and the issue that travelling through the portal can affect your moral health by turning you to the darker side resulting in wonton murder.

*Midnight at the Pera Palace* is based on *Midnight at the Pera Palace: The Birth of Modern Istanbul* by Charles King.

The series was written by Elif Usman and directed by Emre Şahin and Nisa Dağ.

You could argue that hotels and hotel rooms offer dramatically near-perfect opportunities as time portals. For a start they have transitory purpose, in the sense that the people who stay in them are always changing. Then there's the fact that hotels are packed with so many different types of people that a time traveller is unlikely to stand out, at least at first, even if they are wearing clothes from another period. And people who stay in hotels always have a story to tell, so you're never short of subplots. Hotel décor usually reflects its era, but sometimes it has a historical feel, which can cause perhaps some initial confusion as to which era you are actually in. But in hotels there are always newspapers in reception giving you today's date, plus, of course, that obliging concierge who, from an exposition and plot point of view, will fill you in as to what's going on. But the hotel room and hotels in general also have their potential dramatic problems. Who's going to be in your room in the future or past? Security can be tight and since you won't be registered you could find yourself thrown out. Apart from *Midnight at the Pera Palace* there are a few other time portals centred on hotels and hotel rooms, including *Somewhere in Time* (1980) and *Communicating Doors* (1994) a play by Alan Ayckbourn, set in a hotel suite that moves through time from 1974 to 2014. Perhaps too in its own unique way, Stephen King's *The Shining*. In the *Doctor Who* adventure *The God Complex* (2011) an alien prison is disguised as a 1980s hotel, with rooms that contain individual's greatest fears, some of which manifest themselves from their past.

## The Most Unusual Portals and Passageways

### 1 / *The Painted Mirror*

The time portal mirror in *Night Gallery: The Painted Mirror* (1971), teleplay by Gene R. Kearney from a story by Donald Wandrei, offers a black comedy at the expense of that diamond encrusted actress and model Zsa Zsa Gabor. Frank Standish runs an antique shop, but for financial reasons he's had to take on a co-owner, the vile, mean spirited and bullying Mrs Moore, played with relish by the sizzling Zsa Zsa. When Frank's friend Ellen brings in an elegant full-length mirror for sale, Mrs Moore is dismissive of its worth as it's painted over in black. Frank removes the paint and finds that this is no ordinary mirror, for behind the glass is revealed a prehistoric world. Later Mrs Moore's pet dog runs inside the mirror and so Mrs Moore follows in pursuit. So obsessed by finding her pet is she that she doesn't seem to notice she's now in another world and a dangerous one as well. Frank and his sweetheart Ellen are no fans of Mrs Moore, whose garish tastelessness can be seen in everything she says and wears. The couple therefore decide to paint over the mirror glass and as they complete their task, Mrs Moore, still searching for her pet, is spotted by a dinosaur. We must presume that Zsa Zsa became its lunch, but hopefully the dog was quick enough to run away and find a friend.

## 2 / *Timewasters* (ITV 2017–19)

A urine-soaked lift in a rundown block of flats (grandly called New Ellington Mansions) in Peckham is the unlikely time travel device that transports four young Black musicians into the past. Operated by the down-and-out Homeless Pete, the kids refer to it as a time machine (or a 'shit DeLorean'), but it seems the lift shaft itself operates more as a portal taking them to periods keyed in on the floor numbers pad in the lift (a feat only Homeless Pete is able to achieve). This under-rated comedy (created by one of its stars Daniel Lawrence Taylor) managed to smuggle in serious points about racism beneath its lively, rudely comic surface. It also archly referenced the lack of diversity elsewhere in the genre '… people like us never get to time-travel. It's what white people do… like ski-ing, or brunch.'

## 3 / *Primeval* (UK ITV 2007–11)

'Anomalies' as they are called in *Primeval* are what allow dangerous and hungry prehistoric monsters and indeed futuristic creatures onto the streets of modern Britain. *Primeval* was developed by Tim Haines and Adrian Hodges.

## 4 / *Tom's Midnight Garden*

Philippa Pearce's 1958 story is a bona fide classic of children's literature. Tom has to stay with his (childless) aunt and uncle during the summer holidays as his brother has measles. Tom is bored witless and finds the only intriguing item in the whole place is the grandfather clock in the hallway, which he is forbidden to touch. He discovers that when the clock strikes 13 the back door operates as a time portal and leads to a mystical Victorian garden. When he visits the garden Tom seems visible only to one person, Hatty and the two soon develop a close bond. Adapted three times for BBC TV (1968, 1974 and 1980) and made as a film in 1999, it is generally acknowledged that the BBC's 6-part 1980s adaptation is the best screen version of this magical and much loved Time Tale.

## 5 / *Mirror, Mirror*

Another mirror but this time one that specifically allows time travel between two time periods, 1919 and 1995, if the mirror is placed in the exact spot and at the same alignment. In the series two girls – Jo in 1995, and Louisa in 1919 – discover each other in that mirror and that's when the adventures begin. The series was created by Posie Graeme-Evans and co-produced by Australia's Millennium Pictures and New Zealand's NZ on Air production companies. *Mirror, Mirror* ran from 1995 to 1998.

# Potions, Magic, Genii, Artefacts and Other Tickets for The Time Terminal

*Hold Infinity in the palm of your hand / And Eternity in an hour.*
*Auguries of Innocence* by William Blake

TIME MACHINES AND time portals are the most popular means of time travel but there are other methods, including potions, magic and even genii. And, of course, artefacts can also be a Time Ticket to another era. *A Story of the Amulet* (1906), by Edith Nesbit, uses an Egyptian talisman to transport British children back to ancient Gaul and Babylon, and in *The Gauntlet* (1951) by Ronald Welch, a boy finds an iron gauntlet in the Brecon Beacons which allows him to jump back in time to Wales in 1326. In the very first UK TV time travel series *The White Swan* (BBC 1952–53) a young girl visiting her aunt in an old mansion comes across a violin with a colourful history, and, on playing a certain tune, she is transported back to various moments in the violin's past. In *Predestination* (Australia 2014) it's a violin case that proves useful; in *The Two Worlds of Jennie Logan* (1979 US TV) it is an antique dress in an attic that makes the journey to the past possible; in *Prince of Persia: The Sands of Time* (2010) a magic dagger comes in handy and in *The Simpson's* Homer's method of time travel is a dysfunctional toaster that he 'fixed'. In *Click* (2006) a workaholic architect finds a universal remote that allows him to fast-forward or rewind to different parts of his life.

Potions or drugs have also been a popular way of leaping around in time. In *Future Times Three* (*Le Voyageur Imprudent* published in 1943, adapted for French TV in 1982), by French writer René Barjavel, a scientist invents a substance which, if swallowed, allows anyone to time travel and a designer drug does very otherworldly time travelling things in *Synchronic* (2019) and *Trancers* (1984). In Daphne du Maurier's *The House on the Strand* (published in 1969), a biochemist invents a drug that enables him to enter the landscape of the early 14th century. The 1965 novel by Yasutaka Tsutsui, *The Girl Who Leapt Through Time* features a school girl who, as a result of an accidental meeting with a time traveller and exposure to a time travelling drug, is able to time leap and relive the same day. This novel inspired an animated television series (Japan 1972), a TV mini-series in 1994 and successful live-action feature films in 1983, 1997 and 2010. However, it is the 2006 anime version (directed by Mamaru Hosada) which is best known internationally.

A woodland potion is the magic method used in *The Amazing Mr Blunden* (1972, remade for Sky TV in 2021, based on the 1969 novel *The Ghosts* by Antonia Barber) and the combination of an illegal Russian energy drink and a hotel hot tub are the means of the temporal leap in *Hot Tub Time Machine* (2010 – written by Josh Heald, Sean Anders and John Morris). In *Extinct* (US/China 2021 – written by Joel Cohen, John Frink and Rob LaZebnik), Op and Ed are flummels, fluffy rabbit-like creatures from the age of Darwin, who fall into a large flower and find themselves in the future in modern-day Shanghai where they discover that their species is now extinct.

Magic is also a possibility, as with Hermione's Time-Turner in *Harry Potter and the Prisoner of Azkaban* by J.K. Rowling (book 1999, film 2004). In *13 Going On 30* (2004 – written by Cathy Yuspa and Josh Goldsmith), the time change is achieved through wishing and magic and in *The Knight Before Christmas* (2019 – written by Cara J. Russell) it is an Old Crone or witch who sends the medieval Knight forward in time and space to the Ohio of the present day. However, not everyone can be an expert magician and in the children's series *Catweazle* (UK ITV 1970–71), created by Richard Carpenter, when a spell goes wrong, an 11th century wizard called Catweazle finds that he has jumped 900 years into the future to 1969 and is now trapped there. In *Where Do We Go From Here* (1945), a film musical composed by Kurt Weill with lyrics by Ira Gershwin, and written by Morrie Ryskind and Sig Herzig, it is The Genie of the Strange Brass Bottle who sends the hero Bill Morgan across time. Magic, as is sometimes said, is the science of the gods. Not that many of us come across this sort of thing every day. That said, we do have some very strange weather sometimes. Which brings us to lightning.

## Lightning

Electricity and lightning prove crucial to the plot in *Back to the Future*. There's the strike that stopped the Court House clock, plus the hit that essentially sends Doc Brown, now driving the time travelling DeLorean, back to 1885. Oddly enough, *The Clock That Went Backward*, that early time travel story from 1881, also has it that the clock was once struck by lightning, causing its odd temporal abilities. The play *Berkeley Square* (play 1926, movie 1933) by John L. Balderston (in collaboration with J.C. Squire) has a bolt of lightning that seems, at least in part, to contribute to the time travelling protagonist being transported back to the 18th century and few years later in 1933 *Lest Darkness Fall*, an early alternate history novel by L. Sprague de Camp, has its hero struck by lightning and whisked off to ancient Rome. In *That Was Then*, an American television series written by Dan Cohn and Jeremy Miller made in 2002, Travis Glass is struck by lightning and sent back to his high school days, and in *Outlaws*, a television series written by Nicholas J. Corea that ran from 1986 to 1987, five cowboys from the 1880s find themselves in 1986, again the result of a lightning strike.

Flickering lights when the time tourists move on in *Timescape* (1992) suggests some sort of electrical power surge when time travel occurs and something similar happens with the electrical appliances in *The Day Time Ended* (1980), when a supernova opens up a rift in space-time. In *The Final Countdown* (1980) it is a mysterious electrical storm that transports a modern-day nuclear powered aircraft carrier back to World War Two at the time of the attack on Pearl Harbour. *Mirage* (Spain 2018), known in Spain as *Durante la tormenta*, which roughly translates as 'during the storm', has it that a pairing of two electrical storms 25 years apart allows for a connection between two analogue television sets thus sending a message from the future to the past which results in the alteration of the future and a mother losing her daughter. Electricity also plays a part in that other time travelling adventure *The Philadelphia Experiment* (1984 – written by Wallace C. Bennett), when tests in 1943 to render a ship invisible to radar actually result in the vanishing of the ship, transporting crew members into the 1980s. The idea came from a real life experiment where a massive bank of electrical generators conjured up a magnetic field. Similarly, electrical energy is present in *Biggles* (1986 – written by John Groves and based on the books by W.E. Johns) when a modern-day American, Jim Ferguson, is transported back to 1917 and the trenches of World War One where he encounters the famous British air ace. An explanation is given that Biggles and Ferguson are 'time twins', who are united in the past whenever Biggles is in mortal danger. No further explanation is forthcoming about the logistics of the time travel but electrical forces are present at every transfer.

Electricity, or rather more specifically static electricity, is part of the almost accidental opening up of some sort of time portal in *The Evil of the Daleks* (1967 – written by David Whitaker), the final serial of the fourth season of *Doctor Who*. Theodore Maxtible talks about mirrors and reflections which, like many scientific justifications of time travel, is ultimately gobbledegook but does have a certain feasibility if said at a pace. Anyway, the explanation involves 144 electrically charged mirrors, all positive, reflecting images using electromagnetism and static electricity.

But why do so many of the stories feature lightning and electricity? Well, lightning is an uber powerful phenomenon and in many narratives seems to have a special, almost ethereal potency of its own. Gods carry lightning rods and it's lightning that gives birth to creatures such as Frankenstein's monster. And light is the fastest entity in our universe, plus, of course, light represents a sort of timelessness. Just look at the stars in the sky. Many exploded millions of years ago, yet the light they once emitted lives on. Locked together in light and electricity then are concepts of power, life and time itself.

## Other Means of Time Transport are Available

Many stories have it that time gateways or wormholes just happen to exist, for example, *Craighna Dun*, the fictional stone circle that opens around the summer and winter solstices in the novel series *Outlander* (first published in 1991) by Diana Gabaldon. In *Time Trap* (2017) a cave is a gateway to a time moving at a different pace to the outside world, though it is established that it was specially created as a kind of snare. Sometimes time gateways are more or less stumbled upon by accident, for example, Woody Allen's *Midnight in Paris* (2011). In such cases the phenomenon itself, or the reason or science behind it, often remains unexplained.

And then there are technical malfunctions, which can be a useful catalyst event in creating a time travel adventure. In *Past Tense*, an episode from *Star Trek: Deep Space Nine*, written by Robert Hewitt Wolfe, Ira Steven Behr and René Echevarria, it is that tricky transporter beam. A temporal surge is caused by an explosion of a microscopic singularity that shifts the chroniton particles in the ship's hull into a high state of temporal polarisation – *try to keep up* – and as a result, the transporter beam is redirected as it passes through these polarised particles, but not redirected where, but when. It may be gibberish, but it's convincing gibberish.

In *Turn Back the Clock* (1933 – written by Edgar Selwy and Ben Hecht), it is a car accident that sends Joe Gimlet (Lee Tracy) back in time, the same device that transports 21st century detective Sam Tyler (John Simm) back to 1973 in *Life on*

Mars (BBC 2006–07). In Mark Twain's *A Connecticut Yankee in King Arthur's Court* (1889 – sometimes just called *A Yankee in King Arthur's Court*) it is a dream brought about by a knock to the head that sends Hank Morgan into the past. In *A Word of Explanation* Twain says that at Warwick Castle he encountered a stranger who casually said, 'You know about transmigration of souls; do you know about transposition of epochs – and bodies. Wit ye well, I saw it done. I did it myself.' In D.W. Griffith's *Intolerance* (1916), dreaming is also the means of transportation from one time period to another for the waif called Dagover.

In Sam Raimi's *Army of Darkness* (1992) what is required is an incantation, namely, *'Klaatu Barab Nikto'* (which movie fans will recognise from the 1951 film *The Day the Earth Stood Still*). *Berkeley Square* (1926) does have a lightning bolt, but it's the reading of an old diary that is perhaps the true way back to the past, as is, in its own way, Tom Riddle's diary in the *Harry Potter* series.

'Oh Father Time. A cat can't live nowadays – Turn me back to a better age, just for a day' says Felix the Cat in a title card (or intertitle) in *Felix the Cat Trifles with Time* (1925). So Father Time sends Felix back to the stone age in that time-honoured animation fashion of belting him on the head with a truncheon. If there are any younger people reading this, we ask you not to try this method at home.

## Chronesthesia

The poets have always known about this form of time travel but now there is a recognised psychological phenomenon that is called 'Chronesthesia' and it is essentially time travel through the power of the thought. Chronesthesia was tentatively defined in 2002 by Endel Tulving as a form of consciousness that allows an individual to travel mentally in time. This concept is there in a monograph by Thomas Suddendorf and Michael Corballis called *Mental Time Travel and the Evolution of the Human Mind* (May 1997). Put simply chronesthesia is time travel of the mind. This can involve reconstructing events of the past or the mental ability to create possible happenings of the future. Chronesthesia involving future events is similar to the ends-driven technique sports psychologists suggest for athletes when they ask them to picture themselves, for example, kicking the ball into the net at the cup final or soaring over the bar at the Olympics. In other words, seeing it in your head now will make it so in the future. Not, of course, that it always works, as any football or athletics fan will tell you.

Although the term chronesthesia is never used in the script, the character Richard Collier (Christopher Reeve) essentially imagines himself or wishes himself or mind thinks himself into the past in *Somewhere in Time* (1980 – written by Richard Matheson). And Collier, a Chicago playwright, does this in order to meet an actress whose vintage portrait hangs in a grand hotel where he is staying. It's a 'thinking' time travel premise that is similar to *Time and Again* (1970), an illustrated novel by Jack Finney. In this tale an advertising sketch artist becomes part of a government project where movie sets recreating the past and a kind of self-hypnosis together become the means of time travel. Incidentally, *Chronesthesia* was the original title for the movie that is now known as *Love and Time Travel* (2016), a romantic comedy where mysterious messages, dreams and a flurry of coincidences allow the protagonist to change his own life and the lives of others. And let's just mention *Berkeley Square* one more time because you could argue that as well as a diary, a lightning bolt and a portal door, it's really Peter's obsession with the past that leads to the mind exchange across time. Like Collier in *Somewhere in Time*, Peter, as it were, thinks himself into the past.

## Just One of Those Things

There are of course those Time Tales where time travel – or something like it – just happens. *Petite Maman* (2021), written and directed by Céline Sciamma, tells the story of a young girl who meets her mother as a child in the woods. Time travel is mentioned but the movie has more the feel of a fairytale with a visitation from a friendly ghost. In the tale, the young girl's grandmother has just died and her mother is clearing out the grandmother's house. When the girl goes playing in the woods she meets a girl of about her own age and they quickly become friends. Slowly, though, the young girl comes to realise that this girl is her own mother who is also going through a painful loss. As with many Time Tales, *Petite Maman* is about grief, yet this beautiful tale is also about a young girl coming to the understanding that her mother too was once a child. And where better to do that than in a magical time travelling wood?

Ian McEwan's *The Child in Time* (1987) is a disturbing tale of Stephen Lewis, a children's author, whose back-story is the loss of his three-year-old daughter while out shopping. The apparent abduction leads to strains in his marriage but to help save it Stephen visits his wife Julie who is staying in a town he doesn't know. And yet he does, for here he sees his parents as a young couple in a pub before they were married, an event that they themselves later confirm. Has time fragmented? Or is it that time is simply fluid and relative? As often with Ian McEwan, the focus is traumatic loss and the disintegration of a marriage, but the title *The Child in Time* suggests something else and that is a man trapped in the idea of childhood itself. Indeed, Stephen, when looking in at that window, echoes that moment where Peter Pan – that eternal child – describes how he once returned to his home, only to find the window barred and his mother nursing a new infant. From then on, Peter Pan is frozen in childhood and becomes the boy who, through choice, refuses ever to grow up.

In the movie *Last Night in Soho* (2021), written by Edgar Wright and Krysty Wilson-Cairns, it's not exactly clear how the modern-day Eloise Turner, or 'Ellie', not only travels back in time to the Soho of 1960s, but also, when in the past, finds herself in the body of a singer called Sandie, who, she comes to believe, was a victim of murder. Well, let's take the time travel element first. It seems that the way the jump in time is achieved is part location (via a narrow Soho alleyway), part music (the songs of the '60s), part dream (Ellie wakes up when the events of the past become too violent), part the bed or bedroom where Ellie sleeps (the girl who Ellie believes was murdered once had the same attic room) and part reflections (the mirrors in the modern clubs she visits seem to show reflections of the past acting as time windows and these visions end when mirrors in the present day are broken). Yet all is not what it seems and without revealing the big twist let's just say *Last Night in Soho* is an example of that old adage in horror that ghosts from the past often return to haunt the living to achieve a kind of justice. Perhaps then it shouldn't be classified as time travel after all. Or maybe it should, if you accept that ghosts are time travellers. Anyway, why not watch the movie and decide for yourself.

# Time Windows and Time Threads

*It was when I stood before her, avoiding her eyes, that I took note of the surrounding objects in detail, and saw that her watch had stopped at twenty minutes to nine, and that the clock in the room had stopped at twenty minutes to nine. 'Look at me,' said Miss Havisham. 'You are not afraid of a woman who has never seen the sun since you were born?'*
From *David Copperfield* by Charles Dickens

## The Time Window

WE'RE BACK AT base in *The Time Tunnel* television series 1966–1967. The scientists at the facility have a fix on the time period Tony and Doug have travelled to and so are now able to receive pictures of what Tony and Doug are doing but Tony and Doug are unable to see them at the other end. The people at the base cannot communicate directly with the time travellers but occasionally the base can send messages to Tony and Doug via the F-5 in the form of a glowing red brick. Not that this always works. But the important point is, the scientists at the facility do have what we might call a 'Time Window' on the travellers and with their computer database they are able to fill the viewer in on all the historical details. Often this leads to dramatic irony as the watching audience now has more information about what is about to happen to the time travellers than do the time travellers themselves. The time window isn't exactly stable and the facility always needs a fix on Tony and Doug before they can transport them to another time period, but this is usually only achieved in the nick of time due to inevitable technical problems. What's important to note here is that the time window, as with a time machine or time being, is a dramatic construct. It's part of the design of the drama and it's there primarily to enhance and increase the dramatic potential of the stories.

*Déjà Vu* (2006), a film written by Bill Marsilii and Terry Rossio, also had a time window into the past, but, as with *The Time Tunnel*, it's one-way viewing. *Déjà Vu* is a film partly about surveillance in a world where cameras are now everywhere. But, like films such as *Rear Window* (1954), *American Beauty* (1999), *Blow-up* (1966), *Blue Velvet* (1986), *One Hour Photo* (2002) and *Peeping Tom* (1960), *Déjà Vu* is about looking. Voyeurism, if you want to take it that far. This brings us to the concept known as The Male Gaze. This term comes from Film Studies and it was coined by John Berger in 1972 but it's a notion that goes back to Jean-Paul Sartre's idea of *le regard*. In 1983, in an important essay by E. Anne Kaplan called *Is the Gaze Male?*, Kaplan wrote that the gaze is not literally male as such but, as she puts it, 'to own and activate the gaze' is to be in masculine position. It's a big subject, but TV and film are visual media and it is worth mentioning in the context of the time window, particularly as there is an uncomfortable scene in *Déjà Vu* where the time window team are seen staring at a woman having a shower and it takes the only female member of the team to question why it is they are actually looking at something that is essentially private.

The central concept in *Devs* (FX 2020), a TV series written and directed by Alex Garland, is the creation of a time window which uses sophisticated computer software and code to produce visualisations from the past. There is one industry, of course, that is well known for being first out of the traps when it comes to making use of technology and that is 'erotic entertainment', though there is a less flattering noun that could be used. Anyway, several characters in *Devs* cannot resist their carnal curiosity. Although the ultimate aim of the software is to understand the nature of determinism, it should come as no surprise that very early in their experiments the team of boffins, scientists and programmers at the DEVS facility choose to generate, and then voyeuristically enjoy, images of Marilyn Monroe having sex with Arthur Miller. The celebrity sex tape to top them all.

A less contentious time window could be said to be Scrooge's visit to his past in *A Christmas Carol* (1843). The Ghost of Christmas Past tells Scrooge, 'These are but shadows of the things that have been. They have no consciousness of us.' Scrooge is, as it were, inside the window to the past but unable to communicate with what he sees and hears. Incidentally, the description of the transition of time is a curious one:

> Scrooge's former self grew larger at the words, and the room became a little darker and more dirty. The panels shrunk, the windows cracked; fragments of plaster fell out of the ceiling, and the naked laths were shown instead; but how all this was brought about, Scrooge knew no more than you do.

The theme as ever with Dickens is the power of memory but it's intriguing how the description of time passing reads very much like a fast-motion film montage, such as that seen in *The Time Machine* (1960). This effect is, of course, something that Charles Dickens could never have ever witnessed. As ever, Dickens' visual imagination was ahead of its time.

In *Sijipeuseu: The Myth* there's a series of scenes where the computer genius Han Tae-sul and the time traveller Gang Seo-hae move across time as a result of temporal displacement that comes about after they are injected with a drug that alters the brain's biological body clock. Yes, it's that sort of plot. Essentially Han Tae-sul and Gang Seo-hae become invisible, ghost-like entities as they wander through time and into the past. In one scene, they witness the grief of the very young Han Tae-sul following the sudden death of his parents. It's a very emotionally compelling scene and perhaps the writers had in mind the journey Dickens has Scrooge take to his own back-story in *A Christmas Carol*.

The Victorian scientist and inventor Charles Wheatstone claimed his designs for the Electromagnetic Chronoscope, an instrument to measure very precisely small units of time, had been stolen by scientists on the Continent. Perhaps they were stolen but what we can say for sure is that the term Chronoscope was certainly 'borrowed' by science fiction writers, only they changed its meaning and it became another term for time window or time viewer. In his short story *The Dead Past* (1956), Isaac Asimov called the device that can see past events a 'Chronoscope' and the term Chronoscope was also used in Malcolm Jameson's *Dead End*, published in *Thrilling Wonder Stories* in 1941. Incidentally, it has been claimed that a priest named Father Pellegrino Ernetti witnessed a speech by Marcus Tullius Cicero to the Roman senate in 63BC for real on a time viewer he called a 'Chronovisor'. 'Chrono', it should be explained, is a word that comes from *khronos* the Greek word for 'time'.

A curious 1947 novella *E for Effort* by T.L. Sherred features a time viewer built by a guy who uses it to create historical movies. However, a producer in Hollywood exploits this device, first to make historical films, and then political documentaries, only in doing so government corruption is exposed which leads to riots and eventually a nuclear strike. Well, that's meddling with time windows for you. On a more cheerful note there's a story by K.A.W (K.A. Winter) from *Amazing Stories* (December 1926) called *The Time Eliminator,* where an elderly man is able to display on a screen scenes from his courtship. Nowadays, of course, we have our ubiquitous selfies and our data-saving 'Clouds', but in 1926 such a device as a time window to see into the past would indeed have been a wonder and enough to warrant a story by itself.

Other Time Tales with some sort of time window include the movie *The Time Travelers* (1964); the short story *Private Eye* (1949) by Henry Kuttner and C.L. Moore writing together as Lewis Padgett; *I See You* (1976) by Damon Knight; *Millennium*

(1983) by John Varley; *Zig Zag* (1983) by José Carlos Somoza; *Childhood's End* (1953) by Arthur C. Clarke; *The Brightonomicon* (2005) by Robert Rankin; and, in the final episode of *Dark*, there are brief but very moving scenes where Jonas and Martha see young versions of each other through the back of a closet, which is reminiscent of the time window in the classic *Doctor Who* episode *The Girl in the Fireplace* (2006). Oh, and since we've got into the habit of doing this, let's mention once again *Berkeley Square*, for there's a scene in the 1933 film version where the girl in the past looks into the eyes of the time traveller and, with 'eyes burning', sees in a movie montage events of the future known to Peter.

## Time Threads and the Linking of Time Zones

For plot reasons it is sometimes necessary to allow characters in one time period to communicate with those in another. Sending a telegram via Western Union proved to be an inventive method in the *Back to the Future* series and was later borrowed for the television series *Timeless* (NBC 2016–18), only for Wyatt Logan it was less successful. Jiya, also in *Timeless*, fared better when she got stranded in the past and used photographs of her herself in history books to communicate with the team in the present day.

But there are no such problems communicating across the centuries or indeed millennia in *Doctor Who*. Here, mobile phones seem able to get a signal no matter which time zone or era characters are in. Clearly *Doctor Who* writers have never spent a weekend in Norfolk.

A very creepy voice from across time can be found in the horror thriller *The Caller* (2011). Mary Kee, recently divorced from a brutish husband, attempts to make a fresh start by moving into a new apartment. But then Mary starts to receive disturbing telephone calls from woman called Rose, who, it is later revealed, was a previous occupant who hung herself with the telephone cord. Is Rose a ghostly voice or time traveller somehow able to use the phone to communicate with the future? Certainly what is said in the present (Mary's time) changes the past (Rose's time), for example, new walls suddenly appear. The answer then to the ghost or time traveller question has to be time traveller, for it's what Mary says that alters Rose's timepath by making her more resilient. Rose in her now altered past does not die, but instead becomes a killer. And, like the classic 1948 film noir movie *Sorry, Wrong Number*, it is Mary on the other end of the telephone line who eventually becomes the threatened victim. Watch the movie for yourself to see who survives.

Perhaps though the most inventive link across time in more recent years is the television and video recorder that can be found in *Mirage* (Spain 2018). *Mirage* is a romantic thriller and murder mystery with a complex but dramatically rewarding plot. The year is 1989 and the television news has images of the fall of the Berlin Wall. During a 72-hour-long electrical storm, a boy named Nico is recording a video in his house when he hears noises from outside. Nico looks out of the window and witnesses an argument and physical confrontation in the house of his neighbours. He investigates, discovers a dead body and then flees, but, as he runs from the house and onto the street, he is hit by a car and killed. Jump forward 25 years to 2014. A married couple have moved into what was Nico's house and as an electrical storm gathers, very similar to the one 25 years earlier, the husband and wife discover Nico's old television and video recorder. The couple become aware of the death of Nico as Nico's best friend still lives in the neighbourhood and was at dinner with them earlier. In the night, during the storm, Vera when alone switches on the video player and television and sees the boy Nico. Vera warns Nico not to investigate or go outside, otherwise, she tells him, he will be killed. Nico heeds Vera's advice and so does not die in 1989. So far so good, but on waking up the next morning, Vera discovers that as a result of altering Nico's timepath, her own life has drastically been altered.

She is no longer married, nor does she have a daughter. Vera's action in the story as it then unfolds becomes to somehow put right her past in order to regain the present she remembers. It's a very inventive plot and there's a romantic twist that lifts the movie up way beyond your standard time travel tale.

# Time Beings, Time Villains and Time Guardians

*'I could tell you my adventures – beginning from this morning,'*
*said Alice a little timidly: 'but it's no use going back to yesterday,*
*because I was a different person then.'*
*Alice's Adventures in Wonderland* by Lewis Carroll

## Time Beings

IN THE SWIDGERS book series, Swidgers are cosmic beings that are human in form but with a unique energy running through their bodies which allows them to change lives for the better by altering people's timepaths with 'a switch or sway, a shove or a nudge'. Hence the name Swidgers. But not all Swidgers are the same and Granny understands that William, our hero of the tale, has a time ability beyond all others and that to fully access that William must fully understand the nature of time. And to this end Granny takes him to The Royal Academy of Art and asks him to consider a bronze sculpture of two chickens that has been cast as a single egg. It takes William a while but eventually he understands the point, observing:

> 'It's what people say: "Which came first, the chicken or the egg?" But here what the chickens are doing will lead to the egg. So perhaps it doesn't matter which came first because chicken and egg are ultimately one and the same thing?'

And it's this perception of what you might call the 'Oneness of Time' which will eventually allow William to move in time and become a time traveller.

## TIME BEINGS, TIME VILLAINS AND TIME GUARDIANS

Of course there are stories where the protagonist just happens to be born with the ability to time travel. In *There Will Be Time*, by Poul Anderson, the young man has a genetic mutation that allows this, and in the movie *About Time*, the ability to travel in time is passed on from father to son. That's just the way things are in some families, but that's fine because, after all, *About Time* is a family melodrama. In *The Time Traveler's Wife*, Henry thinks of his ability to time travel as a 'condition'. He sees it in terms of a medical illness or genetic anomaly and even consults the geneticist Dr Kendrick who later calls it 'chrono-impairment'. Henry wants help to stabilise his situation as much for his wife as for himself. The central thrust of the story is making a marriage work rather than saving the world from future nuclear catastrophe and the like. Henry's weakness as a time traveller is that he has no control over his time travelling and when he does jump, his clothes don't come with him. Suddenly arriving naked in an unknown time or place has its drawbacks, but it is dramatically a very clever rule to have as it opens up all sorts of potential scenarios both comic and tragic. Similarly, in the Korean time travel series *Alice (Aelliseu)*, written by Kim Kyu-Won, Park Jin-gyeom has little control over where he lands or in which timeline, which also leads to often strange encounters.

The general point here is that time beings are fictional creations and their abilities and vulnerabilities are ultimately designed for their role in that particular Time Tale's story. Or put another way, time beings are dramatic beings. And it's their idiosyncrasies, weak spots and flaws that are just as important as their time travelling capacities. Every time being must have their Achilles' Heel, or their Kryptonite, so to speak. And since not all Time Tales are the same, each time being is constructed differently. Or should be. As cosmic beings put in this world to do good, it is impossible for Swidgers to lie or act violently. Not great for William and Granny as there are moments in the story where their inability not to tell the truth or fight back with fists puts them in danger. Yet such restrictions are an advantage in plot terms because they have to come up with unexpected ways to get out of perilous situations. And isn't that what good storytelling is all about?

Limitations in characters, or perceived chinks in their armour, are all part of the creative dramatic construction of a Time Tale. Take the American television series *Travelers*. Disembodied consciousnesses from the future have been sent to our present but many of them have been put in compromised hosts. Such a thing may be presented as an accident, but you can bet your bottom dollar that the nature of the host was carefully thought through at the pre-production story meetings. One Traveler is believed to have brain damage, another is a junkie and then there's a mom with a baby and an abusive partner, plus, later in the series, a Traveler finds himself in a host body with paranoid schizophrenia and another in the body of a serial killer. With such characters at your disposal, the plots begin to write themselves. And the Travelers from the future can develop problems once here. Trevor, the oldest of the Travelers at 0115, succumbs to Temporal Displacement Aphasia, which means his ability to perceive the passage of time is degraded. Put simply, he freezes. Not good for him, but great for upping the ante in those plot sequences where you're fighting the clock.

In the *Back to the Future* series both Marty and Doc Brown have weaknesses written into their characters which add to the plot's potential. Well, in truth these flaws are only explored in Part Two and Part Three, but that makes the point that they are there to primarily to serve those particular plots. Emmet Brown can't take his liquor, which is a bit of a problem when he gets to the Wild West. Marty's weakness is the question 'Are you chicken?', for he cannot walk away from a challenge. In fact it's Marty's inability to ignore a dare which will ruin his life in the future. But one of the advantages of a time traveller going forward in time is that you can, as it were, learn from your future mistakes. And this Marty does leading to what we believe, or at least hope will be, a happy ever after.

## Orphans Who Learn to Time Travel

In *Alice*, a time traveller of the future, after discovering *The Book of Prophecy* which speaks of the end of time travel, flees to the year 1986 and marries Dr Jang Dong-sik. Unfortunately, this woman dies giving birth to their daughter Yoon Tae-yi, who, in one timeline, later changes her name to Park Sun-young and becomes the mother of Detective Park Jin-gyum, only then she is murdered. However, in another time dimension this same girl grows up to become Professor Yoon Tae-yi, who is investigated by time jumping Detective Park Jin-gyeom, and the said professor, not surprisingly, is the doppelganger of the detective's murdered mother.

Essentially then both Yoon Tae-yi and Park Jin-gyeom grow up as orphans. In a scene packed with dramatic irony, Yoon Tae-yi, now teaching at a university, tells the investigating Detective Park Jin-gyeom that the reason she became a scientist was because of her personal history. Her biological mother left her at the orphanage and disappeared never to return, yet Yoon Tae-yi still remembers her mother's warmth and her scent. And that's why Yoon Tae-yi became a scientist – to invent time travel and so see her beloved mother again. The irony of all this is that Detective Park Jin-gyeom in another time dimension is her son, a son who was close by when his own mother, the spitting image of Yoon Tae-yi, was killed. On top of that, Yoon Tae-yi in another time line is the same Sun-young who took the orphaned daughter – that is herself – to the orphanage, for it turns out that Yoon Tae-yi was wrong to say that this woman was her actual biological mother.

*Sijipeuseu: The Myth* (also known as *Sisyphus*), features more time travelling orphans who, like Yoon Tae-yi and Park Jin-gyeom, are high achievers. Han Tae-sul's parents were killed while helping traffic accident victims many years ago when Han Tae-sul was just a young boy. Han Tae-sul grows up to become a sort of Mark Zuckerberg figure, a socially awkward computer genius whose coding it seems eventually leads to the invention of time travel. But Han Tae-sul is not the only high achieving orphan in *Sisyphus*. There's also Seo Won-Ju who was a classmate of Han Tae-sul. Although Han Tae-sul was always socially awkward he was not, unlike Seo Won-Ju, psychotic. At first, the young Han Tae-sul sticks up for the bullied Seo Won-Ju and it's only when Seo Won-Ju makes himself an orphan by blowing up his abusive father with a mixture of sodium and water, a method incidentally, the science obsessed Han Tae-sul showed him how to do, that Han Tae-sul tells him to go away.

*Meet the Robinsons* is a 2007 American animation science fiction comedy loosely based on the 1990 children's book *A Day with Wilbur Robinson* by William Joyce. Lewis lives in an orphanage. However, his inventor eccentricity scares off potential parents, so he works all night on a machine to scan his memory to locate his birth mother, who abandoned him at the orphanage when he was a baby. Unfortunately, the scanner fails to work when he tries to demonstrate it at the school's science fair. However, Lewis meets a 13-year-old called Wilbur Robinson who claims to be a time cop from the future. Wilbur offers to take Lewis in a time machine to the year 2037, where he meets the Robinson family who at first agree to adopt Lewis, but then change their mind when they discover he is from the past. A mysterious Bowler Hatted Man and a woman called Doris then approach Lewis, and offer to take Lewis to his mother if Lewis agrees to fix the memory scanner he has invented. However, they both betray Lewis and the Bowler Hatted Man then reveals himself to be the adult version of Lewis's roommate, Michael 'Goob' Yagoobian, who believes his life was ruined by Lewis, a scenario not that dissimilar to *Sisyphus*. The credited writers of the screenplay of *Meet the Robinsons* are Jon Bernstein, Michelle Spitz, Don Hall, Nathan Greno, Aurian Redson, Joe Mateo and Stephen Anderson.

But leaving aside the complexities of all these plots let's cut to the chase and ask, why are there so many time travelling orphans?

The orphan's sense of loss or abandonment leaves him or her with psychological scars. And, from a story perspective, people with emotional scars are always far more interesting than those without. Another point is that those who lose both parents early in life tend to be high achievers, as with Lewis, Park Jin-gyum and Yoon Tae-yi. It takes perseverance and resolve when you're left to fend for yourself. However, determination is the sunny side of obsession and that can lead to compulsion and addiction. Hence, the social problems many of these characters go through. It's often said that early loss and grief creates an ocean of emptiness like no other. Psychologically that oceanic void needs to be filled with something – fame, fortunes, possessions, achievement, success – yet rarely does it ever compensate for the sense of loss.

What we have in both *Alice* and *Sisyphus* and, to a degree in *Meet the Robinsons*, is a fascinating opening up of the psychology of the lonely and grieving child as experienced through time travel adventures. The openly emotional scenes in *Alice* and *Sisyphus* explore the dynamics of the Eternal Triangle that is Mother-Father-Child in very affecting, powerful and moving ways. There are numerous scenes across all the various plotlines in these tales of dramatic reuniting and recognition of passed family loved ones. And not surprisingly there are many tears, too. The ancient Greeks loved scenes of *anagnorisis* or 'recognition' and there are many in both the *Odyssey* and the *Iliad*, notably Odysseus meeting his mother in the Underworld, but the number in *Alice* and *Sisyphus* beats even the epic Homer.

It's worth noting here that many time travellers are loners and restless nomads. As one character puts it in Robert Silverberg's 1974 short story *Trips*, 'Not searching *for*, just searching.' And it's another Robert Silverberg tale, *Absolutely Inflexible* (1956), that observes that few time jumpers are family men. And modernist angst, particularly male angst, is often part of the nature of the lone time traveller in Silverberg's stories. In fact, this is a psychological feature that you'll find in many recent time travellers. Compare, for example, the classic Doctor Who character of the 1960s and 1970s with his and her modern incarnations. In fact, in season 13 of *Doctor Who* (2021–2022) a new *mythos* was created around the Doctor being an actual foundling, the Timeless Child, who was in some way the originator of the Time Lords. Doctor Who: the ultimate time travelling orphan.

## The Time Being's Nemesis and Villains of Time

The story guru Robert McKee makes the point that 'a protagonist and his story can only be as intellectually fascinating and emotionally compelling as the forces of antagonism make them.' Yes, but where do terms such as nemesis, villain and shadow fit in? The concept of The Shadow comes from the theories of the psychologist Carl Gustav Jung where those parts of our personality that we fear and repress come together to create The Shadow of the Hero. As Dr Evil knowingly says to Austin Powers, 'We're not so different, you and I.' The word nemesis comes from the Greek, *nemein*, meaning 'to give what is due'. In other words the nemesis character represents retribution, or the matching of the punishment with the crime. For the story theorist Vladimir Propp the villain was simply the initiator of the story who causes the damage or imbalance at the beginning of the tale that the hero must put right. Nowadays the villain comes with a moral dimension and is basically the 'Bad Guy'. But none of these roles is mutually exclusive. In *Doctor Who*, the Doctor's long-standing rival/arch-enemy The Master (sometimes Missy) has taken on all these dramatic functions.

There's a certain bond between The Master and the Doctor precisely because of their shared history and character. Both are outsiders, both are highly intelligent, but morally they are as different as night and day. Or so the Doctor would claim. There is also Davros of course, the creator of the Daleks and all round bad guy, but Davros is not The Doctor's 'Shadow' in the way The Master is. But the general point here is that as with the time being protagonist, the time being antagonist is constructed essentially for dramatic purposes.

A brilliant example of an out-and-out time villain is the 'Weeping Angel' in *Doctor Who*. Weeping Angels (quantum-locked humanoids) appear to be made of stone. Like those still lizards that capture flies with the quickness of their tongues, Weeping Angels are as stone when they are being observed. But that's why you mustn't blink, for it is then that they become, as it were, alive. These angels are cosmic creatures that feed off time – nearly all the *Doctor Who* monsters have a healthy alien appetite of some sort – or at least they steal the energy of unlived lives by sending you back in time, thus taking from you the power of those years. The Weeping Angels are truly frightening monsters and one of the best of the *Doctor Who* revamp.

In THE SWIDGERS book series, the back-story time villain is the Dark Force that puts Time and Life out of kilter at the beginning of the universe. Occasionally, this Dark Force sends part of itself back into the universe to capture and control Swidgers, for it is Swidgers who by their efforts to alter human timepaths are slowly putting Life and Time back in sync. One such element of the Dark Force is The Despiser who seeks out William in book one of the series *The Time That Never Was*, though this is only fully revealed in book two, *The Time They Saved Tomorrow*. In a visit to the Swidger Alicia, William discovers that Granny, William's Mentor, was a victim of The Despiser once herself, but somehow managed to resist its desires. And so must William. To say how William survives the final attack of The Despiser would be to give away the plot. However, what can be said is that understanding the difference between real time and space and the time and space you create with your 'fancy', to borrow a favourite word of Dickens, certainly comes in handy.

## Time Guardians

For Time Lords in the iconic *Doctor Who* television series, it's time that's their thing. It's what they know, it's what they do, it's what they care about. They are, after all, custodians of time. There's also the more metaphysical Mouri in the Temple of Atropos on a planet called Time who hold time and the universe together. However, the majority of time guardians in time fiction operate more like what you could call Time Police. As early as 1951 there was an American television series centring on Captain Z-Ro whose task was to safeguard history from harm by sending people back to sort things out in time when the past had been altered. In the 1970s British television series *Sapphire and Steel* (written by P.J. Hammond), the eponymous protagonists are The Guardians of The Flow of Time, and in *Fringe* (2008–13 created by J.J Abrams, Alex Kurtzman and Roberto Orci) there are beings called Observers, who evolved from humans in a possible future but now exist outside of time and only make themselves known at important historical events. And of course there is also the *Doctor Who* spinoff *Torchwood*, the name being an anagram of the show that gave it birth, an organisation that exists to protect the planet Earth from invaders. Torchwood has a base in Cardiff, which is situated at the end of a time rift and so two different points in time may overlap, resulting in beings and objects coming through time and ending up in Cardiff Bay. Time is something you've really got to keep your eye on. And all the time.

In *The End of Eternity*, the 1955 novel by Isaac Asimov, there are members of a brotherhood called Eternity, an organisation that is 'outside time' that aims to improve human happiness by observing human history and, after careful analysis, directly making small actions that cause 'reality changes'. Its members, known as 'Eternals', prioritise the reduction of human suffering, but it is at the cost of the loss of technology, art, and other human endeavours, which are prevented from existing when judged to have a detrimental effect. Yet why should these Eternals choose what's good for us? It's a little like the politics of Plato's *Republic*, where the elite are put in charge. But what is it that gives any elite the right to control the lives of others? Might we be better off, as the political philosopher Edmund Burke argued, with the wisdom of the 'unlettered man'? Anyway, in the story, the protagonist, Andrew Harlan, is placed in a situation where he must decide whether to allow the Eternity to be founded, or have a world where the Eternity simply never existed. So, which would you go with? The unlettered or the elite?

*El Ministerio del Tiempo* (created by Pablo and Javier Olivares) is a 2015 Spanish television series following the exploits of a team at the Ministry of Time investigating incidents of changes to the present day caused by time travel. In *Time Cop* (1994) there is even a Time Enforcement Commission (TEC) that has been established to prevent the misuse of time travel and in *Beyond the Infinite Two Minutes* (2020), written by Makoto Ueda, two 'time police' show up from the Time and Space Bureau to explain to the group of friends who have a laptop screen that shows two minutes into the future that this is the result of a 'wormhole disturbance' and that their memories must be erased. It seems at first that these time cops are a kind of *deus ex machina* to sort out the complexities of the plot, but when time future doesn't go according to plan, well, something does get erased, and it isn't memories.

In *Loki*, the 2021 American television series created by Michael Waldron, a Time Agency is introduced into the Marvel cinematic world called the Time Variance Authority, a body created by the mysterious Time-Keepers to keep the Sacred Timeline on track. When anyone steps outside of their predetermined timeline, as Loki does, the TVA is there to correct it. If they didn't intervene then there would be branching timelines everywhere and a chaotic number of multiverses would be popping up left, right and centre.

## The Cassandra Complex

'Am I a fraud, a fortune-teller peddling lies from house to house?' Cassandra asks in Aeschylus' *The Agamemnon*. Well, both in a way. Cassandra has knowledge of the things to come, the gods gave her that gift, but her curse is that what she says is never to be believed.

The Cassandra Complex is what one psychiatrist claims that James Cole (Bruce Willis) is suffering from in *12 Monkeys*. It is conjectured that Cole is a fantasist who has created an elaborate story about coming from the future and now that his story is being challenged his mind cannot cope and so he has become violently unstable. Actually, the explanation for Cole's behaviour is much simpler than that: James Cole is angry because, like Cassandra, he's not being believed. And that is something we can all relate to.

The scene where the time traveller tells the truth but is then ridiculed is a popular trope in many time travel tales. Just like poor Cassandra of Greek mythology, cursed to utter true prophecies yet never have them believed, it is when time travellers tell the truth that their words fall only on sceptical ears and lead to mocking laughter. Even just claiming the existence of time travellers is enough to disrupt your life. In *Terminator II: Judgment Day* we learn that Sarah Connor has been incarcerated in a State Hospital where she has become a person-of-interest to the hospital psychiatrist due to her 'incredibly detailed and complex' fantasy about a time travelling cyborg, and a doomed future. In *Trancers* (1985) the time travelling cop Jack Deth only convinces his present-day helpmate that he is from the future when she witnesses a figure disappearing before her very eyes and sees Jack use a time watch from the future which slows down time for ten seconds. And in *Timescape*, even with both present and future versions of Ben Wilson (Jeff Daniels), it still takes a fight with the jailor to secure the present version's release. Even then people don't believe him when he speaks about the approaching meteorite that will destroy the town.

Usually, however, there is eventually some recognition of the integrity of the traveller. In *Time Tunnel*, the opening episode *Rendezvous with Yesterday*, has Dr Tony Newman (James Darren) and Dr Doug Phillips (Robert Colbert) finding themselves onboard the *Titanic*. At first the captain refuses to listen to them, but eventually he says that although his reasoning won't let him accept the idea of time travel, he believes in God's mercy and, if they are telling the truth, their presence will have saved lives. The captain is at least open to the possibility they may be who they say they are and it is even suggested that as a result of what Tony and Doug told him, when the ship does strike the iceberg, the captain makes the decision to give the orders to abandon the ship, so saving 750 souls.

Frustration is the name of the game, but time travellers from the future have something that Cassandra did not possess, and that is proof. Catherine Riley (Madeleine Stowe) eventually believes James Cole in *12 Monkeys* because she recognises him from a photograph in a history book from the First World War. And that too is a moment we recognise in all our lives, when deniers finally see the truth of our words.

# Time Loops and Causal Loops in Time Tales

*There was a young man who was deft*
*At running and cunning and theft.*
*With legs so quick,*
*It was Time he would nick,*
*By returning before he had left!*
Anonymous

## Let's Do The 'Time Loop' Again

A TIME LOOP is where time is, as it were, put on repeat. A time loop, were you able to draw it, would be like an Escher sketch of a staircase that had no exit. If it were a road, it would take you back to where you started, a cul-de-sac, if you will, but with a door at the end that leads to where you began. And if you want to think of a time loop in terms of Greek myths, it would be Sisyphus's worst possible nightmare.

You'll find the time loop principle in *Looper*, *Source Code*, *The Endless* and *Timecrimes*, plus the iconic *Shadow Play* episode in *The Twilight Zone* series. Sometimes a task must be completed, or a discovery made, in order to bring the time loop to an end – you'll find this plot trope played out in *Edge of Tomorrow*, *Happy Death Day*, *ARQ*, *Day Break*, *Retroactive*, *Run Lola Run* and with William in the confrontation in school-corridor in *The Time That Never Was*. There are many time loops as well where some sort of personal growth or redemption must be achieved, for example, *Repeaters*, *Christmas Do-over* and *Before I Fall*.

The classic time loop movie is of course *Groundhog Day* (1993). The Oxford English Dictionary has now added the term 'groundhog day' as a noun for the concept of a day seeming to repeat itself again and again. *Groundhog Day* features Bill Murray as Phil for whom life has not turned out as he hoped it would (male angst is a very common theme in Time Tales – remember Henry David Thoreau's famous observation that 'most men lead lives of quiet desperation, and go to the grave with the song still in them'). Phil asks Gus and Ralph, as they slowly get drunk in a bar in a bowling alley, what they would do it they were stuck in one place and every day was exactly the same and Ralph replies that that about sums up life for him. One of the reasons this film became so popular was because, although a fantasy, in some ways it reflected the endless repetitive daily grind for many people.

Phil then is a man in crisis. Writer/director Harold Ramis said that his fellow screenwriter Danny Rubin used Elisabeth Kübler-Ross's theories on death and bereavement, the so-called 'Five Stages', as a basic template for Phil's process and progress in dealing with his new situation. Strictly speaking, in Kübler-Ross psychological work, these stages are not linear and are not meant to be separated into neat episodes. However, they did become a useful framework for the structure of the movie. Phil undergoes denial, anger, bargaining, depression and finally acceptance. In the 'bargaining period', Phil uses what he discovers about the women of the town whom he finds attractive, such as Nancy Taylor, to persuade them to have sex with him. The exception is Rita, his television producer, who sees through this ruse and recognises it as a dishonest set-up. Rita tells him that the only person he loves is himself. Phil disagrees. He can't love himself because he doesn't even like himself. His misuse of the knowledge he is privileged to as a result of the time loop ultimately leads to failure and even deeper depression.

However, Phil is asked the question, '*What would you do if this were your last day on Earth?*' He's lucky, he can relive that day again and again but it is from this question that he learns one of the greatest things you can do in life is to help others. Eventually this new Phil wins Rita over. She stays the night with him, not for sex, but because she cares for him and likes him. The high-concept theme then is: *Life doesn't change until you change.*

*Groundhog Day* is a modern redemption story, much in the same vein as Charles Dickens' *A Christmas Carol*. *Looper* on the other hand is a time loop tale that is ultimately dealing with the cycle of violence in modern life. And a very moral tale it is too. The director and screenwriter of *Looper*, Rian Johnson, said that his movie was an answer to that classic time philosophy question, *'If you could, would you travel back in time and kill Hitler?'* What happens in the story is that a boy in the present, who has supernatural powers, becomes 'The Rainmaker', a dangerous, monstrous murderer in the future. When this boy is angry, he develops an extraordinary energy that turns him into a killing force. Old Joe, played by Bruce Willis, a character from the future, attempts to eliminate the boy because of who he becomes. In the plot, The Rainmaker of the future has killed Joe's wife, but in attempting to alter the past Old Joe kills the boy's mother and, ironically, it's this event that sets off the circle of violence. What starts with blood ends with blood. Then Young Joe sees it all. The mother who would die for her son. The man who would kill for his wife. A boy who becomes angry and alone. And through this Young Joe sees a path that is essentially a circle going round and round. It's at that moment that Young Joe understands that there is only one way to break it and so he puts a gun to his own chest and shoots. Put simply, Young Joe decides it would be better if he did not exist. He realises that to close the loop will take an act of self-sacrifice. In many ways *Looper* is a mythical fable.

Poor Jonas in *Dark*, who pretty much discovers himself in every time period he visits, takes a while to realise that the only way to end the suffering he finds in these worlds is for him never to have existed. A very literal existential crisis. But *Dark*, like *Looper*, is a powerful fable and such stories force us to contemplate the value of our lives, the contribution, good and bad, that we make to the lives of others. And in a way they prepare us as human beings for our own non-existence and our acceptance of it.

*Before I Fall* is a 2017 American teen drama directed by Ry Russo-Young, written by Maria Maggenti and Gina Prince-Bythewood, and based on the novel of the same name by Lauren Oliver. As with *Dark* and *Looper*, *Before I Fall* is a Time Loop tale of redemption and self-sacrifice. Samantha Kingston (Sam) wakes up on 12 February (so-called Cupid's Day in the story). The teenage Sam plans to lose her virginity to her boyfriend Rob that evening but, foreshadowing perhaps what is to come, her day begins with a class lecture on the legend of Sisyphus. From then on, following a series of complex and interrelated events involving her friends and fellow students, the day does not go according to plan and ends tragically with a car crash. Or so it seems. But this is a time loop story and so in the next moment Sam wakes in her room, where it's Cupid's Day again. Sam, perhaps naturally enough, at first believes the previous 24 hours were simply some sort of nightmare. But as Cupid's Day goes on, similar events occur and it's then that Sam realises that it wasn't a dream and that she is indeed in some sort of time loop. And as in many time loop stories, Sam tries to alter the events that lead to the car crash but nothing she ever does changes the outcome. Only then Sam has a realisation as to what it is she must do and how *she* must change, and so the next time she wakes up, Sam resolves to be kind and considerate as she goes about her day. As for the car crash, that doesn't happen, but when her friend Juliet runs into traffic it is Sam who intervenes to save Juliet. And this proves to be a truly selfless act and one, as with Joe and Jonas, of redemptive self-sacrifice.

There are many task based time loop stories where the hero is given the opportunity to fix a problem and in so doing the time loop will be ended and life can move on. But how do you find new ways of telling this plot? Well, there's the movie *ARQ* (2016). ARQ stands for 'Arcing Recursive Quine', which is basically a self-perpetuating power source. In a rebel attack, this machine is electrically shorted and as a result Renton is put in a time loop. It seems to be a pretty standard get-it-right-next-time scenario but turns out to have a who-can-you-trust subplot. In *Edge of Tomorrow*, Cage, played by Tom Cruise, has a connection with the alien brain of the Mimics which somehow is giving him the opportunity to relive one day in a battle against the alien invaders. The point here is that the plot complication which links these two stories is that it isn't just Renton or Cage who are able, or who have, or who will, relive that day, for these time loop tales have a loop in parallel with the loop.

Other time loop movies include *The Infinite Man* (2014), where a romantic weekend goes wrong with the introduction of a time machine; *12:01* (1993), where a man witnesses a murder and the time loop gives him a chance to save the victim; *The Endless* (2017), where two brothers go to a camp where an entity traps people in time loops allowing it to sadistically enjoy their ever-repeated violent deaths; *Blood Punch* (2014), with the movie tag-line '*Live the same day. Die a different way*'; *Camp Slaughter* (2005), a 'slasher' movie set at a camp near a forest; *Repeaters* (2010), featuring a deranged murderer and *Timecrimes* (2007), again with an insane killer, and *Mine Games* (2012), with – you've guessed it – another killer on the loose.

On a more cheerful note, the time loop scenario has also been adapted for the romantic comedy genre, notably of course *Groundhog Day*, but more recently in *Palm Springs* (2020), *The Map of Tiny Perfect Things* (2021), *Naked* (2017) and the comedy-horror *Happy Death Day* (2017). *Haunter* (2013) also has a time loop scenario but this movie has more of a paranormal flavouring that takes it well into classic horror territory.

*Russian Doll* (2019) is an American comedy drama series created by Natasha Lyonne, Leslye Headland and Amy Poehler. The series follows Nadia Vulvokov, who is a software engineer for a video game developer, who repeatedly dies and relives the same night in an ongoing time loop. Like *Groundhog Day*, *Russian Doll* centres on a self-centred character in mid-life crisis.

There are familiar story tropes such as the initial belief that it's all a dream and the fact that the day itself is special – it's Nadia's birthday – and like Alice in Lewis Carroll's famous tale, it's an animal that leads Nadia down her rabbit-hole as her first 'death' is the result of chasing her cat Oatmeal. However, what distinguishes this series from many others is its inventiveness and its variation in tone from one episode to another, which proves so often to be a surreal existential riff on all that life has to offer.

A left-field take on the time loop tale is where the protagonist – or should we say protagonists – knowing or unknowingly meet versions of themselves or are in fact in some way self creators. The phrase *'you'll meet yourself coming back'* is useful to bear in mind here. And such stories now bring us on to that mind-challenging sibling of the time loop and that is the causal loop.

## The 'Causal Loop'

'Shallow men believe in luck or in circumstance. Strong men believe in cause and effect,' said Ralph Waldo Emerson. And as we've said, belief in causality is a key component of a Time Tale. And never more so than in causal loops.

Causal loops aren't that simple. Trying to explain them can easily do your head in as they deal with backwards-causality, where an event causes a subsequent sequence of events, which in turn is among, or culminates in, the very cause of that first event. In effect, the effect becomes the cause that caused it. *So, how's that head of yours now?*

Anyway, here's perhaps a simpler way of looking at the causal loop. Imagine you are a child with an unusual interest in snooker but you don't know where the attraction came from. All you know is that you get excited when you watch how one snooker ball hits another, setting off a causal sequence of hits on other balls that eventually leads to the black ball being pocketed. This excitement of yours sets off its own series of events in your life that lead – *stay with it* – to time travel into the future where you become the most skilful player of snooker in the world. However, a jealous rival wipes your mind of memories and sends you – that is your apparently blank mind – back to the past into the body of yourself as a child. Yet that love of snooker is so strong it somehow survives the mind wipe and so when you see snooker being played, you become fascinated as to how it is that when one ball hits another it sets off a causal sequence that eventually leads to the black ball being pocketed... and that leads to... and so on and so on...

That, in a nutshell, is an example of a causal loop scenario. And the principle works even without the child and with only the snooker balls themselves, for the whole thing would start again if that pocketed black ball found its way onto the table and the other balls rebounded from the cushion back to where they were in the first place. That is, of course, if there ever was a first place. And there are those scientists who think the universe is essentially in some sort of eternal cosmic causal loop, but more on that elsewhere. It should be said that *Artemis Fowl and the Time Paradox* (published 2008) explores the concept of the causal loop in a similar way to how our fictitious child's interest in snooker came about, only with Artemis Fowl the curiosity is with fairies, who have been known to be even more mysterious than snooker balls.

A very early example of the principle of the causal loop in a Time Tale is F.J. Bridge's 1931 story *Via the Time Accelerator* (F.J. Bridge was a pseudonym of Francis J. Brueckel, a writer of what was sometimes called pulp science fiction). In this story, a time traveller, Anton Brookhurst, takes a trip into the future in a time travelling airplane. Brookhurst has initial doubts about this trip, until he sees himself returning from the future, which reassures him about the success of his voyage, and as a consequence he takes it. Later in the story, when he is in actual danger in the future, he gives himself courage by asking himself had he not seen with his own eyes his return, gliding down into his landing-field? Was he not destined to return to his own age safe and sound? The first cause, as it were, of the causal loop, that is his decision to risk the flight because there he is coming back, acts here as a 'spoiler' of sorts.

# TIME LOOPS AND CAUSAL LOOPS IN TIME TALES

Robert H. Heinlein's title to his 1941 Time Tale *By His Bootstraps* comes from the phrase 'pick yourself up by your own bootstraps', which in a way offers a pretty big clue as to where (and who) the story will eventually take us. And that is a self-creating time paradox. Robert Silverberg acknowledges this story's influence in his Introduction to his collection of short stories *Time and Time Again* and his indebtedness to it specifically is mentioned in his preface to his tale *Absolutely Inflexible*. In fact, Robert H. Heinlein's *By His Bootstraps* became so influential that causal loops are often now referred to as 'the Bootstraps Paradox'. You'll find a reference to it in the *Doctor Who* adventure *Before the Flood* and the German series *Dark*. *Before the Flood* begins with the Doctor directly addressing the camera. Is he breaking the fourth wall or is it a video message to someone unknown? It's never explained, but either way, it's very unusual in the context of how *Doctor Who* is normally presented. Anyway, in this prologue the Doctor offers a thought experiment. Suppose a time traveller who was a fan of Beethoven took all of Beethoven's written work back in time to have it signed by the man himself, only when he arrived in the late 18th century there was no Beethoven? Just conjecture, for this didn't actually happen, says the Doctor. Anyway, not wanting Beethoven's music to be lost, the time traveller essentially became Beethoven. The question then is, who actually composed Beethoven's Fifth? And that question is pertinent to this particular episode because it involves a self-creating aspect of the Bootstraps Paradox in the plot. In *Dark*, there is much talk about how 'The End' and 'The Beginning' are the same thing. Yet, unlike many causal loop tales, in *Dark* there is an origin point and ultimately we find out exactly what that moment was/is.

In the Korean time travel series *Alice*, Professor Yoon Tae-yi has a speech about her motivation for studying time travel and the feasibility of time travel itself. Stephen Hawking, she says, observed that time travel was not possible except through the existence of negative energy, for all objects move in the direction of the applied force, but negative energy moves in the opposite direction. Her research on negative energy, she explains, led to a command program similar to the one found in a Time Card a time traveller gave her. The implication here is that the Time Card, at least in part, will help her in the development of time travel that will lead to the Time Card itself. A causal loop of sorts that's not that dissimilar in principle to the 'chip' found in The Terminator's robotic arm.

A bizarre sort of causal loop can be found in the cult Time Tale *Timecrimes*. There's a deranged pursuer about, so you go back in time an hour or so to escape him, only the events in this new timeline lead you to having a more frenzied state of mind than you did before when once again you encounter that insane pursuer. So you go back in time again, and soon you are almost as unhinged as that mad man who is running about. The scenario is then repeated until it reaches the inevitable 'by your own bootstraps' conclusion.

There are stories too where going back in time is the cause of the very thing you were trying to get rid of. In Philip K. Dick's *The Skull* (1952), Conger is sent back into history to kill a messianic figure who preached against war and later became a cult figure because of his supposed miraculous resurrection. Conger is a typical Philip K. Dick hero, a lowly man who, more by accident than design, goes on to change the world for the better and in a big way. In *The Skull*, Conger, unbeknown to himself (and in the early part of the story the reader), is the very preacher he was sent to assassinate. So how did this come about? Conger accidentally arrives late in the man's timeline. In fact, Conger arrives after the preacher is dead. However, because Conger is seen by people who know him to be the preacher, they, naturally enough, come to believe he has risen from the dead. Anyway, Conger checks the dates and realises he needs to go back further in time, to the moment the preacher began preaching against war. That's when he'll complete the task of the assassination. Or so he thinks. But it's in that time frame that Conger realises that the skull he carries, his only clue to the figure he was sent to kill, is his own. He is the messianic preacher. He knows he will die, that is part of history, but now he has a motive to preach against war. And he does so smiling.

Causal loops in Time Tales can involve people, objects, events or even information. There's the character and story line of Melody/River Song in *Doctor Who* where The Doctor points out that Amy, the mother of River Song, named her daughter after her daughter. In the US series *Timeless*, Lucy's journal, only handed over to Garcia Flynn in the final episode, is essentially the 'first cause' of the causal loop in that without it, Garcia Flynn would never have gone back in time in episode one. There's a neat comic take on the causal loop in *Star Trek: The Voyage Home* when Kirk, who's travelled back in time to 1986, needing money, sells an antique pair of spectacles which were bought in his future by McCoy and given to Kirk for his 50th birthday. This means that McCoy in that future will buy the very gift he's already given in order to give it again. Then there's the antique pocket watch the elderly lady gives Richard Collier in *Somewhere in Time*. This is the very watch he gives to her when he goes back in time to meet her when she was younger. And so the question then arises, *'Were the spectacles and the antique watch ever actually manufactured or do these exist only within the causal loop?'* This question also raises the issue of who actually wrote Lucy's journal in *Timeless*? And, if you pursue all this further, who is it in *Star Trek: The Voyage Home* that invents Transparent Aluminium (or 'Transparent Aluminum' as the Scotty would have it)? Which takes us back again to Doctor Who's question who wrote Beethoven's Fifth?

Well, you could spend a lifetime figuring out these kinds of questions and paradoxes and still end up where you started. Which is a sort of time loop in itself. Perhaps the easiest way to bring it to a close is simply to say, 'It exists because it is and that's all there is to it'. And if, after that people are still asking, 'Yes, but what is or was its source? Where did it come from? Who built it?' simply tell them, as one character does in *The Technicolor*

*Time Machine* (published in 1967) by Harry Harrison, that it came from the same place the missing side of the Möbius strip went. And as Eric Morecambe always said to Ernie, *'There's no answer to that!'*

The causal loop is a fascinating puzzle to challenge the mind. It can be developed in a Time Tale as a study of identity, a motive for change or as a comic subplot or even a horror story. And the latter, when done well, explores and exploits the genuine human fear of being trapped in a vicious cycle from which there is no escape. A rather nihilistic metaphor perhaps for life itself.

As a coda to all this talk of causality it's worth saying that several philosophers, notably David Hume, have been very sniffy about the whole idea. B may follow A but that doesn't mean B happens because of A. Later Ludwig Wittgenstein in *Tractatus Logico* even went as far as saying that belief in 'the causal nexus' was a superstition. As with Hume, Wittgenstein's point was that knowledge requires more than conviction, it needs certainty. Oh but most people are happy enough saying 'I know what I know' and therefore go through life at least wanting to believe that one thing happens as a result of another. And by their nature, most time travel tales endorse that view, even if some very clever philosophers don't.

## Retro-Causality

The time traveller has been called a 'retro-causality engineer', which may sound like someone who looks after an old Victorian sewage system but is in fact a quite reasonable description. An example of retro-causality can be found in *Beyond the Infinite Two Minutes* (2020) where a group of friends have a laptop monitor that shows two minutes into the future and so they begin asking their future selves what to do. But can retro-causality or backward causation ever be reasonable? Isn't causation essentially the cement of our universe that links and makes solid the building blocks of time events that are forever moving forward? Perhaps so, but what if The Big Bang was also The Big Collapse? If our universe comes to an end through gravitational forces compressing matter back to the infinite singularity from which it was born, would it then be reborn, as it were, as a new universe? And would time disappear and then reappear at the universe's reincarnation? Is in fact the universe an infinite elastic yo-yo that has been expanding and contracting forever and ever and ever and ever and ever? And would that explain things like déjà vu and precognition? If you know the answers to any of these questions, please pop them on a postcard and send them to: *The Professor of Big Thinking, The Royal Society, London*, because she doesn't know for sure either.

A curious example of retro-causality in a Time Tale can be found in the horror thriller *The Caller* (2011 – written by Sergio Casci). Divorcee Mary Kee moves into a new apartment and begins to receive telephone calls from mysterious and disturbed woman called Rose, who claims to be calling from the past. Mary doesn't believe her at first but to prove it, Rose makes alterations to the apartment which are then found by Mary. A retro-causality of sorts. Rose is incentivised by Mary to make further and more drastic changes, but when murder is involved Mary cuts off communication with Rose. But, since Rose is in the past, she has all the power. In some ways *The Caller* is a standard woman-in-peril horror flick, but with a time jumping voice on the other end of the phone calling the shots. There's a very sinister scene, for example, where Rose has found the younger Mary and while on the phone threatens the older Mary that she will pour scolding oil on the child. In fact, it's more than a threat, for oil is poured on the younger Mary and as that happens in the past scolding marks and scars suddenly appear on the older Mary's body. *Creepy!*

## Time Cycle

When is a time loop not a time loop? Answer: When it's a time cycle!

*Sijipeuseu: The Myth* takes its name from Sisyphus (who is sometimes called Sisyphos) a character in Greek mythology. Sisyphus was the founder and king of Ephyra (now known as Corinth) who was chastised by the gods for cheating death twice. His punishment was to roll an immense boulder up a hill only for it to then roll back down again as soon as it neared the top. And poor Sisyphus was tasked to do this labour for eternity (this is why actions that are physically intensive yet futile are often described as 'Sisyphean'). However, the aspect of the Sisyphus legend that seems to interest the creators of *Sijipeuseu* is the repetitive nature of the cycle.

The Sisyphus figure could be said to be 'Sigma', also known as Seo Won-Ju/Seo Gil-Bok. Sigma is a psychopathic and revengeful figure who learns to hate the world and everyone in it. His former classmate at primary school (elementary school in the USA and elsewhere) was the computer genius Han Tae-sul, whose coding eventually leads to time travel. At first the young Han Tae-sul is kind to the boy Seo Won-Ju, but, when Seo Won-Ju blows up his own father with sodium and water, not surprisingly Han Tae-sul tells him to keep his distance. Well, you would. From then on, Seo Won-Ju follows the life and career of his old classmate and as the years go on Seo Won-Ju grows ever more envious of Tae-sul's considerable wealth and success. And so a nemesis is born.

The plotting becomes multi-layered and complex but the long and short of it is that Sigma/Seo Won-Ju in the future takes control of the time machine (known as an 'Uploader') that the genius Han Tae-sul will come up with. Sigma, it seems, in the future will send a nuclear bomb back in time and thus create a nuclear apocalypse, though of course the wicked Seo Won-Ju himself will always take precautions and so will survive. It becomes apparent that the psychotic Seo Won-Ju's main aim is simply to witness devastation and death. And, since he now has control of a time machine, he can do this again and again with ever increasing sadistic, smiling pleasure. His other gratification in all this is seeing the humiliation of Han Tae-sul as he repeatedly loses.

However, for this to happen on each cycle Seo Won-Ju has to make sure that Han Tae-sul gives him the computer code that will result in time travel – the first cause, if you will, of the time cycle. And his bargaining chip is always Gang Seo-hae, a time traveller who Han Tae-sul falls in love with. The dilemma is then will it be the world or the girl? Furthermore, there exists the Control Bureau, a government operation policing time travellers, and on each occasion the time cycle happens, the head of this organisation passes on notes to Sigma/Seo Won-Ju as to how next time he should act so as to keep the cycle going. And there are those who play poker who would call this cheating.

Anyway, is all this a time loop or a time cycle? Well, in a traditional time loop, the characters are trapped or at least have found themselves in the time loop unwillingly. And the protagonists in this type of scenario usually know they are in a time loop. Also, in time loop tales, time doesn't move on – how can it when it's in a loop? But in *Sijipeuseu* there is no sense that time doesn't move on in the future and Sigma is not in any way trapped in a time loop. Nor does Sigma have to achieve some task or other to escape the loop, which is also a popular time loop story trope. No, all Sigma wants to do is simply witness other people's pain again and again and again, and, perhaps more importantly, beat Han Tae-sul every time. In a way then you could say it is Han Tae-sul who is the true Sisyphus figure not Sigma. Or if it is Sigma who represents the rock pusher, then it's a psychotic and sadist Sisyphus who relishes pain and loss in others.

## The Time Re-set

If you've ever played the game *Kerplunk*, with all those marbles piled high in a cylinder supported only by plastic straws, you'll know that it is often taking out just one straw that causes the whole marble mountain to collapse. Well, the time re-set is a little bit like that straw.

The time re-set is, in a way, at the opposite end of the spectrum to causal loops and time loops in that the time re-set is that one single action that re-sets time, and can, if so constructed, wipe out those loops or anomalies that time travel has created. For example, in *Looper*, that single re-set action is the death of Young Joe by his own hands, thus resulting in Old Joe and the nightmare loop simply vanishing, and in *Dark*, it is Jonas and Martha telling Tannhauser's son and family not to drive over the bridge, that results in their own non-existence.

The protagonist physically disappearing as a result of altering events in the past is nothing new. There is a classic episode of *The Outer Limits* from 1963 called *The Man Who Was Never Born* (written by Anthony Lawrence), a title which essentially gives away the ending. After accidentally travelling through time as a result of a 'time convulsion', astronaut Joseph Reardon arrives on Earth in the year 2148AD only to find a bleak and desolate landscape. In this future world Reardon meets Andro, a strange-looking mutated human and one of the few survivors of some sort of biological disaster. Reardon in a bid to save humanity from this catastrophe, takes Andro with him on the spacecraft in the hope of finding the space-time rift. Together they go back in time to show people what the future holds if the disastrous outcome that led to environmental devastation is not prevented.

However, as they journey through the space-time rift, Reardon suddenly becomes ill and then mysteriously vanishes, possibly, it is conjectured, as a result of travelling through time twice in one day. But before he dies, Reardon tells Andro to kill the scientist who will cause the biological disaster. It soon becomes clear when he lands that Andro has arrived on Earth prematurely, for the scientist, Bertram Cabot Jr has not yet been born, and his parents, Noelle Anderson and Bertram Cabot Sr, are still only young and not yet married.

Andro, played by the actor Martin Landau, is a mutant and yet through telepathic abilities he is able to hide his ugly disfigurement. Looking perfect normal, Andro convinces Noelle, the future mother of the scientist that caused the apocalypse, of the crucial importance of his mission. In a plot twist, Noelle confesses that she has fallen in love with him. Or at least the version she sees. Noelle then convinces Andro to take her with him to the future, thereby avoiding any possibility that she and Cabot will have the child that will grow up and cause the environmental disaster.

However, the flow of time has now been altered by Andro and Noelle's actions because Bertram Cabot Jr was never born and as a result, the science that made Andro's mutated existence possible never existed. And what all this ultimately means is that Andro himself was never born. Just as the ship arrives in 2148AD, Andro disappears, just as Joseph Reardon had done. Noelle, weeping, is now left to face the future alone.

There's another disappearing act in *Sijipeuseu*. Not giving the wicked Sigma the computer coding he needs to change the future is what ultimately re-sets time. And in that moment of refusal the rockets in the sky that are about to create the apocalypse that gives Sigma so much sadistic pleasure, simply disappear, along with Sigma's gunmen.

In the Korean time travel series *Alice*, there's a re-set not that dissimilar to the one in *Dark*. As in *Dark* with Adam, there is an older version of the main protagonist. In *Alice*, the Older Park Jin-gyeom from another time dimension becomes known as The Teacher and walks around in a monk-like black cloak. The Teacher tells his younger self that he can control time, but is now getting strangled by time. Well, that's old age for you. Anyway, The Teacher says that his gift to Park Jin-gyeom will give him the chance to reign over time, but the younger Park Jin-gyeom does not want this and vows that he will put everything back in its place. And he means it. He, his younger self, says that first he'll save everyone who died and then his own older self. However, it is in fact the self-sacrifice of the mother that is ultimately the re-set, but it is the pain on the faces of her sons that leads her to the act that ends time travel, her own existence and that of her time travelling offspring. *Alice* is a fascinating fable exploring the Oedipal Family Triangle and the final scenes where mother and son meet are very affecting. In fact the whole series is well worth a watch.

In the 2009 film comedy *Frequently Asked Questions About Time Travel*, a funny and engaging Time Tale written by Jamie Mathieson about three lads in a pub discussing time travel, it is, appropriately enough, the spilling of a pint of beer on the notes of one of the lads which is the time re-set button. It's a clever plot that took, to borrow a word coined by the movie itself, a great 'imagineer' to build. Another Time Tale well worth catching.

Explaining the complexities of the 2001 cult classic *Donnie Darko* isn't easy because anyone who tries always comes up with their own version of what has/is/was happening/happened. What you can say is that it is a movie about creative destruction (that's what the writer Richard Kelly claims anyway) and in the moment at the end of the film when the aircraft engine lands on top of Donnie Darko and kills him, time is indeed re-set and a better world hopefully results. Another movie well worth watching, but, Dear Reader, we are guessing that you have probably already seen it. Well, that will be the case, we suspect, of most people reading this book about time travel. But if you haven't seen *Donnie Darko*, why not? *Get to it!*

*Donnie Darko* offers a fresh start and essentially that is what happens in *Travelers* as well. It is a simple email saying 'DON'T SEND TRAVELER 0001' that re-sets Time. Not a time loop, but simply a new beginning. Everything in that timeline, and from the viewer's point of view that is pretty much everything in seasons one, two and three, is negated.

In many of these Time Tales, it is often a simple action that re-sets time. But these lynchpins, as it were, be they a simple refusal to hand over code or the spilling of beer, have been carefully constructed into the complex plotting in such a manner that they are often the only way that a time re-set can be achieved. And what this does is concentrate the mind on those choices made at certain key moments in life. For life can turn on a sixpence. Big moments, or when we look back, moments that at the time seem almost insignificant. All lives have them, the door not opened, the path not taken. The one, according to Robert Frost, 'less travelled by'. What was yours? Did you marry for money not love? Did you in your career do what was expected of you rather than want you truly desired? Is that decision now a regret? And in all these questions, if you could, would go back in time and press a magic start-over re-set button? Or would you maybe be too scared that an alternative timeline would put you in a life even worse than the one you live in? Or do you not ever allow yourself to think about such thoughts? Well, whatever the answer, what can be said is that it's the Time Tale that is able to explore all these questions in literally fantastic ways.

## Most Curious Loops and Cycles and Re-Sets

### 1/ *Shadow Play* (1961)

A Kafkaesque nightmare where a prisoner is tried and executed for murder in public court, but after the execution the whole scenario begins again – and it's the same faces, only this time the character roles of the judge, the lawyers and the jury have been swapped round and recast. *Twilight Zone*, season two, episode 26, original air date 5 May 1961, written by Charles Beaumont and based on his 1956 short story *Träumerei*.

### 2/ *Run Lola Run* (1998)

Pulse-pounding experimental thriller (written and directed by Tom Tykwer) in which our protagonist Lola has 20 minutes to deliver a bag of money to her boyfriend before his criminal boss kills him. Despite frantically running to complete the task, she fails… and time re-sets allowing her another chance. A differently played out set of circumstances still ends in disaster and time re-sets once again… Exhilarating entertainment featuring a breakout performance by Franka Potente as Lola, and a driving soundtrack which complements Lola's relentless running.

## 3/ *Heaven Sent* (*Doctor Who* 2015)

The Doctor finds himself in a castle pursued by The Veil, only able to escape its clutches if he acknowledges the truths of his life. The space and fabric of the castle he is trapped in is in a constant state of re-ordering itself. His day, or whatever time measurement you wish to call it, does eventually begin again. How long is the Doctor in this world? Years? Decades? Centuries? Even perhaps the lifetime of the stars in the sky. Why is he there? To confront truths? To mourn the loss of Clara? To be tested in resilience while entrapped in self-interrogation? Hell is mentioned but theologically *Heaven Sent* is much closer to the Catholic concept of purgatory, which is more about penance than punishment. Plot wise, the original *Doctor Who* series had The Doctor essentially as a Travelling Angel character, who came into a situation and fixed it. The character of Doctor Who still does this but running through the revamped *Doctor Who* is a Doctor persona that is guilt ridden and full of angst. In essence the reboot Doctor is about the nature of The Doctor himself. And Steven Moffat's *Heaven Sent* is arguably the culmination of that arc.

## 4/ *Children of the Stones* (1977)

The key point of distinction between a time loop and what we would call a 'time cycle' is that in the cycle characters are unknowing of the fact that they trapped within a repeated world and, at least for some, that cycle is escapable. The final episode of *Children of the Stones*, entitled *Full Circle* (written by Jeremy Burnham and Trevor Ray), adds the twist that this village is in some sort of time cycle and it reverts to its beginning – the arrival of Hendrick – at the end of the story. However, the main protagonists escape the village, never knowing they have been in a repeating time world.

## 5/ *Triangle* (2009)

Horror slasher set on a boat with a few self-murders thrown in. No, it's not a time loop classic in the mould of *Groundhog Day* but it is well plotted and put together and a welcome variation on the circle of time theme. *Triangle* was written and directed by Christopher Smith.

# The Paradoxes of Time and Time Travel

*I would rather be a man of paradoxes than a man of prejudices.*
Jean-Jacques Rousseau

## Time Paradoxes

A DICTIONARY DEFINITION will tell you that a paradox is something that contains incompatible parts, rendering that something nonsensical. It will also tell you a paradox can be a seemingly absurd statement or proposition which, when investigated, may prove to be well founded or true. Interesting then that the word itself is, well, paradoxical, having contrary meanings depending on how it is used.

But semantics aside, the question is: can there ever be any paradoxes in physics? Well, there are many physicists who state categorically that there are absolutely no paradoxes in physics and if they are believed to exist that's only because those who think that are using inadequate reasoning. Now you may be tempted to reply with the old line, 'Oh, shut up and deal,' but such scientists are in principle correct. The universe is the universe is the universe. Its rules are its rules and they wouldn't be rules if those rules had internal contradictions or exceptions. End of.

Well, that's sorted that out. But really, what would the fun be of physics without paradoxes? Particularly time travel paradoxes. And could it be that the existence of time paradoxes is one of the main reasons people are so interested in the concept of time travel in the first place? Paradoxes Rule OK and KO.

In 1931, *Amazing Stories*, published by Hugo Gernsback, certainly noticed that time paradoxes were becoming a feature of the stories in the magazine and so set a challenge to its readers entitled 'The Question of Time Travel'. One conundrum eventually became known as 'The Grandfather Paradox'. *Amazing Stories* supposed the basic question: Would going back in time and visiting your great-great-great-grandfather and shooting him while he was still a young man and unmarried prevent your own birth? The editor invited readers to comment. A 14-year-old boy named James (Jim) Nicholson, wrote back asking 'who the heck would want to kill his grandpa or grandma?' A similar question, incidentally, is posed in Stephen King's J.F.K assassination time travel story *11/22/63* (published in 2011). Anyway, this young James in *Amazing Stories* then posed this question: 'What if a man were to travel back a few years and marry his mother, thereby resulting in him being his own father?' Not surprisingly perhaps that boy went on to become president of American International Films, the company that made various science fiction classics, including *The Time Travelers* (1964). Incidentally, we have Paul J. Nahin and his brilliant book *Time Machine Tales: The Science Fiction Adventure and Philosophical Puzzles of Time Travel* to thank for drawing our attention to many of the Time Tales in *Amazing Stories* magazine and the history of 'The Grandfather Paradox'.

For many readers, such paradoxes, what you might consider to be 'Thought Experiments' of sorts, are the primary reason, sometimes the only reason, for enjoying the story. Such tales appeal to people who can think round corners. They are the same folk perhaps who also enjoy solving Rubik's cubes, crossword puzzles and Sudoku brainteasers. The unravelling, the deciphering and the resolving are the very point of the game or the challenge. It's not that empathy, emotion or even romance cannot also be enjoyed, but rather that these mind-riddles have great intellectual and mental appeal. And they can be amusing too.

As Nahin points out, Larry Dwyer in his 1971 paper *Time Travel and Some Alleged Logical Asymmetries Between Past and Future*, published in the *Canadian Journal of Philosophy* and later reprinted by Cambridge University Press, had fun with some of the potential legal consequences of time travel. Should a time traveller who punches his younger self (or vice-versa) be charged with assault? *I admit it, I hit me, m'Lud. Yes, and it hurt, you scoundrel!* Should a time traveller who murders someone in the present and then flees into the past be tried for a crime that he has yet to commit? *I'm guilty of murder, m'Lud. Not here and now, obviously, because he isn't dead yet, but, if I get my way, he will be in about fifty years time, mark my words.* And if a married man leaves his wife and escapes into the past, and remarries, is he still guilty of bigamy, even though his other wife will not to be born for a thousand years? *M'Lud, I married her because I love her. And I married another because I loved her, too. Well, I will, once she's born and grown up, if you see what I mean.* These aren't perhaps strictly speaking paradoxes, more ethical and legal questions for a jury to decide. That is, of course, if the jury doesn't think when told about all this time travel nonsense that the man's mad and belongs in a padded cell with only a box set of *Quantum Leap* to keep him company.

## 'The Grandfather Paradox'

The most frequently discussed time paradox is 'The Grandfather Paradox', and that's where we will begin. As said, the originator of this term and concept is thought to be Hugo Gernsback, publisher of the science fiction magazine *Amazing Stories*. The paradox suggests that if you go back in time and alter the timepath of an ancestor, say by murdering your grandfather, you will naturally enough bring into question your own very existence. And obviously, that's not a good outcome. Yet if you are never born, how can you kill anyone's grandfather, never mind your own? And if your grandfather isn't murdered, do you come back into existence again?

In *Travelers*, there is The Oath that their journey back in time from the future is '*At peril of our own birth.*' In one episode, Traveler 117, alias Mrs Bloom, asks whether the deflection of asteroid Helios 685 will alter the course of humanity so much that it is probable that the time era they come from – including the plagues and the wars – will cease to exist. And if that is the case, so will they. And Jonas and Martha in *Dark* face a similar existential challenge. You could argue that the Grandfather Paradox, along with much else in time travel fiction, makes us confront our own mortality and even our potential non-existence. But whatever we may all think of our lives at least those lives were or are being lived, unlike poor Jonas and Martha in *Dark*, who don't really die as such. How can they when they were never born?

On a more cheerful note, meeting ancestors can give us a new understanding and respect for those in our family tree who came before us. That's certainly true in *Back to the Future III*, set in the Wild West. Even in the first *Back to the Future* movie, where Marty has to stop a potential Grandfather Paradox by making sure his parents kiss at the Prom dance, Marty gains a new appreciation for his mom and dad in seeing them so young. And Marty begins to understand too where his father's lack of self-confidence came from.

But now let's return to doom and gloom and death and self-sacrifice, which are never far away in Time Tales. *In the Shadow of the Moon* (2019 – written by Gregory Weidman and Geoff Tock) tells the tale of a cop, Thomas Lockhart, chasing a time travelling serial killer called Rya, but, as Rya is travelling backwards in time, she is killed at what, for Lockhart, is their first encounter. The twist in the plot is that the serial killer is his granddaughter and her motive in killing is to prevent a world-changing disaster in the future. Yes, she probably knows that she will die, but is this really the same type of self-sacrifice as Jonas and Martha? And where is the moral justification for what is essentially murder? Or it is okay to simply tell a crime Time Tale and leave out the exploration of moral complexities?

Rya in *In the Shadow of the Moon* is Thomas Lockhart's granddaughter from the future, but a variation on the Grandfather Paradox is when the time traveller goes back in time and fathers a child, or indeed becomes his own ancestor in order for himself to be born (and in these scenarios it is usually a man). This particular scenario is sometimes called the 'Procreation Paradox' and an example of this is *The Flipside of Dominick Hide* (BBC *Play for Today* 1980, written by Jeremy Paul), where the time traveller is indeed also his own great-grandfather. It's there in a way in *The Terminator* as well. It's John Conner in the future who sends Kyle back in time to protect John's mother and in so doing protects himself, even though he has to be conceived. But that's the point, for John knows that in sending Kyle back in time, it is in fact Kyle who becomes (or will become) John Conner's father. There is also an episode in *Red Dwarf* (*Ouroboros* 1997) where Lister is revealed to be his own dad. Lister thought he was abandoned as a baby under a pool table in a pub inside a box marked something like 'our Rob' or 'our Ross', however, when he becomes a time traveller Lister realises he is in fact his own parent. Lister uses the Time Drive to send himself and his baby back to the Aigburth Arms in 2155. There he explains to the baby that he isn't being abandoned at all, he is simply keeping going the circular procreation causation.

*Ah yes*, you, the intra-diegetic Reader say, *but what about the biology of all this? After all, it takes two to tango*. It is true that to be his own father, the baby Lister would have to have ended up with a total replication of the time travelling Lister's genome (the genome being the complete set of genes or genetic material present in a cell or organism). The chances of this happening are at the jackpot lottery-winning end of probability. But better not to worry about such things. And besides, it is just possible to win the jackpot, even if it is always someone else that gets the millions and never you.

Robert Heinlein took the Procreation Paradox to the Nth degree in *All You Zombies* (1959), which is a Time Tale where everyone is the same someone. That is to say, the main characters – a man and a woman – are really the same person at different stages of their timeline. And Heinlein hoped, as he said to his literary agent, that he had written a story the farthest south in Time Paradoxes. Well, yes, it is pretty far south. Perhaps you could even say it's a tale that is so far south it's fallen off the Antarctic backwards.

Douglas Adams in *The Hitchhiker's Guide to the Galaxy* (1979 – based on the 1978 BBC radio series) and *The Restaurant at the End of the Universe* (1980) has fun with time paradoxes and the Procreation Paradox in particular. In *The Restaurant at the End of the Universe*, Adams, in a classic example of the understated style and the layman ethical thinking that runs through much of his writing, says that there is 'no problem in becoming your own father or mother that a broad-minded and well-adjusted family can't cope with.' And quite right too!

## Newcomb's Paradox

Newcomb's Paradox is a thought experiment that contradicts expected utility theory (the way people make choices) and strategic dominance theory (where one strategy is clearly and demonstrably better than another). In Newcomb's Paradox you, the player, can receive either the contents of a single closed box or the contents of that closed box and another box. The box giver in the game uses an infallible predictive algorithm to accurately work out the choice you will make, and so uses that deduction when filling the boxes. In other words, the one with the boxes is aware what you will do and so knows what choice you will make.

Remember, however, this is a thought experiment and the game itself is not possible in the real world. It has been postulated primarily to illustrate a paradox – and that paradox is that the analysis as to how you should proceed seems to produce conflicting yet logical responses.

The game is that there are two closed boxes, A and B, on a desk in front of you. Box A has inside it £1,000 (in some versions this box is transparent) and that you know to be certain. However, B contains either nothing or £1,000,000, but you don't know which. You are given two options. You can take both boxes, A and B, or just Box B. But here's the thing, the game, as explained, is being run by someone who has made a prediction about what you will do and before making your decision, you are told that the person has infallibility and has never made a prediction that turned out to be wrong. So, what do you do?

Take Box B only. In this choice you think, 'I'll take Box B and leave A. Mistress Infallibility knows that that's what I'm going to do, so it doesn't matter what I do do.' This is the option taken made on the expected utility principle when the probability of the predictor being right is almost certain or certain.

No, take both Box A and B. Here you think, 'I can't influence a decision made in the past by a choice I'm making right now. Such a proposition is irrational. And so I might as well take both boxes. That's clearly the right option. Right?' This choice is based on the strategic dominance principle where one option is, as the chooser says, clearly better than the other. But as said, this thought experiment has a paradox at its centre because the two analyses are both logically sound yet give conflicting answers.

How all this relates to time travel is that time travel creates the ultimate 'predictive algorithm'. In other words, the time traveller, or at least one who has come from the future, should be a perfect predictor of all events up to the date from whence they came. And this issue raises the problem of free will which is at the heart of Newcomb's Paradox from a human perspective. This is because if decisions seemingly made as free are already known by the time traveller, or indeed the soothsayer or prophet or the infallible algorithm, then they are not free at all. And this is the central theme of Alex Garland's series *Devs*.

The Newcomb Paradox was created by William Newcomb of the Lawrence Livermore Laboratory of the University of California and appeared in Martin Gardner's *Mathematical Games* in the March 1973 issue of *Scientific American*.

## The Fermi Paradox

Extra-terrestrial life is highly likely but if this is so, why is there so little proof of such beings? The Fermi Paradox then refers to the apparent contradiction between the probable existence of extra-terrestrial civilisations and the shortage of actual evidence for them. And the Fermi Paradox can easily be adapted to the likelihood of time travel by asking, 'If time travel is possible, where are all future visitors?' And that's a question that was often posed by the physicist Stephen Hawking.

Of course the extra-terrestrial issue can be answered by simply saying they are here, only they live with us in secret, or, from a more practical point of view, that it's such a long way to come to Earth, even if they exist why would they even bother? As for time travellers, well, how do we know they aren't here too? And if they've changed things over the years, how would we know that either? Hitler may have won the war and time travellers from the future went back to 1944 and altered history and it's that action that has given us the world we live in today. Which, incidentally, is the basic plot of *The Time They Saved Tomorrow*, the second in THE SWIDGERS Time Adventure series.

The idea of Fermi's Paradox originates from a conversation between Enrico Fermi and his fellow physicists Edward Teller, Herbert York and Emil Konopinski over lunch in the summer of 1950. They were discussing the recent UFO sightings and the possibility of travelling at the speed of light when Fermi suddenly asked, 'Where are they?' Fermi later came up with a series of calculations around the possibility of planets similar to Earth, the probability of life on those planets, the length of time a civilisation is likely to retain high technology and its likely existence during our own period of life on Earth. Enrico Fermi concluded on the basis of these calculations that Earth has probably been visited many times, but not necessarily within the time frame of our own present-day high technology. Isn't that always the case. You're never in when people you haven't seen for years come round.

## Niven's Law

The science fiction writer Larry Niven is known for his many 'Laws'. On writing he said that you should never be embarrassed or ashamed about anything you choose to write, that it was wrong to waste the reader's time, that if you've nothing to say, then say it any way you like and that the literary term for those who mistake the opinions and beliefs of characters in a novel for those of the author was 'idiot'. All useful and sensible observations.

As for Larry Niven's Law on Time Paradoxes, well, that is sometimes called The Law of The Conservation of the Past. And this is how it works. Say, for example, a message is sent to the past, it naturally follows that the message will change history, but this will ultimately include the very decision to send the message and what was put in it. A 'new' message will then be sent instead, and this too will change the past, only in a slightly different way, and so on, and so on, until, incrementally, some sort of equilibrium is achieved – the simplest being the message isn't even sent at all. You see, Douglas Adams was correct, because, as he put it, 'it all sorts itself out in the end'. And he must be right. We are here after all. Though if there are multiverses, we might be there, there, and there as well.

## Albert's Law

'When you sit with a nice girl for two hours, it seems like two minutes; when you sit on a hot stove for two minutes, it seems like two hours. That's relativity.' The words of Albert Einstein. Not quite a paradox but close, in that we all experience seemingly contradictory notions as to the passage of time depending on the situation. Summer days are long, yet they often seem to go so quickly, while those dark winter nights never seem to end at all. Plus there's the old truth that two minutes of time pass very differently depending which side of the bathroom door you are.

## The Future Paradox and Changing the Future

Theodore Edward Hook (1788–1841), an English man of letters, said that the 'best way to predict the future is to invent it.' In essence, he was arguing that you make your own future. Well, let's see if that works and make a prediction here and now which is that we will end this chapter with the thoughts of Doc Brown from *Back to the Future*. There it is. It's decided. So that means we now know what we are going to do. We have knowledge, if you will, of the future. And any knowledge of the future gives one great power. Yet here's the paradox: that prediction now forces us to follow the path that leads to whatever future we said would be. In effect, the prediction renders us powerless by removing all other choices. Knowing hasn't made us powerful at all. The opposite in fact. Putting all this as simply as possible, the Future Paradox is by nature self-fulfilling. *Beyond the Infinite Two Minutes* (2020), with a laptop screen that shows two minutes into the future, explores this concept in a farcical way because the group of friends who carry the laptop become dependent on their future selves to tell them what they should do next. In fact, they begin to feel obliged to fulfil what they already know will happen and become frightened to contradict it. Well, until one of them accidentally sneezes which causes all sorts of problems. Incidentally, in a Tristram Shandy sort of way, you can now, Dear Intra-diegetic Reader, if you so wish, skip to the end of this section and see if we really do conclude with the thoughts of Doc Brown. Oh, and perhaps check out the page that follows...

Another example of the Future Paradox can be found in a 1928 play called *The Jest of Hahalaba* by Edward John Moreton Drax Plunkett (better known as Lord Dunsany). In it a man reads his own obituary in tomorrow's newspaper and as a result drops dead with the shock, resulting in the very obituary he just read. Well, shock can act as a cause so he had no choice over it. *The Golden Man* (1954) is a Philip K. Dick short story concerning mutants with superhuman mental powers who are seen as a threat to normal humans. One such is the eponymous hero, the 'Golden Man', a beautiful young guy called Cris Johnson who is physically strong, with gold-coloured skin and who has the ability to know the future. Well, his gift specifically is to see all possible outcomes and permutations from any single action, similar to a chess player who can visualise every potential move and counter-move five steps ahead. The short story became the basis for *Next* (2007), starring Nicolas Cage. In the movie, Cris observes that the thing about the future is that when you think about it, it changes, and it changes because you have thought about it – and that's what changes everything. And don't we all to a degree consider future possibilities and scenarios? We weigh them up and try to work out which suits us best. And that future is altered, as it were, as we think about it.

The future paradox in terms of free will is there in one of the earliest of all human dramas, namely *Oedipus Rex* by Sophocles. Oedipus famously went to Delphi to ask about his parentage, but instead of answers he was given a prophecy that one day he will murder his father and have sex with his mother. Not surprisingly, he resolved to leave his home of Corinth and never return, only it's this very action that leads to him killing his father and sleeping with his mother. Oedipus thought he was escaping his destiny, but in fact he was bringing it about. And ideas around destiny have never really left the creative stage, for you can find their essence in many novels, movies and television series which ask the question: *Do we truly have agency over our future?*

There are many Time Tales where the focus is on changing the past, but if you can change what was, why shouldn't you be able to alter what will be? Surely nothing is bound to happen. This conceit is at the heart of the appeal Ebenezer Scrooge makes to the Ghost of Christmas Future when shown his own grave: 'Men's courses will foreshadow certain ends, to which, if persevered in, they must lead. But if the courses be departed from, the ends will change. Say it is thus with what you show me.'

Of course those who know the future, or a potential future, don't always wish to reveal what it is. Tiresias in *Oedipus Rex* wisely refuses to tell King Oedipus what he knows. Likewise Guinan in *Time's Arrow*, an episode of *Star Trek: The Next Generation*, written by Joe Menosky. She was alive when Picard and others time travelled back 500 years, but when Picard becomes stranded in the past she refuses to tell Riker what to do, arguing that 'If I told you what happened in the cavern, it might affect any decision you make now. I can't do that.' History has to fulfil itself in its own way. *Travelers* goes much further for there is Protocol 2H for the Historians which states that 'Updates are not to be discussed with anyone. Ever.' But there is a difference between *Oedipus Rex* and *Travelers* and that is the 'updates' that the historian Philip receives lead only to 'projections' of one or more alternate timelines, as opposed to pre-ordained destiny. Similarly the happenings of the future that Scrooge witnesses in *A Christmas Carol*. The future isn't necessarily as fixed, for our philosophy of life differs greatly from that of the ancient Greeks. At least for most people. Of course, being aware of what may come can give us hope as well as trepidation. But it does raise the very philosophical question: *If we knew how things would end on our journey, would we still make the same decisions? Would we choose a different route?* Contentment is the gift given to those people who are happy to keep to the path they now tread.

Forest in *Devs*, like many characters in Time Tales, is suffering from bereavement, in his case the death of his young daughter. It is the sort of loss where a man tortures himself with guilt in the belief that there was something that could have been done to prevent it. Forest seeks absolution and the machine, he hopes, will give it to him. You see, the DEVS computer is programmed to examine all possible permutations of history and so through it, Forest will discover if there was indeed anything more he could have done to save his daughter's life.

As the story progresses, Lily Chan becomes a bit of a fly in the ointment in the secret world of Forest and DEVS. Her inquiries and investigations into what is really going on there begin to cause Forest and his political and financial backers problems and eventually all is uncovered and revealed. In their final confrontation, however, Lily is offered through Forest and DEVS, an opportunity to view her own future, for it becomes apparent the computer can predict what is to come as well as retrospectively generate what has been. These simulated images are only seconds ahead of real time, but they are enough for her to know how the battle will end. Or rather, how this seemingly infallible computer predicts it will end.

The question becomes will the Future Paradox force her into making that predicted decision or will she choose another path? In other words, will the determinist computer be wrong and her actions show that she does after all have the free will to ultimately choose what she will?

Of course, seeing your future, even if only for a few seconds ahead, as is the case in *Devs*, could be a double-bluff. In the Future Paradox there is always the possibility that telling you that doing X and not Y will bring about Z may well be what makes you do Y, which is what actually was going to bring about Z all along. Oedipus certainly learnt that. Anyway, in the end, Lily does not do as the computer predicted. The chain of cause and effect is broken just as it was in the German television series *Dark*. You could say then that the concept of the Future Paradox is broken as well and the good news there is that free will is a possibility. The bad news, however, in this story at least, is that both Lily and Forest die. Well, sort of. You see, there's another twist, for Lily and Forest somehow become part of the computer simulation in a world as real as reality itself.

*Devs* is a tale with many layers. The series explores bereavement (both Forest and Lily are recovering from loss of loved ones), voyeurism (the time window is used to generate images of Marilyn Monroe and Arthur Miller having sex) and even God is there in the mix too because in Latin the letter V is an allograph and so DEVS is really DEUS, the Latin word for God. Ultimately though the focus of the series is the exploration of those perhaps unanswerable questions about the nature of pre-determination and its relationship with our belief in free will. And an imaginative and fascinating exploration it is too.

Knowing the future, or having a sense of it, is sometimes there in Time Tales that deal with crime. The film *Minority Report* (2002), again from a 1956 short story by Philip K. Dick – this time set in 2054 – features Delphic-like 'PreCogs', mentally-altered humans who are now able to predict the future to such an accurate degree that special cops are tasked with arresting killers before a crime is even committed. Philip K. Dick had personal doubts about the agency of free will and in his original story Chief John Anderton, the Precrime Program Commanding Officer, goes through with the murder. But then destiny encountered Hollywood in the form of Steve Spielberg and Tom Cruise. And when Tinsel Town got hold of the rights to the tale, the bleak outcome not surprisingly changed and John Anderton was able to change his future. So too, it might be added, did the physical appearance of the main character Chief Anderton, who was no longer ageing as in the original story, but instead, with Tom Cruise on board, time went unsurprisingly backwards, and a much younger and more vital John Anderton became the hero.

*Five Days to Midnight*, styled as *5ive Days to Midnight*, is a five-part mini-series written by Robert Zappia, David Aaron Cohen, Anthony Peckham and Cindy Myers which ran on the Sci Fi Channel in 2004. The series concerns J.T. Neumeyer, a physicist who discovers a briefcase containing post-dated documents and evidence suggesting he will die five days into the future. Another crime tale is *Time Lapse* (2014), a murder mystery of sorts, which deals with a strange machine that takes pictures of events 24 hours before they occur.

We all know the old line, 'It's difficult to make predictions, especially about the future.' But who said it first? And are we certain who that is? Was it Niels Bohr? Samuel Goldwyn? K. K. Steincke? Robert Storm Petersen? Yogi Berra? Even Mark Twain? It has been traced to a Danish parliamentary debate in 1937, but with no attribution specified. It seems it made its first appearance in English in a 1956 academic publication called the *Journal of the Royal Statistical Society* where it is said to be an aphoristic joke of Dutch origin. But again, no name is given. Ironically, even with the most famous gag about predicting the future, nothing is known for sure. And isn't that in a way its own paradox?

There was irony too in the making of *FlashForward* the American television series (2009–10) based on the 1999 novel by Robert J. Sawyer. The show revolved around a mysterious event which causes nearly everyone on the planet to simultaneously lose consciousness for two minutes on 6 October 2009 and in this blackout people see what seem to be visions of their lives six months hence. The final episode of season one of *Flashforward* showed visions of happenings 20 years into the future, only it was filmed before it was known the show would be cancelled and there wouldn't be a season two. Well in the future, perhaps even in 2030, the 20 year anniversary of the show, someone will re-commission *FlashForward* to see if those visionary predictions were correct.

But not everybody wants certainty as to the future. Isn't it cheating in a way? As Liz Cooper observes in the movie *Next*, isn't life supposed to be a surprise? But knowing something of the future isn't all bad news, after all, in *Next* it's Cris's ability to see into the future that saves Liz's life.

In book one of THE SWIDGERS book series, Aloysius has a parchment which seems to speak of William's future, but, like those Delphic oracles, what it says – 'the past will be your future and there you will willingly choose death' – is somewhat cryptic. Granny later tells William, 'Don't worry yourself too much over what Aloysius said, for words can have many meanings.' Indeed so. And isn't that the truth, in a way? We have a vague idea we may know what could happen, but exactly how it will work out, well, that's always a little misty, until the event itself occurs. And it's only when it does that those mysterious foretellings begin to make sense. Or at least we find a sense in them.

But perhaps the last word should be left to Doc Brown. In *Back to the Future* he says that nobody should know too much about their own destiny. Jennifer Parker brings back a note from the future, only now it's erased. And what that means, Doc Brown tells her, is that their future hasn't been written yet. In fact, no one's has. It's the old line, your future is whatever you make it. The future really should be a blank page.

# The Stories and Plots of Time Tales

*The best thing about the future is that it comes one day at a time.*
Abraham Lincoln

## Time Correction and Time Disruption Plots

WE ALL WANT to make the world a better place. It is part of human nature to put right life's past mistakes. And what Time Tales do is stretch that principle to include what are perceived as mistakes in history that have led to an unjust and less pleasant world. An example of this might be Stephen King's *11.22.63*, where a man travels through a time portal back to 1963 in the hope of preventing the assassination of J.F.K, thus fixing the world. However, as Stephen King has noted, it's not a wise thing to fool with Father Time. In the novel, saving J.F.K has unexpected consequences and things in the new timeline end up being far from perfect.

More personal stories usually have better outcomes. In *See You Yesterday*, two Brooklyn teenagers, C.J. Walker and Sebastian Thomas, build a makeshift time machine to go back in time and save C.J.'s brother from being wrongly killed by a police officer. The driving force here is injustice. *Erased*, known in Japan as *Boku Dake Ga Inai Machi*, is a Manga series written and illustrated by Kei Sanbe (a live-action film was released in 2016 and a television drama series followed) and features a character called Satoru Fujinuma, a young man who possesses an ability known as 'Revival' that can send him back in time to moments before a life-threatening incident occurs, thus enabling him to prevent it from happening.

The timeline disruption plot is the other side of the coin in that it normally features someone going back in time with the intention of creating an imbalance in the present to give them some sort of personal advantage. This scenario is one of the most popular in time fiction as it usually involves a counteraction to stop it. 'When the Omni's red, it means history's wrong. Our job is to get everything back on track.' Those were the words of Phineas Bogg in the opening narration of *Voyagers!* the 1980s television series that featured a hand-held device much like a pocket watch, called the Omni. Stories included preventing Abraham Lincoln from being kidnapped, saving Teddy Roosevelt from being shot by Billy the Kid, rescuing the Mona Lisa from the *Titanic* and assisting Thomas Edison in his discovery of electricity. All in a day's work for your average time traveller.

In a similar vein there are numerous 'stop-the-bomb' scenarios, where the time traveller is tasked with preventing some sort of terrible catastrophe or explosion (*Déjà Vu*, *Source Code*, plus several time storylines in the television series *Heroes*). A bizarre take on the bomb scenario is *Tomorrow I'll Wake Up and Scald Myself with Tea* (written by Josef Nesvadba). Needless to say the plot is as strange as its title and involves death by a bread roll and a portable hydrogen bomb taken back in time to Hitler's Germany. It's a brilliant and very funny movie. One for the Time Tale connoisseurs.

Averting catastrophes is the theme of the television series *Seven Days* (1998–2001 written by Christopher and Zachary Crowe). The premise here is that a secret branch of the US National Security Agency (NSA) has developed a time travelling device based upon alien technology found at Roswell that is capable of sending 'one human being back in time seven days'.

A more up-to-date version of this type of Time Tale is *Timeless* (created by Eric Kripke and Shawn Ryan), where a Time Task Force is put together in order to stop interventions in history from a renegade time traveller. The mission team of agents seek out Garcia Flynn, a rogue NSA operative who seems to be set on a crazy course of revenge. However, as the series goes on, he and the team of agents work together to stop the true threat to American life which is revealed to be a secret organisation called Rissenhouse. It's never absolutely clear what the ultimate goal of Rissenhouse is. However, you can assume from its members – Henry Ford, J.P. Morgan, Joseph McCarthy – and those people Rissenhouse wants to kill – Connor Mason, J.F.K and Harriet Tubman – that its long-term aims aren't civil rights. *Timeless* is an adventure yarn with lots of action, good jokes and great characters, but the underlying theme is America under threat from the far right. It probably wasn't Donald Trump's favourite show. But *Timeless* is an example of what a Time Tale, even of the adventure yarn variety, is capable of when it has a social conscience.

## 'The Butterfly Effect' and Accidental Interference

A tenet of chaos theory is that the outcome of a series of consequences is always dependant on its starting point, as in the poetic observation *'the flap of a butterfly's wings in the jungle can cause a tornado in Kansas'*. Or, as Jonas says in *Dark* 'We change a grain of sand, and with that, the whole world.'

The concept is thought to have originated with an American meteorologist called Edward Lorenz who in the 1960s said that one flap of a seagull's wing would be enough to alter the course of the weather elsewhere. However, the principle itself can be found in Ray Bradbury's short story *A Sound of Thunder* (1952) where the catalyst for change is a butterfly. In 2055, time travel has been commercialised and there is a company called Time Safari Incorporated that offers excursions into the past. On a trip to the late Cretaceous period 66 million years ago, all one innocent time traveller did was accidentally tread on a butterfly, but even this small seemingly insignificant single action had consequences and these led to a different present when the traveller returned to his own time. And it's called *A Sound of Thunder* because that is what is heard at the end of the tale, the implication being that he is now unable to live with himself and his clumsy foolishness and so takes his own life. The story is parodied in the *Time and Punishment* section of *The Simpsons* episode *Treehouse of Horror V,* where Homer accidentally turns his broken toaster into a time machine, travels to prehistoric times and swats a mosquito, resulting in Ned now ruling the world. *The Sound of Thunder* became *A Sound of Thunder* (1989) as a story in *The Ray Bradbury Theater* TV series 1985–1992 on TV-14. Incidentally, the movie *The Butterfly Effect* (2004) explores a similar idea, but expands on it. In this story, a traumatised man is able to re-do certain parts of his past experiences, only when he does, it results in vastly different alternate futures. And these are often worse than his present situation. A time traveller in *Midnight at the Pera Palace* (Turkey 2022) put it well when he compared altering events in the past as 'playing Russian Roulette'.

The principle of the seemingly inconsequential act causing chaos can be found in *The Rift in Time* storyline of *The Tomorrow People* (Roger Price). John warns his fellow time travellers in an ancient Roman tavern that even swatting a tiny fly could have unforeseen consequences. If that fly had not been hit, explains John, it might well have gone on to land on a Roman soldier's meal, giving him food poisoning which in turn would have then prevented him from fighting in battle. But with the fly now dead because a time traveller had killed it, that soldier would, in the newly created timeline, be well enough to fight and who knows who he would now kill and whose untimely death would drastically alter the future.

Accidental interference can come in many forms and one of the most curious can be found in Philip K. Dick's *The Variable Man* (1953), where 'histo-research' inadvertently scoops up someone from the past. This person though from the distant past turns out to be an expert mechanic and as a result of his abilities manages to alter the future world he has found himself in.

And there's a particular type of accidental interference plot where the protagonist has to take the place of a pivotal figure in history who is accidentally killed in order to protect and restore the original timeline. In fact, the entire series of *Midnight at the Pera Palace* is based on this premise. But it's a popular story trope in other time travel stories, for example, in *Past Tense* (1995), an episode from *Star Trek: Deep Space Nine*, written by Ira Steven Behr and Robert Hewitt Wolfe, with René Echevarri, a problem with the transporter beam sends Lieutenant Dax, Doctor Bashir and Commander Sisko 300 years back into Earth's past. Their presence in 2024 results in the untimely death of Gabriel Bell, one of the heroes of a rebellion that later altered Earth's history, and because of this intervention Sisko decides to take on the identity of Bell and becomes a key player in hostage negotiations with the aim of restoring the timeline. Another and very bizarre replacement tale can be found in *Once and Future King*, a 1986 episode of *The Twilight Zone* (adapted by *Game of Thrones* creator George R.R. Martin from a story by Bryce Maritano), where an Elvis Presley impersonator travels back to 1954 and finds himself in a brawl with the real Elvis, who as a result is impaled on a broken guitar and dies. Gary, the impersonator, then takes it upon himself to become Elvis and does so for the next 20 years. Great work if you can get it! A variation, incidentally, of the substitution/replacement story trope can also be found in the 2016 *Tiempo de leyenda* (*Time of Legend*) episode (written by Angela Aranda Lamas, Javier and Pablo Olivaros) of *The Ministry of Time* (2015–2020) involving El Cid.

In *Terminator II: Judgment Day* (1991) it is the damaged CPU and right arm of the original Terminator that is found and becomes the basis for Cyberdyne's work on Artificial Intelligence that is the 'butterfly wing' that will eventually create Skynet. Thus the presence of that arm from the future creates (or at the very least, hugely accelerates) the scientific research which will result in the downfall of man.

It's a frightening thought however that every action no matter how small has the capacity to alter everything. Ultimately we couldn't live our lives if, before we went about everything we did, we considered the potential long-term consequences. But aren't we flattering ourselves here? Most of the actions we take hardly change a darn thing but perhaps the thought that they do is why we like Time Tales so much. They give us an inflated sense of the importance of what we do or didn't do, or won't do, when the truth of life is that little of what we actually do amounts to a hill of beans. Ah, but we don't want to believe that, do we?

## How Do You Get to Know What You Can't Possibly Know?

Of course, writers have to be creative in coming up with ways by which protagonists can know the result of their interventions, accidental or otherwise. If you intentionally alter a past event, how is it that you can be certain of the consequences before they have even taken place? In fact, part of the appeal of Time Tales is how this puzzle is dealt with. In *Travelers*, the historian Philip gets 'update' downloads of the ever-changing future via both his computer, and bizarrely, his eyes and brain. But these updates are only for him, for *Protocol 2H* tells him he must never reveal the contents of these updates to his team, no matter what the circumstances. Also of course in *Travelers*, there is the fact that the most recent arrivals from the future can tell the team what changes the mission has already achieved.

In *Quantum Leap* (1989–1993 – created by Donald P. Bellisario), Sam Beckett has help from the project's supercomputer, Ziggy (by way of a hologram, Al) and this to some degree is able to tell him the historical consequences of his actions. On the other hand, Marty in *Back to the Future* partially gets round the whole conundrum of possible futures by having a photograph in his pocket of him with his family in the future. It's at those points in the story when Marty is seemingly unable to complete his task that people in that picture begin to fade one by one. This idea of fading images is also used in *Timeless* in an episode with J.F.K where a coin briefly shows the face of Richard Nixon.

The historian in *Timeless*, Lucy Preston, can't actually say for sure what will happen but her knowledge at least offers a guide to the potential consequences of the team's action. But if historians, photographs and supercomputers are not available then there's always the possibility of a trip to the local library and their archive might offer some help.

## Time Tourism

'Give our love to the dinosaurs' is a phrase repeated in *Tomorrow I Shall Wake Up and Scald Myself With Tea,* a comedy movie featuring a plot involving the misuse of time tourism. And the exploitation of such possible adventures is often a key part of the time tourist plot, for someone is always breaking the rules of non-interference that are often so important in such tales. The time tourism plot can be seen as a variation of the 'Accidental Interference' plot, as in *A Sound of Thunder* where it's the clumsy stepping on a butterfly that creates an alternative future on the traveller's return. However, it is not always accidental as in *Tomorrow I Shall Wake Up and Scald Myself With Tea* where a gang of right-wingers secretly plan to use the time tourism industry to achieve their aim of giving Hitler a hydrogen bomb to help him win the War.

A variation on the time tourist scenario can be found in *Timescape* (1992 released on video as *Grand Tour: Disaster in Time*). Ben Wilson discovers that the guests in his hotel are actually time tourists who are visiting scenes of catastrophic disasters. He uses one of their 'time passports' to travel back in time to save many people in the town from the disaster, a gas explosion, thereby changing his future and the time travellers' past.

## Endangered Futures

The challenge of our time is climate change, and so it shouldn't come as any surprise that the environment and green issues feature very strongly in contemporary Time Tales. A variation on the correction plot then is 'Endangered Futures', the main difference being that with this scenario, our present day is the time traveller's past.

A primary example is the popular televisions series *Travelers*. The concept here is that the world of the future is so threatened by our actions in the current day that a team from the future, in fact many teams, must be sent back to our time to make the necessary corrections to save themselves. What makes this series a little different is that it's a disembodied consciousness that is sent to our world and it is this consciousness which then takes over a host's body at the moment of their historical death. Think *Invasion of the Body Snatchers* meets *The A-Team* with a strong environmental message thrown in.

In *Travelers* there is much talk of wars, famine and disease in the future, but clearly all is not well politically either, for in that future, a 'Faction' has developed and our era has become the battle ground. As the Faction battles with The Director, the AI machine which comes up with the various missions, numerous assassins are sent back in time to do their worst, often giving the series a Terminator vibe. This was particularly the case in one episode where a young girl called Anna Hamilton, an important future American president (the 53rd President to be precise), needs to be protected at all costs.

In *The Terminator* itself, of course, a Bad-Guy Android is sent from the future to kill Sarah Connor, whose as-yet unborn son is the leader of the rebellion against the androids. In the sequel, *Terminator II: Judgment Day*, a Good-Guy Android is also sent back in time to impede or disrupt any further plans to kill Sarah Connor or her now young son John. And both movies are great action yarns. *Returner* (2002) incidentally is a Japanese science fiction film that follows a similar scenario in that aliens, Dagga, have conquered Earth and so someone is sent back in time to kill the first alien scout and in the cult science fiction movie *A.P.E.X.* (1994) the threat to the future is people carrying a deadly virus.

*Sijipeuseu: The Myth (Sisyphus)* is essentially an endangered future story plot very similar to *The Terminator*. In fact, the writers make a direct reference to *The Terminator* storyline in the series. Gang Seo-hae is sent back in time and her task is to make sure that Han Tae-sul, a Mark Zuckerberg techno-genius kind of guy, does not create the code that results in the building of an 'uploader' time machine that will, in the endangered future, lead to nuclear war and a deadly apocalypse.

*The Lazarus Project* (2022), written by Joe Barton, is a television series where time travellers prevent extinction level disasters by means of a time loop. The movie *Millennium* (1989) offers a twist on the endangered future concept for it involves time travellers from years hence, where the human race has become sterile, abducting aircraft passengers who, as in *Travelers*, would have died anyway and taking them to that future to repopulate the world.

There are also Time Tales that are set in a dystopian or endangered future. An example of this is *La Jetée*, set in the aftermath of World War III in a post-apocalyptic Paris and its remake *12 Monkeys*. Others include *Diverge* and *2067*, plus the Indie 2011 psychological thriller *Sound of my Voice*, and of course *Star Trek IV: The Voyage Home*. In this popular '80s movie, Kirk's Earth of the future is in grave danger from an alien probe that seeks to make contact with the now-extinct humpback whale. The only solution is to go back in time to our 1986, collect a whale – no easy task as it turns out – and then take said whale back to the future in time in order to reply to the probe before it destroys the entire planet. Such stories as *La Jetée* or *Star Trek* may actually be set in the future but as with most Time Tales they are really about the concerns of our present day, be it war and conflict, or the environment.

The German television series *Dark* is a bleak and tragic fable. Its focus is not really the environment but it is partially set in the year 1986, the time of the nuclear accident at Chernobyl. In both of *Dark*'s complex time loop scenarios, there is an apocalyptic accident at the nuclear power station in the fictional Winden and much of *Dark* is set in a post-apocalyptic future. Grim indeed.

There are certainly many zeitgeist Time Tales around at the moment centring on the concept of changing the past to help the future. And they're not all centred on environmental issues. In fact there are people jokingly offering the suggestion that the political world we live in is so messed up it can only be explained by time travel. Someone, they say, must be constantly going back to the year 2016 and trying to fix the world, only each time they do they alter things in such a way that makes everything worse. Well, that's one explanation. And given the bizarre state of the world politics at this moment in 2023, perhaps not that far-fetched. Dear Reader of The Future, we hope, if you bought this book in a charity shop in 2033, you are now living in a better world. Are you shaking your head at our stupidity in believing that things couldn't get worse? Or smiling indulgently because, well, after those aliens landed on Christmas Day in 2029, the world became one of peace and goodwill among men and Slozzerborgs.

## Stranded in the Wrong Time

In *Doctor Who*, the Doctor has found himself left high and dry in the wrong time on many an occasion. In fact, you could argue that, with the TARDIS disabled by the Time Lords, much of the Third Doctor era with Jon Pertwee, 'John Smith' is essentially stranded in the 20th century. The Weeping Angels famously stranded the Tenth Doctor (David Tennant) in 1969 in *Blink*, a plot which was essentially reworked as *Village of Angels* with the Thirteenth Doctor (Jodie Whittaker).

*Star Trek* of course has explored the stranded theme many, many times, notably in *The City of the Edge of Forever* and the movie *Star Trek IV: The Voyage Home*. And in the *Star Trek* reboot movie, Spock finds himself locked into the new timeline. *Deep Space Nine* (1993–99) used the stranded plot in *Little Green Men*, *Trials and Tribble-ations*, and *Past Tense*. The latter episode is set in 2024, and with the prescience of many a science fiction drama, *Past Tense* does quite accurately speak of our socially divided society, with people without jobs or places to live.

But it's not just folk with spacecrafts and time machines that get stranded in the wrong era. *Outlaws* (1986–87) was a television series about five cowboys from the 1880s who, as a result of a freak lightning strike, found themselves in 1986. With no way to get back home, the men use their skills to start a detective agency in order to make a living. Other Time Tales on the theme of being stranded include *The Adam Project, Timeless, Dark, Phil of the Future, Demolition Man, Futurama, Adam Adament Lives!* and *Catweazle*.

## Parallel Worlds

An example of a parallel world would be *Doppelgänger*, the 1969 British science fiction film written by Gerry and Sylvia Anderson and Donald James (also known as *Journey to the Far Side of the Sun*). In this film, astronauts return to a sort of 'back-to-front' Earth and eventually realise they are on a near literal mirror-image version of our planet, rather than the one they journeyed from. In the parallel world scenario, the other world or universe is independent of our world, but always in parallel time with it.

But what about *It's a Wonderful Life*? Is that a parallel world movie? Well, not really because Pottersville has only just come into existence as a result of the angel Clarence asking his superiors to create a world without George Bailey so George can see the importance of his life. It might be better to say that Bedford Falls and Pottersville are alternate worlds in that Bedford Falls is the world where George Bailey is alive and Pottersville is the world where he was never born. Besides, in the end, Pottersville ceases to exist, for George, in the redemptive nature of the story, is essentially 'reborn' when he chooses life over death. The clue after all is in the title of the movie: *It's a Wonderful Life*.

## Schrödinger's Cat and the Mess it Made

Imagine a sperm fertilising an egg. In the usual scenario, once the egg is fertilised, the sperm closes the egg off from all its rivals, which then simply die. But suppose those sperm don't die. Suppose each creates their own individual embryo. There'd be millions of them. It would mean Dr Evil Mini-Me's from *Austin Powers* to the power of infinity. A frightening thought, except of course, if each Mini-Me were given their own private little universe.

In a way, the scientific justification for the multiverse or Many Worlds Interpretation (MWI) is not that far removed from this concept. Except we are not in the realm of biology but rather quantum mechanics as pioneered by Hugh Everett III (1930–1982). Hugh Everett III (and how appropriate that there were at least two others in the universe with that name) famously rejected what was known as the Schrödinger equation.

The German physicist Erwin Schrödinger basically said that in quantum theory until a particle is measured or observed it exists in all the possible states it could be in. Put another way, all potential possibilities are possible (what mathematically would be called a 'non-zero possibility') until a consciousness decides or observes which one of these possible possibles will be more than just possible, but will actually be. And when this happens, that future possible has a probability of 1, whereas all the other possibles not observed now have a probability of 0 (that is, they cannot be). This is commonly referred to as the collapse of the wave function.

Schrödinger's Cat is the name of the thought experiment that explored this nature of existing and not existing in quantum physics (Schrödinger incidentally did have a cat in the 1930s, which he called Milton, so let's go with that name as we look at the thought experiment itself). You put pussy cat Milton into a box with a radioactive substance that has a fifty-fifty chance of killing said moggie. You then close the lid. Until the box is opened, Milton could be said to be both alive and dead.

It exists and it does not exist until we can be sure either way. Smart Alecks have pointed out that cats meow a lot, and what about Animal Liberation and the RSPCA? I mean, you can't go around putting cats in radioactive boxes just because you want to prove a point that's about not being able to prove a point. However, that is the point because this thought experiment, from Schrödinger's perspective, was simply to show how weird quantum physics can be. And, one supposes, quantum physicists for coming up with such ideas. Einstein thought that quantum physics involved a lot of what he called 'spooky action'. Yes, and clearly spooky people too.

Anyway, in 1957, in his Princeton doctoral dissertation, Hugh Everett III argued against Schrödinger and his pussy cat Milton and thus opened a whole can of worms. Indeed entire multiverses of cans of worms. Hugh Everett basically conjectured that the wave function does not collapse at all, but rather 'splits' at every moment a choice or decision is made. To turn a well-known remark upside down, *Time allows not only everything to happen all at once but there are multiple every wheres and every whens to do it in.*

Oddly enough, and well before the era of quantum physics, this was an issue that worried Descartes (1596–1650) in his *Meditations*, but he solved the problem by coming up with the idea that God perhaps constantly recreated our world moment by moment, fixing it, as it were, to be the right and only world. Anyway, the long and short of all this is that according to Everett there are out there, somewhere and whenever, a multitude of physical realities beyond our imagining. And this idea of the Multiverse Universe (or Universes) became known as the Many Worlds Interpretation (MWI) of quantum mechanics. Knowing that in this universe there are at least 140 billion galaxies is enough to fry your brain, but multiverses on top of that? Well, that's your brain sautéed with every known pepper and chilli stirred by Uncle Tom Cobley and all.

A brief word on the possible evidence for multiverses. The term Mandela Effect came about when people began to claim they had witnessed the death of Nelson Mandela in the 1980s, when in reality he died in 2013. But many others followed saying exactly the same thing. They too had seen on television Mandela's funeral and even the speech given by his wife, years before he really died. And the conclusion that some people came to was that what these people were actually really seeing were glimpses into a parallel world where Mandela died earlier than he did in ours. The explanation other people came up with for what then became known as the 'Mandela Effect' was that it was a result of false memory syndrome or confabulation. There was, as well, the suggestion that it was all part of a vast world power conspiracy. Quietly in the background you could also hear the very politically incorrect observation that these people were simply bonkers. Mad or multiverse? Confabulation or conspiracy? The choice is yours.

## Time Tales and Their Multiple Worlds

In multiple world Time Tales, two or three, or sometimes an infinite number of worlds are created, usually as a result of different choices made somewhere along a timeline that then splits and leads to alternative consequences and so alternate worlds. This can be seen in *If I Hadn't Met You, (Si no t'hagués conegut)*, the ten-part 2018 Catalan television series written by Sergi Belbel. In some of these worlds, time can move faster or more slowly than ours, which, of course, prevents them from being in parallel. It also explains why Eduard does not recognise that the elderly Dr Everest (a name not too far removed from that of Everett the multiverse theorist) is really his wife from another timeline.

The principle of *If I Hadn't Met You* can be found in Dr Everest's supposition that the universe doesn't have just one story, it has all the stories that are and can be possible. If you want to get theological here then this might be an appropriate moment to bring in good old Gottfried Wilhelm Leibniz (1646–1716) and his contention that we live in 'the best of all possible worlds.' Leibniz was no slouch philosopher and as a natural scientist, his mathematical theories rival Newton's. But what about his logic? The Leibnizian argument basically goes like this: because God is all knowing, he knew which possible world was the best and, being pure goodness, in creating our existing world, God created what has to be the best of all possible worlds. I mean, come on, why would God create anything less than such a thing?

But suppose the number of worlds God created is in fact infinite, there could then be no single world that is best. For any given good world, there will always be another world that is better in some ways and almost certainly worse in others. It's possible you might suppose to aggregate goodness, but that ends up turning God (and morality) into little more than an adding machine. Besides, life is full of greys and would-be and could-bes make those greys even more complicated. Anyway, Leibniz digression over and back to those imperfect worlds of *If I Hadn't Met You*.

Eduard suffers a terrible tragedy when his wife and children are killed in a car crash. His trauma is made worse because he believes he is, at least in part, responsible. When Dr Everest offers the chance to go to different universes, Eduard takes the opportunity in the hope of finding a better one. Only it doesn't work out like that. Yes, coincidence certainly conspires to bring Eduard and his wife Elisa together through music and the movies, but equally it is car accidents in the different universes that bring tragedy. There simply is no best possible world.

In *Donnie Darko* (2001), a jet engine from a parallel world crashes into Donnie Darko's bedroom at the stroke of midnight. Luckily, Donnie is far away, watching over the town from a hilltop. The arrival of the jet engine sets off a metaphorical ticking clock counting down the next 28 days. After the arrival of the unexplained jet engine falling out of the sky, nothing in this world seems to go right for people. A very negative vibe has seemingly entered into this world from somewhere. Whatever this vibe is it has given Donnie himself some sort of superpower which allows him to put an axe in a metal statue that stands outside of his school and the strength to cause the school to flood. A strange rabbit then begins to appear, which is ultimately revealed to be a character called Frank in a costume. It is as if this rabbit has somehow entered Donnie's world from a parallel world, just like the negative vibe. And this scenario is what the writer and director Richard Kelly has suggested is going on, though who or what is doing all this is never quite clear. The Universe? God? The Rabbit? The ghost of Charles Lutwidge Dodgson? Anyway, Donnie is ultimately being manipulated like a puppet where the ultimate aim is to realign the universe, re-set time and separate the two universes. This will be done when the ticking clock of the 28 days runs out. And when that happens, Donnie is in his bedroom giggling. This time, however, the falling jet engine kills him. It is then that time is re-set to where it was and the rip in space-time through which the 'first' jet engine fell, is healed and closed. Does Donnie know his death or self-sacrifice will lead to all this happening? Hard to say, so perhaps better not ask. Just enjoy this strange and enigmatic cult Time Tale for the classic it is.

The multiverse universe concept is a major feature of *Avengers: Endgame*, where there is only one version of the world that can save them and that demands the self-sacrifice of Iron Man. The moral is: Yes, you can have what you want, but you'll have to pay for it. *Spider-man: Far From Home* (2019) has a more playful relationship with the multiverse concept. In fact, in this movie it's a bit of a red herring and used primarily to put the young hero off the truth about the duplicitous 'Mysterio'.

Over in the DC movie universe, *The Flash* (2023) features the Barry Allen version of The Flash travelling back in time to prevent his mother being slain and his innocent father being jailed for her murder. However, the chain of events that his meddling brings forth endangers the whole DC multiverse as the different realities collide with devastating effect.

The nexus of time and space and the multiverses they create in *Dark* are about as complicated as it gets. As one of the many Marthas says, 'The question isn't what time, the question is what world?' In fact there are three worlds in *Dark* but two are full of pain and misery, and worse, these worlds are trapped in eternal time loops. The final episode reveals that only a self-sacrifice can bring about a world without suffering, only for Adam and Eva, it's not just death that they must accept, but the fact that they must never even have existed.

Ultimately the creation of the two worlds in *Dark* boils down to the attempt of Tannhaus, The Watchmaker, to alter history by building a time machine to save his family from a car crash. It is established that when the time machine was first switched on, time stopped and cause and effect was suspended and in that moment the world divided into two timelines and two time loops bringing eternal pain and misery to the people of Winden. There are many moral messages to be found in *Dark* and in this instance it seems to be: Don't try and alter the past for in doing so there will be unforeseen consequences and these could well be tragic and even apocalyptic in their actuality. *And there endeth the Lesson.*

A more individual and personal multiverse scenario can be found in the movie *Mr Nobody* (2009), written and directed by Jaco Van Dormael, which tells the story of a 118-year-old man who is now the last mortal on Earth as everyone else has now achieved quasi-immortality. Nemo, with his memory fading, thinks of the three main loves of his life, of the divorce of his parents and later the hardships he endured. Three critical junctions in his life are identified and they are at the ages of 9, 15 and 34. Alternative life paths branching out from each of these crossroads are examined and as a result Nemo Nobody 'remembers', as it were, different possible futures for himself. As has been said on many occasions before and will be again, the curse of time is the contemplation of what never was but might have been. Happy the man perhaps who fully understands The Prayer of Serenity: 'God, grant me the serenity to accept the things I cannot change, the courage to change the things I can, and the wisdom to know the difference.'

## Time Splits and Duel Existence in the Same World

In *The Man Who Haunted Himself* (1970, written by Basil Dearden, Michael Relph and Bryan Forbes and based on a book by Anthony Armstrong), Harold Pelham (Roger Moore) as he is driving along the road suddenly appears possessed and this results in a serious car accident. Later, on the operating table at the hospital, for a moment there appear to be two heartbeats on the monitor. When Harold recovers and goes about his life as before, people begin to claim they have seen him in places he has never been. More importantly, this other self is making decisions he, Harold, would never ever make.

Identical twins are common in human life, but usually they are very similar both in appearance and nature. But suppose there was an exact version of yourself in looks, but who was completely different in temperament and disposition? In the classic *Star Trek* episode *The Enemy Within*, the transporter malfunctions – as it so often does – and Kirk is split into two antithetical people, and in *Mirror, Mirror*, the transporter malfunctions yet again and sends Kirk and his party to a cutthroat parallel universe where promotion is achieved through assassination. Many stories in the original *Star Trek* series were essentially moral fables, and with *The Enemy Within* and *Mirror, Mirror*, the theme is what you may call the darker side of human life. Its 'Shadow', to borrow the Jungian concept.

In the Korean time travel series *Alice*, the Kuiper Institute Director, Seok Oh-won, explains to Park Jin-gyeom that there isn't just one world, for there are countless dimensions and with time travel death will become meaningless and so he'll get to see his mother again. But Park Jin-gyeom replies that though there might be countless versions 'I only have one mother. Also, the fact that you killed my mother will never change.' The plot later reveals that the Kuiper Institute Director did not kill Jin-gyeom's mother (lots of people did, but not him), yet the son's point is still well made. No matter which dimension you are in, you could only ever have had one mother.

The rule in *Alice* is that as dimensions connect, the doppelgangers in them more closely sense each other's thoughts. The Alice Time Agent Yoo Min-hyuk asks Yoon Tae-yi, the genius physicist, if he's been experiencing déjà vu since encountering Jin-gyeom's mother because when doppelgangers from two time dimensions meet their memories and emotions mix. This turns out to be bad news for Park Jin-gyeom for in one particular dimension his counterpart is a psychopathic killer. In fact, Park Jin-gyeom in different dimensions is variably detective, architect and matricidal killer. That said, there is a dimension where the mother (Yoon Tae-yi/Park Sun-young) kills her other self. The last act of *Hamlet* has nothing on *Alice*.

The Director Seok Oh-won in one dimension is the man trying to keep time travelling in operation, and in another, where he is killed, he is trying to prevent time travel. 'Who are you?' becomes 'Which are you?' and that for the viewer can lead to confusion as the plot does occasionally get lost in a labyrinth of its own complexity.

There are several scenes in *If I Hadn't Met You, (Si no t'hagués conegut)*, when the two Eduards from different universes meet. The most moving encounter is where they share their grief, one for the loss of both his parents, the other for the death of his wife and children. What unites these different Eduards is the fact that the tragedies in each universe came as a result of car accidents, and each Eduard blames himself for the deaths of his loved ones.

*Sisyphus*, the Korean time adventure series, uses the idea of computer coding as a means to time travel. This is achieved by an 'uploader' and a 'downloader', as it were, which allow data to be transferred across time. But what happens if the person who came from the future was yourself with identical data? Well, it is possible for two sets of data to co-exist in the same time world, but, as physical bodies get into close proximity, memories become mixed up – there's a similar time rule in *Alice* – yet *Sisyphus* goes even further, for, as put by one of the bandit brokers, 'one of you goes *kapow* and is gone'. Actually, we only get to see that happen with physical objects in a scene where two identical family lockets from different time worlds are brought together. As the computer coder Han Tae-sul says, holding two lockets side by side, it's like copying a file to another drive when it's impossible for the original data and copy data to exist in the same place. In time travel there is a time designation and if data, that is objects, ever overlap in the same time phase then the two become one. And, as if by magic, the two lockets he holds merge into one.

There are numerous *Doctor Who* episodes with multiple Doctors, but according to the Fugitive Doctor (Ruth Clayton) in *Fugitive of Judoon* (2020), if her TARDIS were to find itself too close to the Thirteenth Doctor's TARDIS there could be 'a temporal feedback loop'. In *Back to the Future II* (1989), the Doc warns Marty not to communicate with his other self. This, he argues, could have devastating effects on the time continuum, creating a time paradox that ultimately would destroy the very fabric of the universe.

Dumbledore has fewer concerns in *Harry Potter and the Prisoner of Azkaban* (2004) and even prompts Hermione to use her Time-Turner to go back in time and save Buckbeak. That said, she, Ron and Harry are cautious not to bump into their other selves. In *Frequently Asked Questions About Time Travel*, there is a scene where the three lads in the story end up in the distant future. It turns out that in this future they are thought of and celebrated as 'heroes', so much so that they attend a tribute party to themselves where all the guests are dressed up in costume, as at sci-fi conventions, as the legendary time travellers. It's a neat gag about meeting yourself in the future as well as the world of the fandom convention. Any way you look at it, meeting yourself or avoiding yourself is a useful dramatic device in any Time Tale, whether it's there to increase the jeopardy or enhance the comedy.

There's a scene in *The Time Traveler's Wife* where two adolescent Henrys are found together under the bedsheet and in *Austin Powers: The Spy Who Shagged Me* (1999), the two

Austin Powers, Austin and Austin-ten-minutes-from-now via the time machine want to take things even further ('What's the policy on *ménage à trois?*'). But there is no love lost between Old Joe and Young Joe in *Looper* for they are essentially antagonist and protagonist. In *Star Trek* (2009), the two Spocks, who you would have thought would know about such things as double identities and the time continuum, have no qualms at all about meeting. The final scene between the actor Zachary Quinto and Leonard Nimoy isn't strictly necessary to the plot, it is part of the story's resolution rather than its climax, but nevertheless, it is a touching handing-on-the-baton moment that is much loved by fans.

Of course, one simple solution to the doppelganger problem is murder. Reichenbach is a time tourist in Robert Silverberg's short story *The Far Side of the Bell-shaped Curve* (1982) who breaks the rules of time travel by re-entering a time-span where he is already present. His aim is the removal of a sexual rival (a theme in several of Silverberg's tales) but the twist is they are in the era of Robespierre and the 'other' Reichenbach accuses the murderous Reichenbach of being an aristocrat, which would of course result in an immediate and almost certain death in revolutionary France.

The doppelganger problem can be complicated enough, but what if the time travelling doppelganger is a twin? *Tomorrow I Shall Wake Up and Scald Myself With Tea* (which surely wins first prize in The Weirdest Title for a Time Tale competition) is a *Comedy of Errors* type farce centring on twin brothers, one good, one bad. The plot is simple enough, a group of fascists in the present want to change history so that the Germans win the Second World War, so they travel back in time to give Hitler a hydrogen bomb. And the pilot who is meant to help them is the bad twin, only he dies choking on a bread roll and the good twin accidentally takes his place in charge of the time machine. The whole plan goes pear-shaped and the film becomes an insane farce. But the plotting has the problem of getting rid of the double existence of the gang members when they return to their original time. And as this movie isn't just a farce but a black comedy, the deaths include trampolining off the top of a high building and melting away in a bath as the result of the accidental spillage of dissolving washing up liquid. Yes, it's that sort of movie. As for the hero, the good twin, well he takes the place of his brother the bad twin. And, as *Tomorrow I Shall Wake Up and Scald Myself With Tea* is also a romantic comedy, each end up with the girl they love.

## Multiple Existences Across Time and Living Another's Life

*The Inner Light* (1992), written by Morgan Gendel, is one of the most popular and admired episodes in *Star Trek: The Next Generation*. It is a poignant tale where Captain Jean-Luc Picard, after an energy beam probe hits him, wakes up to find himself on Kataan, with a wife, Eline, who tells Picard that he is Kamin, an iron weaver recovering from a fever. Picard tells her of his life on the Enterprise, but Eline tries to convince him that his memories are only dreams. Of course it is Kamin's memories that are the dream and the Enterprise that is real, but when he awakes, Picard comes to understand that the purpose of the probe was to give life to the memory of Kamin's race, long after the death of their civilisation over a thousand years ago from the radiation from the planet's sun. And when the probe is brought on board for analysis, it is found to contain Kamin's flute, which Picard mastered during his 40 years as Kamin.

Is *The Inner Light* a time travel tale? Well, yes and no. It's not a Time Tale with a machine with levers or a portal – Picard after all never moves from the floor of the bridge and his time under the influence of the beam is no more than 25 minutes – and yet in another way it's a Time Tale as old as human life itself, for its theme is memory and the need for remembrance to give life purpose. And since it is very personal and moving, let's call it warm glow time travel.

Strictly speaking reincarnation or body take-over stories are not time travel tales, yet there is something about the past life memories explored in *On a Clear Day You Can See Forever* (1970) that makes it at least worth mentioning. It tells the story of Daisy, played by Barbra Streisand, who is a kooky five-pack-a-day chain smoker who goes to psychiatrist Marc Chabot, played by Yves Montand, for help to kick her smoking habit, only when she does, she becomes unintentionally hypnotised. During this period, it is discovered that Daisy is in fact the reincarnation of Lady Melinda Winifred Waine Tentrees – what a name and what a Lady – a seductive 19th century coquette who was born the illegitimate daughter of a kitchen maid. These hypnotic sessions continue, and as they do Chabot begins to fall in love with 'Lady Melinda', Daisy's exotic former self, whereas the present-day Daisy begins to fall for Chabot. When Daisy accidentally hears a tape recording of one of her sessions and discovers that Chabot's interest lies only in Lady Melinda, she runs away.

But all is not lost. The two have one final meeting where Daisy mentions 14 additional lives, including a future life as 'Laura' and her marriage to the therapist in the year 2038. It's a 'girl-meets-boy, girl-loses-boy-to-past-life-girl, girl-gets-boy-when-she's-a-future-girl' sort of plot. The title song with lyrics by Alan J. Lerner explores an idea that can be found in spiritual philosophy and that is that it is possible to feel a connection across time and space by means of a bond with the cosmos itself. If you don't know the song, it's worth a listen. You'll certainly hear it well enough with Barbra belting it out.

In *Requiem for Methuselah*, written by Jerome Bixby, an episode from the original *Star Trek* series, Kirk and his party encounter a man who calls himself Flint and claims he was born in 3834BC, and, after falling in battle, discovered he could not die. Flint says he has lived many 'lifetimes' across time, using hundreds of aliases, including Methuselah, Solomon, Alexander, Merlin, Leonardo, and Brahms. Yet all those he loved died and so he built 'Rayna', a humanoid robot, to be his immortal mate, but

Rayna needed to learn how to love and so he used and manipulated Kirk to achieve this. This is all a bit of a plot contrivance but the themes here are similar to Shakespeare's *The Tempest*, with Prospero, the old magician, tiring of life alone with his young daughter Miranda. *Requiem for Methuselah*, as the title suggests, is a reflective fable on mortality and Flint, by the end of the story, has accepted the possibility of death as his fate.

The most curious character in exploring multiple identities across time has to be Virginia Woolf's Orlando. The novel *Orlando: A Biography* was first published on 11 October 1928. It is a high-spirited romp inspired by the tumultuous family history of the aristocratic poet and novelist Vita Sackville-West, who was Woolf's close friend and lover. *Orlando* is in part a satire on the history of English literature and in part a take on sexual identity. The book describes the adventures of a poet who changes sex from man to woman and lives across many centuries, meeting the key figures of English literary history, some great, some not so great. It's a study of gender and sex, biological or otherwise, and is now one of the key texts when looking at the history of transgender identity in the novel.

The central concept of THE SWIDGERS is that Time is out of joint with the Universe. In the creation myth of Swidgers, the Universe came about when there was a divide of Cosmic Energy into Time, Space and Pure Energy. And Pure Energy, as our own science will tell you, later became matter and, ultimately, life. But somewhere in the mix there was a Dark Force that was against the very existence of life and so put Time and the Universe out of sync, resulting in our imperfect world.

But where does all this leave Time itself? Well, in the Swidger way of thinking, Time is a sentient entity of sorts and its primary duty is to avoid too many paradoxes or inconsistencies in Time. That said, Time occasionally allows options to be created. Maybe a time loop or split identity here and there, but ultimately there can be only one timestream. In book two, *The Time They Saved Tomorrow*, Time does allow a divide and this results in two distinct timepaths with split identities but later it is revealed that Time has gone one step further and allowed there to be a parallel world, dependent on a time loop that can't exist forever. What this means is that at some stage Time must choose between these two time worlds. But Time is more logical than moral. It favours no one side over the other and not even Swidgers can be sure exactly what choice Time will make.

In allowing Time to split two Williams and two Grannys have been created. However, as the existence of double identities in the same place is not possible, the choice for Time is either to allow them to amalgamate or choose between the existence of one or the other. As it happens, there is a physical meeting between both Williams and both Grannys and they do become as one and in doing so the two Williams and the two Grannys share each other's memories and knowledge.

Of course in writing *The Time They Saved Tomorrow* there was the practical problem of how the reader, with two of the same character in the same room, is able to distinguish between these dual identities. Writers and film-makers have to come up with practical solutions that help their readers or viewers. For example, in *Alice*, the 'bad' Park Jin-gyeom has a noticeable rash of red spots. In *The Time They Saved Tomorrow* it just so happens that the William and Granny the reader has been following have just come through a dusty coal-tunnel and so their dirty faces distinguish them from their doppelgangers.

But what of that parallel world that is dependent on the time loop mentioned earlier? Well, this new world to Granny and William is revealed to be a very wicked place. As for their old world, well, that now hangs in the balance and its survival depends on the continuing existence of a time loop which William must become a part of. To go into too many details would give away the climax of the entire series, but it soon becomes apparent that William and Granny might never be able to return to the world they knew, nor that that world, our world, is certain of survival. Time alone will decide.

# The Dramatic Devices of the Time Tale

*The day will come when the man at the telephone will be able to see the distant person to whom he is speaking.*
Alexander Graham Bell

## Message in a Time Bottle – Communication Across Time

FOR PLOT REASONS it is sometimes necessary to allow characters in one time period to communicate with those in another. The *Back to the Future* series came up with a clever, if somewhat complicated wheeze, as to how this could be done. When the Doc Brown of 1955 gets stuck in 1885 and Marty comes to rescue him the Doc Brown now living in 1885 wants to know how 'future boy' can know he's in 1885 if the 'me' of the future is now in the past. And to answer that Marty holds up a letter.

Using Western Union proved to be such a brilliantly inventive method that it was later borrowed for the television series *Timeless*, only for Wyatt Logan that telegram was less successful. Jiya in *Timeless* fared better when she got stranded in the past and used photographs of her herself in history books to communicate with the team in the present day.

Weirdly in *Travelers*, messages are despatched from the future and delivered to the present by temporarily taking over the consciousness of children (adults, it is explained, could not survive the process). These children are then sent to wherever the Travelers are. 'Where is my mom?' is then often what they say when they are released from being what is essentially an incarnated talking telegram. Yet how this bizarre communication is actually achieved is never fully explained. Doubtless there is an explanation, but sometimes why bother explaining what is an impossibility anyway. Instead simply get on with the story.

Those clever people back at Project Tic-Toc in the 1960s *The Time Tunnel* series use the radiation left on their time travellers after their 'radiation bath' to locate them in time. There is also a means of sending messages to the time travellers via a location probe, the F-5, but frustratingly this doesn't always work. Still, that F-5 often proves useful in constructing the plot.

In the Korean time travel series *Alice*, there's a scene where two time travellers are in the same space but different time dimensions. But there's no need to worry, not when you have sticky notes you can simply put on the wall. Sometimes solving the problem of a dislocation in the space-time continuum is as easy as pie.

Communication between different time periods via a radio is a key feature in the crime movie *Frequency* and the romantic South Korean drama *Ditto* (2000). In the (highly recommended) 2022 Irish film *Lola* – a black and white found-footage mockumentary – two sisters in the 1940s create a device that can pick up radio and TV broadcasts from the future, opening up a delightful cultural fast track but also creating the possibility that the technology, in the wrong hands, could change the future for the worse.

Contact between the young people in *Your Name* (2016) is achieved not surprisingly via their smart phones. In *The Lake House* (2006), a remake of the South Korean film *Il Mare* (2000), it is an old-fashioned mailbox that allows an architect living in 2004 and a doctor living in 2006 to communicate. In the movie, with Keanu Reeves as the architect and Sandra Bullock as the doctor, letters are left in the mailbox in real time two years apart, but somehow the red arrow pops up immediately in the other time period and when Keanu and Sandra open the box, there they are. The best postal service that has ever existed in any era. Well, perhaps it's because *The Lake House* is a romantic time drama which of course has a huge advantage over any other type of time drama for, as we all know, 'Love will always find a way'.

# Message in a Time Bottle – *Doctor Who*'s *Blink* Episode

In one episode of *Doctor Who* writer Steven Moffat had a bit of a challenge. In season three of the reboot with the Tenth Doctor David Tennant, they were apparently running out of cash and so Moffat had to come up with budget-aliens. And so he devised the Weeping Angels, who are only ever seen as stone statues. No expensive CGI there, then. Another issue was that there's usually an episode in each *Doctor Who* season which doesn't feature the time travelling Doctor that much. This is in order to allow the actor a break of sorts during the arduous shooting schedule. And so, in *Blink*, Moffat had The Doctor stranded in 1969 by the Weeping Angels, and in 1969 we only ever see him and his companion on a TV screen. So far, so good. But then you have the plot problem of how to communicate with the present day from 1969 and how to get the TARDIS in 2007 back to 1969? Well, to solve both issues, Moffat came up with ingenious scenario featuring Sally Sparrow (Carey Mulligan), who is arguably the true hero of the episode, who acts as both receiver and courier of messages across time and is crucial in getting the TARDIS back to its owner.

Sally enjoys taking photographs in abandoned buildings (cheap to hire) and while exploring Wester Drumlins, she finds a strange message written directly to her under peeling wallpaper which appears to have been left by someone called 'The Doctor'. That same night Sally meets Larry Nightingale, brother of her friend Kathy Nightingale. Larry has on display numerous screens playing 'Easter Eggs', hidden messages encoded into DVDs, that feature a man talking to camera in a weird one-sided conversation.

Kathy joins Sally on her second visit to Wester Drumlins and whilst in the house, they notice peculiar looking stone statues. There's an unexpected visitor at the door and so Sally goes downstairs, leaving Kathy behind. The visitor, Malcolm, claims to be Kathy's grandson. Baffled, Sally returns to ask Kathy for an explanation, only to find that she has vanished. In a nod perhaps to *Back to the Future*, Larry then delivers a message from Kathy from 1987 in the form of a letter that had to be delivered on that exact day and that exact time. Kathy, it seems, vanished back in time to 1920 as a result of encountering one of the Weeping Angels. Sally then visits Kathy's brother Larry at work in his DVD shop and passes on a message in the 1987 letter telling Larry that Kathy loves him and has 'gone on a trip'. While there, for a brief moment, Sally seems inexplicably able to interact with the 'Easter Eggs', meaning the man in the pre-recorded video in one-sided conversation. Prompted by a worker in the DVD shop where Larry works, Sally goes to the police with her story about the missing Kathy and the potential dangers of Wester Drumlins. There she meets a young and handsome officer called DI Billy Shipton who is also sent back to 1969 as is the Doctor's TARDIS. And it's here the message in the bottle is explained. Sally meets Billy, now an old man, in her own time. It was the Doctor, also in 1969, who got Billy to put all the Easter Egg messages on the DVDs, for in his new life in 1969 Billy became a publisher and later a producer of DVDs.

Sally and Larry go to Wester Drumlins and here they play the pre-recorded Easter Eggs on a portable DVD player. As they watch, Sally discovers she can converse with the one-way conversation of the Doctor's in 1969, as he, the Doctor, somehow possesses a copy of the complete transcript that Larry is at that very moment compiling. The Doctor explains all about the Weeping Angels and how they now want the time energy in the police box, meaning his police box time machine, the TARDIS. To see exactly how the Doctor gets his TARDIS back and how the Weeping Angels are tricked you'll have to watch the episode itself, but needless to say it's as ingenious as the rest of the plot.

Essentially then the whole episode is plotted around how to communicate across time and so get a stranded time traveller his time machine back. It's convoluted certainly and feels at times more like a purpose built puzzle than a problem that needs a solution, but who cares? *Blink* is a now a favourite with the *Doctor Who* community and rightly so. It has truly frightening alien, an intricate and inventive time plot, plus a great performance by Carey Mulligan as Sally Sparrow.

## Gifts from the Future

Several stories use the knowledge of time travellers from the future to offer some sort or help or gift to those in the present. Including themselves. Winning the pools or the lottery can be found in *The Flipside of Dominick Hide* and *The Time Traveler's Wife*. In *Sisyphus* there's a neat twist on the lottery scenario. In fact in the story, the lottery is said to have been created specifically to fund the Control Bureau, an organisation that polices illegal time immigrants from the future. Not only that, in a rather clever way the lottery becomes one of the main methods of tracking down such illegals as many try and use the lottery as an easy route to making money. Find the big winners and they're likely to be time travelling criminals. The mysterious Sigma character however, avoids this trap by putting on small sure bets at the race track and then taking that cash to buy and sell stocks and shares. And it is this stealth way of creating mammoth wealth which, somewhat indirectly, leads to the creation of the time machine itself.

Medical cures from the future, notably cures for cancer, are key plot elements in both *Sisyphus* and the American television series *Travelers*. A cure from the future becomes more of a comedy moment in *Star Trek IV: The Voyage Home* when Dr McCoy restores to health a patient who then starts running round the hospital shouting about it.

## *'Read All About it! Tomorrow's News Today! Read all About it!'*

Several stories use privileged information from the future as the central plot device. And often that knowledge comes in the form of a newspaper from the future telling of events yet to happen.

An early example of this is the one-act play *The Jest of Hahalaba* (1928) by the Irish author Lord Dunsany (or Edward John Moreton Drax Plunkett). The drama is set in the final hours of 1928. Sir Arthur Strangways enlists an alchemist to summon the unpredictable and mischievous spirit of Laughter. Though the alchemist warns of possible dire consequences, Sir Arthur's greed leads him to invoke the spirit, but when he does he receives a shocking surprise. Sir Arthur is given a copy of the next day's newspaper and in it he reads his own obituary. As a result, Sir Arthur drops dead with the shock, resulting in the very obituary he just read. Undoubtedly the dark spirit of Laughter found his joke very funny.

A few years later, H.G. Wells wrote a short story called *The Queer Story of Brownlow's Newspaper*, which first appeared in the February 1932 issue of the *Ladies' Home Journal*. The tale takes place on 10 November 1931 and opens with the protagonist, Mr Brownlow, accidentally being delivered a newspaper dated 10 November 1971. The intriguing arrival of a newspaper 40 years hence allows Wells to speculate on what he thought the future might hold. As he reads, Mr Brownlow notices that there is no mention of the British Empire, the Soviet Union or even France or Germany. The narrator of the short story then observes:

> Now to me this is a very wonderful thing indeed. It means, I take it, that in only forty years from now the great game of sovereign states will be over. It looks also as if the parliamentary game will be over, and as if some quite new method of handling human affairs will have been adopted. Not a word of patriotism or nationalism; not a word of party, not an allusion. But in only forty years!

The newspaper edition from 1971 has colour photos throughout, which didn't prove exactly correct for the real 1970s, and we're not quite there yet even in the present era, except of course, for online newspapers, which will, in time, most probably take over the print medium entirely. Wells' more accurate predictions based on news items and articles in Brownlow's paper include a world with a lower birth rate, the use of geothermal energy and concerns over endangered species (in his 1971 world gorillas are already extinct). The newspaper itself unfortunately gets put 'down the chute' by the cleaner, but a couple of small pieces are later found confirming its existence:

> I said at the beginning that it was a queer story and queer to my mind it remains, fantastically queer. I return to it at intervals, and it refuses to settle down in my mind as anything but an incongruity with all my experience and beliefs. If it were not for the two little bits of paper, one might dispose of it quite easily. One might say that Brownlow had had a vision, a dream of unparalleled vividness and consistency. Or that he had been hoaxed and his head turned by some elaborate mystification. Or, again, one might suppose he had really seen into the future with a sort of exaggeration of those previsions cited by Mr. J.W. Dunne in his remarkable *Experiment with Time*. But nothing Mr Dunne has to advance can account for an actual evening paper being slapped through a letter-slit forty years in advance of its date.

But who is this Mr Dunne? And what is his remarkable *Experiment with Time*?

Mr Dunne's full name was John William Dunne, but he was known in the publishing world as simply J.W. Dunn. He was a soldier, an engineer and a philosopher. His seminal book *An Experiment with Time* (1927) develops a theory around the idea that the moment of 'The Now' cannot be described and pinned down by science. Dunne's way of thinking about time led to the notion of an endless sequence of higher dimensions of time or 'Serial Time'. In some way these speculative theories are similar to the philosophical explorations of the 19th century philosopher Georg Wilhelm Friedrich Hegel, where Hegel talks about our passageway through and along various dimensional flows of time. Hegel's philosophical writing is not always that easy to comprehend to say the least but he does seem to suggest that if we, human beings, were capable of some sort of higher form of thinking then that would allow us to rise, as it were, above the singular nature of 'The Now' and so witness and experience the fullness of time itself. And Dunne's thinking is not in principle that different. For Dunne though, it's our wakeful world that prevents us from seeing beyond the present moment, but, he argues, when we are dreaming, needful attention fades and we gain the ability to see along our timeline, allowing fragments of our future to appear in the form of precognitive dreams. However, for Dunne anyway, precognitive visions can only foresee future personal experiences of the dreamer and not more general events. Dreams, Dunne says, are personal and so it is only what is personal that can be foretold.

Dunne's book *An Experiment with Time* became very influential in the 1920s and 1930s and led the novelist John Buchan, a writer not exactly known for science fiction and fantasy, to pen *The Gap in the Curtain* (1932), a Time Tale which explores the theories of Serial Time put forward by J.W. Dunn. And, like Wells' *The Queer Story of Brownlow's Newspaper*, it uses the device of a newspaper of the future.

In the novel *The Gap in the Curtain*, the narrator, Sir Edward Leithen, is introduced at a house party to the brilliant physicist and mathematician Professor Moe, who, like Dunne, has been working on a new speculative theory of time. Moe believes that he has found a way to enable people to see, as if through a 'gap in the curtain' – hence the title of the novel – future events. Several house party guests are persuaded into an experiment where they concentrate, with the aid of an unspecified drug, in order that they may see a chosen page in *The Times* newspaper a year from hence. The guests are then asked to turn their eyes inwardly and indeed images do appear, but the effort in bringing all this about proves too much for Professor Moe, who promptly dies on the spot. The novel then follows the fortunes of various guests over the next 12 months. And in each case, what they saw and what was predicted comes true, though often in unexpected ways.

*It Happened Tomorrow* is a 1944 American movie loosely fashioned on Lord Dunsany's theatre play *The Jest of Hahalaba* (1928), but it develops the bare bones of that tale considerably. And more towards the supernatural. In *It Happened Tomorrow*, set in the mid-1890s, Lawrence Stevens (Dick Powell) is a journalist and obituary writer who becomes fascinated by the musings of an elderly newspaper man called 'Pop' Benson, who keeps talking about the possibility of seeing right then and there, in the present, newspapers of the future. Lawrence Stevens says that as a journalist he wishes such a thing were really possible, but 'Pop' Benson warns Stevens to be careful what one wishes for as 'it's no good to know the future.' However, the wish comes true when the old-timer 'Pop' Benson somehow does give Stevens the next day's newspaper, a full 24 hours ahead of its publication. Ever the journalist, Stevens uses the information he reads in the headline (a robbery the next day at a theatre's box office) to get a scoop on his rivals, but that brings him under considerable suspicion from the police as to how he knew about the crime ahead of it taking place. But Stevens is a wily character and manages to talk his way out of trouble. At least for now.

The next day, Stevens is given yet another newspaper from the next day by 'Pop' Benson. This time though he sees a different sort of benefit in knowing the future, for he intends to use the racing results to win at the racetrack, as Biff does in *Back to the Future III*. But there's a problem, for our journalist Stevens, as in *The Jest of Hahalaba* and also one of the characters in *The Gap in the Curtain*, reads a story in the newspaper about his own death that night. In the supernatural plot twist, Stevens is told by the other newspaper men that his benefactor 'Pop' Benson actually died the night he was musing about newspapers from the future, and so the 'Pop' Benson who gave Stevens the two newspapers must have been some sort of ghostly spirit. As to what actually happens to Stevens, well, let's just say it's best not to believe everything you read in the newspapers.

*Early Edition* is an American fantasy drama television series which ran between 1996 and 2000. And as with *It Happened Tomorrow*, the action was set in a newspaper office. The location this time was Chicago, Illinois, and here *Early Edition* followed the adventures of Gary Hobson who every day mysteriously receives a copy of the *Chicago Sun-Times* newspaper a full 24 hours before it is actually appears on the streets. Each episode then had Gary Hobson taking advantage of this knowledge to prevent whatever terrible event was there in the headlines. In an odd twist of life imitating art, the series was apparently commissioned after a mock-up newspaper presented as the real thing sparked a fiery conversation in the pitch meeting itself. Only at the end of the pitch was it revealed to the television executives that the edition, dated the next day, wasn't actually real.

*Early Edition* has been compared to *It Happened Tomorrow*, but it's creators, Ian Abrams, Patrick Q. Page and Vik Rubenfeld, have argued that their series is in no way based on that film. And in a way that is fair because for anyone dealing in time fantasy, tomorrow's newspaper is now hardly a new idea hot off the press.

Another prophetic newspaper tale is Robert Silverberg's *What We Learned from this Morning's Newspaper* (1972) which features neighbours in a suburban block in New York who are at first mystified and then excited at the realisation that next week's newspaper has just landed on their doorsteps. But perhaps they should have watched *It Happened Tomorrow* and heeded 'Pop' Benson's wise words that 'it's no good to know the future.' In fact, in Silverberg's story, trying to take advantage of news from the future is no good for anyone, for in their attempt to play the stock market and change the future, space-time is somehow corrupted and an 'entropic creep' begins to blur out the paper. And not only the newspaper, but eventually everyday life itself.

Newspapers from the future continue to be a standard device for time fantasy writers. Newspaper headlines past, present and future featured throughout the *Back to the Future* series, both for key plot reasons and expositional purposes. In book two of THE SWIDGERS *The Time They Saved Tomorrow*, William discovers the terrible nature of the oppressive and tyrannous world he has found himself in by looking through newspapers he finds that are lining a sock drawer. Oddly enough, it isn't the front page headlines that reveal the horrible truth of this wicked world but rather the photographs of crowds at a football match.

## Time Gadgets (Patents Pending)

Very conveniently, the TARDIS, the means by which the Doctor in *Doctor Who* travels through space and time, has a 'translation circuit', which is a gift of the TARDIS. Very wise of it to give The Doctor such a plot hole get-out-card. In simple terms the translation circuit is a telepathic field stretching from the TARDIS that gets inside your brain and translates what the aliens are saying. But, as with many things relating to the TARDIS, the system isn't infallible. On some occasions, the telepathic field is limited to a certain radius around the TARDIS. Also the translation circuit isn't 100 percent accurate, for it has a swear filter, which means that if an alien or even a speaker of ancient Greek uses a rude phrase, all potentially impressionable young viewers would only ever hear is something like 'You're all a bunch of naughty melon pluckers!' or some such innocuous nonsense that disguises the original expletive. *Doctor Who* did begin as a children's tea-time show after all.

There have been occasions when the translation circuits have failed to work or even been hacked. The Master's odd humour came into play when he disrupted what the Doctor was saying by altering the telepathic circuits of the TARDIS with the bizarre result that when the Doctor's own words were fed back to him they came out backwards. The TARDIS does however seem able to deal quite cleverly with accents, as when Donna arrived in

Pompeii and met one Latin speaker who thought she was Celtic. But maybe the bigger clue was in her red hair.

The Korean time travel series *Alice,* stays firmly on Earth and so doesn't have any alien languages to worry about. That said, those clever people at Alice did come up with a one brilliant gadget that surprisingly hasn't been fully exploited yet on the commercial market. Older looking time travellers when they travel back in time to see a loved one simply put in their ear some sort of device that allows their older selves to look 30 years younger. For some people, this would undoubtedly be an invention far more important than time travelling itself, yet in the series it is never fully explained or even developed all that much. Ah well, we'll all have to stick to Botox.

The wormhole timepiece carried around by travellers in *Dark* is about the size of a cricket ball, but trust Korean technology from Alice to come up with something even smaller. You see, travellers in *Alice* carry a Time Card, no bigger than a credit card, which, when pressed, allows them to travel in time. Detective Park Jin-gyeom's mother Yoon Tae-yi did have one, but hers was damaged. Jin-gyeom asks her doppelganger, Professor Yoon Tae-yi, to examine it and inside she finds various mathematical equations that are similar to those she has been working on. There are hints here of a causal loop, that is, something that itself is not invented but rather comes from the future to the past where it becomes the cause of that which it will become. Put simply, if you take the technology of a time machine back in time, you can then use that wizardry to put together the very time machine that took you. Causal loops have the big advantage of saving you lots of hard work in the lab and inventive brain thinking.

## Time Buried Treasure

Discovering something hidden that has been especially placed there to be found at a later date, is a popular plot device in Time Tales. The DeLorean left in the mine shaft in *Back to the Future III*, for example. In *Stranded*, a 2016 episode of the series *Timeless*, Lucy, Wyatt and Rufus are left high and dry in 1754. However, Rufus leaves a literal message in a bottle inside the damaged Lifeboat for Mason Industries to locate and find in 2016 buried underground in what is now a suburb of Pennsylvania. However, it would be best if the message could only be understood by those at the base. Anyway, Rufus manages some repairs in 1754 but is more worried about the cryptic message being too cryptic. As it turns out the message is eventually understood by Jiya in 2016 to be a reference to *Star Wars* and from that Jiya is ultimately able to guide the team and the Lifeboat back to base. In *Time's Arrow* a 1992 episode of *Star Trek: The Next Generation*, it isn't so much a message in a bottle more a message in a skull. Data's skull to be more specific, which in a time travel story is discovered in a cave from 500 years ago. The message is about the importance of closing down the time portal and is decoded by Data when he is reunited with his head.

Bill and Ted in *Bill and Ted's Excellent Adventure* discover a set of keys behind a bush that they themselves apparently put there in the future knowing that they would be needed. A neat gag on this Time Tale trope that cleverly solves a plot hole. *Need something, dude? Whoa! Simply leave that something in the past and let ourselves find it when it's wanted. Excellent!* In *Dark*, the younger Claudia Tiedemann in 1987, uses a map given by her older self to find the exact spot behind her house where the time machine was buried by the older Claudia Tiedemann in 1954. This allows the 1987 Claudia to travel in time to 2000. Here perhaps there's a warning for all gardeners, be careful where you dig out your vegetable patch with your shovel. You never know what a time traveller might have left there in 1883, which might, if you hit it too hard, send you back to the era. Still, Victorians loved gardens, so you'd always be in work.

# The Rules of Time and Time Codes

*Lost time is never found again, and what we call time enough, always proves little enough.*
Benjamin Franklin

THE RULES OF time in a Time Tale should be absolute and irrevocable. And it's your Time Tale, so you can decide what those time rules are. But the point here is that once that world of yours has been imagined and created, like the scientific laws of our own universe, those time rules must be kept to and never broken. Especially regarding time travel. If you start changing your fundamentals mid-story, your Time Tale will lose all credibility.

As with time beings, your time rules are primarily created for dramatic and thematic reasons. In *Dark*, it is established that cause and effect is halted in the moment that Tannhauser's time machine is switched on. The stopping of the relationship even for a second allows two timelines to be born. It's a simple but ingenious concept. The complexities that follow may well bring about a bewildering labyrinth of interconnecting lives but the fundamental principle of how time works in the *Dark* time world is always consistent.

Rules then vary depending on the story, some have limits on how far back the protagonist is able to travel in time, or indeed where they cannot go. For example, the Mission Team in *Timeless* are only able to travel to a period within their own lifetimes, likewise, Tim in *About Time*. This is usually the case as well for Henry in *The Time Traveler's Wife*, but there are exceptions. In Poul Anderson's *Flight to Forever*, the protagonist's machine runs out of energy and so can only move forward in time and not back. Others have it that events can be witnessed, but not interfered with, for example, Daphne du Maurier's *The House on the Strand*, and Charles Dickens' *A Christmas Carol*. But there are some time worlds where there are no rules, or at least within them what is Time is purely random. And this time world belongs to *Slaughterhouse-Five* by Kurt Vonnegut.

The rules of time travel in *Travelers* are to some degree flexible in that they are dependent on ever-changing technology and the Artificial Intelligence of the future. However, even here there are principles that must be kept to, one being that time travel is limited to the computer age, as the quantum technology that allows for Time Travel in *Travelers* is dependent on computer programming. No visits to the world of the dinosaurs, then. *Travelers* also has other rules such as it is only possible to go back as far as the most recent Traveler and so it is not possible to do 'do-overs' as this would create 'ripples in space-time'. This latter rule you'll find in most Time Tales, and it makes sense, for in your story, if you didn't get things right the first time and all you have to do is do it again, where is the jeopardy?

What about establishing a rule as to how quickly time passes in the different time spaces? The same? More quickly? More slowly? In *Bill and Ted's Excellent Adventure*, the clock ticks the same in both worlds, the past and the present, but in Stephen King's *11/22/63* no matter how long you spend in the past, when you return only two minutes have gone by in the present.

And what about clothes or anything else you can take with on your time journey? In *The Time Traveler's Wife*, it's only Henry's physical body that can journey in time and so Henry always arrives naked. Difficult for him, yes, but in a way this has dramatic advantages, for Henry is forced to find inventive ways of getting round the problem. A similar rule exists in *The Terminator*. Bizarrely, Austin Powers' newly cleaned teeth in the '90s revert back to being dirty and yellow when he travels to the '60s. However, Austin has already looked into the camera and winked and told us not to worry too much about all that time travel logic.

Is the time journey a one-way ticket or a return? Scientifically speaking, a wormhole time journey would definitely be one way. In *The Terminator* the TDE (Time Displacement Equipment also known as the Time Displacement Generator) is definitely a one-way trip, and that suits the story. *In the Shadow of the Moon*, it is established that the journey is in one temporal direction only. That suits the story too. But again that's the whole point: construct the rules around the story you wish to tell rather than make up rules then create a story round them.

What are the potential side effects of time travel? In the Korean time travel series *Alice*, radiation from time travel can cause problems and that's why Yoon Tae-yi who is expecting a child stays in the past to single-handedly raise her son, Park Jin-gyeom. But some damage has already been done to the unborn child and Park Jin-gyeom, because of radiation from time travel is born with Alexithymia, that is, a lack of empathy and emotional connection. And that turns out to be an important element in his character.

## Time Codes

As Granny says in book one of THE SWIDGERS, 'Rules are like pie-crusts, they are made to be broken.' Breaking guidelines can lead to drama and in fact *The Time That Never Was* opens with William ignoring one of the key Swidger strictures, which is not to follow those people whose timelines you alter. William knows he must do this to save the man's life, but it also sets William up as different to his fellow Swidgers. But in a way, scenarios in Time Tales are built around how far time codes can be pushed. And that is ultimately the narrative purpose of all time codes in Time Tales.

In *Travelers* as with many series, there are strictures concerning how to behave in a time travelling situation and these are called Protocols and they include: leave the future in the past, do not interfere and do not reproduce. You could argue that dramatically the entire series of *Travelers* is built around how and why these Protocols occasionally must be broken. The mission itself in *Travelers* is always to make changes in our era to help the world in the Travelers' own future, but with Time Tales, as in life, moral and practical ambiguities abound. And it's around dilemmas and quandaries that many episodes are based. For that's where drama lies.

## The Prime Directive

The overall objective of the team mission in *Travelers* is to alter the future, save it in fact, but in Time Tales where there is no assignment, then the default protocol, or prime directive to borrow a term from *Star Trek*, is usually 'non-intervention'. Or put simply, 'Don't leave your footprint in history'.

As Doctor Who says in *The Witchfinders* (2018), 'The most important thing about dips into the past: Do not interfere with the fundamental fabric of history.' The Doctor is then asked if that includes even when something isn't right and the Doctor basically says yes. The rule for time travellers then is that no interventions should be made, even if positive, for the simple reason that consequences further along the timeline could be catastrophic and even create a worse situation than that which currently exists. Yes, the present may not be perfect, but it's all we have and all we can be sure of. Better the devil you know, and all that. Plus, as the Doctor says to Yaz in *Demons of the Punjab* (2018), 'The wrong word in the wrong moment, you could interfere yourself out of existence.' But that's the very premise of course of the famous 1967 *Star Trek* episode *The City on the Edge of Forever*, where the Enterprise itself is interfered out of existence. Yet, here's the thing: non-intervention is the rule, but break it and you get great drama.

## Travelling in Time but Not Space

There are two issues here. A time machine that journeyed backward through time and yet didn't move in space would face a very troublesome problem – it would simply crash into itself. Scientists have dubbed this 'the double occupancy problem'.

The other issue is that even if the time machine doesn't move in space, the Earth itself does. It's spinning round right now. And isn't the Earth also orbiting the Sun? So perhaps the real question for time travellers, who, shall we say, want to travel back in time to 1812 to witness Russia's successful defence of its territory from Napoleon isn't so much 'When is 1812?' but 'Where is 1812?' If you don't move in space as well as time you might find yourself floating in Earth's orbit but millions of miles from your intended destination. However, on the whole, Time Tales tend to ignore that issue.

Of course, H.G. Wells' time machine travelled only in time, not space, and to a degree Wells in the early chapters does address the issue of double occupancy. In the story itself the only occasion the time machine is moved is when the Morlocks push it into the Sphinx and this creates problems for the Time Traveller. But jeopardy such as this never does any harm to a story. The DeLorean car in *Back to the Future* clearly moves in space. And it needs to be fast too in order to hit the 88 mph mark and so do its stuff, yet it cannot 'jump space' in the way the TARDIS can, or even that phone box in *Bill and Ted's Excellent Adventure*. But the DeLorean's limitation is actually an advantage for it raises more danger and jeopardy for Marty, particularly in *Back to the Future III* where the bridge across the ravine is still unfinished in 1885 and so Marty has to risk driving over it in the hope he will travel into the future where there will be a bridge in 1985. As with any story rule, code or stricture, the space-time rule here is designed to suit and fit the individual plot. And here we again see the brilliance of the *Back to the Future* structure and plotting.

## Where the Dead Don't Die – The Death Reversal

None of us want to die and we don't want those we love to die either. But death is part of life and we must learn to accept this. And in their own way, Time Tales are creative stories that explore this area of human experience with numerous stories around loss and bereavement.

The attempt to prevent a past death is often a key part of a Time Tale. Wyatt Logan, whose wife was killed in violent circumstances, is not the only character in *Timeless* who knows or has witnessed grief. Flynn, the supposed 'villain' of *Timeless*, jaunts to NASA in 1964 to save the life of his half-brother Gabriel, who he knows will die of an allergic reaction to a bee-sting without an immediate antihistamine injection. This is not a selfish act, for it was the grief and sadness Flynn saw in his mother who witnessed this terrible accidental death that was the motivation for this particular death reversal.

In *Timecop* (1994, written by Mark Verheiden and Mike Richardson), Max Walker has the job of preventing time travellers from altering time, yet is tempted to do so himself to prevent his wife's death. And even Superman, when Lois dies, flies around the world in the opposite direction to its spin, thus causing the Earth to 'turn the clock back', as it were, and so reverse time and bring Lois back to life. Strictly speaking, travelling fast, according to Einstein's theory anyway, simply wouldn't do this, unless, like those mysterious tachyons, Superman went all FTL – that is, Faster-Than-Light. Anyway, this saving act of Superman does go completely against what his father had taught him and that is a cost to Superman, for a trust and a promise has been broken. Such actions have their consequences, as there are for Barry Allen when he attempts the same thing – travelling faster than light to go back in time to try and prevent the death of his mother – in 2023's *The Flash*.

There are a few attempted turnarounds for the dead in the *Harry Potter* world. In *Harry Potter and the Prisoner of Azkaban*, Hermione uses the Time-Turner to save Buckbeak, though in *Harry Potter and the Cursed Child* (play 2016), using the Time-Turner to meddle with time to save Cedric results in unexpected and disastrous consequences elsewhere. A rare success in preventing a death is *Happy Accidents* (2000), except here the time travellers, or 'back-travellers' as they call themselves, only reveal to the central character Ruby at the end that it is her death they have stopped.

In *The Time Traveler's Wife*, young Henry is with his mother when she is killed in a car crash. Of course, when he grows older he tries to reverse this but nothing he does can change things. His attempts only result in Henry having to witness his mother's death many, many times. Eventually, Henry comes to accept that what happened is irreversible and moves on.

Lazarus is the exception, not the rule.

# Dreams, Foretellings and Memory

*In a Wonderland they lie,*
*Dreaming as the days go by,*
*Dreaming as the summers die:*
*Ever drifting down the stream –*
*Lingering in the golden gleam –*
*Life, what is it but a dream?*
Lewis Carroll (Charles Lutwidge Dodgson) from
the poem A *Boat Beneath a Sunny Sky*

## Dreaming

LITERATURE HAS DREAM stories in abundance and two of the most famous are the Alice stories, namely *Alice's Adventures in Wonderland* and *Alice Through the Looking-glass*. Scientists believe that when you dream, the rational, cognitive and reflective parts of the brain are put on hold and that allows the intuitive, instinctive and creative parts of the brain to go into overdrive. Nature's free 'high'.

A fascinating aspect of time as experienced in dreaming is how its dynamics become all mixed up. What would be an extensive period of time in the waking world, travelling long distances, for example, becomes condensed into a single point. Or a single moment in time in a dream, finding yourself in a place you don't want to be, becomes extended and seems to go on forever. Dreams then distort time or at least our sense of its duration. And that is an idea explored in many Time Tales, notably those such as *The Jacket* and *Jacob's Ladder*, where dreaming is key.

## Life as a Dream

The ancient Chinese philosopher Chuang Tzu woke up one morning and remembered he'd been dreaming he was a butterfly. But then came the big question, 'Was I Chuang Tzu dreaming I was a butterfly, or am I now a butterfly dreaming that I am Chuang Tzu?' You might ask Jean-Luc Picard a similar question in *The Inner Light* written by Morgan Grendel, an episode from *Star Trek: The Next Generation*. As a result of a strike from an alien probe, Picard lies prostrate on the bridge in enforced or induced dreaming (his 'neurotransmitter production is off the scale') which is somehow making him believe he has become, in a very real and physical way, Kamin on the planet Kataan. In *Alice Through the Looking-glass* the nature of Alice's very existence comes alarmingly into question when she sees the Red King dreaming. Alice is told it would be best not to wake him as the Red King may be dreaming of Alice herself, and so, if the King woke, she would simply disappear, like a snuffed out candle. And dreaming in this sense becomes a metaphor for being, a theme explored in *Dark*, where the existence of Adam, like that of Alice, could soon end.

In fact dreaming is a *motif* that runs throughout the entire series of *Dark*. Many episodes actually begin in one of Jonas' dreams – often more like nightmares – for Jonas to discover when he wakes up that none of it was real. Ironic indeed, because in the last episode of the final season, pretty much everything – Jonas, Martha, Adam, Eva, the eternal time loops created when time stops – all come to an end as if a mere fantasy. In fact, across all three seasons, it's only that dinner party in the last episode that is 'real'. The rest is as if it were an all too soon forgotten dream.

Perhaps not surprisingly then, the dream motif is there in many Time Tales. Marty in *Back to the Future* several times wakes up and immediately starts asking for his mom and saying he's just had a terrible dream. *Last Christmas* is the 2014 Christmas episode of *Doctor Who*. As with many episodes in the series, *Last Christmas* works within a specific genre and this particular story is a riff on *Alien* and the '80s *The Thing*, with a few dollops of *Ghostbusters* and *The Santa Clause* thrown in for good measure. But it's the dream-within-a-dream concept found in *Nightmare on Elm Street* and *Inception* that is the key element in the plot, for the monsters are Dream Crabs which slowly devour your brain but to stop you noticing they anesthetise your mind by putting you in a happy dream state – hence the arrival of a jolly Santa Claus and his elves. Incidentally, in this episode the Doctor points out that we are all time travellers when we dream, but the downside is that since dreams appear to be real, it's difficult to break their hold.

We might mention here as well *Things Past* (1996), an episode from *Star Trek: Deep Space Nine*, written by Michael Taylor. Okay, it's not strictly speaking a dream plot, but one where 'morphogenic enzymes' in Odo are activated by a 'plasma storm' which in turn initiates a 'telepathic response' which reaches out to other changelings, but finds only Sisko, Dax and Garak, who become comatose. Events from Odo's memory are relived for real by Sisko, Dax and Garak in a dream-like state. But there's jeopardy here because physical injury in the 'dream' manifests itself as real in the sleeping dreamer. And that's a problem because the people Sisko, Dax and Garak have become are due for execution. *Der-de-de-de-dud-der!!!*

## Dreams and Time Tales

Dream foretellings are not time travel tales in the way *The Time Machine* is. Yet, as we've seen with Ebenezer Scrooge, what we are shown of a possible future can have a great effect on that future as it is truly lived. Dream foretellings are worth mentioning because they are a key part of stories such as *Minority Report* and *Stranger Things*, plus stories dealing with chronesthesia, the psychological phenomenon of mental time travel that is there in movies such as *Jacob's Ladder* and *The Jacket* (based on the American novel *The Star Rover* written by Jack London).

But the time travel element of dreams is rarely rational or consistent. And there have been those who have wanted to explore that side of dreams and their relationship to time. *Un Chien Andalou (An Andalusian Dog)* is a 1929 Franco-Spanish silent surrealist short film created by Spanish director Luis Buñuel and artist Salvador Dalí. *Un Chien Andalou* – coming from the Spanish saying, 'the Andalusian dog howls, someone has died!' – has no plot in any conventional understanding of the word. Its scenes are disjointed and seemingly unconnected. Time is meaningless and the title cards jump around between 'once upon a time', 'eight years later' and 'sixteen years ago' without the characters or settings changing that much. *Un Chien Andalou* was inspired by Freudian theories around the concept of dream logic, where images of displacement (one thing instead of another) and condensation (bringing two ideas together as one) predominate. Buñuel was keen to avoid what was rational or had psychological or cultural explanations. The only rule was that no idea or image that might lend itself to a rational explanation of any kind would be accepted. And that included the nature of time itself.

But here's the irony of Buñuel and Dalí. They used a dream form to explore the idea that life has little meaning. And that means *Un Chien Andalou (An Andalusian Dog)* does have a meaning, which is to explore the idea that life has little meaning. The problem with life and dreams is that even if they have no meaning human beings can't help giving them meaning and purpose.

What though if you never dream?

In THE SWIDGERS book series, it is revealed that our Swidger teenage hero William has never experienced dreaming. Ever. In fact, he does not believe Swidgers even can dream. But Granny understands that in the battle to come with the Dark Force which seeks William, imagining and a corkscrew way of thinking will be essential. And so to that end she takes him on a visit to Dungeness, where, under a starry night sky Echo tells William the Swidger fable of The Universe's Dream. The Universe, says Echo, was once dreaming it was a real Universe and then woke up to discover that it was. And that made it shake in fear:

> 'One night, long ago, after a dog-weary day, perhaps on an evening such as this, the Universe was fast asleep. Dreaming. And what was its fantasy? It was dreaming it had become a real Universe. Oh, such happy thoughts. But then the Universe was shaken from its sleep. Something disturbing had frightened it. The Universe slowly began to open its eyes. "Oh my," it said, suddenly seeing the deep blackness of the night, "it was only meant to be a dream." The Universe then shuddered for that night sky was now as real as real can be. And cold. And lonely. And lost. Oh, if only it could go back to its dream, thought the Universe, it had been such a happy dream where all was good and pure and in its place. So that's what the Universe tried to do. Remember its dream. But somehow it was always just out of reach. But, William Arthur, our Universe never gave up. It's still hoping, one day, to dream its dream again. If Time will allow. And when it does, all will be well once more.
>
> 'You see, that is what we are, young Swidger,' Echo whispers to William, 'the hope of a dream in a world, a sad world, that awoke too soon.'

Just a silly story, thinks William, but that night, our Swidger hero dreams for real for the first time and in the dream's absurdity, William finds, as is often the case with dreams, a new understanding of himself. Later in the tale William comes to appreciate the true meaning of that Swidger fable, for it was waking too soon that put Time and the Universe out of joint. And in a way it's by understanding the full meaning of Echo's elusive dream tale that allows William to become a Swidger Time Traveller.

## Prophecy

The Bible repeatedly warns against those who prophesy false dreams (Jeremiah 23:32; Zechariah 10:2; Deuteronomy 13:1-3), but equally there are those characters in the Bible such as Daniel and Joseph who are called upon to interpret dreams, including those which are about the future. And God Himself took time out from His busy schedule to appear to Abimelech in a dream (Genesis 20:3).

In the Korean time travel series *Alice*, there exists *The Book of Prophecy*. The back-story of *The Book of Prophecy* is that it was discovered by a woman who then fled to the year 1986 and married a man called Dr Jang Dong-sik. Unfortunately, she died during the birth of Yoon Tae-yi. *The Book of Prophecy* essentially foretells the fate of time travellers and the future, as it were, of time travel itself. The book is, therefore, a much sought after prize. One night, robbers come to steal it and in the process Dr Jang is killed, but not before he gives the key last page to his young daughter, Yoon Tae-yi. Alice Time Agents arrive moments later and neutralise the killer. They then take possession of *The Book of Prophecy*, but without realising the final page is missing, which, it is later revealed, the young Tae-yi hid in the pocket of her nightie.

As the series progresses, the contents of *The Book of Prophecy* are slowly revealed. As with Delphic oracles, the words and phrases of *The Book of Prophecy* turn out to be somewhat cryptic with lines about a child born while opening The Door of Time controlling Time and a destroyer son who can only be killed by the mother's marvellous creation. There's a scene where some of the leading characters try to make sense of it all. There are many ancient books, says one, that call Time the murderer of all beings. And isn't there something in ancient civilisations that says that Time is the Absolute Being, invisible to our eyes, yet it creates everything?

At least in part, what keeps the interest going in *Alice* is the mystery behind exactly what the predictions in *The Book of Prophecy* mean and what will be the result if they do come to pass. Also, who is the son and what is the price? Is Park Jin-gyeom the child born while opening The Door of Time? Is Park Jin-gyeom also her 'marvellous creation' or is that a reference to time travel itself?

## Premonitions

As Doctor Who once observed, a premonition is remembering in the wrong direction. In Time Tales, premonitions as with prophecies are usually left ambiguous for dramatic reasons. In the film *Premonition* (2007 – written by Bill Kelly), with Sandra Bullock as Linda Hanson, the police call on Linda, a young wife, and tell her that her husband has been killed in a car accident, yet the next day she wakes up and there he is downstairs having breakfast. And waking up on another day her husband is dead again, yet the following morning she finds him there in the shower. What the heck is going on? Are these premonitions or is time somehow fracturing? Or indeed is the husband definitely dead and what Linda is going through is a mental breakdown? The film remains intentionally ambiguous throughout, partly for suspense purposes but mainly because the bigger theme is forgiveness (Linda discovers her husband intended to have an affair, but didn't go through with it). Anyway, whether it's a supernatural premonition, a breakdown, or a rift in space-time, the film is ultimately about the need sometimes just to say sorry. And on those terms it is an effective grieving story.

To list every story that involves premonitions or precognition would take many hours – and that's just a good guess rather than actual precognition – but here is a brief selection: *The Dead Zone* (2002), where a man wakes up from a coma with the ability to see into other people's futures; *Night has a Thousand Eyes* (1948), a phony stage mentalist mysteriously begins to see the future for real; *Clementine's Enchanted Journey* (1985–1987), an animation series featuring a young girl who has precognitive dreams; *Unbreakable* (2000), where a man learns extraordinary things about himself following a terrible accident; *Final Destination* (2000), a young man has a sudden premonition of an air crash; *Heroes* (2006–2010), ordinary people suddenly develop special gifts, including one which enables the character to see into the future; *FlashForward* (2009–2010), every person on Earth suddenly experiences black-outs and awakens with a vision of their future; *Next* (2007), a Las Vegas magician who can see into the future two minutes ahead and so is asked to help the FBI prevent a nuclear attack. And we add *The Time That Never Was*, for in the first scene of the story our young Swidger hero experiences some sort of mental aberration where events happen, but then time stops, only to restart again with those events reversed and different scenarios taking their place. Are these visions of the future? But if so, how can they keep changing? Or maybe it's Time that is somehow fracturing? The why and how of all that is happening to William isn't fully revealed until much later, after all it is mystery story. But what can be said is that William discovers he an extraordinary time being – and there has never been a Swidger like him.

## Memory and Identity

'The only thing that bound them together into a feeling of identity was continuity of memory.' So says Robert Heinlein in *By His Bootstraps*. And it's memories that determine for most of us what the past is and so it is our memories that also determine, at least to some degree, what and who we are. In *Travelers*, people from the future, using something called The Theory of Quantum Entanglement, travel to our century – 'Welcome to the 21st' – and when here, their consciousnesses take over the bodies (and minds) of those they knew through their historical records were about to die. In their previous world these consciousnesses did exist in human form, but they never had a name, they were just numbers. And most had never seen the blue of the sky or ate an apple off a tree, for they lived within a protective dome and consumed only a protein based gruel.

## DREAMS, FORETELLINGS AND MEMORY

But now the Travelers have a life where they can breathe the air, see the sun, touch the sand and even eat real fruit and vegetables. Sensorial memories are created which they could never have experienced before. Yet some host memories, especially those that are defining and strong, live on in the host's brain. Some Travelers are more dispassionate than others, but there are those who are deeply moved by these memories that have somehow been left behind. For example, Special Agent Grant MacLaren, Traveler 3468, is nearly killed in a plane crash, but as he lies on the operating table, some of the residual memories of his host's former life begin to surface and haunt him. Not many perhaps, but those that still do exist are powerful and loving. And it's these memories that give Grant a new perspective on who he is. Or was.

In another episode, the body of Marcy must be 're-set' to save her physical body, but this means starting again from scratch ('Control-Alt-Delete'). All the memories which Marcy (or her consciousness) has built up in the body of her host will be lost. In effect, this induced 'amnesia' will mean that Marcy will not remember the sensual times she had with her lover David, including sexual intimacy and the emotional connection she had made. Marcy recognises that these memories are now part of who she is, for flesh and blood and sex and love matter in what it is that makes us human and alive. Nevertheless, she has no choice but to go ahead with the procedure. Yet afterwards she finds a way, by means of an ice-cold bath, to access these precious 'lost' memories. Love doesn't always obey the rules of science. Or at least when you're shivering in freezing water.

As the series goes on there is an increasing use of something called a Memory Inhibitor. The Memory Inhibitor is usually used on non-Travelers to prevent the uncovering of the secret network, but sometimes after a difficult mission or one that is morally ambiguous, the Memory Inhibitor is used on Travelers themselves at their own request. This happens, for example, when Grant MacLaren's mission is to kill a child, Aleksander, who was on a timepath to become a force for ill. Even so, he's still a child. A *would-you-kill-Hitler-when-a-baby?* type scenario. As it happens, Aleksander was not shot by Grant MacLaren, but by another Traveler who took over Grant's body and that why Grant's memories of that day were wiped. Yet some memories are so strong they somehow survive. So who did kill Aleksander? Grant? He remembers doing it but was it really him? As for Marcy, was she no longer Marcy when she couldn't remember David or did she once again become Marcy when she could recall her lover? And it's often these philosophical tangents on the nature of human identity and their relationship to the memory of times past which makes *Travelers* so fascinating and engaging.

## Memory Wipes and Time

Accidental and intentional memory loss are both explored in numerous novels, movies and plays. *Eternal Sunshine of the Spotless Mind* (also simply known as *Eternal Sunshine*) was a 2004 American romantic comedy written by Charlie Kaufman and directed by Michel Gondry. Memories of a break up became so painful, that the lovers Joel Barish and Clementine Kruczynski have their memories erased. The title of the film is a quotation from a 1717 poem *Eliosa to Abelard* by Alexander Pope, which, in part, is about a passion reawakened through memory. And that's a theme that has echoes in the Samuel Beckett play *Krapp's Last Tape*, where a lonely lover is listening to an old tape recording he made of a now lost love. Memory gives you the gift of the past but on the other hand memory can become a cruel hole to fall down when only loss and regret remain. Perhaps that's why the man suffering from melancholia in Charles Dickens' *The Haunted Man* chooses to have his sad memories wiped. *Doctor Who* touches on this kind of memory loss in *Gridlock*, set in a dystopian world where there are drugs that induce amnesia sold in patch form with the name 'Forget'.

If memories do determine for most of us what time past is, what we are or were, and even love itself, then loss of memory could be said to be equivalent to losing time, love and even yourself. And anyone who has witnessed a loved one's memory slowly disappear would probably agree. But some people are willing to exchange memory and time for big bucks. *Paycheck* by Philip K. Dick tells of Jennings, a talented electronic engineer, who accepts a contract for a secret project after which he will have his memory erased and in compensation be paid an inordinate sum. However, he discovers after the memory wipe that he chose to forego the money and instead he now finds himself with trinkets which, as the plot progresses, lead him to the discovery that the project involved a machine that could see into the future. Then there is *Total Recall* (1990) based on Philip K. Dick's 1966 novelette *We Can Remember It For You Wholesale*, and Robert Ludlum's *The Bourne Identity* (published in 1980). There are also stories where criminals lose their memory, notably Robert Silverberg's *The Second Trip* (1972), and instances too of memory wiping monsters, for example, 'The Silence' in *Doctor Who* being a creepy and very frightening example.

But a memory wipe can prove advantageous as well, for there's the *Doctor Who* episodes *Human Nature/Family of Blood* (2007) where memory loss becomes a convenient way of maintaining disguise. The Doctor is being tracked down so the Chameleon Arch is used to transform his biology into a human being while his essence is kept in a biodata module in the shape of a fob watch. The TARDIS invents a life story for the Doctor where he is an ordinary schoolteacher, one 'John Smith', living in 1913. But if something can be remembered, even if held in a fob watch, it can come back, a theme which is also explored in a later Amy Pond storyline.

## Memory and the Time Traveller

If the original time world of the time traveller is changed, it is usually only the time traveller who knows this on their return. That's the rule, for example, in *Back to the Future* and *Timeless*. It's a trope that's neatly referenced in the 2023 *The Flash* when Barry Allen finds himself in a future where time has been altered and discovers that Eric Stoltz (who was originally cast in the film) – rather than Michael J. Fox – is the star of *Back to the Future*! But rules can be broken or at least varied. In Robert Silverberg's *Needle in a Timestack* (published 1970, made into a film in 2021) when a time traveller alters events of the future to their advantage – an 'unhappen' as it's referred to in the plot – there are a brief few hours when those who have had their lives altered can remember their previous time track. A giveaway sign that a time 'phase' has happened is a taste of cotton in the mouth. In Silverberg's tale such intentional changes are a 'time-crime' but such wrongdoing is difficult to prove for the simple reason that the crime by definition took place on a time track that no longer exists. Talk about destroying the evidence.

In the movie *Mirage*, Vera is the only one who can remember and has knowledge of her original timeline but this results in her being supposed a woman who is having a nervous breakdown of some kind. The police officer she turns to doesn't appear to believe her incredible story, but nevertheless is sympathetic to her situation. Vera's claim is that she sent a message to the past warning a boy not to venture outside the house otherwise he'd be killed and somehow this has altered her own timepath, for her current life is unrecognisable to her. But her having no memory of that present life doesn't mean that other people don't and the big twist of *Mirage* is that the boy she saved becomes entwined in the story, only she doesn't recognise him. When she does it's an unexpected ignorance-to-knowledge moment. There's another point to be made here and that is that Vera is the reflector character. It might have been possible to make the boy the focus and follow his narrative, but the choice was made to tell the tale from Vera's point of view. And when you discover who the boy is that decision makes perfect sense.

In the *Doctor Who* episode *A Christmas Carol*, the nature of memories and how they are created are explored in a very logical time travel way. The Doctor visits Kazran Sardick, the Scrooge of the story, when a child and the older Kazran Sardick is in the future watching on a screen his past change before his very eyes. The Doctor in the past explains to the older Kazran that as the events of his past change, so too will his memories. The older Kazran denies such a thing has happened. Well, until it does. It's an idea that is also explored in the American television series *Timeless*, where the people in the present back at base develop new memories of events which the time travellers to the past managed to change.

Another *Doctor Who* episode, *The Big Bang* (2010), takes the idea of lost memories much further, for, when history collapses, whole races are deleted from existence and become 'fossils in time' and 'footprints of the never-were'. Yet all is not lost and through Amy Pond the memory of the universe returns. For Amy herself, however, it will be like a dream, which is itself but a story. And according to Doctor Who that's what we all become in the end. Stories. But, as The Doctor says, what's important is to make your story, your dream, a good one.

## Déjà Vu

> We all have some experience of a feeling, that comes over us occasionally, of what we are saying and doing having been said and done before, in a remote time – of our having been surrounded, dim ages ago, by the same faces, objects, and circumstances.

So said Dickens' David Copperfield. We now call that feeling déjà vu. *Dark* ends at a dinner party where one guest has a strange sense of déjà vu, which, as some believe, might be glimpses into timelines that never happened but do somehow exist in another dimension. A shadowy echo of a memory, perhaps, of what might have been. Or even was. It's an idea that's there too in *The Adam Project*. In one scene, Adam points out to Laura that if he destroys time travel then he and Laura may never meet. But Laura isn't so despondent and argues that even if the timestream is corrected she believes that somewhere in them will be the 'echo' of this timeline and that echo will help the lovers find each other in another way. And it's an idea that is also explored in *Life after Life*, the 2013 novel (and later television series) written by Kate Atkinson. The tale's central character, Ursula Todd, repeatedly lives different lives but it is only through a particularly strong sense of déjà vu of these half-remembered existences that she realises she has indeed lived before.

## Anterograde Amnesia

Anterograde amnesia is the loss of the capacity to make new memories resulting in an inability to recall the recent past. This is in contrast to retrograde amnesia, where stored or past memories are lost as a result of a traumatic event of some sort but new memories can still be created. *Memento* is a 2000 mystery thriller written and directed by Christopher Nolan. It tells the story of Leonard Shelby, played by Guy Pearce, who suffers from anterograde amnesia as a result of an accident. Although he can recall some details of his life before this accident, Leonard cannot remember what happened 15 minutes ago, where he's going, or why. In the story, Leonard is searching for the people who attacked him and killed his wife. He does this using an intricate system of Polaroid photographs and tattoos to track information he cannot remember. In the movie, Christopher Nolan uses reverse-chronology as a means of putting the audience in the mindset of its brain-damaged detective. And it's this aspect more so than memory that makes *Memento* recognisably a Time Tale.

# Ageing, Immortals and Ghosts

*Time is the soul of the world.*
Pythagoras

## Refusing to Get Old

IT'S AN OLD joke but it's worth repeating and that is that time is a great healer but a lousy beautician. And even in those Time Tales where there are those who are given apparent eternal youth, it rarely lasts. In Jonathan Swift's 1726 satirical tale *Gulliver's Travels*, there live in the land of Luggnagg humans called Struldbrugg who are born seemingly normal, but are in fact immortal. They do not die, but the catch is they continue to age. And in this satire Swift mercilessly depicts the downside of immortality without the benefit of eternal youth.

In *She: A History of Adventure* by Henry Rider Haggard published in 1887, Ayesha finds immortality in The Pillar of Fire but when 'She' steps into it for a second time, the Spirit of Life in the fire rejects Ayesha and she quickly returns to her true age of over 2,000 years. And no moisturiser could do anything about those wrinkles. In a similar vein, there's that famous painting in the attic in Oscar Wilde's *A Picture of Dorian Gray*, published three years after *She: A History of Adventure* in 1890.

In these stories, time, or at least the ravages it wreaks on the human body, is held back or suspended. However, in what you might call 'body supplanting tales' the human lifespan is expanded by putting minds into replacement physical bodies, thus allowing people, or at least minds, to live beyond what Nature and Time would normally permit.

But taking over someone else's body and life and so escaping death is to cheat Time. And Father Time and his ever-present companion the Grim Reaper do not like that. *Freejack* (1992) has a plot where time travelling 'Bonejackers' take bodies from the past to allow wealthy people to escape death by a mind transfer or transmigration of souls. In *Self/Less* (2015), a human being who is slowly dying pays a great deal of money to take over the body of another who is willing to sell it to help his family and a similar body-takeover plot can be found in John Frankenheimer's *Seconds* (1966). Yet the span of one life should not be taken from another's. Although these stories end very differently, the moral seems to be, *Don't be greedy for Life, for what makes it special is its limitation*. And that's why those immortal Greek gods in Olympia in a way envied human beings, for if you are immortal you cannot possibly understand the precious and precarious nature of life which for us is what makes it so special.

## The Quest for Immortality

Most Time Tales accept the realities of mortality. In *Groundhog Day*, for example, Phil fails to keep the vagrant he befriends alive – 'He was just old. It was just his time,' says the medic at the hospital.

Time Tales often see those who seek immortality as dangerous. A popular *Doctor Who* story that deals with this very issue is *The Five Doctors* (1983). Lord President Borusa seeks immortality in The Tomb of Rassilon but foolishly doesn't understand the warning that states that 'to lose is to win and he who wins shall lose'. Rassilon offers Borusa his ring as the key and means to immortality, but when donning the ring, Borusa disappears, only to quickly reappear as a living stone that is part of Rassilon's tomb. Borusa now will live forever within the stone of the tomb, alongside all the others who foolishly sought out immortality. Yes, the tomb foretold immortality, yet it was also a warning and those who ignored it must pay the cost with incarceration in stone.

Then there is the M.R. James short story *Lost Hearts* (1895), a macabre tale of Mr Abney who seeks immortality by removing the hearts of children. Thankfully, as with most of Monty's tales, there is a supernatural element, and when the life of an orphan boy is threatened, the ghosts of those who previously lost their hearts haunt and kill Mr Abney. And good for them. Immortality is not for us humans, seems to be the message of these Time Tales. And it's a moral you'll also find explored in *Gilgamesh*, that most ancient of all myths.

In THE SWIDGERS, there are those who William comes across who seek an immortality of sorts. But Granny, William's friend and early Mentor, is wise and tells William that nothing can stop the advancement of Time. In the story, these men live in a kind of time 'bubble', but events on the outside world would eventually have brought an end to their existence. Anyway, it never gets that far for those who seek immortality in the tale act foolishly and ultimately bring about their own end.

## The Immortals

In Time Tales the search for eternal youth is rarely seen as a good thing. *Time Trap* (2017) is the bizarre yarn featuring a cave in which lies The Fountain of Youth (more a murky pool, actually), but the various caverns protect these special waters by slowing down time as you approach The Fountain. The cave then acts as an entrapment of sorts, and at its centre it looks like a room in Madame Tussauds with dozens of historical figures all moving at the pace of sleeping snail. An eternal youth of a kind is achieved, but at a seemingly deadly slow speed.

But what if you don't need magical waters? Suppose you are born immortal. In *Highlander* (1986 – story by Gregory Widen), Connor MacLeod (Christopher Lambert) is a Scottish swordsman of the 16th century who, when in battle, discovers he cannot die. His villagers believe him to be of the devil and so he is banished. MacLeod then meets Ramirez, who is another like himself, and Ramirez teaches MacLeod that the only way to kill another immortal is to take his head with a sword.

MacLeod journeys through time at the same pace as everyone else. The difference for him is that everyone he loves eventually dies. And this is painful for him to see, so he decides to abandon the possibility of love. In 1990s New York, however, he meets Brenda Wyatt (Roxanne Hart) who explains his predicament well when she says of him that being afraid to die is not his problem, his problem is being afraid to live. Immortals such as Connor MacLeod may have a more varied diet than their counterpart, the undead vampire, but ultimately they are equally unliving.

*Eternals* is a 2021 American superhero movie from the Marvel Comics stable. It was directed by Chloé Zhao, who, with Patrick Burleigh, Ryan Firpo and Kaz Firpo, also wrote the screenplay. The Eternals are an immortal alien race who have emerged from hiding after thousands of years in order to protect the Earth from their ancient counterparts, the Deviants. Like many in the Marvel canon, *Eternals* is a movie that is aware of story traditions and there are a number of intertextual references to legends and folktales both ancient and modern, such as the myths of Peter Pan, Icarus, Troy and Gilgamesh. The plot itself is essentially a team mission scenario and like many team mission tales there is a betrayal at its heart. It turns out that the true purpose of the Eternals wasn't to protect Earth as such, but rather to increase its population ready for the Celestials to harvest humans at the time of 'Emergence'. The Eternals were inadvertently protecting planet Earth to be used for human farming. But many among the Eternals had grown quite fond of the place and as a result fought back against the devouring Celestials.

What about robots? Data, for example, in *Star Trek: The Next Generation*. *Time's Arrow* is a time travel story where Data's head is discovered in a cavern after laying untouched for 500 years. Although at first it is unclear how it got there, Data is not at all upset by the knowledge of his own 'death'. Far from it.

In fact, Data argues that knowing he is going to die makes him feel more human. Other stories with immortals or an immortality theme are *A.I. Artificial Intelligence* (2001), *The Old Guard* (2020), *Deadpool* (2016), *The Fountain* (2006), plus of course Captain Jack in *Doctor Who*. Not all are time travel tales as such, but they are worth mentioning in the wider context of how stories see and explore time.

## Are Ghosts Time Travellers?

In Christopher Marlowe's *Doctor Faustus*, written somewhere around 1592/3, Faustus, at the request of the Emperor, asks Mephistophilis to summon characters from the classical world. What we then see is the Emperor Alexander killing Darius. Towards the end of the play even Helen of Troy makes an appearance – 'was that the face that launched a thousand ships, / And burnt the topless towers of Ilium?' – but even she cannot make Faustus 'immortal with a kiss', for now the game is up. But leaving the problems of Faustus aside, could it be argued that Helen of Troy, the Emperor Alexander and Darius were the first ever time travellers? Well, there's no concrete evidence of course that Helen was even a real person, the Trojan War, even if it was based on some sort of conflict across the Mediterranean Sea, was probably more artistic invention than history. As for the time travelling nature of these characters in the play, it's important to note that they are not 'real' in the way Socrates, Joan of Arc and Abraham Lincoln are real in *Bill and Ted's Excellent Adventure*. The manifestations conjured up in Marlow's *Doctor Faustus* are spirits in the shapes of Alexander, Daruis and Helen in what is essentially an Elizabethan theatrical dumb show. But boundaries in stories often blur. What to make, for example, of the armoured men in the museum who are magically brought to life in *Bedknobs and Broomsticks* (1971). They are both in their time and yet out of time. And then there's the baseball players in *Field of Dreams* ('If you build it, he will come.') Yes, the field has a magical quality and those who appear are very real and physical, yet the rule is they cannot leave the field. Are they ghosts or phantoms of time? Or maybe a bit of both.

Ghost tales come in many forms and there is what you might call the 'Time Slip' ghost. These ghosts are not haunters with chains, decaying flesh and removable heads, but rather spirits from another time going about their business as they would have done in that era. For example, Charles Dickens' *The Ghosts of the Mail*, where a living character from the present joins a mail coach and mixes with people from an earlier time. Often encounters with such spirits (if that's what they are) involve no interaction, for the simple reason they unable to see the living. For example, in Amelia B. Edwards' *Was it an Illusion?* (1881) there is this encounter:

> 'Can you tell me', I said, 'if I am right for Pit End, and how far I have to go?'
> 
> He came on, looking straight before him; taking no notice of my question; apparently not hearing it.
> 
> 'I beg your pardon,' I said, raising my voice; 'but will this path take me to Pit End, and if so—'
> 
> He had passed on without pausing; without looking at me; I could almost have believed, without seeing me!

So was it an illusion or time jump or a ghost or something else? The tale ends by saying,

> Ay, indeed! that is the question; and it is a question which I have never yet been able to answer. Certain things I undoubtedly saw – with my mind's eye, perhaps – and as I saw them, I have described them; withholding nothing, adding nothing, explaining nothing. Let those solve the mystery who can.

*The Open Door* (1882) by Margaret Oliphant is a classic Victorian ghost tale that concerns the return of a wastrel son who, when he hears that his mother is dead, cries out at the door 'Oh, mother, let me in! O, mother, mother, let me in!' Only that was years ago and now there is no door, it is but a ruin. Yet that pitiable scene still goes on and is witnessed by several observers. The narrator, one of the witnesses, describes what he sees 'as if it had been real':

> I seemed to explain it all to myself by saying that this had once happened, that it was a recollection of a real scene. Why there should have seemed something quite satisfactory and composing in this explanation I cannot tell, but so it was. I began to listen almost as if it had been a play.

Later there is another encounter with what amounts to the same scenario:

> To me it seemed as if — Heaven help us, how little do we know about anything! — a scene like that might impress itself somehow upon the hidden heart of nature. I do not pretend to know how, but the repetition had struck me at the time as, in its terrible strangeness and incomprehensibility, almost mechanical, — as if the unseen actor could not exceed or vary, but was bound to re-enact the whole.

The idea that a moment of emotional trauma in time 'might impress itself somehow upon the hidden heart of nature' – an emotional residue, if you will – has been a feature of modern ghost tales, but as we can see here the idea is in fact an old one.

There's a more benign encounter with a lady from the past in George MacDonald's *Uncle Cornelius His Story* (1869):

> I am not good at observing, and I am still worse at describing dress, therefore I can only say that hers reminded me of an old picture – that is, I had never seen anything like it, except in old pictures. She had no bonnet, and looked as if she had walked

straight out of an ancient drawing-room in her evening attire.

Often when someone converses with you in Victorian and Edwardian ghost stories it's only at the end of the tale that it is revealed that the figure was actually dead at the time that conversation took place. This is popular trope and can be found in Robert W. Chambers' *A Pleasant Evening* (1896) and Charles Dickens' *The Portrait-Painter's Story* (1861).

It's true that all these tales can – and perhaps should – be classified as ghost tales, even if they do involve a 'time shift' or 'time jump' element. But what of E.F. Benson's *In the Tube* (1923) which begins with a philosophical refection on the nature of time itself:

> 'It's a convention,' said Anthony Carling cheerfully, 'and not a very convincing one. Time, indeed! There's no such thing as Time really; it has no actual existence. Time is nothing more than an infinitesimal point in eternity, just as space is an infinitesimal point in infinity. At the most, Time is a sort of tunnel through which we are accustomed to believe that we are travelling. There's a roar in our ears and a darkness in our eyes which makes it seem real to us. But before we came into the tunnel we existed for ever in an infinite sunlight, and after we have got through it we shall exist in an infinite sunlight again. So why should we bother ourselves about the confusion and noise and darkness which only encompass us for a moment?'

The narrator is having an after dinner conversation with his friend Carling in front of a log fire. Carling, says the narrator, goes on to say that the finite is more difficult to comprehend than the infinite because with the finite you have to imagine a beginning, but that leads to the question what was before that beginning. Eternity however is something that never began and will never end. It is not a quantity but a quality. The narrator's philosophising friend next develops the concept of when a crime begins and listens as Carling puts forward the idea that the commission of the act is merely the material sequel of resolve. Carling then speculates what those who have 'second sight' are seeing when they observe spirits are re-enactments of wrong-doings – 'For it seems certain that the spirit of a man, after the death of his body, is obliged to re-enact such a crime, with a view, I suppose we may guess, to his remorse and his eventual redemption.' Carling then goes on to describe how he saw what he calls a 'phantom of the living', whom he knows, throw himself onto the line of an on-coming tube train. Yet it's only Carling, who is on a crowded platform, who actually witnesses this event. 'The flimsy veil of Time had been withdrawn from my eyes, and I had seen into what you would call the future.' Carling decides not to warn the man of what he had seen because doing so might lead to the action itself (the Future Paradox). 'Might not the fact of my telling him what I had seen put the idea into his mind, or, if it was already there, confirm it and strengthen it?' But it happens as Carling saw it and he knows this because he reads of the man's suicide a few days later in the newspaper.

What we have here is surely more time travel than a ghostly visitation. Yet there's a twist in the tale when the dead man appears before them in a concealing haze with his 'chest crushed in and drowned in the red stain, from which broken ribs, like the bones of a wrecked ship, protruded.' Most definitely ghost on this occasion.

Ghosts, as with time travellers, come from another world, and with ghosts it is usually a lost or forgotten era. Ghosts of the past, like time travellers from the future, bring with them warnings. Ghosts tend to be harbingers of doom because they have witnessed the darker actions of society and those who live in it. As a result, ghosts are often seekers of justice and retribution, who wish to expose wrongdoing and even evil, or simply have an unfinished project to complete or have a need to say sorry. In this sense they might be said to be enablers, and the same could be said of time travellers. Ghosts are lonely and abandoned creatures, unhappy in a world they do not understand. And in this they have much in common with many nomadic and restless time travellers. And ghosts, as with time travellers, often seek to defeat death. Or at least don't always want to move on just yet.

The tradition in supernatural stories that ghosts are really coming back to help or for help is very cleverly explored in the psychological horror movie *Last Night in Soho*, written by Edgar Wright and Krysty Wilson-Cairns. The 2021 modern-day Ellie seems to go back in time to Soho of the 1960s and into the body of a girl singer called Sandie. At first Ellie believes that Sandie was the victim of murder, yet ultimately it is revealed that Sandie was in fact a serial killer and her victims were the grubby, sleazy men of Soho. Not only that, but it is their ghosts who are now driving the visions she is having. So are the ghosts time travellers or not? Is it that the ghosts are bringing the past to Ellie or is she going back in time with them to witness the events that led up to their death? Or doesn't it matter, for the logic of the supernatural set-up allows both versions. A discussion about ghosts being like time travellers could perhaps go on ad infinitum. Let's just leave the similarities there for now, and acknowledge there are at least some parallels.

However, there is one film, where the ghost is definitely a time traveller, or at least is able to make contact with people on other timelines. *Haunter* (2013) is a time loop scenario where the ghost, Lisa Johnson, and her family are all trapped in the day and the house where they were murdered. However, by communicating with the past residents and victims, Lisa is able to break the loop and in doing so, ultimately saves herself and her family. Only then of course she stops being a ghost.

# Utopias/Dystopias, Counterfactuals, Time Sleep and Time Stopped

*'All my life,' he said, 'I have been strangely, vividly conscious of another region — not far removed from our own world in one sense, yet wholly different in kind — where great things go on unceasingly, where immense and terrible personalities hurry by, intent on vast purposes compared to which earthly affairs, the rise and fall of nations, the destinies of empires, the fate of armies and continents, are all as dust in the balance.'*
The Willows, Algernon Blackwood

## Utopian/Dystopian Fiction and Time Tales

THE FRENCH PHILOSOPHER Betrand De Jouvenel argued that tyranny could be found in the womb of every Utopia. Dystopian fiction and Time Tales sometimes have a symbiotic relationship and there is an entire genre to be found when the two come together. And there are many such tales in both books and the movies, including, for example *Lost Horizon, Planet of the Apes* and *A Wrinkle in Time. Back to the Future II* could even be said to be a dystopia, where Hill Valley becomes like the nightmare version of Pottersville in *It's a Wonderful Life*, only more so. And the problems resulting from Biff's gambling success in this alternative world have clearly had major and widespread political repercussions for there is a frightening headline about Richard Nixon seeking a fifth term and vowing to end the Vietnam War by 1985.

Two positive thinking utopian tales are worth a particular mention here and they are *Sultana's Dream* and *Beatrice the Sixteenth: Being the Personal Narrative of Mary Hatherby, M.B., Explorer and Geographer*, for both are early feminist narratives. *Sultana's Dream* is a Bengali feminist Utopia and was written in 1905 by Begum Rokeya, a Muslim social reformer. It is a fantasy of sorts where gender roles have been reversed. Strictly speaking it's a time sleep tale not time travel, and it's a very short tale too. However, in its brief telling it depicts a world where science better serves society. Here's the exchange between the new arrival and the lady she meets who tells her of this new world and how it came about:

> 'While the women were engaged in scientific research, the men of this country were busy increasing their military power. When they came to know that the female universities were able to draw water from the atmosphere and collect heat from the sun, they only laughed at the members of the universities and called the whole thing "a sentimental nightmare"!'
> 'Your achievements are very wonderful indeed! But tell me, how you managed to put the men of your country into the zenana. Did you entrap them first?'
> 'No.'
> 'It is not likely that they would surrender their free and open air life of their own accord and confine themselves within the four walls of the zenana! They must have been overpowered.'
> 'Yes, they have been!'
> 'By whom? By some lady-warriors, I suppose?'
> 'No, not by arms.'
> 'Yes, it cannot be so. Men's arms are stronger than women's. Then?'
> 'By brain.'

*Beatrice the Sixteenth* is about a time traveller who discovers a lost world that turns out to be a Utopian post-gender society. It was written in 1909 by Irene Clyde, a writer and lawyer, who was transgender. In the story, the explorer Mary Hatherley receives a kick from a camel while journeying through Asia Minor which sends her into another time period and a place called Armeria, which is ruled over by Queen Beatrice the Sixteenth of the title. The Armerians are strict vegetarians and their life partnership, known as a 'conjux', appears to be based on love and companionship, rather than sex. Their language, a combination of Latin and Greek, contains no gendered pronouns. Mary forms a conjux with Ilex, one of the leading figures in the kingdom, and even when offered a way to return home by the court astrologer, she decides to remain. However, Mary is able, with the astrologer's help, to send a manuscript to a friend in our world, who then arranges for it to be published by Irene Clyde.

The key point about any utopian/dystopian tale is that you are not being shown what is, but rather what could be, be that good or bad. And in seeing these alternatives, you are able to re-evaluate your own society and understand it in a new light.

## Counter Factual and Alternate Histories

Alternate histories, sometimes called speculative fiction or counter factual, should only really be classed as a Time Tale when the change from what we know to be reality is caused by a time split or time travel. *Lest Darkness Fall* (1939) is definitely in the time travel category, whereas Len Deighton's *SS-GB* (1978), Quentin Tarantino's *Inglorious Basterds* (2009) and Philip K. Dick's *The Man in the High Castle* (1962) offer essentially challenging maybes and what ifs about the outcome of the Second World War. *2009: Lost Memories*, also a Second World War narrative of a sort, is a 2002 South Korean science fiction action movie that is set in a universe where the United States of America and Japan joined forces to fight the Nazis in the 1930s. However, as this change was brought about by altering a previous event in history in 1909, it is a time travel tale.

In L. Sprague de Camp's *Lest Darkness Fall* (published 1941), set in 1938, Padway is struck by lightning and he finds himself in Rome in the year 535 AD. After making certain changes, Rome continues to be able to share its knowledge. Darkness does not fall, that is to say the Dark Ages, when much of the accumulated knowledge of the ancients was lost, do not occur.

A more recent example of an alternate history can be found in Richard Curtis' *Yesterday*, where the whole world experiences a 12-second electrical flicker and it is at that exact moment that singer and songwriter Jack Malik is hit by a bus. When Jack awakes, he slowly comes to realise that The Beatles never happened (and neither incidentally did the *Harry Potter* book series by author J.K. Rowling) and so he uses his extensive knowledge of the Lennon and McCartney songs to pass them off as his own. Increasingly, alternate histories/speculative/counter factual stories have an environmental aspect and these are usually called 'apocalyptic fiction futures'. The reasons why the apocalypse happened range from disease, social collapse, technology, war and impact events to alien invasion, monsters, biologically altered human, zombies and even ghosts. The time travel element, if there is one, usually centres around going back in time and stopping the catalyst event that caused the change in the status quo.

*The Time They Saved Tomorrow*, book two of THE SWIDGERS Time Adventure series, involves an alternate history where World War II was lost. Granny and William discover that their world, the one where the Allies were victorious, was only a possible world. And it was only made possible by the intervention of a Swidger in a time loop who is now dying. To say any more would be to give away too much of the plot, but what can be said is that Time will eventually have to choose between these two worlds and even though the world Granny and William know came about through the intervention of a Swidger, that does not necessarily mean it takes priority. In fact, the default world is actually the tyrannous and authoritarian world they now suddenly find themselves in.

## 'Time Sleep' Tales

There is a sub-genre of Time Tales that could be called the 'Time Sleep' story where a sleeper for some reason awakes in a different era (these stories are also sometimes called 'suspended animation tales'). As a plot, it is as old as *Sleeping Beauty* but specifically dealing with time travel it is a scenario that dates back as far as 1771 and *L'An 2440, rêve s'il en fut jamais* (literally *The Year 2440: A Dream If Ever There Was One*), which is usually rendered in English as *Memoirs of the Year 2500*. This novel by Louis-Sébastien Mercier features an unnamed man who falls asleep in Paris but wakes up centuries later in a world he hardly recognises. It's a work that is now regarded as the first example in utopian fiction that is set in the future rather than the past.

Washington Irving's story *Rip Van Winkle* has a similar plot, in that a colonial American meets a mysterious Dutchman who plies him with a drink and as a result he wakes up 20 years later and in a very changed world, having missed out on the American Revolution. One of the biggest selling novels of the Victorian period was Edward Bellamy's *Looking Backward: 2000–1887* (published 1888), again featuring a slumberous time lapse. In this story, America has become a socialist utopia. The novel at one stage even inspired 'Bellamy Clubs' that propagated and spread the book's social and societal principles.

A very different take on the falling asleep and waking up in the future scenario is Philip Francis Nowlan's 1928 novella, *Armageddon 2419 A.D.*, for this is the book which eventually led to the swashbuckling hero we know as Buck Rogers. In *Armageddon 2419 A.D.*, Anthony Rogers was working for the American Radioactive Gas Corporation in 1927 when he was sent to investigate an unusual phenomenon in an abandoned coal mine. Here he was exposed to radioactive gas which put him in a state of suspended animation. These forty winks last 492 years and when Rogers eventually wakes up he finds himself in the year 2419. In this new world Rogers joins a gang where the combat skills he learnt in the First World War are put to good effect. Buck Rogers appeared in *Amazing Stories*, and later on radio in 1932, plus a serial film and several television adaptations.

There are in fact many Time Sleep stories where a protagonist comes out of some sort of hibernation and finds themselves in a changed world. These include *The Sleeper Awakes*, the 1910 novel by H.G. Wells, and *The Man Who Woke*, the 1933 novel by Laurence Manning, where Norman Winters puts himself in suspended animation for 5,000 years at a time and when he wakes has to try and make sense of the society he finds himself in. Of course, the idea of suspended animation or being cryogenically frozen has been used many times in movies too, notably in Woody Allen's *The Sleeper* (1973). Then of course there's the *Austin Powers* series and more recently *Idiocracy* (2006) with Luke Wilson as Joe Bauers. These time skip tales often turn into 'stranded' stories' or 'fish-out-of-water' tales in that once the time travel element is established, the situation itself remains unaltered. *Outlaws* (CBS 1986–87), for example, was a television series about five cowboys from the 1880s who, as a result of a freak lightning strike (always a useful catalyst event in a Time Tale), find themselves in 1986. With no way to get back home, the men use their skills to start a detective agency in order to make a living. *Phil of the Future, Demolition Man, Futurama, Catweazle, Adam Adament Lives!* and *It's About Time* also explore this time skip concept.

One of Russia's most popular home grown Time Tale movies was *Ivan Vasilievich Changes Profession* (1973) directed by Leonid Gaidai (in the United States the film has sometimes been sold not surprisingly under the title *Ivan Vasilievich: Back to the Future*). It tells the tale of Ivan Vasilievich who time swaps with Ivan the Terrible. In 1973 it was one of the most attended movies in the Soviet Union, with more than 60 million tickets sold.

These stories are often dismissed as pulp fare and pure entertainment, and nothing wrong with that, but apart from its dramatic and comic potential, the 'fish-out-of-water' premise can resonate deeply with people who, in their own life, see themselves as outsiders. Plus, of course, the 'fish-out-of-water' concept allows comparisons between society's cultural values then, or whenever, and now. And sometimes if it is an imagined future, that future comes true. Laurence Manning's *The Man Who Awoke* is set in a world that has had a sexual revolution, suffers from global warming, and where there is a form of Artificial Intelligence and even Virtual Reality. Time Tales really can be a peek into the world of tomorrow.

## Time Stopped

> The sun stood still, and the moon stopped, until the nation avenged themselves of their enemies. Is it not written in The Book of Jashar? And the sun stopped in the middle of the sky and did not hasten to go down for about a whole day.

A verse from Joshua 10:13. The poem is usually interpreted to mean that the sun delayed its setting, remained in the zenith of the heavens rather than set in the east. Luke 4:5 has a different type of stopped time when the devil takes Jesus to a high mountain and shows him all the kingdoms of the world in 'a moment of time', or, a 'twinkling of an eye' as the 1599 Geneva Bible puts it. How the sun remained in the sky without setting or how the devil could stop time, if that is what is meant, opens up a can of worms beyond our ken, but we mention it here simply to illustrate that the concept of time being frozen has existed for several millennia at least.

For obvious dramatic reasons, centring an entire plot around the concept of time stopped would not be easy but *The Guests*, a 1964 episode of *The Outer Limits* written by Donald S. Sanford is worth a mention. In the story, a drifter called Wade Norton, finds an old man dying by the side of a remote country road. Wade picks up the man's pocket watch and takes it to a nearby mansion with the intention of seeking help. However, those living there appear oddly uninterested. Wade then tries to leave through the front door, but finds himself being forced backward upstairs where he discovers an amorphous jelly-like alien being who, it is revealed, is keeping the inhabitants of the large house suspended in time in order to understand the nature of humanity. And this experiment could last an eternity, for, as the creature says to Wade, 'I have more Time than forever.' On returning downstairs, the drifter attempts to flee but discovers the windows are blocked and doors lead back where he started.

Inside the pocket watch there was a picture of a young woman and this same woman then leads Norton to an escape route, a gate adjacent to a cemetery plot which is accessible from the mansion. However, she also tells him that if she leaves all her years will catch up with her and she will die. Wade chooses to remain in the house with her but, realising he will be trapped among them for eternity, the young girl exits through the gate and, without the protection from the passage of time that the alien offers, withers and turns to dust. Yet the creature in seeing this has discovered two important aspects of humanity: love and self-sacrifice and as a result the mansion returns to its true reality, an enormous alien brain, and then disappears leaving Wade Norton behind and alone. A fascinating tale for this drifter to tell, but who'd ever believe him?

There are several Time Tales where time is stopped, for example, *The Magic Boomerang* (ABC Australia 1965–66), *Clockstoppers* (2002), and *Bernard's Watch* (ITV 1997–2005), though in these stories time is only stopped on a temporary basis. Likewise in Charles Band's *Trancers* (1984 – written by Danny Bilson and Paul De Meo), our protagonist time traveller Jack Deth is equipped with a wristwatch which slows time, stretching one second over a 10-second period. You might also include *A Matter of Life and Death* (1946), though this is more a supernatural story where time can be stopped by an intervening angel or spirit. In the Korean time travel series *Alice*, Park Jin-gyeom has the power to stop time. Where this ability came from isn't clear but perhaps it's because his mother went through The Door of Time when she was pregnant with him, and, *The Book of Prophecy* says that the child born while opening The Door of Time will eventually control Time.

In *The Time That Never Was*, there is a character who claims to be able to stop Time, but this gift is misused and selfishly so. We must move on in life. We must grow up. The inspiration behind *The Time That Never Was* is in some ways J.M. Barrie's *Peter Pan*. It's always useful to remember that the subtitle of Barrie's play was *The Boy Who Wouldn't Grow Up*. Originally the word was 'couldn't' but Barrie then realised that making it Peter's choice with 'wouldn't', results in it becoming a modern tragedy.

## The Malleability of Time

It should be said that not all Time Tales are about time travel, time stopping or time displacement. There are stories where characters suddenly age in their bodies but remain at the same mental or sexual age (*Big*, *Going On 30*) or in fact don't age at all (*The Picture of Dorian Gray*). There are also tales where a character's life is lived continuously through history as themselves (*Intolerance* and *The Navigator: A Medieval Odyssey*) or as themselves but with shifting chameleon-like identities (*Zelig*) or as themselves but becoming a different gender (*Orlando*). Or even indeed not lived at all (*It's a Wonderful Life*). There are stories too where time in effect goes backwards (*Tenet*) or leads to a life lived backwards (*The Curious Case of Benjamin Button*). None of these stories are time travel tales as such, but instead they play with the malleability of time itself.

## Stories Within Stories

There are tales where a character is reading a book, or watching a film or engrossed in a television series or even listening to a song, and then, through a strike of lightning or whatever, becomes part of that fictional world. Tales where a character enters and becomes part of a made-up world, particularly a well-known or established fictional world, is sometimes called a meta-fiction or an inter-textual narrative. The films *The Purple Rose of Cairo* and *Pleasantville* are examples of this. Here, it's not so much the past that these characters become a part of, but rather a specific fictional world set in the past. That said, is the difference in practice or in storytelling terms that different? And does it matter? If not, these stories become Time Tales by default.

# Time Tales and Genre Crossovers

*Don't classify me, read me. I'm a writer, not a genre.*
Carlos Fuentes, Mexican novelist and essayist

## What is Genre?

GENRE SIMPLY MEANS what kind of story it is – the category you would put it in based on its particular style or content. Think here of all those shelves in bookshops that have labels saying Romantic Fiction, Gothic Horror, Science Fiction, Westerns and so on. Genre then is that aspect of a work that deals with its classification. The word genre comes from the French, literally meaning 'a kind', and is based on the Latin word *genus*, meaning 'birth, family or nation'. Yet is there such a thing as the Time Travel genre? *Somewhere in Time* and *The Terminator* are certainly both Time Tales, but does it feel right that such different stories should share the same shelf? Larry Niven argued that science fiction (SF), including time travel stories, wasn't a genre at all – 'SF is a matrix in which genres are embedded.'

Of course a unique advantage of a Time Tale is that it can take on a period style or indeed a genre particular to that era, plus it can imitate other narratives. *Quantum Leap* in the '80s, time travelled back to the late '50s with a distinctly *Good Morning, Vietnam* vibe going on in the episode *Good Morning, Peroia* about a radio station playing decadent rock'n'roll and there's a seasonal episode of *Doctor Who* called *A Christmas Carol* (2010). In fact, *Doctor Who* often enjoys playing with genre, notable examples include the Robin Hood legend (*Robot of Sherwood*) and pirate ship tales (*The Curse of the Black Spot*). Occasionally television time travel shows seem to be as much about a trip back to a genre developed in a particular time in cultural history as the actual time period itself. This was certainly true for *Life on Mars* and *Ashes to Ashes*. In the *Travelers'* episode *The Day Reagan Was Shot*, Jiya and Lucy even go by the names Cagney and Lacy, characters of course from the popular '80s cop series *Cagney and Lacy*.

What is important with genre is familiarity. The new narrative must fulfil the characteristics of the story but in an unexpected way. Tales that play with genre have to be as inventive as the original stories on which they were based. Let's now look at a few, including the action movie, the sitcom, the rom-com, the sitcom, the crime detective story, horror and the western.

## The Action Movie Crossover

What is it that makes a great action movie? What are the plot requirements? And what are its essential ingredients? Before the arrival of *The Terminator* in 1984, the time travel action movie was a rarity. And even if it did exist, it never made money. But then came the blockbuster success of *The Terminator*, and now the Time Tale action movie thriller is a genre in its own right.

In the typical action movie the events themselves take place in an unfamiliar and hostile environment to the protagonist. Bridges must be burnt, metaphorically or literally, so that there is a point of no return with no possibility of going back. If your protagonist is new to this lark, you should take them 'from Zero to Hero', as the saying goes, and if they are seasoned professionals there should be a low moment, the nadir, when they are near death, which then, through their own ingenuity, becomes a moment when they leap from apparent failure to glorious triumph. In an action movie there is usually a ticking clock so that whatever needs to be achieved must be done within a finite time period, with usually only seconds to spare at the climax. And the stakes are always high, at least death for you, but better still the threat of death for anyone you care about. The hero and the antagonist villain should not be evenly matched, for the hero must always be somehow weaker or out-numbered. If the hero is male and there is a girl in the story, then there is usually a sex scene. No matter how fast the clock is ticking, there must always be room for rumpy-pumpy. Oh, and every 20 minutes or so there should be a fight or a chase, and in the end some sort of seemingly unwinnable battle or confrontation. To put all this in one golden takeaway nugget: *Don't ever, ever make it easy for your hero*.

So how does *The Terminator* (screenplay by Sacha Gervasi and Jeff Nathanson, with story by Andrew Niccol and Sacha Gervasi) stack up to that very prescriptive list of requirements? Pretty well, actually. Burning bridges? Well, there's no turning back because for Kyle Reese time travel is a one-way ticket. Unfamiliar environment? Most Time Tales have someone travelling to a different era, so that box is ticked. Ironically for Kyle, in 1984 it is the agents of law enforcement that turn out to be the most hostile to him. Is the villain more powerful than the hero? Er, you bet. The Terminator is a killing machine, Kyle Reese is a vulnerable human being. Yes, a trained soldier, but still flesh and blood not reinforced steel. And Kyle is literally only flesh and blood for he arrives naked and so is immediately at risk. *The Terminator* of course has joint heroes, Kyle and Sarah, and it's certainly Zero to Hero for Sarah the waitress who eventually, and alone, destroys the seemingly invincible Terminator. Not that this villain is that easy to wipe out. Truth is, in good action movie tradition, he/it just won't lie down and die. The Terminator certainly seemed to be trashed after the explosion of the gas tank, only then there is that famous slow emergence of his skeletal figure from the flames which became one of the movie's most iconic moments. Guess what, there's more work to do to stop him/it permanently.

The obligatory sex scene between Kyle and Sarah is far from gratuitous from a plot point of view as Kyle has been sent back by John Connor precisely because John Connor knows that Kyle will become his father. What about a ticking clock? Strictly speaking, there is no ticking clock in *The Terminator*, or at least not one with the flashing digits of a bomb as in the 007 type movie. That said, The Terminator is pretty much indestructible and so it seems it will be only a matter of time before Sarah is killed. But Sarah is a quick learner. In the final confrontation, it is the new born hero Sarah Connors, close to death herself as the genre rule must have it, who ingeniously tempts the villain into a metal pressing unit that is his/its doom. It takes a machine to kill a machine. Or what's left of it, as bits weirdly crawl along.

*The Terminator* became seminal in influencing all those time travel action movies that have followed, such as *Deadpool*, *Source Code*, *X-Men* and *Men in Black*. One big difference between *The Terminator* and say action adventure series such as *Travelers* or *Timeless* or the movie *Timeline* is that *The Terminator* has a hero–villain dynamic, whereas in the others the dynamic is more that of the team mission.

## Romantic Comedy Crossover

The term 'soulmate' first appeared in the English language in a letter by Samuel Taylor Coleridge in 1822, but the idea had been around for a while, since in fact the writings of Plato in classical Greece. In Plato's *Symposium*, Aristophanes tells the story of how Zeus feared human beings so much that he split them into two halves. According to Greek mythology, humans originally had four arms, four legs and a head with two faces. They were very powerful and physically perfect creatures, and so Zeus, fearing humans would rise against him, chopped these human beings down the middle, creating male and female counterparts. The body, now cut into two, yearned for its 'other half', the half that had been severed. Love is simply the name given by the Greeks to the desire and pursuit of that whole. As a matter of fact, in Greek thought, there were three sexes in nature: man, woman and androgynous, which literally means man-woman in Greek. Men were children of the Sun, women were children of the Earth and androgynous were children of the Moon, born of the merging of the Sun and Earth. But whichever your sex or gender, binary, non-binary or whatever way you identify your sexual nature, there is a strong romantic tradition that somewhere out there is your 'other half' who will make you complete. And, uniquely, what Time Tale crossover romantic dramas can do is have distances across time as one of the obstacles to be overcome. Or more positively have time itself lead you to the love of your life.

Modern romantic comedies often work like this. A and B are together (or A would like to be with B). B in this scenario is usually very good looking and seemingly perfect. But there's C to add to the equation. C may be a friend or someone new who comes along. C is often more quirky or sometimes emotionally damaged, but whatever the case they are never as perfect or good looking as B. Eventually, however, A comes to realise that though they thought they were in love with B, they discover that it is C they truly want to be with. B usually magnanimously accepts this and so it is A and C who ride off into the sunset. And you'll find this basic formula in such films as *Sleepless in Seattle*, *Crossing Delancy* and *When Harry Met Sally*.

So how does this basic formula work with Time Tales? Well, what a Time Tale inevitably does is add a time twist. In *When We First Met* (2018 – written by John Whittington), it is Noah who longs for Avery, but Avery is engaged to Ethan. Carrie at this stage is a friend in the background. On a night out, Noah discovers a magical photo booth that can take him back to the day he and Avery first met and so he decides to travels back in time to make sure it is he, Noah, that Avery falls for and not Ethan. Noah doesn't succeed at first, so he goes back to the photo booth and tries again. After many disastrous attempts, Noah is eventually successful. He finds himself married to Avery but unhappy because he hates his rich life and besides Avery is discovered to be having an affair with Ethan anyway. Noah discovers destiny doesn't like things being changed. It's very obdurate. Perhaps that's why they call it destiny. Anyway, during these repeated days, Noah has been thinking a lot about

Carrie and realises that it is Carrie that he truly loves. Once this is understood, everything turns out all right. *Ahhh!*

*Sliding Doors* (1998 – written by Peter Howitt) is a popular Time Tale with a similar theme, though it is presented in a slightly different way. In *Sliding Doors*, there is not a time machine, just a chance moment on the London underground as doors close. But in this story, even if chance seems to work against you, destiny will eventually find a way for you and the person you are meant to be with to come together. Circumstances may change, the sliding door may close too early, but take comfort in the belief that your destiny will remain open for you until you will find your love. An even bigger *Ahhhhhh!*

Cara J. Russell's *The Knight Before Christmas* (2019) is more an old-fashioned romance that uses the standard movie formula of boy-meets-girl, boy-loses-girl, boy-gets-girl. Only the getting and the losing are done in different centuries. It's a festive story concerning a medieval Knight from 1334 who is magically sent to contemporary Ohio by an Old Crone and falls in love. It's a fish-out-of-water story with predictable jokes about airplanes that look like 'flying steel dragons' and that television in the corner is a 'magic box that makes merry'. Of course, he, the Knight, eventually returns to his own time back in 1334 but once back he realises his one true love is actually living in Ohio in the 21st century. The Old Crone takes pity on him and returns the Knight to his modern maiden. And verily, I say unto you, they all lived happily ever after. All together now... *Ahhh!*

## Sitcom Crossovers

The comic possibilities of time travel have been explored many times but rarely as consistently as in *Family Guy* (Fox from 1999) which features a returning strand in which Stewie the Griffin family baby (a self-styled scientific genius and diabolical mastermind who inexplicably speaks with an English accent) and Brian the family dog (a pompous talking canine with ambitions above his breed) use Stewie's time machine to enjoy fantastical adventures, that often begin as attempts simply to solve an argument about something that happened in the past. Whether these trips are real or just the products of Stewie's fevered imagination, may be a moot point, but *Family Guy* creator Seth MacFarlane – a self-confessed sci-fi fan – has explored (and subverted) many traditional Time Tale tropes in this recurring set of stories. *Blackadder Back and Forth* (1999) uses the device of a time machine to allow us to meet some old incarnations of the Blackadder family, plus some new (to us) historical characters. Lost-in-space sitcom *Red Dwarf* (BBC from 1988, later DAVE – created by Rob Grant and Doug Naylor) has also featured time travel episodes. There are as well series that pivot on the very idea of time travel, like *Goodnight Sweetheart* and *Timewasters*, and others that use time travel in their opening episodes to set up their premise, like *It's About Time* (CBS 1966–67) and *Futurama* (Fox from 1999).

## The Crime and Detective Crossover

As Seneca said, '*Veritatem dies aperit*' ('Time reveals the truth') and the Time Tale certainly lends itself to crime genre. There is the 'Fugitive Narrative', for example *Time Trax* (1993–1994), *Trancers* 1984, sometimes called *Future Cop*) and *Mirai Sentai Timeranger* (2000–2001), where time criminals are tracked and pursued. There is also the more traditional detective story but with a time element added. In Anthony Horowitz's *Crime Traveller* (1997) for example, Jeff Slade (Michael French) uses a time machine to witness crimes in the past but later solve them in the present. *New Amsterdam* has the twist that John Amsterdam is a homicide detective who is immortal and in fact 400 years old and therefore able to use his knowledge acquired across time in solving murders. The movie *Time After Time*, from the 1979 novel by Karl Alexander, features H.G. Wells himself travelling in time to the 1970s in search of Jack the Ripper. And then there are the fish-out-of-water series *Life on Mars* and *Ashes to Ashes*.

## The Supernatural and Horror Crossover

*Happy Death Day* (2017 – written by Scott Lobdell) is set on Tree Gelbman's birthday, the day she gets murdered – hence the film's title. But, in proper Bill Murray fashion, Tree is able to relive this day again and again. The problem for Tree is that her mystery killer takes no chances and even if she escapes the knife in the alleyway, her murderer is there waiting for her in the bedroom. Many unhappy returns indeed. *Happy Death Day* (and its sequel *Happy Death Day 2U* – 2019) is a 'slasher'-come-romantic-comedy-come-Time-Tale. Like Phil the Bill Murray character in *Groundhog Day*, Tree goes through various stages, including denial and anger, and, like Phil, eventually she decides to assist people along on their life journey, including helping one guy to accept that he's gay as well as healing the emotional rift with her own father. And so to this slasher-comedy-time mix you can add the concept of the 'redemption story'. There are some terrific final twists that are truly inventive and the film ends with a nod to the movie that clearly inspired it when in a coffee shop Tree tells new friend Carter Davis that she's never seen *Groundhog Day*. Perhaps not, but she has lived it, bless her.

*Tru Calling* (2003–05 – created by Jon Harmon Feldman) combines time, crime and the supernatural. In the show, Eliza Dushku as Tru Davies, is a 22-year-old medical student working in a morgue. One night, a corpse 'awakes' and asks Tru to prevent her untimely death for, it is revealed, Tru has the power to relive the previous day.

## The Western Crossover

In *Back to the Future III*, director Robert Zemeckis has great fun with the western. Marty's arrival in 1885 was shot in Monument Valley, a favourite location of the director John Ford, he calls himself 'Clint Eastwood' (who consented to the use of his name and was said to be pleased with the reference) and other actors in the film include the John Wayne stock company regular Harry Carey Jr who appears in the saloon, plus Dub Taylor and Pat Buttram. It's a shame though there wasn't a real time machine to allow the return of the wonderful Walter Brennan. These movie 'in-jokes' are intended for those in the know. Just like the names of Doc's children, Jules and Verne.

*Time Stalkers* (1987), a television movie written by Brian Clemens also had a distinct Wild West vibe. Dr Scott McKenzie, is a college professor and fan of the Old West. When McKenzie enlarges some faded photographs, he notices one of the gunslingers, named Cole carrying a .357 Magnum from the 1980s and becomes convinced that this Cole is a time traveller. Eventually McKenzie tracks him down, but Cole flees back in time to 11 July 1886. McKenzie follows him there, and in a one-on-one duel, kills him. In an earlier era *Time Stalkers* would probably have starred Gary Cooper and Eli Wallach, with Barbara Stanwyck running the local saloon.

# The Science of Time

*Time flies like an arrow; fruit flies like a banana.*
Sometimes attributed to Groucho Marx

## What is Time?

SAINT AUGUSTINE FAMOUSLY enquired, 'What is Time then? If nobody asks me, I know; but if I were desirous to explain it to one that should ask me, plainly I do not know.' We use the word time in so many different ways. Time has duration (*'I'm playing Solitaire, well, it passes the time'*), frequency (*'I've told her time and time again'*), motion (*'Oh how time flies!'*), direction (*'Time is like a river, forever moving onwards to the sea'*), rhythm (*'He's one of those musicians who can't keep time...'*), limits (*'Five, four, three, two, one... you're out of time!'*), numerous qualities and connotations (*'It was the best of times; it was the worst of times...'*, *'Winnie and me had a hot time!'*, *'Reggie is in Wormwood Scrubs doing time...'*) and, of course, Time is transformative (*'I loved you once... but time changes everything'*). Yet we also speak of Time as having power and being a decider (*'Can England reach the final? Only time will tell'*) and occasionally we give it human or at least living attributes (*'When our eyes met... oh... it was as if Time itself stood still...'*, *'We went for a walk round the shops – well, it killed some time'*, *'He's 78 and his legs are none too steady. Well, time catches up with us all.'*).

But is 'Time' a thing? Solitaire is played, fun is had and feet walk, be they slow or fast, but as these things happen isn't Time more an onlooker than a protagonist? Augustine isn't around to answer his question, but in some ways asking 'What is Time?' is at the heart of both the philosophy and science of Time.

## Sir Isaac Newton, Albert Einstein and Kurt Gödel

Until Einstein, the theory of gravity used by science was that of Sir Isaac Newton, but whereas Newton's theory keeps time and space separate and distinct, the Einsteinium universe suggests that time and space are intimately intertwined. In Sir Isaac Newton's view, time and space could exist even if there was nothing, but Albert Einstein in his *General Theory of Relativity* argued that time and space would cease to exist if the universe were empty.

From 1905 it had been known that Einstein's *Special Theory of Relativity* allowed time travel into the future (from a paper published on 26 September 1905 entitled *On the Electrodynamics of Moving Bodies*). Time as we know it, said Einstein, is not universally absolute, for the rate of passage depends to a great extent upon the velocity of an object. For example, the faster a person travelled relative to the Earth, the slower the tick-tock on the traveller's wrist watch compared to that of an identical watch left on terra firma. Put simply, time is not the same everywhere, it depends on local conditions.

But that was only Einstein's *Special Theory of Relativity*, the *General Theory of Relativity* (final form published in 1916) took things even further. And it was Kurt Gödel's 1949 paper that showed that the *General Theory of Relativity* also allowed time travel into the past, but only under certain conditions. Kurt Gödel used Einstein's mathematics to show for the first time that general relativity does not forbid time travel into the past. In retrospect, Kurt Gödel's paper was a pivotal event in establishing the respectability of a scientific approach to time travel.

However, theory should be distinguished from imaginative fiction. These were mathematical calculations and essentially belonged to the theory alone, but that didn't stop storytellers with a speculative fancy from taking these thoughts as starting points for Time Tales in novels and movies. But what was the big idea anyway?

Kurt Gödel was a great mathematician (and outed as a Swidger in THE SWIDGERS book series) and he calculated that movement of mass energy could be achieved not only through space but also backwards in time along trajectories in space-time that have now been called Closed Time-like Lines or Curves (CTL/CTC). What is being talked about here is a material particle that is 'closed', that is it returns to its starting point. Such lines are finite in length but have no 'ends' as such. In other words, the line forms a closed loop in space-time. These lines or trajectories are such that if a human travelled along them, and always at a speed less than light – that is 'time-like', but not exactly at that speed – everything around that traveller would be happening in normal causal order, but eventually those CTLs/CTCs would close back in on themselves and the traveller would be, in effect, in the past. In this sense a region of space-time containing closed time-like lines could be said to be a 'time machine'.

However, all this is only theoretically possible in certain cases and for Kurt Gödel's mathematical calculations this meant a rotating, infinite, static universe composed of a perfect liquid at constant pressure. Or put another way, Kurt Gödel's space-time universe satisfies the general relativity field equations, but the fly in the ointment is that universe's time travel property does not match the space-time universe in which we live.

One solution that has been put forward is negative energy or negative mass and there are those who have designed time machines using this method. However, once again the problem is that negative energy or mass exists mathematically but does not actually exist in life, or at least scientists haven't discovered any yet down the back of the sofa. The mathematician Frank Tipler did conceptualise a time machine that does not require negative energy but the problem with his design was that it did require more energy than actually exists in our universe. When it comes to energy you can't win, can you? There's either too little of it or not enough of the negative/minus sort.

What all this means is that is that the time travel world might as well be Neverland, Narnia, or The Wonderful Land of Oz. Besides, the emphasis in Kurt Gödel's 1949 paper is not based on the idea that time travel to the past is achievable, but rather that general relativity does not forbid it, which isn't quite the same thing. There is a subtle difference. In theory, there is nothing to forbid Yeovil Town before the decade is out from winning the European Cup. But let's get real, it just ain't gonna happen.

And there are other issues too. According to Professor Paul J. Nahin in his excellent book *Time Machine Tales*, the speed at which the time traveller would have to move in Kurt Gödel's space-time universe is about 71 percent of the speed of light (a 'time-like' speed indeed) and for this to happen, argues Nahin, the size of the fuel tank needed for such a journey would be the equivalent of several trillion ocean liners. And before you even build that tank, of course, you'd need to find the right sort of universe. So, until those Dilithian Crystals are discovered and available from John Lewis, Time's arrow is one way. And the best Yeovil Town can hope for is an unexpected win in the FA Cup.

## Wormholes or the Einstein-Rosen Bridge

Apples have real wormholes, with real worms that munch their way through real Granny Smiths one end to the other. Annoyingly bookworms do the same with novels. In time travel science fiction, a 'wormhole', a name borrowed from that hole the hungry worm makes, is sometimes called an Einstein-Rosen Bridge, named after Albert Einstein and Nathan Rosen. But such a 'bridge' isn't real in the way an apple and a worm are real. This bridge is essentially a speculative structure that could link disparate points in space-time. But 'could' isn't 'does'. Einstein's *General Theory of Relativity* predicted the possibility of the existence of wormholes in space-time; masses that create pressure in different parts of space that could, in theory, link up and create a type of connection between them. This has been envisaged as a tunnel with two ends at separate places. The concept itself is there in the writings of Ludwig Flamm (1885–1964), who worked in various areas of theoretical physics and quantum mechanics and who was the first to describe solutions that lead to connections, or these etymological 'wormholes'. But note the words 'theory', 'speculative' and 'possibility'. Ah, but such caveats have never put off science fiction writers.

In the movies, Einstein-Rosen Bridges are sometimes illustrated by someone taking a flat piece of paper and writing 'A' and 'B' on opposite edges, and then folding it in half or making a cylinder of said piece of paper, thus bringing points 'A' and 'B' together. And indeed mathematical wormholes do work on paper. However, as Stephen Hawking has pointed out, they are so unstable that they could only truly be theoretical. Add one molecule, he said, and the whole thing would destabilise and disintegrate. Again, that bit tends to be glossed over by writers of fantasy.

There are other problems too as set out in Paul J. Nahin's book *Time Machine Tales*. For example, the enormous gravitational gradient would dismember anything approaching it, and even if you could sort out that issue, your journey would almost certainly be a one-way trip. However, if you do fancy building one, the instructions can be found in M.S. Morris and K.S. Thorne's *Wormholes in Space-time and Their Use for Interstellar Travel: A Tool for Teaching General Relativity* published in the *American Journal of Physics* in May 1988. In fact, the science fiction writer Carl Sagan (1934–1996) approached Kip Thorne for help in making plausible the interstellar travel or 'subway system' imagined in his 1985 novel *Contact* (later made into a film starring Jodie Foster).

In 1949, Kurt Gödel's 'time machine' mathematics required an entire rotating universe but everything in science eventually gets smaller and that's where F.J. Tipler comes in handy. In 1974, Tipler wrote *Rotating Cylinders and the Possibility of Global Causality Violation* and in it he stated that general relativity suggests that a sufficiently large enough rotating cylinder was all you needed to create a time machine. You see, you didn't need the whole universe at all! Other patents pending include J. Richard Gott's 'cosmic string' (incredibly thin filaments of energy that are thought to run from one end of the universe to the other) and Miguel Alcubierre's 'warp bubble', that surrounds a spaceship with warped space-time. Well, there's two suggestions to add to Santa's list.

## Time Dilation

Time Dilation (or *Zeitdilatation* to use Einstein's term) means the altering of the rate of timekeeping as calculated by a standard clock either by motion, gravity, or, in Time Tales, some other force. In Einstein's theory of special relativity, a non-accelerating observer will experience the passing of time differently to that of one who is accelerating. 'Time', suggested Einstein to his friend Michele Besso in 1905, 'cannot be absolutely defined and there is an inseparable relationship between time and [the] signal velocity.' And this we now know to be true because, technically speaking, the US astronaut Scott Kelly, after travelling at great speed while orbiting the Earth in the International Space Station, came back a few milliseconds younger than his twin brother who stayed home. An imaginative fictional twist on this concept can be found in B.W. Aldiss's *Man in His Time* where an astronaut returns from Mars three minutes ahead in time from everyone else.

But how practical is time travel via time dilation? Photons that travel at light speed have energy and momentum, but no mass. A human being does have mass, so what would happen if a human being suddenly moved at the speed of light? Well, your mass would become infinite – and that's pretty big. As biggest as you can get, if not bigger. Besides, the energy needed to achieve that speed would be that of an exploding star. All in all, not very practical. It should be noted too that time dilation as established in Einstein's *Special Theory of Relativity* allows for time travel into the future only. But don't tell Kal-El that as he tries to save Lois in *Superman* (1978).

*Planet of the Apes* is a plot that relies on a relativist time dilation, in that for the astronauts returning to Earth from a mission in deep space, only 18 months have passed by, but here on Earth, it's more like 2,000 years. The Icarus/Liberty 1 spacecraft isn't designed to be a time machine as such but it becomes one simply by way of its speed. As said, time passes differently for someone fast moving compared to someone standing still. If Icarus/Liberty 1 did travel close to the speed of light then that would in theory explain the time dilation. And of course what happens in the movie is that the returning astronauts find a dystopian Earth future. This though is a change to the original book and it was made by Rod Serling of *Twilight Zone* fame, who also gave the twist of the Statue of Liberty at the end. Yes, it was after all Earth to which the astronauts had returned, not another planet.

The time dilation concept has expanded in many Time Tales to include time beings, where people (or aliens) move in time at different time speeds in comparison to those around them or space dilation, where a specific geographical location operates at a different time speed to those next to it. An inter-dimensional temporal rift is what Doctor Who calls the cave in the episode *The Easters of Light*. You find this basic concept as well in the musical *Brigadoon* (stage 1947, movie 1954) with book and lyrics by Alan Jay Lerner and music by Frederick Loewe. An example of time beings that exist at a different speed can be found in *Wink of an Eye*, a *Star Trek* episode from 1971, where time-accelerated aliens take over the Enterprise and attempt to use the crew as breeding stock. Similar ideas can be found in *Timelash*, an episode in the 1970s UFO series, and the 2002 film *Clockstoppers*.

In book one of THE SWIDGERS Time Adventure series, *The Time That Never Was*, time dilation is possible through both a place, the Old Coach Inn, and the time being who rules there, the wicked Aloysius. What this means is that when

Granny and William return to London in book two, *The Time They Saved Tomorrow*, time in the capital has moved on much quicker. Their stay in the Old Coach Inn was just a few months but in the world they return to time has moved on three years.

In Steven Moffat's *The Girl in the Fireplace*, a *Doctor Who* episode from 2006, the Doctor is on a spaceship and here he discovers an adjacent space through a time portal that leads through a fireplace to 18th century Versailles. Here, Doctor Who meets a young girl called Reinette. However, this 18th century space seems to exist at a different temporal speed to that of the space ship, and so when he returns to see the young girl again, she has aged. The Doctor later meets her once more, only now she's a woman. They fall in love, plus he saves her life from invading aliens. And then there's the final journey through the portal, only now Reinette is leaving Versailles for the last time – in a coffin in the carriage drawn by black horses. It is a popular *Doctor Who* episode with enthusiasts for it is a rare romantic interlude among the usually fast moving action adventures.

*Old*, the 2021 American thriller written and directed by M. Night Shyamalan, is based on the French-language Swiss graphic novel *Sandcastle* by Pierre Oscar Levy and Frederik Peeters. In the story, Guy and Prisca Cappa are going through a divorce and, to avoid upsetting their young children Maddox and Trent, they have a final family vacation in a tropical resort. But as the children play on the sand they rapidly turn into teenagers, while other members of the group suddenly become ill and even die. The beach is ageing them at a rate of one year every 30 minutes. But all is not what it seems, for it is revealed that the resort is a front for a research team conducting clinical trials. Drugs have been administered to guests by spiking their cocktails and since the beach naturally accelerates the lives of the guests, the scientists have been able to complete the lifelong drug trials within a day. The director M. Night Shyamalan saw the story as a way of looking at the human relationship to time, where some are unable to cope and others find peace.

*Here and Now and Then*, a time travel novel by Mike Chen, has a time traveller from the Year 2142 stranded in contemporary San Francisco after a botched mission. A rescue team from the future does eventually arrive but not until 18 years later, the time rule being that although 18 years have gone by in modern-day San Francisco, only a few weeks have passed in 2142. The film *Time Trap* is a 'let's-explore-this-cave' scenario. In the story, the young explorers discover as they go deeper that there are areas of the cave where Time is moving at a much slower pace than in the outside world. Much, much more slowly. Years and centuries pass above while below it's just minutes and hours. And the plot reveals that these layers and pockets of delineated time are running incrementally more slowly the further down they go. It is eventually revealed these time bubbles are ultimately there to protect The Fountain of Youth. Time dilation and its relationship to the ageing process is a feature of the Utopian novel *Lost Horizon* (1933 – written by James Hilton), later adapted into a film which in turn became a movie musical and you'll find it also in the Stephen King story *Green Mile* that then became a successful movie. In *The King: Youngwonui Gunjoo (Eternal Monarch)*, written by Kim Eun-sook, there is a character, Lee Lim, who travels across parallel worlds and subsequently ages at a different speed to those who don't have such a capacity.

## Black Holes and the Singularity

General relativity predicts that a sufficiently massive star – roughly four times greater than our dear little sun – when its fuel is nearly exhausted, will experience a total gravitational collapse. So fuel-starved and destabilised, its radiation pressure would be no longer able to keep this large but weakened elderly star inflated against the force of its own gravity. As a result, it would implode and crash into itself creating what is called a black hole, a dramatic term coined in 1967 by the Princeton physicist John Wheeler (1911–2008) in an address before the American Association for the Advancement of Science.

A black hole then is an object with a gravitational field so strong that even light cannot escape it, hence why it is called 'black', and at its centre is something called a singularity, a region even smaller than an electron, into which everything is drawn, hence the word 'hole'. It's a very difficult concept for the human mind to contemplate, especially when most of us can't even fit all our socks into the same drawer. Anyway, as gravity, as it were, runs out of control, space-time smashes itself out of existence at this singularity. Or, as Stephen Hawking put it, 'a singularity is a place where the classical concepts of space and time break down as do all the known laws of physics.' Maths gone bonkers. Or, as physicists sometimes put it, a space-time singularity is where God starts dividing by zero.

But writers of science fiction like nothing more than those places where 'all the known laws of physics break down'. To such places and ideas they will themselves gravitate. And a pretty strong gravitational field it is too. But be warned, black holes are dangerous, for they are essentially one-way trap-doors, and not, as many would have it, a gateway to dinosaurs.

A singularity, it has been suggested, was the origin of The Big Bang itself. In fact, there are those who have conjectured the universe created itself through time travel, not unlike those time travellers such as Dominick Hide in *The Flipside of Dominick Hide* who become their own ancestors (or his own great-grandfather in the case of Dominick). There is also the theory that the universe is like an elastic band that expands and contracts across eternity. Philosophers have also raised the interesting question that if time was created at the moment of The Big Bang, would time disappear if the universe collapsed in on itself and became a black hole and once again a singularity? Most physicists don't believe the universe has enough mass to do this, nor do they support the 'elastic band' theory. Maybe so. But could it be that they just haven't looked hard enough for the mass that is required. Might it not be simply hiding down a rabbit-hole somewhere?

## The Fourth Dimension

Aristotle said that three dimensions were all we had and that these dimensions were spatial. Put simply, there's up and down, front and behind (or fore and aft), and right and left. Breadth, length and thickness. That's enough surely, isn't it? Well no, not for physicists. They want to include time, after all, what will be an object's breadth, length and thickness tomorrow? And next week? Or in a trillion billion years time? For Einstein, space is a three-dimensional arena, but it really needs time to add a fourth co-ordinate and that involves time directions. And H.G. Wells' *The Time Machine* goes into great detail as to why Einstein will be proved right and Aristotle and Euclid were wrong:

> 'Clearly,' the Time Traveller proceeded, 'any real body must have extension in four directions: it must have Length, Breadth, Thickness, and – Duration. But through a natural infirmity of the flesh, which I will explain to you in a moment, we incline to overlook this fact. There are really four dimensions, three which we call the three planes of Space, and a fourth, Time. There is, however, a tendency to draw an unreal distinction between the former three dimensions and the latter, because it happens that our consciousness moves intermittently in one direction along the latter from the beginning to the end of our lives.'

Wells' fantasy was written in 1895 but a few years later the concept of The Fourth Dimension, well, took on another dimension. When Hermann Minkowski gave his famous address *Raum und Zeit* (*Space and Time*) in 1908 he spoke of a 'world-point', he then went on to talk of a 'world-line'. Every 'where' and every 'when' has something perceptible and from that we have the everlasting career of the substantial point, a world-line. He goes on to say that in his opinion physical laws might find their most perfect expressions as relations between these world-lines and so the three-dimensional geometry of Euclid becomes four-dimensional

21st century physics. It seems that creative fiction writers took three concepts from this presentation and started using them in science fiction. And those words were 'between' and 'four', which became more of a modifier when added to the third important word, 'dimension'. And we've all heard the sort of dialogue that writers use to explain unexpected arrivals. 'Where did the aliens come from?' 'The Fourth Dimension!' 'Where's that?' 'Somewhere between their universe and ours.'

In *Dimensions* (2011) time travel is possible using, not surprisingly, other dimensions. And more words have emerged from this concept of the 'Fourth Dimension' such as 'subspace' and 'hyperspace'. Exactly what they mean scientifically is rarely expanded upon, sometimes it's simply enough to say, 'They were hiding in subspace' or 'We will travel more quickly if we go into hyperspace'.

In *The OA*, a television series built around the concepts of 'dimensions', it is suggested that in a Near Death Experience (NDE), if someone 'comes back' that person must have come back from 'somewhere', that is another dimension. *The OA* is part science, part metaphysics, part LSD trip, for it is the only time travel story in history to feature a telepathic octopus. Even Doctor Who, who has travelled to the universe and back, has never yet managed to shake hands (or tentacles) with one of those.

What we are finding with all these justifiable scientific terms is that fiction writers take the bits of the concept that suit their purpose and then run with them. Of course they love the catchy phrases that sound legit, but ignore the parts of the theory that say it is just that, theory and one that is not possible in our universe. But who cares? Certainly not most scientists, who, by the way, tend to be the biggest fans of science fiction.

## The Shape of Time

The Greek philosopher Plato thought of time as something of a closed loop, as having a beginning, but, in his concept, time did not have an infinite future. He imagined it rather curving back upon itself, which, when you think about it, is a reasonable way of thinking for a natural philosopher as everything Plato observed in nature has its seasons, its tides. The day starts over at the end of night and the day begins again, so why can't time do the same? Stephen Hawking in his book *A Brief History of Time* concludes with a similar idea, with a collapsing singularity and The Big Bang. But this concept is older than both Hawking and Plato, for circular time is there in the image of the world snake or worm ouroborous eating its own tail (the sideways figure of eight is now our sign of infinity). There is also the Ankh symbol – a cross surmounted by a loop and known in Latin as a *crux ansata* – which is thought to have originated in Africa and later became the image of eternal life in ancient Egypt. An Ankh, incidentally, features in *Berkeley Square* as the connection across time for the two lovers.

However, endings and beginnings are also rooted in our everyday conception of time and, on the whole, theologians at least have argued for a beginning of time, as have ancient storytellers with their many creation myths (from the Greek *mûthos* meaning story). The date of creation, according to Bishop James Ussher, a 17th century Biblical scholar, was 23 October 4004BC. Martin Luther also argued for a date around 4000BC, but geological time now puts the creation of our universe at about 13.8 billion years ago. How old God was then nobody knows.

Philosophers being philosophers disagree about pretty much everything, and time is no exception. For example, Aristotle in *Physics* said the heavens were finite, but time itself was infinite. Emmanuel Kant on the other hand was in favour of a finite past, a belief sometimes called 'temporal finitism', but he did accept an infinite future. Saint Thomas Aquinas, however, tended towards an infinite past, but with God somehow and mysteriously on the outside of it.

Laurence Sterne's *The Life and Opinions of Tristram Shandy, Gentleman* (also known as simply *Tristam Shandy*) hilariously plays with the whole concept of a 'beginning' by trying to tell the story of his life from the beginning. But what constitutes his beginning? His birth? His conception? Either way he fails in his task because the book ends even before it 'began', in that it finishes before he's even conceived. Incidentally, to illustrate the absurdity of an infinite past there is the Tristram Shandy Paradox, named after the book and it goes like this: Suppose Tristram Shandy writes his biography so slowly that for every day that he lives, it takes him a year to record that day. That would be difficult enough if he had lived a finite past, but suppose Shandy had always existed, that is, in a universe that had no beginning. In this scenario Shandy wouldn't just get further and further behind, he would get *infinitely* further and further behind. And no modern publisher would be happy with that sort of timeframe. 'Any chance the book will be ready for the Christmas market?' 'No. Unless you're okay with the second Thursday in October in the year after forever.'

But isn't all this a bit tangential in a book about time travel? Perhaps so, but most of *Tristram Shandy* is made of up of curious tangents and digressions, so that's our excuse too. Besides, recollections of events that have happened in our lives make up our daily adventures with time travel that we call memory. And most of those, as with the events in Tristram Shandy's life, are also mainly fiction.

## The Arrow of Time

The 'Arrow of Time' is simply the idea that time has a direction and that there is a difference between past and present. Or, put another way, as Ray Cummings did in *The Girl in the Golden Atom* (1919) and also in his tale *The Time Story* (1921), 'Time is what keeps everything from happening at once.' This line is sometimes attributed to others, including Albert Einstein. Perhaps Einie was a Cummings fan. But now consider this speech from a Time Tale:

> Time is a condition, not an essential. Viewed from the Absolute, the sequence by which future follows present and present follows past is purely arbitrary. Yesterday, today, tomorrow; there is no reason in

the nature of things why the order should not be tomorrow, today, yesterday.

From the movie *Tenet* or *Interstellar*? No. These are the words of Professor Van Stopp in *The Clock that Went Backward* written by Edward Page Mitchell as far back as 1881. And here are some more:

> 'We hear much,' said the Hegelian professor, reading from a notebook in his usual dry, hurried tone, 'of the influence of the sixteenth century upon the nineteenth. No philosopher, as far as I am aware, has studied the influence of the nineteenth century upon the sixteenth. If cause produces effect, does effect never induce cause? Does the law of heredity, unlike all other laws of this universe of mind and matter, operate in one direction only? Does the descendant owe everything to the ancestor, and the ancestor nothing to the descendant? Does destiny, which may seize upon our existence, and for its own purposes bear us far into the future, never carry us back into the past?'

The ideas expressed here come from the philosophy of Georg Wilhelm Friedrich Hegel. Hegel's thoughts on time can be found and are explored in various publications, including *The Phenomenology of Spirit* (1807), *The Encyclopaedia of the Philosophical Sciences* (1830) and in *Lectures on Philosophy of Religion*, published in 1832 a year after his death. Hegel's philosophical writings on time are notoriously difficult to comprehend, partly because he is dealing with speculative philosophy but also because his illustrations and metaphors are themselves limited to temporal human sensibilities, for time, as he sees it, is outside of lived experience. ('You do not grasp the return of the Itself into Itself through its Otherself? Well, you will, sometime,' says Professor Van Stopp in *The Clock that Went Backward* to his bemused student.) To put it simply, in

Hegel's thinking, the Past, Present and Future, are 'moments of becoming' which pass into the Oneness of The Eternal Now. And that is about as simple as it gets with Hegel. The point is, don't think of the shape or form of time as linear. It isn't a straight line, in fact it isn't a shape at all. For Hegel, the Time Present is merely something that distinguishes itself from Time Past, and Time Present itself 'is not' because Time Future 'is' and exists too but only as an as yet unfilled form of sensibility. As Marty McFly might say, 'That's heavy, Doc!' But that said, it is possible to see how Hegel influenced writers such as Edward Page Mitchell and indeed how Hegel's thoughts continue to have an impact on modern writers and creatives such as Christopher Nolan. Indeed, the theories of Hegel are the bedrock upon which time travel is possible in *The Time They Saved Tomorrow*, book two of THE SWIDGERS Time Adventure. In fact, Hegel even gets a name-check in the book, as does Kurt Gödel.

Human beings certainly have a consciousness that gives them a sense of time moving forwards, but might it not be quite interesting to live your life backwards, as Benjamin Button did/does/will? Such a life must be a strange one, as Merlin says in T.H. White's *Once and Future King*, 'I unfortunately was born at the wrong end of Time, and I have to live backwards from in front, while surrounded by a lot of people living forwards from behind. Some people call it having second sight.' It does, however, work well for the White Queen in Lewis Carroll's *Alice Through the Looking-glass*, if not for poor Alice:

> 'It's jam every other day: today isn't any other day, you know.'
>
> 'I don't understand you,' said Alice. 'It's dreadfully confusing!'
>
> 'That's the effect of living backward,' the queen said kindly. 'It always makes one a little giddy at first—'

> 'Living backward!' Alice repeated in great astonishment. 'I never heard of such a thing!'
> '—but there's one great advantage in it: that one's memory works both ways.'

This idea of reverse time can also be found in the Philip K. Dick short story *The World Jones Made*, plus *The Mysterious Stranger*, the unfinished novel attempted by the American author Mark Twain which he worked on intermittently from 1897 through to 1908.

There are characters in Time Tales that travel in linear timelines but in an opposite temporal trajectory. The movie *In the Shadow of the Moon* has a cop tracking a female serial killer, Rya, who appears every nine years, 1988, 1997, 2006 and 2015. It is revealed that she is travelling in a one-way direction from the future, killing as she goes. The tale is a reflector narrative presented from the perspective of the cop who shoots her dead on their first meeting, which for him is in 1988. This naturally enough creates some confusion when she repeatedly 'reappears' later. Of course she didn't come back to life, it's just that she isn't dead yet.

## The Second Law of Thermodynamics

The Second Law of Thermodynamics states that any entity in a system that is free of external influences, that is it is within a closed system, will continually evolve towards maximum disorder, or thermodynamic equilibrium, as physicists prefer to put it. The future state always has greater randomness than does the beginning state (entropy will be low in the past and high in the future). And entropy, to put it as simply as possible, is the measurement of that disorder. The lowest state of entropy was at the moment the universe came into being, the greatest state of entropy is right now. Yes, the 'now' as you read that very word is the maximum entropy has ever been. Oh, and the universe just got even more disordered as your eyes passed over that last sentence. Perhaps if you are a teenager whose mum keeps telling you to tidy up your bedroom you might mention this particular scientific fact to her. You can say, 'What's the bloody point, mum, in me doing any tidying when the universe is on an unstoppable journey towards an ever increasing magnitude of ultimate chaos?' She might, however, apply the same principle and say, 'In that case, I might as well not bother doing your dirty washing,' but that's consequences for you.

*Tenet*, the Christopher Nolan film, had a lot of fun reversing this fundamental law of the universe. In interviews, Nolan said that he wasn't reversing time as such, but rather that in reversing entropy, time itself was put in reverse. A subtle but important difference. The key phrase from the definition of The Second Law of Thermodynamics from a temporal point of view is 'continually evolve towards'. Put another way, entropy seems to define the direction of time and for that reason entropy has now come to be called The Thermodynamic Arrow of Time. Yet despite the best imaginative efforts of Mr Nolan, time really is only in one direction.

Or is it?

*Sisyphus* centres on Han Tae-sul, a genius computer programmer whose coding will one day lead to the invention of a time machine called an 'Uploader'. In a kind of fragmented-in-time flashback, there is a scene where Han Tae-sul and his time travelling friend Gang Seo-hae witness the young Han Tae-sul with his older brother after the death of their parents. The older boy, in that typical way people deal with grief when talking with younger children, says that one day, if they are both good, they will both be reunited with their mother and father. However, the young Tae-sul uses the cold reasoning of The Second Law of Thermodynamics to explain that time is irreversible. There's a certain irony in that it's the time travelling Tae-sul who is witnessing this sad exchange. Yet the impossibility of time travel is made possible. And even the very, very clever and rich Mark Zuckerberg computer genius has never managed that.

## Is the Past Fixed?

Could we go back in time and save the RMS *Titanic* from sinking? The simple answer is: No. Does that mean the past is fixed? Yes, because you can't change history. Well, that's the answer a scientist would give, for science is a bit of a party pooper when it comes to Time Tales. Philosophers and theologians tend to agree with the scientists. Aristotle in *Nicomachean Ethics* (written around 340BC and probably named after or even set out for his son who was named Nicomachus), said that even God could not make undone something that had been done. Saint Thomas Aquinas (1225–1274) said essentially the same thing, but being a theologian he put the emphasis rather differently, writing that what involves a contradiction cannot be done, rather than that God could not do it. In effect, Aquinas was arguing that God is always bound by his own rules and laws.

## The Block Universe, The Rigid Universe and the Space-time Continuum

The movie projector is sometimes used as a metaphor for what is sometimes called the 'Block Universe' or 'Rigid Universe' (a phrase used by Wells in a serial version of *The Time Machine* but not in the final book). The idea is that The Now – or the present – is the instant the 35mm film frame goes through the projector, resulting in time happening as a beam of light cast onto a screen. Yet the part of the movie reel that has gone through doesn't just disappear, it still exists. Not only that, the future is already fixed and waiting to happen in the next part of the ever turning reel. And it's the same principle whether the movie is by Jean-Luc Godard or Alfred Hitchcock. The philosopher Hans Reichenbach in *The Direction of Time* (1956) poo-poohed this idea and pointed out that the analogy breaks down because 'the flow of time of a movie is unreal'. 'Is the present,' asks Reichenbach, 'more than our cognisance of a predetermined pattern of events unfolding itself like an unwinding film?'

The idea of a rigid or fixed universe had been around for much of the 19th century. Pierre-Simon, Marquis de Laplace (1749–1827) had said that the universe's past, present and future was reducible to a formula. If, speculated Laplace, there was an intelligence which could comprehend all the forces by which nature was animated, then nothing would be uncertain. But that idea of a fixed universe goes back as far as the 5th century BC and the Greek philosopher Parmenides who argued that universe was uncreated and indestructible. Moreover it was complete, immovable, and without end. And the Now of time was all at once, 'a continuous one'. However, it was Hermann Minkowski in the early 20th century who gave scientific legitimacy for this way of thinking.

Hermann Minkowski (1864–1909) was Albert Einstein's mathematics teacher while Einstein was a student in Zurich. In 1908, Minkowski gave a famous address called 'Raum and Zeit' or 'Space and Time' that he himself described as radical. There's a point in space at a point in time and these he brought together in what he called a 'world-point' and from this 'everlasting career of the substantial' we obtain what he named the 'world-line'. Putting the concept of the world-line as simply as possible: what was (the past) still 'is', and what will be (the future) already 'is' too. In effect, what Minkowski did was give the concept of the fixed universe a kind of mathematical justification. And from all this the idea of the 'space-time continuum' was born.

The term block universe is thought to have originated from Francis Herbert Bradley's 1883 book *Principles of Logic* in which he sees time as a river down which we float with blocks of houses that we get off to visit as we go by, and, 'all this while, the firm fixed row of the past and future stretches in a block behind us, and before us.' Marcus Aurelius in his *Meditations* also wrote that time is like a river made up of events which happen and as soon as a thing has been, it is carried away, and another comes in its place. Thomas Aquinas put it another way when he said that God's knowledge of the movement of time in His eternity was comparable to the way a person standing on top of a watchtower is able to see at a single glance a whole caravan of passing travellers. And the overseer and the river image were combined in the 1926 play, *Berkeley Square*, where Peter, the time traveller, asks a sceptic to imagine being in a boat, seeing what is on the banks as they pass. It may be clover now, but the grove that was passed is still there, though it is no longer in view. That's the perspective from the boat, but Peter then puts it to the doubter: what if you were in the sky in a plane, then you'd see it all at once, including what was around the next bend. And that, says Peter, is 'real Time' and exists in the mind of God.

Water has proved a popular metaphor when thinking about time. In *The Time They Saved Tomorrow*, a time traveller offers William many metaphors of Time, including the concept of a river, but also a lake and even rain. In the story the purpose of these conflicting ideas is to make William connect with the mystery of Time itself in order to become a time traveller. Paul J. Nahin in his book *Time Machine Tales*, suggests an alternative 'water' image: Time as a snowball, where the beginning is the centre with the ever new present increasing the surface 'as the snowball rolls down the hill of history!' But Nahin is not at all keen on the whole block universe/flowing river concept and argues that it's 'fatalism disguised as physics' and a 'denial of free-will dressed up in geometry.' Strong words. And, going back to Hermann Minkowski, a space-time in which all 'worldpoints' are completely determined would indeed be a fatalistic view of the universe, with no free will. Who's right and who's wrong depends on your own philosophical view of the world. As for the man in the boat, well, suppose he should suddenly decide to steer it to the bank, get out, and never even see what's round the bend. Or, to be more fanciful, a bird could drop a poo in his eyes, causing him to crash, sink and die. Or any number of possibilities unseen and undreamt of by that 'man in the sky', be he on a plane or some supposedly omniscient He floating in His heavenly clouds.

But the 'river of time' way of thinking does exist in one sense and that is through memory, because no one disappears or truly dies until they are forgotten. This is the philosophy underpinning the hugely popular Disney movie *Coco* and the old epigram that 'We are alive for as long as our name is spoken'.

## Science and The Time Tale

Albert Einstein is referenced in many Time Tales, *Back to the Future* has Doc Brown's dog, Einie, named after him. Kurt Gödel features in *The Time They Saved Tomorrow*, and, like Hegel, is an important cog in William's discovery of time travel. But most Time Tales don't have an Einstein or a Gödel and so they make do with the device of 'The Explainer' who operates much like Basil Exposition in the *Austin Powers* series. For example, in *Déjà Vu*, there is a scene with an 'explainer' called Denny, a non-scientist named Doug, who wants everything put in plain words, plus the true scientist whose name is Shanti. Denny is talking about bursts of energy enhancing the sensitivity of optical telescopes and creating enough energy to warp 'the very fabric of space'. Doug wants all this put more simply, so Denny takes a sheet of paper and holds it flat, saying that's how we are used to seeing and thinking of space. But then he adds, folding the paper, that when space is folded you create an Einstein-Rosen Bridge or wormhole. Then Shanti sums it up by saying that what they are essentially doing is creating an instantaneous link between two distant points. The dialogue is spoken incredibly quickly, but it's said with conviction and once this explanation is over and done with, the science of the 'time window' in *Déjà Vu* is pretty much left alone.

You'll find similar scenes and exchanges in many Time Tales. There's usually some science, a few questions from someone who doesn't understand it and then it's all explained again in layman's terms. You'll hear phrases such as 'time continuum', 'looped quantum gravity' and 'bend in the fabric of space'. Plus there's usually a time MacGuffin that takes care of all the practicalities.

In *Back to the Future*, much is made of the 'flux capacitor' and in *Doctor Who* there is the 'vortex manipulator' used by the Time Agency of the 51st century, though it can take its toll on organic beings as a result of direct exposure to the time vortex. Such detail often enhances credibility. Another trick is to take some legitimate mathematics and then embellish it with fairy-tale science. Much of the first half of *Primer*, for example, is taken up with complicated sums and laboratory gobbledegook.

In *Dark*, there is quite a bit of talk about the Einstein-Rosen Bridge. There's also references to Ernst Wilhelm Brücke, who was interested in a variety of scientific areas, including experimental physiology, and the physicist Peter Higgs who gave his name to the Higgs particle. The design of a device that allows time travel in *Dark* came into the hands of The Watchmaker, Tannhauser. Essentially the device generates a Higgs field, increasing the mass of Caesium that is placed inside it. An electromagnetic pulse then turns this into a black hole, or wormhole, through which time travel is achieved. Simple really.

But science oddly enough is rarely what time travel stories are about. Essentially Time Tales are fantasies that explore consequence in people's lives and in history, which is to say, why do things happen the way they do? In this sense, Time Tales are more essays in philosophical speculation than scientific theory. But they are human tales too. Take *The Time Traveler's Wife*. Yes, it's a plot that is dependent on a fixed or Block Universe, as Henry aged 28 says to Henry aged 7, 'Whatever you do, something's going to stop you.' But a chance to analyse the theories of Minkowski is not why people have recommended the book. The story uses time travel to explore childhood trauma and the damage it does, particularly to Henry. But it's also about healing and the capacity to change. And on top of that there's the romance and the marriage and the problems resulting from both. In words, or in one word, it's about Life.

# The Philosophy of Time

*There was a young man who was deft*
*At running and cunning and theft.*
*With legs so quick,*
*It was Time he would nick,*
*By returning before he had left!*
Popular limerick

## Philosophical Viewpoints

THERE ARE, IT could be said, essentially two views of the universe. The first is The Atomist perspective. Here the universe is seen as merely a load of atoms, randomly bouncing about in space. Life has accidentally come about, and we may be very thankful for it, but ultimately there is no real meaning or purpose to it all. As Professor Stephen Hawking used to say, 'The universe is just one of those things.' Yes, it is what it is and stuff just happens. It's ultimately all down to dumb luck and the roll of the dice.

The opposite perspective is that of The Destinist. Here we have a philosophy where life has purpose and certain things are meant to be. There is often a Greater Power or Cosmic Force behind such philosophies, but sometimes it is simply what the Greeks called *Ananke*, the primordial personification of Necessity and the guiding 'Force of Fate'.

That there is a 'Big Plan' and that certain things are meant to be, is at the heart of the vast majority of Time Tales. And it's this underlying philosophy and view of life that is, perhaps, their greatest appeal. You'll hear lines in Time Tales such as, 'And if you have to die, it won't be in vain.' And the character can say that in the story because she or he knows the historical consequences of the self-sacrifice that is being made to save mankind. In short, the Time Tale gives meaning to our actions. Of course, everything we do has consequences, but only in The Destinist view of the universe do these have an ultimate and discernible purpose. And it's time travel stories that are able to explore and can even demonstrate this, for human beings like the idea that life has purpose and meaning.

But all this surely is just philosophical musings for the sake of something to talk about over a glass or bottle of wine or two? Perhaps, but plots in Time Tales are dependent on whether your time world is fixed and rigid or uncertain and changeable. *Berkeley Square* and *The Time Traveler's Wife* are essentially dependent on a fixed universe, whereas *Back to the Future* and *The Terminator* need a changeable timeline to make their stories work. It's not that one is right and the other is wrong, but rather that the time world view matches the plot. *Doctor Who* cleverly has it both ways, for there are some events that are certain and immutable (or 'time-locked') and others that are uncertain ('The future is not fixed,' says the Thirteenth Doctor, Jodie Whittaker, in *Orphan 55* 'it depends on billions of decisions, and actions'). Well, that duality of thought makes sense in a series with several hundred episodes. And there are greys too, because even in a changeable universe there is also the idea that 'The Big Plan' is bigger than any of us as individuals. Yes, we can to a degree, do what we like, but Father Time will discover a means of getting his own way in the end. Think of those alternate timeline stories where lovers still somehow end up meeting in the final scene such as *The Adam Project* and *Sliding Doors*.

## God and Time, Aristotle's Concept of First Cause and 'The Origin'

The principle of the 'First Cause' assumes that each natural thing comes about as the result of something other than itself. You had a mother and father, and they had mothers and fathers of their own. And there are further assumptions with first cause: one, there cannot be an infinite series of causes, and, two (and arising from that) there must therefore be a 'First Cause' whose existence is not caused by something other than itself or anything that came before it. Saint Thomas Aquinas called such a thing 'God', while others have named it 'The Big Bang'.

The most influential Christian philosopher before Aquinas was Saint Augustine and in Book XI of *The Confessions*, Augustine argued that time belonged to God. In effect, God is the creator of time and made time a part of the universe when He created the universe. Time wasn't something that was already there, as it were, all along, that God found behind a bush. As Augustine says, 'What time could there be that You had not created? Or how could ages pass, if they never were? Thus, you are The Maker of all Times.' To say anything other would be heresy. So where does that leave the time traveller in a time machine? Isn't such an invention going against the rules of time and ultimately God Himself?

Until the 19th century, it was only God who could move in time, but then along came H.G. Wells who in *God the Invisible King* rejected the very idea of God the Creator. And it was H.G. Wells, of course, who wrote *The Time Machine,* the plot of which broke those strictures of Saint Augustine. Then there was the American writer Mark Twain, a well-known religious sceptic, who wrote about a human being who travelled into the past. Perhaps one of the reasons why there never had been a time travel story before the 19th century (or none that could be said to be serious in philosophical or theological terms) was because such a story would by definition be heresy and sacrilegious. To travel in time, and potentially change time, what God Himself had decreed, would be tantamount to challenging, or worse, altering, God's will. For Saint Augustine and Saint Thomas Aquinas, time was God's domain and God's creation, not Man's. It is not possible to prove that fear of prosecution for blasphemy was the reason that no Time Tales were ever printed before the 19th century, but it is offered as a possibility.

So, what in Heaven and Earth would Aquinas and Augustine have made of *Dark*? *Dark* is a Time Tale that uses the iconography of religion and the traditions of the Bible, but then inverts them in order to create a very secular fable. In *Dark*, The Watchmaker, one H.G. Tannhaus – those initials look very familiar – builds a time machine he intends to use to go back in time and save his family from a car accident. By creating this machine, Tannhaus causes a stoppage in time that halts the cause-and-effect relationship of time and thus two timelines – or two worlds – are created, each with unforeseen and tragic consequences, including in one a nuclear apocalypse. The Watchmaker – often a by-word for God – creates two seemingly eternal and infernal time loops of near hellish damnation for the people of Winden. A painful and never ending déjà vu of despair. Jonas and Martha, who later become Adam and Eva – familiar names if you've read *Genesis* – learn that they are at the centre of the 'Origin' of this damnation, a 'First Cause' of sorts, and the only way out of the 'Endless Loops' that have been created is to bring an end to their own existence. When this happens the loops will be broken and a free world will be born. In effect, our new Adam and Eva create this new world, this new Paradise, by this self-sacrifice.

What John Milton, or even God Himself, would have made of all this, well, perhaps we'll never know. Unless they both have a streaming subscription up there in the clouds. What can be said is that *Dark*, a secular parable in its own way, has taken the potential of what a Time Tale is capable of beyond pretty much all that has gone before it. *Dark* is essentially a Genesis Creation Myth in its own right, and as the music of Soap&Skin singing *What a Wonderful World* brought it to an end, it was a reminder that our Wonderful World is The Now.

## Atomic, Genetic and Mechanical Determinism

In *Devs*, written and directed by Alex Garland, a team of computer scientists create a time window to rival the eyes of God Himself. The title *Devs* gives you the clue to the theological and moral philosophy underpinning the series because, in the classical alphabet, the sound or phoneme for what we write as 'U' looks like a 'V', but for a long time there was no 'U' and so the 'V' was an allograph, that is, a letter or grapheme that has a variation of pronunciation where it is used in another context or situation. What all this linguistic jiggery-pokery means in practice is that *Devs* can be pronounced *Deus*, the Latin word for God. But before concerning ourselves too much with the Almighty, let's first look at the science and philosophy of *Devs*.

Human beings are contingent by nature, that is, we are subject to change and that change is brought about by cause and effect. *Devs* puts forward the theory that to access a person's past you need, first, the right software and code; second, a huge computer with impossibly large processing power; and third, collected data of every previous historical cause and effect. Then, working cause and effect backwards from effect to cause, you would be able to have access to all the events of the past. And that includes anyone's past. Incidentally, in principle, this is an idea that goes back to the French philosopher and mathematician Pierre-Simon, Marquis de Laplace, who in 1814 argued that if there was an intelligence that could comprehend all the forces by which the universe was animated and that data was submitted for analysis then nothing would be unknown or uncertain – and 'the future as the past would be present to our eyes.'

What *Devs* added, however, was a GPS system and a computer screen in order to generate those images of that past. Pixelated, yes, and mere simulations, but visualisations for our inquiring eyes nevertheless. That is what DEVS is. Not, though, that these images strictly speaking would be from the past, this time window would not be the actuality of an event, but rather computer-generated projections of high probability.

The long and short of it is that we live in a predetermined universe. And that you just now read the sentence 'We live in a predetermined universe' was itself predetermined. Forest in *Devs* argues that the universe is deterministic and defined, not by God or morality, but only by physical laws. Neo-Darwinists would add perhaps genetic laws here as well. What seems to be life's chaos is actually based on tramlines that are prescribed and undeviating.

The key point *Devs* makes is that immutable physical laws offer no room for flukes, or quirks, or whims, or accidents, or arbitrary events. There are no spokes in the wheel of cause and effect. Put simply, there is no such thing as chance. Everything that happens or will happen is potentially knowable because all events are the result of those unchanging universal laws. Those tramlines Forest talks about are set and there are no crossroads, no forks or junctions. The open road is an illusion. Or put all this another way: there is no such thing as free will. We may believe we have choices and options, but ultimately, since thinking and consciousness is itself the result of predetermined movement and interactions of atoms and electrical impulses in our brains, we don't and we never had.

But maybe all this is just a silly load of nonsense. Perhaps it's simply that science does not yet fully understand the potential randomness of its own laws. Stochasticity rules KO. Surely randomness is built into subatomic science. And anyway, didn't Albert Einstein and Stephen Hawking say something about all those so-called immutable laws of the universe becoming meaningless and breakable when lots of gravity comes into play? Oh yes, very mischievous are those weird singularities. And isn't chance built into our genetic nature? That DNA code of ours must allow for some possibility of randomness because don't species survive as a result of infinite variety? Then there's quantum physics. Doesn't that depend on uncertainty as in Heisenberg's uncertainty principle? Not only that, since the subatomic particle has no past or future, how can there be a way of predicting which way it will move? And on top of all this, aren't we forgetting Dark Matter? That stuff that scientists assume must be out there because their equations don't quite add up otherwise. What's that doing that we don't know about? Is Dark Matter, which we can't see and yet may be everywhere, subject to the same physical laws as the rest of the universe? And what about Hugh Everett and his multitude of multiverses and the principle that if something could exist it does? And if there are billions of universes out there, don't they make a single predetermined universe standing all by itself look very silly indeed? Many questions, oh but few answers.

And we haven't even mentioned cats yet.

*Cats?*

Yes, cats. Those of us who have cats as pets are laughing extraordinarily loudly at those scientists who believe the universe is governed by actions that are fixed and determined. Have these idiots never opened a door for a meowing feline? Try it. You open the door only to watch said creature just stand there. Then it makes a move to exit. No, it doesn't. It stops mid-movement, meows again, and then turns round and looks at you as if to say, *'Why did you open the door, you're letting a draft in? Stupid human.'* The point is, our everyday experience tells us the uncertainty principle is ever present in our lives. And most definitely in the lives of our feline friends.

Well, if moggies are no help, how about God? Can theology aid us in any way in deciding this question of determinism?

Not really, for every Calvinist would immediately be at loggerheads with every Catholic. The Calvinists, who, since God is all knowing, would be arguing very loudly for a predestined universe. The Catholics, on the other hand, who agree God is all knowing but believe that is more about the possibilities of outcome than its singular actuality, would (perhaps here citing Aquinas' Just War Principle) get together with the Anglicans and fight to the death on the hill of Free Will. And it wouldn't be the first time, of course, that that lot got involved in actual fisticuffs.

If God can't help, how about secular morality? Well, this soon comes a cropper if you believe in determinism. This is because the very idea of choosing between right and wrong can be thrown out straight away because doesn't predeterminism, or whatever you choose to call it, get us all off the hook for all our life choices, be they good or bad? As the scorpion famously said as it killed the well-meaning frog that offered to take it across the river, 'I can't help it, mate, it's my nature.' To quote the German philosopher Arthur Schopenhauer in chapter five of *On the Freedom of the Will*, 'Man does at all times only what he wills, and yet he does this necessarily. But this is because he already is what he wills', which Albert Einstein then paraphrased in his essay *My View of the World* (1931): 'A man can do as he will, but not will as he will.' THE SWIDGERS book series incidentally has as its hero a boy called Will (or William). And that name was certainly not chosen at random.

That sense, however, of being let off the moral hook is central to *Devs*. Forest, played by Nick Offerman, devastated by the loss of his young daughter, built the computer system with the issue and question of predeterminism in mind. DEVS (the system itself), says Lily Chan (played by Sonoya Mizuno), who herself has experienced a significant loss, is how Forest has put himself on trial. If it works, determinism will have triumphed over free will, and so he's 'absolved' of any wrongdoing. But of course if it doesn't work, he had choices and that makes him guilty. Determinism, says Chan, in a moral sense 'gives us all a free pass'.

But there's a twist in *Devs* and that is the free choice taken by Lily. She was the person the imperious Delphic-like computer could not predict. And in that free choice, there is hope. Well, a hope of a kind, for Lily and Forest in our real world fall to their physical deaths inside the computer, but, as a result, become part of the computer programme itself. Exactly how this comes about is never quite explained, but we go with it because by now the philosophical ideas have taken precedence over both the science and the fiction. And that act of free will leads Lily and Forest into the 'reality' of the computer-generated world itself. And here they can choose what they wish do with their new lives. Or at least they believe that to be the case. Which is, I suppose, the best they can hope for... until that moment when someone comes along and pulls the plug or offers us a choice of a red or blue pill.

## Predestination and Predeterminism

In *Oedipus Rex*, it was running away from his Destiny that ironically led Oedipus to it. Had Sophocles rewritten his classic play as a time travel tale – a fanciful notion maybe – perhaps he would have done so with multiple timelines, where each, though slightly different, would ultimately end in the same outcome. The point for the ancient Greeks was that the greatest power, greater even than Zeus himself, was *Ananke*, or what we would now call Necessity and Fate. And you can't escape that no matter how many timepaths you create. Yes, you can try to change history, but history and Father Time often have other ideas. In *Timeless*, J.F.K is warned by the Time team not to go to Dallas, Texas, but that doesn't stop him being assassinated in Austin, Texas, instead. Sophocles and all those Greeks would have approved of that, for Destiny will find you, one way or the other.

The Calvinists like the Greeks also believed in predestination or fatalism. Time travel in the Calvinist philosophy is therefore heresy on stilts, for to go back in time and alter what God has already put into place – essentially change God's mind for Him – would be complete anathema.

But what about those time travellers, human or otherwise, who don't believe in God or a Cosmic Plan? In a godless universe is there ever a right choice or a morally right side of history?

There are modern atheistic philosophers who, though they have no religious faith in predestination, do believe in its secular kinsman and that is predeterminism. Which takes us back to the German philosopher Arthur Schopenhauer and Man not being able to will what he wills. Schopenhauer's point was that if our choices are determined by our desires, then our freedom of choice depends on whether our desires are free in the first place as opposed to simply existing as part of our nature. Arthur favoured the second. Nature rules all, so for Schopenhauer, free will is the ultimate delusion, for in his philosophy it is our nature that ultimately controls our choices. The scorpion's nature wins out over even over his best intensions. Maybe so, but surely there has to be an element of will in life or why should we bother?

The philosophy of Schopenhauer underpins much of the German television series *Dark*. In the endless Times Loops throughout *Dark*, the actions taken by characters may differ slightly in each timeline due to circumstances, but the final result is always the same. Our nature is our ruler. And sometimes a very cruel one at that.

But *Dark* adds another element to the equation. Jonas tries to end his own life in the hope of bringing about an end to the time loop, but he is told by Magnus that 'Time won't let him.' Time itself seems to be making choices. It is as if time is an entity in its own right. Eventually Martha and Jonas (or Eva and Adam), as they repeatedly witness the terrible consequences as a result of that well-meaning choice made by The Watchmaker, decide the only option is the complete elimination of the Endless Loops and this can only be achieved by taking away the choice made by The Watchman. But to do this will end their own existence. But maybe that elimination isn't as complete as it seems, for *Dark* ends at a dinner party where one guest has a strange sense of déjà vu, an echo, perhaps, of what might have been. It's a neat metaphysical note on which to end a fascinating and thought-provoking series.

# The Appeal of The Time Tale

> *Ocean is more ancient than the mountains, and freighted with the memories and the dreams of Time.*
> H.P. Lovecraft

THE NUMBER OF adventures, both in literature and on-screen, that feature time travel within their framework is at an all-time high. Time travel has escaped the confines of hard sci-fi to appear in all manner of new stories that seem to encompass every genre. Why this recent explosion of time travel mania? Why does it suddenly hold such great appeal?

There are a number of factors in play here but one of the main triggers is the enduring appeal of a few key works. The successful return of *Doctor Who* in 2005 is one such pivotal moment. The global success of the new series, with its upgraded effects and more lavish production values, sparked renewed interest in time travel as a storytelling device. At the same time the 1980s *Back to the Future* film trilogy was proving to be something of a classic, with the originals delighting new generations and various spin-offs (video games, comic book adaptations, television versions) ensuring its retention in the public psyche and eventually resulting in a prestigious (and highly regarded) musical stage version. The 1993 time loop, romantic comedy *Groundhog Day* (created by Harold and Danny Rubin) was similarly achieving 'classic' status, making numerous 'Best Comedy Lists' and proving timeless in its appeal, with its title used universally to describe the time loop phenomenon. It too spawned a stage-musical version, a sure sign that a title has transcended its cinematic origins. Biggest of all was *The Terminator* franchise, which exploited the most cutting edge special effects, in its continuing story of time travelling cyborgs and the fight to alter the timeline to prevent an apocalyptic future. The fact that such titles as these were proving to have such lasting (and cross-generational) appeal, meant that the idea of time travel as a storytelling device was moving into the mainstream.

Other factors in play included the rise of the multi-channel and streaming TV services which resulted in scores of new outlets for all forms of storytelling (including fantasy themed material) many of which – in the way of game-changing – were from non-UK and non-US territories, the majority of which were in original languages (with English subtitles) and thus presented ideas and themes from different outlooks and perspectives.

Time Travel's universal appeal has intrigued film-makers from all over the globe. The massive South Asian film industry (now preferred over the term 'Bollywood' which is seen by many as derogatory) being no exception, with films like 1991's *Adita 369* (in the Telugu language), co-written and directed by Singeetam Srinivasa Rao, in which a group of children use a time machine to investigate a robbery; *Fun2shh ... Dudes in the 10th Century* (2003 – in the Hindi language) co-written and directed by Imtiaz Punjabi where three guys who are fleeing due to being wrongly accused of a crime, crash into a wall and find themselves back in the 10th century; *Love Story 2050* (2008 – in the Hindi language) co-written and directed by Harry Bajewa, in which a man travels to the future to try and bring his girlfriend back to life; and *24* (2016 – in the Tamil language) written and directed by Vikram K. Kumar, a musical extravaganza in which a scientist's invention of a time machine leads to a clash between his evil brother and his son.

Then of course there has been the plethora of comic book adaptations both on film and on TV, most of which tell fantastical stories, and many, think here of *Doctor Strange*, Marvel's *Agents of Shield, Superman, Avengers: Endgame: X-men: Days of Future Past, The Flash, The Umbrella Academy*, incorporate time travel as an integral part of their plot. Once a new generation of creators are willing to embrace time travel as a legitimate area of storytelling, the potential of the device can be explored to the full. The concept of time travel in all its manifestations (loops, portals, alternate histories, time machines etc) opens up numerous avenues and plot lines. The fact that time travel has outgrown its sci-fi origins to cross into other genres (rom-coms, thrillers, horror) has expanded horizons and allowed creators to extend the boundaries of storytelling. This can be witnessed by just looking at one streaming service (Netflix) and the titles they were grouping together (for example in May 2023) under one subject title they called 'Adventures in Time Travel':

*The Adam Project* (2022)
*Dirk Gently's Holistic Detective Agency* (2018)
*In The Shadow of the Moon* (2019)
*Midnight at the Pera Palace* (Turkey 2023)
*Always a Witch* (Columbia 2019)
*Captain Nova* (Netherlands 2021)
*The 7 Lives of Lea* (France 2022)
*Needle in a Timestack* (2021)
*If Only* (Spain 2022)
*Time Trap* (2017)
*Alice* (South Korea 2020)
*ARQ* (2016)
*See You Yesterday* (2019)
*Back to 15* (Brazil 2022)
*Synchronic* (2020)
*When We First Met* (2018)
*Still Time* (Italy 2023)
*Star Trek* (1968)
*Mirage* (Spain 2018)
*Terminator III: Rise of the Machines* (2003)
*Rik and Morty* (2021)
*The Knight Before Christmas* (2019)
*Mr Queen* (South Korea 2020)
*13 Going on 30* (2004)
*Austin Powers: International Man of Mystery* (1997)
*Lucid Dream* (South Korea 2017)

*Couple on the Backtrack* (South Korea 2017)
*The Door into Summer* (Japan 2021)
*Time Hustler* (Brazil 2022)
*Hello Me* (South Korea 2021)
*Inuyasha* (Japan 2000)
*Revisions* (Japan 2018)
*Thermae Romae Novae* (Japan 2022)
*Love Destiny: The Movie* (Thailand 2022)
*My Only Love Song* (South Korea 2017)
*Back to 1989* (Taiwan 2016)
*Krotkahisteriaczasu* (Poland 2005)
*Rooftop Prince* (South Korea 2012)
*Day of Destiny* (Nigeria 2021)
*A Chinese Odyssey: Part One - Pandora's Box* (China – HK – 1995)
*A Chinese Odyssey: Part Two - Cinderella* (China – HK – 1995)
*Holiday on Mars* (Italy 2020)
*Eggnoid: Love & Time Portal* (Indonesia 2019)
*Back to Q82* (Kuwait 2017)
*Que peso mas guay* (Spain 2012)
*Sisyphus: The Myth* (South Korea 2021)
*Dark* (Germany 2017)

# If Time Travel is Impossible, Why Are We So Keen on Such Nonsense?

There have always been those who claim to see the dead from times gone by, plus those who say they see the future. Charlatans they may be but there is one world where we all become time travellers and that is in our dreams. Perhaps that's why we accept the scientific nonsense of time travel. But why have there been so many Time Tales since H.G. Wells' classic and why are we so accepting of them?

Perhaps one reason is photography and especially film recordings. On 7 January 1839, members of the French Académie des Sciences were shown an image that would forever change how we saw the world: a photograph. No other human before then had seen time captured as a single moment. Suddenly there existed a way of holding onto to a Now and making it permanent. And if you were able to hold that Now in your hand could it not still be existing in some way elsewhere? Put another way, from then on the past never quite disappeared. And that notion becomes even stronger with the invention of moving images. Besides all this, isn't science knowledge in general, especially now with the creation of Artificial Intelligence, moving ahead at such a pace that it's possible to imagine a technology capable of jumping about in time?

But isn't our acceptance of time travel much more simple than all this? We believe because we want to believe. At a psychological level, it's pure wish fulfilment. Regrets. What ifs. If onlys. All these can be explored in Time Tales and more importantly fixed and put right. Okay, not by us the reader or viewer in our actual lives but vicariously through the time traveller. Much of the action with Marty's dad in *Back to the Future* is comic but what of the son watching the movie who knows the family history of his own father's youthful mistakes which put him on the wrong track? *Back to the Future* then becomes, as they say, a whole different ballgame. But let's not get too heavy here, not all Time Tales are sci-fi versions of the novels of Marcel Proust.

There is, however, a strong case against time travel stories and that is that surely we should tell tales which celebrate The Now? That is where our focus should be. Stop moaning on about the past or worrying unduly about the future. As Joseph Campbell suggests in *The Power of Myth*, there is no some time later or some long ago, for 'the experience of eternity right here and now, in all things, whether thought of as good or as evil, is the function of life'.

He has a point. However it is the nature of story that tales about the past and the future are invariably filtered through the present at the time of their creation and writing. As said, most Time Tales are about The Now. Anyway, the continuing popularity of time travel stories is testament to our need for them, and the current obsession with such tales may indicate that they are needed even more at present. And if the need is there, people will provide for it.

## When the Design is Right

Sid Sheinberg, who was in charge of Universal Studios when *Back to the Future* was made, said, 'That screenplay is like a Swiss watch.' And indeed he was right. There's not a plot beat that doesn't advance the story or enhance the characters. In fact, it's somewhere near perfection in construction. And there is great pleasure too in the inventiveness with which the writers Bob Gale and Robert Zemeckis deal with the many challenging anomalies, contradictions and paradoxes that time travel always raises. Somehow *Back to the Future* never fails to be logical and so avoids the plot holes many Time Tales find themselves falling down. And the explanation is always concise and simply presented, as when Doc Brown draws lines on a blackboard showing the creation of an alternate 1985. And there's a real joy in watching how these carefully constructed time travel rules are played out in this entertaining fast-moving comedy adventure series. Amazing then that the original screenplay was rejected 42 times because, as Bob Gale was repeatedly told, 'time travel movies don't make money.' Clearly some people in Hollywood did not have their eye on the future.

As said before, the design of your time world, its rules and restrictions, is created for the purpose of the story. Content always dictates design, and never the other way round. And, as Steve Jobs used to say, 'Design is not just what it looks and feels like. Design is how it works.'

Yet the fascination and appeal of the Time Tale goes way beyond the clever concept idea or the rules played out, for Time Tales are fundamentally 'Thought Experiments', where speculative intellectual and moral questions are posed and explored. Put simply, Time Tales are the ultimate '*What If*' stories.

## The 'Hitler...' Question

There is a famous question often posed to first year students of moral philosophy: *If you could go back in time and kill Hitler when he was a new born baby, would you do it?* It's a question that raises many other questions. Killing is wrong, we take that for granted, but surely the greater good would be served by the death of this monster? Or is murder murder no matter who the victim is? Besides, can you really be sure that killing Hitler as a baby wouldn't result in an even greater tragedy than the Second World War? Difficult to imagine anything much worse but when the Law of Unintended Consequences comes into play anything can happen. Indeed, this is the premise of *Making History*, the novel by Stephen Fry. But the Hitler-and-the-time-traveller scenario has been around since the 1940s. There is a tale called *I Killed Hitler*, written by Ralph Milne Farely (pseudonym for Roger Sherman Hoard), in the July 1941 issue of *Weird Tales*. In it an unnamed narrator says to a friend 'If I can travel back to the time and place where the Dictator was a boy, why can I not kill him, and thereby prevent there ever having been this little man who now "bestrides this narrow world like a colossus"?' The friend, a Hindu, replies that travelling back in time can be arranged but 'the Gods of Karma will build up another Dictator, to take his place; for this man is but the symbol of what must be.' And that is what happens, though to find out who becomes the Dictator you'll have to read the story. Perhaps it's worth mentioning here that Stephen Hawking, who probably didn't believe in Karma, wrote a paper called *Chronology Protection Conjecture* in 1991 in which he expressed his belief that scientific reality does not allow the appearance of closed time-like curves. In his own words, the laws of physics 'make the world safe for historians.'

There is a *Doctor Who* episode called *Let's Kill Hitler*. However, Hitler himself becomes little more than a sideshow (he's locked in a cupboard for most of the time) in what is essentially the origin of River Song. Nevertheless, the moral dilemma of the Hitler Question is at the heart of the classic *Doctor Who* storyline *The Genesis of the Daleks* (1975). In the final episode, The Doctor (Tom Baker) has in his hand the wires that could kill the Daleks at birth. But he chooses not to. His rationale is a fine piece of philosophical thinking about what is and what isn't justifiable in the relationship between what is good and what is bad. And similar scenarios are played out in many Time Tales.

*In the Shadow of the Moon* has a time traveller going back in time to kill those who are seen as a threat to the future. Perhaps they are, but the weakness of the movie is the morality of this is never even discussed. *Looper* on the surface is a shoot and kill 'em film but at its heart it is a moral fable about the cycle of violence. Old Joe's self-sacrifice to break the circle is a moral choice. It's a far more reflective movie than others of its kind. *Terminator II: Judgment Day* arguably lies somewhere between the two. The computer technician, Miles Dyson, working on the chip that came from the future, does not know its origin, nor, of course, to what it will lead. When he is confronted by Sarah Connor, Miles points out she is judging him on things he hasn't even done yet. And it's a tough day when you learn you're responsible for the death of billions. *Terminator II* shows Miles' domestic world, with his loving wife and children. He's no monster. And of course when Sarah does have the opportunity to kill Miles face-to-face, she cannot pull the trigger. Ultimately the Hitler Question boils down to an extreme version of the Utilitarian argument of the Greater Good versus a Moral Absolutist position. As said before, a natural home for moral questions are stories which allow us to explore dilemmas in, as it were, the safe environment of fiction. And Time Tales (or at least the good ones) do that exceptionally well.

## Who Are We?

Clare says of the many Henrys she encounters in *The Time Traveler's Wife* that they are the same Henry, 'just shuffled'. But to use a different metaphor, are we different slices from the same pie or a series of newly baked pies that are all distinct from each other? And what are the ingredients which make up the pie in the first place? We might mention here David Hume's 'bundle' theory of self in *A Treatise of Human Nature* that says the self or the mind is 'nothing but a bundle or collection of different perceptions, which succeed each other with an inconceivable rapidity, and are in a perpetual flux and movement.'

The nature of identity is a key theme in many Time Tales. It's certainly there in Robert Heinlein's *By His Bootstraps* ('No sane person ever expects to see his own face hanging on another') but in that story which one is the real Bob Wilson? As Lewis Carroll's Alice says, 'it's no use going back to yesterday, because I was a different person then.' Time changes who we are into what we become. And this leads us onto the question what makes us who we become? What is our 'cause'?

The Korean time travel series *Alice* explores multi-dimensions. There's a scene where Professor Yoon Tae-yi asks Seok Oh-won Director of the Kuiper Institute of Advanced Science how a morally good version of the Park Jin-gyeom she knows could in another dimension have become the ultimate killer. Seok Oh-won tells the tale of a monster who kidnapped a woman's son. For the son to be released the mother had to answer correctly whether the monster would kill her son. The wise mother said he would, and that was the right answer so the monster couldn't kill her son. Yoon Tae-yi says that's simply a paradox where the question contradicts itself, but Seok Oh-won goes on to say that life is made up of paradoxes and contradictions, yet there are always answers and consequences. But the story isn't finished for the monster in the tale saves the son, but then kills the mother – and in so doing turns her son into a monster like himself.

What and who makes us who and what we are? In an alternative dimension and an alternative life, would we be that different? Do our old sins cast long shadows or can we learn to accept and forgive and move on?

## What Is It That Makes Our Families What They Are?

*Mirai* is a 2018 Japanese animated adventure fantasy film written and directed by Mamoru Hosoda. Kun is a four-year-old boy born to a hard-working executive mother and an architect father. The family live in a stepped house that Kun's father designed around a tree and it's here that Kun spends most of his days playing with his dog, Yukko. When Kun's sister Mirai (Japanese for 'future') is born, Kun is at first very happy but slowly grows jealous as his parents focus all their attention on her. After one tantrum, Kun stomps off to the garden and here he meets a strange man who claims to be the 'prince' of the house. The man whines on about how he lost all the attention when Kun was born, and as he speaks Kun realises that this man is actually his dog Yukko turned human. Kun sees Yukko's tail on the man and when Kun removes it and places it on himself, he too transforms into a dog.

Later, in the same garden, Kun encounters a school girl who claims to be Mirai from the future and this is confirmed when Kun sees a birthmark he recognises on her right hand. Mirai has somehow come back in time from her futures. She has done so, she reveals, because she is concerned that after Hinamatsuri (Girls Day), the family didn't put away the traditional dolls – and every day they are left out adds one year before she can marry. However, the future Mirai, along with Kun and Yukko's help, put away the dolls.

But the time travelling has only just begun. In fact, in the course of the film, Kun is transported years back to the past where he meets a little girl whom he recognises from family photos as his mother and later encounters his great-grandfather, who has recently died, as a young man. With each encounter Kun comes to a better understanding of people in his family history and in so doing becomes more open-minded. This culminates in a magical journey which ends when Kun and baby Mirai land in the tree, which houses the family's past. Kun sees how his father was too weak to ride a bike when he was young, how his much loved dog Yukko left his mother to become a pet, how Kun's own mother stopped wanting a cat when she saw a stray one kill a bird, and how World War II left his great-grandfather's leg badly injured.

We all have our back-stories that have changed our lives, yet it's impossible to offer the next generation an insight into those struggles that made us who we are. Well, except, as Kun learns, through time travel. *Dark* incidentally takes the idea that when the past haunts our parents, it becomes our present. And in *Dark* that present is a bleak one, but though it may try to explain people's behaviour, it never makes an attempt to excuse.

## A Peek into the Olden Days

There is obviously the historical appeal of time travel stories. It's not just cats in life who are curious, for which historian hasn't wanted to see for themselves what really happened at the court of King Whatever the Fourteenth? A time machine gives you a front row seat at The Theatre of History.

*Doctor Who* was in part conceived as a series for children in order to introduce them to historical characters and events, and recently returned to this idea in a story about the American activist Rosa Parks. This theme of historical enquiry was also there in the 1970–1971 children's television series *Timeslip*. Although the case in favour of *Bill and Ted's Excellent Adventure* is that it is very funny, the plot itself is about two students who go back in time in order to round up historical figures who might be able to help write their school assignment. And who hasn't thought when wading through a dry history book that it would have been quite fun to meet Ching Shih, Boudicca, Sappho, Nefertiti and Eleanor of Aquitaine for real.

That said, the ethics of the historical time tourists in *Timescape* are morally questionable. *Timescape*, released on video as *Grand Tour: Disaster in Time*, is a 1992 move directed by David Twohy with a screenplay by him very loosely based on the 1946 novella *Vintage Season* by Henry Kuttner and C.L. Moore (writing as Lawrence O'Donnell). The movie's scenario involves human-like beings from the future, where it's a seemingly perfect world, travelling back through time to witness the 'spectacle' of natural disasters, such as the San Francisco earthquake. However, when visiting a small American town that is about to be destroyed by a meteorite strike, the hotel owner Ben Wilson, played by Jeff Daniels, becomes suspicious when the local driver who picked them up tells Ben that it's odd these apparent tourists carry no cameras. Ben later discovers that their cameras are somehow in their brains and these tourists are in fact from the future. One tourist claims his reason to be on the trip is not voyeuristic but purely academic. In fact, he goes as far as calling himself a 'retropologist', which he says is one who studies the past first-hand.

Time tourists are not unique to *Timescape*. *Thrill Seekers* (also known as *The Time Shifters*) was a 1999 science fiction television movie featuring Tom Merrick. Tom is a TV reporter who films a fire at a power plant and spots a strange-looking man, Murray Trevor played by Julian Richings, whom Tom later sees in pictures of other disasters, including the sinking of the *Titanic* and the explosion of the *Hindenburg* airship. It is later discovered that Murray is a time traveller using an enterprise company called Thrill Seekers, which sell trips to the past allowing travellers to witness a catastrophe, and then return to their own time before getting killed.

The theme of both *Timescape* and *Thrill Seekers* could be said to be voyeurism. Yet in a way aren't we all guilty of that when we watch a disaster movie, especially one based on a real event? In principle, are we any less a voyeur than those time travellers? Yes, a movie isn't real but what we seek is the same as that which the time tourists want, namely thrills and spills. We could argue that we are merely watching to understand, say, why the *Titanic* sank, but does that – excuse the pun – really hold water? We can call ourselves 'retropologists' if we like, but we're kidding no one.

A more fun and certainly more family friendly academic is Mr Peabody in *Mr Peabody and Mr Sherman* (2014), an animated science fiction comedy film, where Mr Peabody is in fact a dog, and Mr Sherman is a seven-year-old boy who together have time travelling adventures. Mr Sherman on his first day at school is none too impressed by the history being taught in class. And he should know because he was there! *Mr Peabody and Mr Sherman* is an adventure story but it is also packed with witty lines and historical curiosities. A long way from the dry history lessons of 1066 and all that.

In *The Time That Never Was*, William's Mentor Granny comes from a different era. It's never explicitly said which time period but as it is established she can't read or write and that she only ever went to Sunday School, it's possible to assume it was before the 1891 Elementary Education Act. Granny isn't a time traveller as such, it's just that Swidgers, though human in appearance, age more slowly. And, if she spent a year or so in the Old Coach House, where Time passes at different rate to our world, when she returned to our world she would be more out of her Time. Anyway, being from another era, Granny is able to introduce William not only to shillings and tanners, but ideas, experience and thinking that come from a different century. And the language and expression she uses makes him laugh! *Stop fratching!*

## Social Commentary

In the movie *In Time* (2011 – written and directed by Andrew Nicco), time is the new human currency where money is time, for you 'pay' in minutes and hours. 'Time is money', that platitude of life, has now been made literal so when you talk about the cost of living that expression too takes on an entirely new meaning. There's social commentary in lines such as 'For a few to be immortal, many must die' or 'The cost of living keeps rising to make sure people keep dying.' There are a few fun lines too, as when someone buys a car and is told that it will be '59 years, plus tax'. *In Time* is ultimately a Bonnie and Clyde/Robin

Hood action thriller but it's an action thriller with a social conscience concerning the redistribution of wealth – 'The truth is there's more than enough. No one has to die before their time.' A message the Ghost of Christmas Present and the children hidden under his robes would share.

## 'It's About Today, Stupid!' – The Social Politics of Time Tales

The irony of most time travel adventures is that they are not really about the past or future at all, for their focus is nearly always on the world we live in today. The past is a mere backdrop for our modern concerns. This is as true for the contemporary series *Timeless* and *Travelers* as it was for *The Planet of the Apes* in the '70s, or for *Quantum Leap* in the '80s, or indeed H.G. Wells' *The Time Machine* in the late 19th century. And will it be long before someone comes up with a scenario where a time traveller from the future goes to the year 2019 and intentionally creates the COVID-19 pandemic as the only way of preventing global warming destroying the planet in their time? You see, scientists in the year 2458 worked out that only a catastrophic worldwide event, such as a pandemic in the early part of the 21st century, could stop carbon emissions to the degree that was necessary to prevent the world becoming a dead desert of sand. Except in some ways that plot has already been used in episode five of season two of *Travelers* (2017), *Jenny*, where a deadly virus is intentionally spread all over the world. Oh, how life imitates art. Or was it that the Chinese government were fans of *Travelers* and when the Chairman saw this episode it offered him a good idea as to how to bring down the Western liberalism?

As a matter of fact, ecological catastrophe, global warming and worries about pollution are not topics that have only concerned the 21st century generation. You'll find ecological scenarios in 1970s episodes of both *Doctor Who* and *Timeslip* where there are underlying concerns about the quality of the air and the lack of trees and grass. And Peter Fonda's 1973 *Idaho Transfer* is a Time Tale movie where people learn of future environmental problems. But that's science fiction writers for you: always ahead of their time.

Future nuclear wars or nuclear accidents feature regularly in the back-story (or should that be 'ahead-story') of Time Tales. It's there in *World Without End* (1956), *The Terminator* (1984) and *In the Shadow of the Moon* (2019), plus television series such as *Travelers* and *Dark*. There are occasions when you'd think, watching a Time Tale that time machine fiction was actually created for the sole purpose of allowing political writers to explore issues such as civil rights, the environment, sexual freedoms and the rest. And in a way you wouldn't be far wrong, for it was a divided and unequal society that was the theme in H.G. Wells' seminal novel *The Time Machine*, way back in 1895.

Of course *Star Trek* in the 1960s was well known for smuggling in moral messages into its storylines. And in its casting too. *Star Trek* was way ahead of its time when it came to diversity and gender representation in the starship crew (you might add here the cast of *The Tomorrow People,* running from 1973 to 1979, which was always racially inclusive and, importantly, made little reference to skin colour). Of course, *Star Trek* had the first interracial kiss on American television, but having Chekhov on board was just as controversial as it assumed that the Cold War between America and Russia had long ended. *Star Trek* had a utopian ethos about journeying out in peace and friendship. That was the '60s for you: *Make love, not war*. Of course, it didn't exactly work out like that... but people had a damn good time trying.

## The Personal

Away from the cerebral and political appeal of Time Tales, there is also the personal. It is a natural human want to help people, even fix them if necessary. And this can equally apply to ourselves, for who has not wanted to go back in time and have a conversation with their younger self and try to come to an understanding of why they did what they did? Think of Time Tales then as Therapy Tales.

'Regret', is the one word answer that Gang Seo-hae gives in *Sisyphus* when she is asked why people want to travel through time. It can be more complicated than that but regret is perhaps the key word in the motivation of time travellers. There are often people who are dealing with psychological flaws or traumas that have to be confronted. In certain tales, a time traveller is given the ability somehow to change their life or even live it again. These plots are called the 'Re-do' scenario or the 'Second Chance' story, for the tragedy of life isn't so much that an opportunity passed you by, but rather an opportunity was ignored in favour of an easier option. It's a popular type of Time Tale for it can show that in the past you may have underestimated yourself and your capabilities, and that your potential went further than you thought possible and that the other path would have taken you there.

*17 Again* (2009 – written by Jason Filardi), starring Zac Efron, is about Mike O'Donnell who is unhappy about how his life has turned out. After trying to save the life of a janitor jumping from a bridge – in a nod perhaps to *It's a Wonderful Life* – O'Donnell finds himself going through a time vortex and when he returns to where he was staying he finds that he's 17 again.

*Twice in a Lifetime*, a Canadian television series created by Steve Sohmer that ran from 1999 to 2000, features individuals at the end of their lives who are offered the chance to speak to their younger selves and try to convince them to make different choices at key moments across the years. *That Was Then*, an American series made in 2002 created by Dan Cohn, Jeff Kline and Jeremy Miller, has James Bulliard as the 30-year-old Travis Glass who believes he can pinpoint his downward spiral to a single week in high school in 1988. One night, as he listens in bed to *Do It Again* by the Kinks, Travis is struck by lightning and sent back in time to his teenage days. *Do Over*, created by Rick Wiener and Kenny Schwarz, has Joel Larsen (Penn Badgley) at the age of 34 who is involved in an accident that sends him back to 1981, when he was 14. But his adult memories remain intact and he sets about setting right the wrongs that befell his family. This American fantasy sitcom ran from 2002 to 2003. Curiously all these Time Tales were created round about the Millennium. It was almost as if looking back was a theme in the zeitgeist itself.

But Time Tales as therapy are nothing new. Arguably it was Charles Dickens in *A Christmas Carol* who got that ball rolling in 1843. As said, you'll find many protagonists in Time Travel stories who are psychologically damaged or coping with the impossibility of grief, notably in *La Jetée*, and, more recently, the young widower Wyatt Logan in *Timeless*. But dwelling on the past or reliving it isn't always that straightforward. In *Je t'aime, Je t'aime*, a suicide survivor, who intends to travel back a year to relive a single minute, finds himself trapped in a vortex confronted by key moments in his marriage.

Male angst is the theme of both *Groundhog Day* and the cult low budget movie *Primer*. You might add here Ian McEwan's *The Child in Time* (1987) which is about a man who feels lost and in a way is still trapped in his childhood. *Primer* is a kind of Faustian story where life has not turned out as expected or as it was hoped to have been. The Faust legend comes into play when the question is asked, *What would you do if it were possible to do something without impunity?* Time travel gives Aaron his wish and, without revealing too much of the plot, let's just say it's not peace on Earth and goodwill to all men. *Primer* is a jigsaw puzzle with more than half the pieces missing so it's impossible to say exactly what was done, but you get the impression that it didn't work out well, for it destroys the special bond between best friends Aaron and Abe.

*Mr Destiny* (1990 – written by James Orr and Jim Cruickshank), is a comedy where Larry Burrows, played by James Belushi, believes it was one mistake while in high school during a baseball game that resulted in the unhappy life he lives now. An Angel, played by Michael Caine, offers Larry a drink called 'Spilt Milk' which transports him to an alternate universe where that mistake was not made. In this world Larry is more successful, but the wife he had in his other life is married to someone else in this one.

On a more cheerful note there is *Peggy Sue Got Married*, (1986 – written by Jerry Leichtling and Arlene Sarner), in which Peggy Sue gets the opportunity to meet her grandparents. And *The Time Traveler's Wife* is especially moving when the grown up Henry meets his mother before her death and likewise, Henry's time travelling daughter seeing and meeting him after his. Time travel tales are especially good at those moments.

The most personal episode of *Time Tunnel* is where Tony Newman goes back to the days before the bombing of Pearl Harbour and meets his own father who he knows dies in the attack. Of course Tony tries to save his father (it wouldn't be a Time Tale if he didn't), but his father is a Navy man and therefore must do his duty. However, the older Tony does save himself, the Young Tony, plus Tony's friend and the friend's mother by telling them to run to the hills. The scene of Tony's father dying in the arms of his son is heartbreaking and in many ways the series was never bettered. And it's similar in many ways to *Father's Day*, the episode in *Doctor Who* where Rose was able to go back in time and briefly meet her father. Such scenes as these, plus those in *Peggy Sue Got Married* and *The Time Traveler's Wife*, are pure emotional wish fulfilment for those of us who lost parents at a young age.

# LGBTQI +

There's a scene in Russell T. Davies' *Queer As Folk* where a guy takes another guy back to his place for sex. Only sex suddenly becomes secondary when the guys discover they have a shared passion for *Doctor Who* and so the night is spent not between the sheets but talking about and watching their favourite episodes. Well, one has to have the right priorities in life, after all.

But what is it that makes the Doctor Who character and the series itself so important to so many gay/trans/bi/queer people? Well, there is that immediate sense of other and difference. Just look at how the Doctor dresses. Even in the '70s Jon Pertwee's Doctor had a touch of the Oscar Wilde. But it goes beyond outward appearance. The Doctor is an outsider who goes through life protecting those who are misunderstood. Think of all those episodes where his/her arrival saves someone from the ignorance of those who would do them harm. And the Doctors don't just accept difference they embrace it. The appearance of Alpha Centuri isn't what you'd call conventional, but that's of no matter to the Doctor, for they become dear friends. Then there's the literal escapist element of the time travel stories themselves which can take you to another world. Sometimes a more tolerant world.

In more recent series there have been numerous gay/trans/bi/queer characters but that sense of otherness around sexuality was occasionally there in the classic series of the '60s, '70s and '80s. Need we say more than Ace and Harry Sullivan? But nothing could be too overt, for a degree of subtlety was required. Well, kind of. In *The Ark in Space* (1975), written by Robert Holmes, the Fourth Doctor (Tom Baker), says when a human asks for medical help: 'Well, my doctorate is purely honorary, and Harry's only qualified to work on sailors.' A remark that had many closeted teens giggling away all the way down to the bottom of their flares. And *Carnival of Monsters* (1973) – also written by Robert Holmes – even had a few exchanges in the gay language of Polari for those 'in the life'.

*Doctor Who* was not alone in the 1970s. The premise of *The Tomorrow People* was that there were teenagers who were discovering themselves to be different and struggling with the inner changes that came with that otherness. Oh, but once the struggle was over what exciting and fun lives they would have! But sci-fi series have often been ahead of their time in this area. The closing exchange, for example, in the *Quantum Leap* episode (written by Robert Duncan) *Running for Honor*

(1993) – Admiral Al Calavicci: 'Well, was Tommy gay or not?' Dr Sam Beckett: 'Does it matter?' – was an iconic moment in American television. And it's sci-fi series such as this that have now made that question asked by Admiral Al Calavicci seem oddly anachronistic.

## The Moral

In the Korean series *Alice*, the story arc of the series belongs to time travel genius Professor Yoon Tae-yi. She tells Detective Park Jin-gyeom why she became a physicist. Her biological mother left her at the orphanage, but she can still remember her scent and warmth. Even then she thought of time travel, to be with her again, and that's why she became a scientist. And all this is addressed to the man who in another time dimension *is* her son, a son who was there when *his* mother died, who was a doppelganger of Yoon Tae-yi herself.

You can certainly understand Yoon Tae-yi's good intentions but her view changes as the series develops, for later she says to Park Jin-gyeom that she now believes that no matter where you go and who you meet, the people of the past are not as precious as the people who know you and are around you now. Yes, the importance of 'The Now' comes up again. Park Jin-gyeom argues that she could meet those she can't meet here instead, but Yoon Tae-yi replies that wouldn't change things because even if you met them you couldn't stay with them forever. Yoon Tae-yi in the final episode goes even further when she says when interviewed by a journalist that time travel shouldn't be invented. Retain the past in memory, but turning back time is just greedy. And when she talks with Director of the Kuiper Institute of Advanced Science, Seok Oh-won, Professor Yoon Tae-yi essentially ends the possibility of time travel once and for all by giving up her study of the subject. As she says to Seok Oh-won, she thought time travel would make people happy. Mend heartbreak. But she was wrong, for wounds, despair and sorrow are all necessary in human life.

## Emotion or Intellect – *Are you Tin Man or Scarecrow?*

It is sometimes said that science fiction stories appeal to 'thinkers' over 'feelers', that is those people who enjoy conceptual ideas and Thought Experiments rather than romance and sentiment. Solving Rubik's cubes and Sudoku games always wins out over sunsets and holding hands under duvets. Yet when you look at series such as *Doctor Who* and *Star Trek: The Next Generation*, you will often find that the most popular and enduring episodes are those with the biggest emotional heart. For example, *The Girl in the Fireplace*, where Doctor Who falls in love, or *The Inner Light* where Captain Jean-Luc Picard lives a lifetime of someone else's memory, with a wife and family on a now dead but at least not forgotten planet. These are the ones that stick in the mind precisely because they're about the complexities of the human heart. The heart the Tin Man so wished to have.

It is true that when it comes to the Grandfather Paradox and the potential of killing your own grandfather, physicists think mainly in terms of cause and effect and billiard balls and it's left to philosophers and therapists to ask, *'So, why you do want to kill your grandfather?'* Of course the appeal for physicists, particularly theoretical physicists, is that Time Tales allow them to explore the logic of what could happen in space-time if factors allowed it. The emphasis is on 'could' and 'if', but that is why they are called speculative physics in the first place. Such brainwork would appeal to the Scarecrow who so wanted to be an expert in 'thinkology'.

## New Words for the OED and the Metaphors of Time

The 'coulds' and 'ifs' of time travel also raise the intellectual and indeed emotional challenge of coming up with new language for an imagined or speculated world. Some even end up being added to the Oxford English Dictionary.

Let's start with Dilithium crystals. Is that an existing word or made up? Well, Dilithium exists, it's a molecule made from two Lithium atoms bonded together, but Dilithium crystals do not. As far as we know. Mugwump? This is a wonderful old word for a fence-sitter and it is also to be found in William S. Burroughs' *Naked Lunch*, but now it is also a well-known term for having your face in one half of a time-space and your backside in the other. Kate Mascarenhas' novel *The Psychology of Time Travel* even has a glossary of 'Time Words'. There is 'Liebestod', meaning a trip to see a lover for the last time before death and which can trace its etymology back to Wagner's *Tristan and Isolde*. Then there's 'Zeitzorn', meaning feeling angry with someone for something they haven't done yet. Neat. Oh and 'Me-timing', which is sex with yourself in another time period. Check out *The Time Traveler's Wife*. But be kind on Henry and his 'Me-timing', for that word is a great twist on Woody Allen's observation that you shouldn't mock masturbation as it's only 'sex with someone you love'.

It's doubtful whether 'Me-timing' will catch on, you'd need time travel for real for that, but some time travel words and phrases do make it to the OED. 'Warp-drive', for instance. It's a phrase that's almost conventional now. Of course, 'warp' already existed as a word. In science, both the power of gravity and travelling at the speed of light can 'warp' space-time. 'Warp-drive' is merely the fictional superluminal (meaning faster than light speed) propelling force of the spacecraft itself. As said, it's a common expression in everyday use. But not for everyone. When the veteran British actress Beryl Reid was at the read through of her episodes playing Captain Briggs in *Earthshock*, *Doctor Who* (1984), she was apparently a little confused by the term. 'Send the ship into Warp Drive.' 'Warp Drive?' she said again, looking over her script at her fellow actors, 'Is that like "Acacia Avenue"?' Much laughter ensued, but Miss Reid still remained puzzled. The language of science fiction will always be a mystery to some.

# THE APPEAL OF THE TIME TALE

## Sometimes it's the Small Things that Bring the Greatest Pleasure

Time travel tales often have scenes in them where the time traveller is doubted or even mocked. This happens in *12 Monkeys*, *The Time Traveler's Wife*, *The Terminator*, *Back to the Future* and *Star Trek*. Of course, this is often a set-up for the pay-off later in the story where the doubter sees a flash of light and then the traveller suddenly vanishes into thin air. That dropping jaw of the doubter is always worth the wait. A small pleasure maybe, but a rewarding one. For example, the jailor in *Timescape* who locked up Ben Wilson (Jeff Daniels) in a police cell after he claimed the tourists in his house were all time travellers. The police officer has been quietly counting coins and then in walks Ben Wilson 'number two', who did some time travelling himself, and now, with the jailor in shock, the piles of coins drop to the floor.

Solving the practical problems of time travelling such as in those plots where a time traveller arrives naked and needs to find some clothes sharpish, can also be quite fun. Equally entertaining though can be the looks on the faces of time travellers who journey to the past when they are suddenly confronted by ancient plumbing and sanitary conditions. Sometimes characters need a quick buck now they're in their new world. If the future is known, the easiest option is a big win on the lottery, for example in *Travelers* and in *The Time Traveler's Wife*, but back in the '70s, the only option was a football pools win, as was the case in the plot of *The Flipside of Dominick Hide*.

Sometimes how a character uses their knowledge of the future to get themselves out of a scrape can be inventive and engaging. Hank Morgan in *A Connecticut Yankee in King Arthur's Court* remembers that a major eclipse is due that day and that is his means of threatening the Court. It has been suggested that this idea in Mark Twain's novel was inspired by a real incident where Christopher Columbus used his knowledge of an eclipse to get his way with the native Arawak Indians when he first came to America. Of course, selfish misuse of certain knowledge can lead to a dystopian world, as in *Back to the Future II*.

The names people call themselves in the future can be creative and help set a mood and tone for the story itself. *Futurama*, for example, has names such as Ziodberg, Cartridge Bot, Flex o, HG Blob, Morbo, Pazazu, Slurms McKenzie and Head Cat. Someone had fun thinking those up. Yet there can be a serious side to all this. In *Just Imagine* (1930), people of the future no longer have names but simply refer to each other as RT-42 and J-21, giving the dystopia an inhuman feel. In the television series *Travelers*, again the people of the future have no names only numbers. A small detail but it gives us a glimpse into the nature of their broken society.

## Time Can Be Fun, Too!

Time Tales aren't always deep thinking meditations on the nature of the human condition. They can be fun too! Early science fiction comics even boasted of '*Sensational Fiction with No Philosophy*'. Yes, Time Romps can be pure schlock and hokum – think *Austin Powers: The Spy Who Shagged Me, Hot Tub Time Machine, Deadpool, Galaxy Quest*. Many of these can be laugh out loud hilarious. And if you don't find *Bill and Ted's Excellent Adventure* funny perhaps you should time leap your mind back to that hormonal period in your own life when you would have done. As for *Palm Springs*, well, that genuinely is a witty and smartly constructed farce from director Max Barbakow and writer Andy Siara. It features Andy Samberg as Nyles who really is a guy who's seen it all before. And will do again. And again. With hilarious consequences, until of course he finds love, because *Palm Springs* is also a fun rom-com too. And for more big laughs who can forget the gags in *Back to the Future* where Marty is called Calvin because the name 'Calvin Klein' is written all over his underwear or when Marty tells Doc Brown that the President of the United States in 1985 is Ronald Reagan and Doc then asks if the Vice President is Jerry Lewis.

It's often the smallest detail that the eagle-eyed movie viewer finds the most fun. There are those who believe the three path layout of the town square in *Back to the Future* is deliberately designed in the shape of the three pronged flux capacitor. Maybe. But what can't be denied is the name of the Mall. In the first feature, have you ever noticed the pine trees? In 1985, when Marty leaves the parking lot of Twin Pines Mall to go back to 1955, he is going at such speed that when he arrives in the past, the DeLorean immediately destroys one of the young saplings and as a result of this, on his return to 1985, the shopping mall sign instead now reads Lone Pine Mall. It's a subtle joke from the production team, but one that fans love. And you can even buy Twin Pines Mall and Lone Pine Mall paperweight souvenirs.

In fact, there are numerous fun background moments to enjoy all through the *Back to the Future* series. In *Back to the Future II*, The Hill Valley Theatre can be seen to be under construction and the clock tower clock is there in one shot being unloaded from the train. And if you look closely at the loose change Marty takes out of his pocket in the diner, you can spot a guitar pick, which all good guitarists would always carry, setting up Marty's readiness to play with the band at the school dance.

There are quite a few industry in-jokes in *Back to the Future* as well. The non-speaking part of the photographer who takes the picture of Marty and Doc in the Wild West is none other than Dean Cundey, the actual Director of Photographer of all the *Back to the Future* movies. There's also a few not so well hidden 'Easter Eggs' for movie nerds. In the window of the 'antique' store in *Back to the Future II* there is a VHS copy of *Jaws*, which was of course the hit movie directed by Executive Producer Steven Spielberg. Also in that window, if you look closely, you can see a JVC camcorder similar to the one used by Marty to record Doc Brown's first experiment. There is as well a *Who Framed Roger Rabbit?* doll, merchandise from the movie directed by Robert Zemeckis, the director of all three *Back to the Future* features. Movie buffs will pick up on how when Marty disappears towards a cinema in his nuclear DeLorean, the sign above says what's showing is, appropriately enough, *The Atomic Kid*, a 1954 movie starring Mickey Rooney and Robert Strauss. 1955, the year *Back to the Future III* is partially set, marked the film debut of Clint Eastwood in *Revenge of the Creature* and it's actually the poster of that movie which can be seen on the walls when Marty is seen in his 'cowboy' outfit. Later, when Marty returns on the railway line, the sign has changed to 'Eastwood Ravine' rather than 'Clayton Ravine'. It was originally called 'Clayton Ravine' after Clara Clayton, but the past has been altered and Clara was saved, so now it is 'Clint Eastwood', the pseudonym Marty used in the Wild West, who, it must have be assumed, fell to his death.

The pseudonym-joke was taken up in *Timeless*, where the Time Team, when they travel into the past, give themselves aliases such as 'Wesley Snipes', 'Agent Mulder' and 'Hans Gruber' and 'John McClane'. There's a nice touch too in the Classic Hollywood 1941 episode of *Timeless*, *Hollywoodland* (2018) where there's already talk of a *Jurassic Park* screenplay.

*Fiddlers Three*, written by Angus MacPhail and Diana Morgan, is a 1944 British comedy where a pair of Jolly Jack Tars on shore leave, take a Wren, a female sailor, to Stonehenge and get caught up in a Time Warp transporting them to ancient Rome. *A Hitch in Time*, written by T.E.B. Clarke, a Children's Film Foundation production from 1978, features Patrick Troughton as Professor Wagstaff, who can never get his time machine called OSKA to work properly. But two children come along and he sends them back in time where they meet the ancestors of a bullying teacher. Oh yes, nothing wrong with a bit of popcorn fun on Saturday morning at the flicks. And on the subject of food, the comic relief in *Travelers* is usually food related for the Travelers from the future haven't a clue about the proper stuff because they've been living on a diet of what sounds like protein based gruel. Hot Dogs are a complete mystery to them, and as Trevor, Traveler 0115 says, 'I knew corn existed. I knew popcorn existed. I just never made the connection.'

A rare television sitcom Time Tale is *Timewasters* (another being *Goodnight, Sweetheart*). The premise of *Timewasters*, which ran from 2017 to 2019, is a struggling black jazz band from contemporary South London who are propelled back in time to the 1950s. As with many other Time Tales, the series includes social commentary, mocking and exposing bigotry and the ridiculous attitudes of the '50s. The novelist Dexter Palmer famously wrote in *Version Control*, 'I can't comprehend why any black man with even a lick of sense would have the slightest bit of interest in time travel. Going backward in time? A black man? You have got to be out of your mind.' In a way, that's a perfectly sensible observation, but, as *Timewasters* showed, and *Timeless* too, such a premise does open up many dramatic and even comedic possibilities.

## Music

Did Cher have a crystal ball when she was starting out in the business? Or maybe even a time machine? *If I Could Turn Back Time* features in quite a few Time Tales, including *Deadpool 2* and even *Dark*. And of course *I Got You, Babe* was the wake up song every morning in *Groundhog Day*. And Cher always looks so young. Probably cosmetic surgery but can a time machine be ruled out?

Music generally is often a very enjoyable feature of a Time Tale. Think of Marty 'inventing' rock'n'roll in *Back to the Future* or even Bing Crosby adding a bit of swing to the medieval minstrels in the movie version of *A Connecticut Yankee Arthur's Court* (1949). And in *Highlander* Connor MacLeod may be centuries old but that doesn't stop him from enjoying the music of Queen. Sometimes it is there to help set the time period and sometimes to comment as it were on the action or the theme. *What a Wonderful World* features in this way in both *Dark* and *12 Monkeys*.

## The Pitfalls of the Time Tale

This book's aim is to celebrate the inventive nature of the Time Tale and see how it can explore ideas and even help us understand who we are. But there are pitfalls too. Terry Pratchett talked about what he called the 'make-it-up-as-you-go-along-eum', where time travel story problems are solved with a one line contrivance. It's perhaps useful here to remember Samuel Taylor Coleridge's phrase concerning 'the willing suspension of disbelief', and although this is not the process by which a story is experienced or enjoyed, it is sensible not to push that initial willingness to accept a fictional world too far. Yes, enjoy what is strange and intriguing, but keep in mind that the dividing line between weirdness and absolute codswallop can sometimes be very thin indeed. And aligned to this point is that sometimes stories can become so convoluted that they begin to lose their focus. Yes, Time Tales can be packed with fascinating conceits and much philosophising, but please don't neglect a coherent plot.

Inconsistency is another potential pitfall in a Time Tale. Time rules when set, just like the laws of our own universe, should from then on be unchangeable. Yet programmes such as *Star Trek* and *Doctor Who* because they are in series form have it both ways when it comes to the Rigid Universe verses Uncertain Universe question. Then there are those niggly issues in *Timeless* such as how come there are two versions of Rufus Carlin, the one who died and the one who is now alive, when the series is meant to operate on a single timeline basis? *The Terminator* is also a single timeline universe, yet *Terminator Genisys* (2015) introduces the possibility of a multiverse. Make up your mind (or minds). And the idea of the multiverse raises the issue of empathy and sympathy for the multitude of characters. *Dark* is a brilliant Time Tale, yet with so many versions of incarnations past, present and future, even diehard fans are wont to ask, 'Which one am I meant to care about and root for?'

Another issue is that you're a hostage to the fortune if you set your story in the near future because time comes round quicker than you might think. 21 October 2015 was the future in 1989. The day in fact that Marty journeyed forwards in time at the beginning of *Back to the Future II* and so a big date for fans of the franchise when it came round for real. Marty (Michael J. Fox) and Doc Brown (Christopher Lloyd) even appeared on *Jimmy Kimmel Live* and discovered that in the real 2015 flying cars and hover boards hadn't been invented. The car licence plate in their fictional future was a barcode, yet oddly enough, by 2015 barcodes were everywhere except on licence plates. The fictional newspapers of 2015 also proved far from prophetic. Queen Diana? Sadly that never happened. A female US President? Well close, but no cigar. *Back to the Future II* also got it wrong that fax machines would still be in operation and now the scene where Marty is fired by fax seems oddly anachronistic. But getting the future wrong is understandable and forgivable, but surely making mistakes about the past perhaps is not. If you care to look, you'll find numerous examples of historical anachronisms in the Goofs section on IMDb for *Back to the Future*. But the simple answer to such criticisms is surely, 'Who cares? It's a movie! Pass the popcorn!'

Both *Travelers* and *Timeless* began as adventure series with great characters, strong narrative hooks and unexpected plot twists, but with both, the dramatic emphasis moved away from exciting escapades and more towards the complex domestic relationships between the characters themselves. Mission adventure became weekly soap opera. And then there's the issue of too much navel gazing. The classic *Doctor Who* protagonist of the '60s and '70s was essentially a Travelling Angel character. In many tales of this period the Doctor would arrive somewhere, get involved in some sort of ongoing problem and then find a way of solving it before travelling to his next adventure. The point about Travelling Angel characters is that they are essentially fixers who themselves don't need fixing and the stories of the classic period were rarely about the Doctor until it came to their regeneration. For example, the Jon Pertwee Doctor is made to face his greatest fear, the implication is that being so afraid means the time for his next regeneration has come. Although the modern era *Doctor Who* series still has the Travelling Angel concept, it is become much more about the nature of the Doctor.

Samuel Goldwyn supposedly asked his writers to come up with some new clichés. His point was that stories and plots do repeat themselves and what he was after was new versions of the sure fire hit. Yet sometimes watching a Time Tale can leave you with a feeling you've heard that before. For example, T.S. Eliot's line about the end being a beginning is quoted not only in *Dark* but also *Arrival* and *Needle in a Timestack*.

And one final pitfall to avoid in Time Tales: don't allow your story to be called *Space Man From Pluto*. That was the title suggested by an executive at Universal Pictures for *Back to the Future*. It was a serious memo but Steven Spielberg cleverly sent a note back saying, 'Thanks for the new title you sent over. It gave us all a big laugh! Keep 'em coming!' And so that was the end of that. Or indeed the beginning of something else.

## *The Adam Project*

Some people found *The Adam Project* – written by Jonathan Tropper, T.S. Nowlin, Jennifer Flackett and Mark Levin – to be a glorious romp, others a derivative hotchpotch. Either way *The Adam Project* certainly ticks the boxes of many Time Tale story tropes.

In the movie, time travel is made possible by projecting a wormhole in front of a spaceship and simply flying through it. As with many other time travel tales there is a lot of gobbledygook to explain all this such as 'with a powerful enough pulse you could generate a utilitarian wormhole in space.'

*The Adam Project* has one of those Time Tale plots where the villain, Sorian, takes control of time travel and so is able to interfere with the timestream in order to make her rich and powerful in the future (compare, for example, *Sisyphus)*. To do this, Sorian broke the protocol that time must not be altered, another typical story trope of the Time Tale, and as a result this has now caused a 'divergence' in time. The only option to prevent this happening is stop the possibility of time travel itself, again another regular story trope of the Time Tale.

But before all that there is Adam's immediate problem on arriving in present day, 2022, after travelling from the future, 2050, and that is he and his wormhole-creating time travelling spaceship are damaged and until it fixes itself (machines of the future can do that) Adam is essentially stranded. And stranded is yet another Time Tale story trope. And even when the spaceship has mended itself there's the problem of starting it up again because it will only respond to his DNA and that had been damaged in an attack before he went through the wormhole. So, in order to start up his time machine, Adam visits himself as a boy, who, of course, has his undamaged DNA. Again past and future selves meeting is a popular time travel story trope.

The older Adam, wearing his father's old jacket, has a moving scene with his mother, who, in the older Adam's time, is deceased. And the son or daughter meeting their dead mother or father is yet another classic scene in the Time Tale canon. On a less serious note there are numerous nods to other time travel stories. For example, whereas Doc Brown has a dog called Einie, named after Albert Einstein, Adam has a dog called Hawking, named after Stephen Hawking. And the dog naturally enough loves both Adams. There are various cinematic references and allusions to movies such as *The Terminator, E.T., Star Wars, The Last Starfighter, Flight of the Navigator, Field of Dreams* and *Top Gun*, plus the movie has a great soundtrack of rock music that occasionally reflects what's happening in the plot.

Time Tales always have to decide what to do about the issue of double identity in the same time. In *Alice*, for example, it causes all sorts of problems, whereas in the rebooted *Star Trek* it's not a problem at all. In *The Adam Project* the double identity question is referred to as 'parallel contact' and the rule is that it is possible to meet yourself and interact with them without too much fuss. In fact, the older Adam interacting with the younger Adam is essentially the whole plot of *The Adam Project*. And there's a joke with it too when Laura witnesses them together and Adam replies that she always wished she'd met him earlier.

Another well-known Time Tale story trope is the 'echo' or déjà vu, where a lost alternate time world somehow finds an echo in the one that survives. Adam points out to Laura that if he destroys time travel then he and Laura may never meet, but Laura isn't so despondent. In the story, the two time travelling Adams do indeed disappear when time travel is stopped (again compare *Sisyphus* and also films such as *Looper* and the German series *Dark*), for once time has been re-set their future selves logically must cease to exist. But this moment happens, perhaps not surprisingly, when the two Adams are playing catch with their father (a reference perhaps to *Field of Dreams*). As for Laura and her belief in that 'echo', well, there is a postscript scene where the older Adam does indeed meet Laura and another where the younger Adam shows more kindness to his mom.

So, *The Adam Project*, is it a glorious romp or derivative hotchpotch? Or could it even be both, depending perhaps on which timestream you're living in…

## 'Time is Out of Joint'

'Time is out of joint'. So said Hamlet. And typical of that young prince, he thinks it's all about himself – 'Oh curs'd spite, / That ever I was born to set it right.' Yet suppose time really is out of joint. Suppose too at the beginning of Creation, Time and the Universe were deliberately put out of kilter by a life-hating Energy. That is the premise of the Swidger Universe. But the Cosmos fought back with beings tasked with putting Life, Time and the Universe once again back into sync. And these beings of course are called *Swidgers*. And although cosmic beings, Swidgers are human in form, but unlike that self-absorbed Danish prince, Swidgers don't curse their role, they relish it.

Uniquely THE SWIDGERS bases its concept of Time on an idea in speculative science and that is known as Group Field Theory (GFT), a branch of quantum gravity that aims to establish the fundamentals of what everything from light and matter to space and time is actually made of.

All theories around the creation of the Universe ask the question 'Where did it come from?' and 'What was there before?'. THE SWIDGERS suggests that the Universe originated from an Energy that existed without Space or Time and therefore the questions of where or before are irrelevant as there was no where or when. And this idea is partly based on the field of science known as Condensate Cosmology, which is an area of physics that postulates the existence of mysterious algebraic entities named 'Spin Networks'. These networks constitute what Space and Time are made of and the central idea is that somehow they condensed to produce the Universe. Don't worry, reading THE SWIDGERS doesn't require a PhD in Physics for none of this speculative science is even discussed. After all, Granny in the story can't even read and William is a very young teenager, but the ideas do underpin its philosophy.

Most cultures and peoples have their own creation myth and the Swidgers are no different. For them the Universe came about when there was a divide of Power into Time, Space and Pure Energy. And that Pure Energy later transformed itself into Matter – stars, moons, custard – and ultimately of course Life. But in this mix there was a Dark Force Energy that didn't approve of Life, and so, in a wicked act of spite, put Time and Life out of sync, thus giving us the imperfect world in which we live. And that's why the Cosmos hit back with Swidgers. Yes, Time is, as Hamlet would say, 'out of joint', yet *Life*, *Time* and the *Universe* can be put once again in sync. Swidgers are only able to make tiny adjustments to our timepaths, small changes, one at a time. But, as the saying goes, *'Every Little Helps'*.

And that is the main theme of THE SWIDGERS: the smallest good, can right the biggest of wrongs.

And this is perhaps a good note on which to end our thoughts about time travel in a book where you can, like a time traveller, approach it in whatever order you see fit. Leap straight into those chapters which sound the most fun and then go back in the future to the ones with big words. Skip some altogether, as time travellers might skip those historical events that hold no interest to them, such as general elections in Belgium, the War of Jenkin's Ear or the invention of the shoe umbrella...

# Steven Moffat Interview

STEVEN MOFFAT HAS tackled more than his share of Time Tales, from contributing to – then becoming showrunner of – *Doctor Who*; toying with time shifts in both *Sherlock* and *Dracula*; and adapting *The Time Traveler's Wife* for television. We asked Steven his thoughts regarding the concept of Time and Time Travel.

**Were there hard and fast rules regarding time travel in the *Doctor Who* universe?**

SM: There isn't a big book of how time travel works in *Doctor Who*. For the most part time travel in *Doctor Who* works to deliver the Doctor somewhere interesting, where he has an adventure and leaves. So it's a bus. I tended to do more messing about with time travel but for the most part *Doctor Who* is a delivery system of the Doctor into a particular adventure. The big thing is, does it make any sense to change Time? I'm sure that the Doctor would answer something along the lines of 'Time happens once. You're not getting a second go.' And then he would elaborate, 'But of course if you did change Time you wouldn't know, would you? Because instantly Time would have always been that way.' But how would you know? The debate on *Day of the Doctor* – which is the one where he averts the destruction of Gallifrey – is did he change Time? Did he alter the outcome of that event in his memory? Or did it go one way and then the other? Embedded in that is a complete misunderstanding. Time happened once and if you changed it that's the way it always happened. But I think that this just probably demonstrates that time travel isn't possible.

As for the rules of Time, I think in *Doctor Who* they operate like this: I think they're specific to the story. In some stories the Doctor talks as if Time can be rewritten and we've used that line, and in other stories he behaves as if it is immutable, whatever he does it will turn out the way it always did. We get round it because the Doctor has some flummery about how there are 'fixed points', there are some things that change and some things that can't be changed – 'and I with my giant Time Lord brain can understand it and you, mere mortals sitting in the audience, don't have a hope.' So it's a get-out, because we have used both versions, sometimes in the same story but, you know, none of us are alone in this. *Back to the Future* in the space of one movie does both. Is the current version of that town the result of Michael J. Fox's intervention? Well in some respects no because he goes back in time and gives that guy in the café the idea of becoming mayor, which he already is back in the future, but in other respects Marty changes everything. So the question in time travel is always: if you are going to time travel are the changes you are going to make tomorrow already in place before you leave? Or, nonsensically, do they only appear after you've done the journey? *Back to the Future* has it both ways in the space of one movie. And that's not a criticism of it, it's a fantastic movie.

**It's true that time travel tales have their own peculiar problems.**

SM: There's a famous *Doctor Who* story, '*City of Death*', where the Doctor has to run and get a taxi to get to the TARDIS to travel back in time to stop the baddie changing history. Why doesn't he stop for lunch? I mean what difference does it make if he's going to run to a time machine?! And if the guy had succeeded in doing this, he would already have succeeded. It would have happened instantly or always or whatever. Any of those things. Or none of those things. I mean, you can cut the scene where he runs back and you're pretending it's an emergency but that's one of the big ones in *Doctor Who*. The Doctor is always running. He owns a time machine. He doesn't have to run anywhere.

**Isn't that a hangover from a time where he couldn't travel anywhere with accuracy?**

**SM:** And that's the classic version of *Doctor Who*. And they were quite sensible suggesting that he can't actually work it, so he's unable to use it in the middle of the adventure.

**Unlike most stories, *The Time Traveler's Wife* has a Block Universe, one where time can't be changed.**

**SM:** The time travel in *The Time Traveler's* Wife by Audrey Niffenegger is very strict, nothing changes at all. It's a Block Universe it's just set and it doesn't matter what he [Henry, the Time Traveler] does, it's going to be the same. That doesn't mean he can't make decisions, he does make decisions, but he knows what the results are going to be. And I think there what you've got is an acceptance particularly of death and there are so many tales where time travellers go back to try to put a death right, stop the death happening and I haven't really found one where it works, it's almost as if one of the morality questions is saying death is simply part of life.

**With *The Time Traveler's Wife* adapting the book to your series, how do you make something dramatic when you know everything that's going to happen?**

**SM:** To me it was fascinating. Yes, we know *we* know but she didn't know that Henry would be a husband and finding the right perfect dramatic moment for her to find out struck me as being one of the keys to it. Because – oddly – that moment doesn't happen in her book [see the section **Story Information and the Television Adaptation** of *The Time Traveler's Wife* on page 60 for details of Moffat's adaptation]. And I used ruthlessly the death of Henry's mother to say that nothing can be changed. It's one thing for Audrey to write very beautifully about it in the prose about how that works but that's not a scene. If you want somebody to remember something, attach it to an emotion, otherwise it just goes. So it had to be something awful.

**What's the appeal of the time travel story? One of the things we've been thinking about, especially after COVID, is whether it's simple wishful thinking: if only we could go back and fix things. Is that a zeitgeisty thing?**

SM: It could be it. I suppose the thing I think about time travel is that given that today physicists and theorists of this field – many of whom are *Doctor Who* fans by the way – absolutely reject the idea that this will ever be possible. So why do we dream it all the time? Why do we accept it unequivocally in fiction that we can travel in time? We don't accept every impossible thing in a story. We have an idea that sits inside in our heads that, of all the impossible things, it is somehow acceptable to me logically, but someone who can turn himself into the colour blue isn't. There's loads of stories we don't tell because we think they are ridiculous, genuinely impossible. The biggest objection that everyone raises to Superman is the glasses. The fact that a pair of glasses can disguise who he is. Everyone knocks this but not the fact that he can fly! There are many things that we would not accept in fiction because it's too stupid – and I've written a few of them – but we *are* willing to believe time travel and that means something about the world.

# Index

**Literature and Plays**

11/22/63 (Stephen King 2011) 135, 191

*Absolutely Inflexible* (Robert Silverberg 1956 short story) 107, 121

*Alice's Adventures in Wonderland* (Lewis Carroll 1865) 197

*Alice Through the Looking Glass* (Lewis Carroll 1871) 197–198, 255

*All You Zombies* (Robert A. Heinlein 1959 short story) 138

*Anacronópete, El* (Enrique Gaspar y Rimban 1887) 68, 70,

*Armageddon 2419 A.D.* (Philip Francis Nowlan 1928) 225

*Aura* (Catols Fuentes 1962) 65

*Beatrice the Sixteenth: Being the Personal Narrative of Mary Hatherby, M.B., Explorer and Geographer* (Irene Clyde 1909) 221–223

*Berkeley Square* (John L. Baderston play 1926) 60, 62, 88, 91–92, 99, 252, 260, 264

*Bourne Identity, The* (Robert Ludlum 1980) 207

*By His Bootstraps* (Robert A. Heinlein 1941) 121–122, 204, 281

*Child in Time, The* (Ian McEwan 1987) 93, 289

*Christmas Carol, A* (Charles Dickens 1843) 11, 19–41, 97, 116, 145, 191, 208, 231, 289

*Clock that went Backwards, The* (Edward Page Mitchell short story 1881) 68, 88

*Communicating Doors* (Alan Ayckbourn play 1994) 83

*Connecticut Yankee in King Arthur's Court, A* (Mark Twain 1889) 91, 295, 299

*Day with Wilbur Robinson, A* (William Joyce 1990) 106

*Dead End* (Malcolm Jameson 1941) 98

*Dead Past, The* (Isaac Asimov 1956 short story) 98

*Doctor Faustus* (Christopher Marlowe play c1592) 215

*E for Effort* (T.L. Sherred 1947 novella) 98

*End of Eternity, The* (Isaac Asimov 1955) 110

*Erased* (AKA *Boku Dake Ga Inai Machi*, Kei Sanbe 2012–16 Manga series) 152

*Experiment with Time* (J.W. Dunn 1927) 183–184

*Far Side of the Bell-shaped Curve, The* (Robert Silverberg 1982 short story) 172

*FlashForward* (Robert J. Sawyer 1999) 148

*Flight to Forever* (Poul Anderson 1950) 190

*Gap in the Curtain, The* (John Buchan 1932) 184–185
*Ghosts, The* (Antonia Barber 1969) 87
*Ghosts of the Mail, The* (Charles Dickens 1837 short story) 216
*Gianni* (Robert Silverberg 1982 short story) 52–53
*Girl Who Leapt Through Time, The* (Yasutaka Tsutsui 1965) 87
*Girl in the Golden Atom* (Ray Cummings 1919) 253
*Golden Man, The* (Philip K. Dick 1954 short story) 143–144
*Green Mile* (Stephen King 1996) 248
*Gulliver's Travels* (Jonathan Swift 1726) 211
*Harry Potter* (series J.K. Rowling from 1997) 87, 91, 171, 195, 224
*Haunted Man*, The (Charles Dickens 1848) 206
*Here and Now and Then* (Mike Chen 2019) 248
*Hitchhiker's Guide to the Galaxy, The* (Douglas Adams 1979) 65, 139
*House on the Strand, The* (Daphne du Maurier 1969) 87, 190–191
*I Killed Hitler* (Ralph Milne Farely 1941 short story) 279
*I See You* (Damon Knight 1976 short story) 98–99
*In the Tube* (E.F. Benson 1923 short story) 218–219
*Jest of Hahalaba, The* (Edward John Moreton Drax Plunkett 1928 play) 143, 182, 185
*Lest Darkness Fall* (L. Sprague de Camp 1933) 88, 223

*Life After Life* (Kate Atkinson 2013) 210
*Life and Opinions of Tristram Shandy, Gentleman, The* (Laurence Stern 1759) 49, 252
*Looking Backward 2000–1887* (Edward Bellamy 1888) 225
*Lost Hearts* (M.R. James 1895 short story) 213
*Lost Horizon* (James Hilton 1933) 221, 248
*Man in His Time* (Brian Aldiss 1965 short story) 245
*Man in the High Castle* (Philip K. Dick 1962) 223
*Man Who Woke, The* (Laurence Manning 1933) 226
*Many Mansions* (Robert Silverberg 1973 short story) 64
*Memoirs of the Year 2500* (Louis-Sébastien Mercier 1771) 225
*Memories of the Twentieth Century* Samuel Madden 1733) 68
*Midnight at the Pera Palace: The Birth of Modern Istanbul* (Charles King 2014) 82
*Millennium* (John Varley 1976) 98–99
*Mysterious Stranger* (Mark Twain 1916 unfinished story) 256
*Needle in a Timestack* (Robert Silverberg 1970) 208, 302
*Open Door, The* (Margaret Oliphant 1882 short story) 216–217
*Orlando: A Biography* (Virginia Woolf 1928) 175, 229
*Outlander* series (Diana Gabaldon from 1991) 90
*Paycheck* (Philip K. Dick 1952 short story) 45, 55, 67, 207

# INDEX

*Picture of Dorian Gray, A* (Oscar Wilde 1890) 211, 229
*Pleasant Evening, A* (Robert W. Chambers 1896 short story) 218
*Portrait Painter's Story, The* (Charles Dickens 1861 short story) 218
*Private Eye* (Henry Kuttner and C.L. Moore 1949 short story)
*Queer Story of Brownlow's Newspaper, The* (H.G. Wells 1932 short story) 182–184
*Rip Van Winkle* (Washington Irving 1819) 68, 225,
*Second Trip, The* (Robert Silverberg 1972) 207
*She: A History of Adventure* (H. Rider Haggard 1887) 211
*Skull, The* (Philip K Dick 1952 short story) 44–45, 122
*Slaughterhouse-Five* (Kurt Vonnegut 1969) 47, 191
*Sleeper Awakes, The* (H.G. Wells 1910) 206
*Sound of Thunder, A* (Ray Bradbury 1952 short story) 154–155, 158
*SS-GB* (Len Deighton 1978) 223
*Star Rover, The* (Jack London 1915) 199
*Story of the Amulet, A* (Edith Nesbit 1906) 86
*Sultana's Dream* (Begum Rokaya 1905) 221–222
*Swidgers, The: The Time That Never Was* (Steve Nallon 2022 + sequels) 13, 50–51, 59, 63, 81, 102–103, 109, 141, 148, 175–176, 187, 192. 200, 213, 224, 242, 246, 255, 270, 285, 304–306

*Sziriusz* (Ferenc Herczeg) 71
*Tale of the Ragged Mountains* (Edgar Allan Poe 1844) 68,
*Technicolor Time Machine, The* (Harry Harrison 1967) 124
*There Will Be Time* (Poul Anderson 1972) 103
*Time and Again* (Jack Finney 1970) 91
*Time Machine, The* (H.G. Wells 1895) 53–54, 67–71, 76, 82, 194, 199, 250, 258, 265, 286–287,
*Time Story, The* (Ray Cummings 1921 short story)
*Time Traveler's Wife, The* (Audrey Niffenegger 2003) 21, 48, 50, 60–63, 103, 171, 181, 190–191, 196, 262, 264, 280, 290, 294–295, 307, 309
*Tom's Midnight Garden* (Philippa Pearce 1958) 85
*Toynbee Convector, The* (Ray Bradbury 1984 short story) 17
*Trips* (Robert Silverberg 1974 short story) 64, 107,
*Uncle Cornelius His Story* (George MacDonald 1869 short story) 217
*Variable Man, The* (Philip K. Dick 1953) 155
*Version Control* (Dexter Palmer 2016) 299
*Via the Time Accelerator* (F.J. Bridge 1931 short story) 120
*Vintage Season* (Henry Kuttner & C.L. Moore 1946) 283–284
*Was it an Illusion* (Amelia B. Edwards 1881 short story) 216
*We Can Remember it for You Wholesale* (Philip K. Dick 1966) 207

*What We Learned from the Morning's Newspaper* (Robert Silverberg 1972 short story) 186
*World Jones Made, The* (Philip K. Dick 1956) 256
*Zig Zag* (José Carlos Somoza 2006) 99

**Films**

*12 Monkeys* (1995) 16, 72, 112–113, 160, 295, 299
*13 Going On 30* (2004) 87
*17 Again* (2009)
*41* (2007) 80
*2067* (2020) 160
*A.I. Artificial Intelligence* (2001) 215
*A.P.E.X.* (1994) 159
*About Time* (2013) 103, 190
*Amazing Mr Blunden, The* (1972 & 2021) 89
*Arrival* (2016) 65, 302
*Austin Powers: International Man of Mystery* (1997 + sequels) 48–49, 79, 108, 163, 171, 191, 226, 261, 296
*Avengers: Endgame* (2019) 167, 274
*Back to the Future* (1985 + sequels) 11, 13, 19–41, 43, 58, 72, 75–77, 88, 99, 104, 137, 143, 149, 157, 171, 177, 180, 185, 187, 194, 198, 207–208, 221, 226, 238, 261–262, 264, 273, 277–278, 295–299, 301–302, 308
*Bedknobs and Broomsticks* (1971) 215
*Before I Fall* (2017) 114, 117
*Berkeley Square* (1933) 60, 62, 88, 92, 99, 252, 260, 264

*Beyond the Infinite Two Minutes* (2020) 111, 124, 143
*Big* (1988) 229
*Biggles* (1986) 89
*Bill and Ted's Excellent Adventure* (1989) 73, 189, 191, 194, 215, 283, 296
*Blood Punch* (2014) 118
*Brigadoon* (1954) 246
*Caller, The* (2011) 98–99, 125
*Camp Slaughter* (2005) 118
*Chien Andalou, Un* (1929) 200
*Clockstoppers* (2002) 228, 246
*Curious Case of Benjamin Button, The* (2008) 229, 255
*Day Time Ended, The* (1980) 88
*Dead Zone* (2001) 203
*Deadpool* (2016 + sequel)) 215, 234, 296, 299
*Déjà Vu* (2006) 96, 153, 261
*Demolition Man* (1993) 162, 226
*Dimensions* (2011) 251
*Ditto* (2000) 178
*Diverge* (2016) 160
*Doctor Strange* (2016) 274
*Donnie Darko* (2001) 130, 166
*Doppelgänger* (AKA *Journey to the Far Side of the Sun* 1969) 162
*Edge of Tomorrow* (2014) 43, 114, 118
*Endless, The* (2017) 114, 118
*Erased* (AKA *Boku Dake Ga Inai Machi* 2016) 152
*Eternal Sunshine of the Spotless Mind* (2004) 206
*Eternals* (2021) 214
*Evil Dead: Army of Darkness* (1992) 91
*Extinct* (2021) 87,
*Felix the Cat Trifles with Time* (1925) 91
*Fiddlers Three* (1944) 298

# INDEX

*Field of Dreams* (1989) 215, 303–304
*Final Countdown* (1980) 88
*Final Destination* (2000) 204
*Flash, The* (2023) 167, 195, 207–208, 274
*Fountain, The* (2006) 215
*Freejack* (1992) 212
*Frequency* (2000) 178
*Frequently Asked Questions About Time Travel* (2009) 80, 130, 1771
*From Time to Time* (2009) 80
*Fun2shh ... Dudes in the 10th Century* (2003) 274
*Galaxy Quest* (1999) 296
*Girl Who Leapt Through Time, The* (2006) 87
*Groundhog Day* (1993) 16, 26, 58, 115–116, 118, 133, 212, 238, 273, 289, 299
*Happy Death Day* (2017 + sequels) 114, 118, 238
*Harry Potter and the Prisoner of Azkaban* (2004) 171
*Hellzapoppin'* (1941) 49,
*Highlander* (1986) 213, 299
*Hitch in Time, A* (1978) 298
*Hot Tub Time Machine* (2010) 72, 87, 296
*Idiocracy* (2006) 226
*Infinite Man, The* (2014) 118
*Inglorious Basterds* (2009) 223
*Intolerance* (1916) 91, 229
*Idaho Transfer* (1973) 287
*It Happened Tomorrow* (1944) 185–186
*It's A Wonderful Life* (1946) 27, 40, 162, 221, 229, 288
*Ivan Vasilievich Changes Profession* (1973) 226
*Jacket, The* (2005) 46, 197, 199

*Jacob's Ladder* (1990) 46–47, 49, 199
*Jetée, La* (1962) 160, 289
*Kate & Leopold* (2001) 80
*Knight Before Christmas, The* (2019) 87, 236
*Lake House, The* (2006) 178
*Last Night in Soho* (2021) 93–94, 210
*Lola* (2022) 178
*Looper* (2012) 13, 58, 114, 116–117, 128, 172, 280, 312
*Lost Horizon* (1937) 221, 248
*Lost Memories* (2002) 223
*Love and Time Travel* (2016) 91
*Love Story 2050* (2008) 274
*Man Who Haunted Himself, The* (1970) 169
*Map of Tiny Perfect Things, The* (2021) 118
*Mare, Il* (2000) 178
*Matter of Life and Death, A* (1946) 228
*Meet the Robinsons* (2007) 106–107
*Memento* (2000) 210
*Men in Black* (1997 + sequels) 234
*Midnight in Paris* (2011) 90
*Millennium* (1989) 160
*Mine Games* (AKA *The Evil Within* 2012) 118
*Minority Report* (2002) 147, 199
*Mirage* (*Durante la tormenta* 2018) 23, 27, 89, 100, 208
*Mirai* (2018) 282–283
*Mr Destiny* (1990) 289
*Mr. Nobody* (2009) 168
*Mr Peabody & Mr Sherman* (2014) 285
*Navigator: A Medieval Odyssey, The* (1988) 229

*Needle in a Timestack* (2021) 208, 302
*Night has a Thousand Eyes* (1948) 203
*Old* (2021) 247
*On a Clear Day You Can See Forever* (1970) 174
*Palm Springs* (2020) 18
*Peggy Sue Got Married* (1986) 290
*Petite Maman* (2021) 92–93
*Philadelphia Experiment, The* (1984) 89
*Planet of the Apes* (1968) 221, 246, 286
*Pleasantville* (1998) 230
*Premonition* (2007) 203
*Primer* (2004) 45, 72, 262, 289
*Purple Rose of Cairo, The* (1985)
*Repeaters* (2010) 114, 118
*Run Lola Run* (1998) 114, 131–132
*Seconds* (1966) 212
*Self/Less* (2015) 212
*Shining, The* (1980) 83
*Sleeper* (1973) 226
*Sliding Doors* (1998) 236, 264
*Spider-man: Far From Home* (2019) 167
*Split Infinity* (1992) 80
*Somewhere in Time* (1980) 60, 83, 92, 123, 231
*Sound of my Voice* (2011) 160
*Source Code* (2011) 114, 234
*Star Trek IV: The Voyage Home* (1986) 16, 123, 160–161, 181
*Star Trek* (2009) 161, 172, 303
*Superman* (1978) 195, 246, 274
*Sziriusz* (1942) 71,
*Tenet* (2020) 229, 254, 257
*Terminator, The* (1984 + sequels) 43, 46, 70, 112, 122, 138, 156, 159–160, 191–192, 231–234, 264, 273, 280, 287, 295, 300, 303
*Time Bandits* (1981) 80
*Time Flies* (1944) 72
*Time Lapse* (2014) 147
*Time Machine, The* (1960) 76, 97
*Time Trap* (2017) 90, 213, 248
*Time Travelers, The* (1964) 98, 135
*Timecop* (1994) 195
*Timecrimes* (Los cronocrímenes 2007) 114, 118, 122
*Timeline* (2003) 234
*Timescape* (1992) 88, 112, 158, 283–284, 295
*Tomorrow I'll Wake Up and Scald Myself with Tea* (AKA *Zltra vstanu a opaří Čajem* 1977) 153, 158, 172–173
*Total Recall* (1990) 207
*Trancers* (1984) 87, 112, 228, 237
*Triangle* (2009) 18, 57, 133
*Turn Back the Clock* (1933) 90
*Unbreakable* (2000) 203
*Wayne's World* (1992) 49
*When We First Met* (2018) 235
*Where Do We Go From Here* (1945) 88,
*Wrinkle in Time, A* (2018) 221
*Yesterday* (2019) 224
*X-Men* (2000 + sequels) 234, 274
*Your Name* (2016) 178
*Zelig* (1983) 229

**TV and Streaming**
*Adam Adamant Lives!* (BBC 1966–67)
*Adam Project, The* (Netflix 2022) 162, 209, 264, 302–304
*Agents of S.H.I.E.L.D.* (ABC 2013–20) 274

# INDEX

*Alice* (SBS TV 2020) 103–105, 107, 121, 129–130, 169–170, 176, 178, 188, 192, 202–203, 228–229, 292, 303

*ARQ* (Netflix 2016) 114, 117–118

*Bernard's Watch* (ITV 1997–2005) 228

*Blackadder Back and Forth* (BBC 1999) 237

*Captain Z-Ro* (KKTV) 1951–56) 74–75, 110

*Catweazle* (ITV 1970–71) 87, 162, 226

*Children of the Stones* (ITV 1977) 132–133

*Christmas Do-Over* (ABC Family 2006) 114

*Class* (BBC 2016) 80–81

*Clementine's Enchanted Journey* (Antenne 2 1985–1987) 208

*Crime Traveller* (BBC 1997) 237

*Dark* (Netflix 2017–20) 13, 16, 45, 49, 71–72, 99, 116–117, 121, 128–129, 137, 146, 154, 160, 162, 167–168, 188–190, 198, 209, 262, 266, 272, 283, 287, 299–300, 302, 304

*Doctor Who* (BBC from 1963) 17, 23, 29, 56, 72–76, 79–80, 83, 89, 99, 108–110, 121 123, 132, 161, 171, 179–181, 187, 193, 198, 203, 206–209, 212, 215, 231, 246–247, 251, 262, 264, 273, 279–280, 283, 286, 290–294, 300–302, 307, 328–31

*Devs* (FX 2020) 96, 140, 145–146, 266–270

*Early Edition* (CBS 1996–2000) 186

*Erased* (AKA *Boku Dake Ga Inai Machi* Netflix 2017) 152

*Family Guy* (Fox from 1999) 236–237

*Five Days to Midnight* (SF 2004) 147

*FlashForward* (ABC 2009–10) 148, 204

*Flipside of Dominck Hide, The* (BBC 1980) 128, 181, 249, 295

*Fringe* (Fox 2008–13) 110

*Futurama* (Fox/Comedy Central/Hulu from 1999) 162, 226, 237, 296

*Goodnight Sweetheart* (BBC 1993–99) 80, 237, 299

*Heroes* (NBC 2006–10) 153, 204

*If I Hadn't Met You,* (AKA *Si no t'hagués conegut* TV3 2018) 48, 165–166, 170

*In the Shadow of the Moon* (Netflix 2019) 137, 192, 256, 280, 287

*It's About Time* (CBS 1966–67) 226, 237

*King: Youngwonui Gunjoo (Eternal Monarch), The* (SBS TV 2020) 248

*Lazarus Project, The* (Sky from 2022) 160

*Legends of Tomorrow* (CW 2016–22) 77

*Life After Life* (BBC 2022) 210

*Life on Mars* (BBC 2006 + sequels) 90–91, 237

*Loki* (Disney + from 2021) 111

*Magic Boomerang, The* (ABC 1965–66) 228

*Midnight at the Pera Palace* (2023) 79, 82–83, 115, 156

*Ministerio del Tiempo, El* (LA 1 2015–2020) 111,

*Mirai Sentai Timeranger* (TV Asahi 2000–2001) 237
*Mirror Mirror* (Network 10 1995) 85, 169
*Naked* (Netflix 2017) 118
*New Amsterdam* (Fox 2008) 237
*Next* (2007) 144, 148, 204
*Night Gallery* (NBC 1970–73) 83–84
*OA, The* (Netflix 2016–19) 251
*Old Guard* (Netflix 2020) 215
*Outer Limits* (ABC 1963–65) 128, 227
*Outlaws* (CBS 1986–87) 88, 162, 226
*Phil of the Future* (Disney 2004–06) 162, 226
*Primeval* (ITV 2007–11) 85,
*Quantum Leap* (NBC 1989–93) 79, 136, 157, 231, 286, 291
*Ray Bradbury Theater, The* (HBO/USA 1985–92) 155
*Red Dwarf* (BBC/Dave from 1988) 138, 237
*Russian Doll* (Netflix from 2019) 118–119
*Sapphire and Steel* (ITV 1979–82) 110
*See You Yesterday* (Netflix 2019) 77, 152
*Seven Days* (UPN 1998–2001) 153
*Sijipeuseu: The Myth (Sisyphus* JTBC 2021) 79, 97, 105, 125, 159
*Star Trek* (NBC 1966 + sequels) 17, 31, 76, 82, 90, 145, 156, 161, 169, 173–174, 189, 193, 198–199, 214, 246, 287, 293, 295, 300

*Stranger Things* (Netflix from 2016) 199
*That Was Then* (ABC 2002) 88, 288
*Thrill Seekers (*AKA *The Time Shifters* TBS 1999) 284
*Time Stalkers* (CBS 1987) 39
*Time Traveler's Wife, The* (HBO 2022) 48, 60–63, 307, 309
*Time Trax* (Primetime 1993–94) 237
*Time Tunnel, The* (ABC 1966–67) 60, 78–79, 95–96, 113, 178, 290
*Timeless* (NBC 2016–18) 72, 99, 123, 153–154, 157–158, 162, 177, 189–190, 195, 207, 209, 234, 271, 273, 286, 289, 298–301
*Timewasters* (ITV 2017–19) 84, 237, 299
*Tom's Midnight Garden* (BBC 1980) 85
*Tomorrow People, The* (ITV 1973–79) 155, 287, 291
*Torchwood* (BBC 2006–2011) 110
*Travelers* (Showcase/Netflix 2016–18) 16, 58, 104, 130, 136–137, 145, 157, 159–160, 177, 181, 191–193, 204–206, 232, 234, 286–287, 295–296, 298, 301
*Tru Calling* (Fox 2003–05) 238
*Twice in a Lifetime* (CTV 1999–2001) 288
*Twilight Zone* (CBS 1959–64) 114, 131, 156, 246
*Umbrella Academy, The* (Netflix from 2019) 274
*Voyagers* (NBC 1982–83) 153

Also published by **LUATH PRESS**

**The Time That Never Was**
Swidgers Book One

Steve Nallon

ISBN: 9781910022610 PBK £8.99

HE CAN'T LIE, HE CAN'T HARM BUT HE CAN SAVE LIVES

William Arthur is no ordinary teenager. He is a Swidger, a person who can sense future catastrophes and hinder your timepath to certain peril. Only now he's discovering that his time-bending powers go far beyond mere accident prevention.

After a mind-boggling incident leaves him confused and questioning his place in the world, William is rescued by a wise and bizarre lady by the name of 'Granny'. Together they embark on an epic journey of hilarity, danger and intrigue. Will he learn the true nature of his gift? And can he evade the dark forces that would use his powers for evil?

ALL WILL BE REVEALED... IN TIME

*Grabs you from the beginning and doesn't let go. Steve is a master mimic and uses all his skills to create a powerful and dramatic tale of mystery!*

RORY BREMNER, BAFTA winning writer and performer

*A rambunctious riot of a book with a totally unpredictable plot – I never knew where I was going to be taken next! –*

JOSEPH ELIOT, author of *The Good Hawk, The Broken Raven* and *The Burning Swift*

*Beguiling, inventive and magical: Nallon has conjured up a perfect world and a perfect read. A dazzling piece of fiction.*

JONATHAN MAITLAND

*Steve Nallon is an experienced and formidable talent and this departure into YA fantasy may win him a whole new generation of fans.*

JENNY LECOAT, screenwriter, novelist and author of *Hedy's Girl and Another Mother's Son*

Details of books published by Luath Press can be found at:
**www.luath.co.uk**

# **Luath** Press Limited

*committed to publishing well written books worth reading*

LUATH PRESS takes its name from Robert Burns, whose little collie Luath (*Gael.*, swift or nimble) tripped up Jean Armour at a wedding and gave him the chance to speak to the woman who was to be his wife and the abiding love of his life. Burns called one of the 'Twa Dogs' Luath after Cuchullin's hunting dog in Ossian's *Fingal*.
Luath Press was established in 1981 in the heart of Burns country, and is now based a few steps up the road from Burns' first lodgings on Edinburgh's Royal Mile. Luath offers you distinctive writing with a hint of unexpected pleasures.
Most bookshops in the UK, the US, Canada, Australia, New Zealand and parts of Europe, either carry our books in stock or can order them for you. To order direct from us, please send a £sterling cheque, postal order, international money order or your credit card details (number, address of cardholder and expiry date) to us at the address below. Please add post and packing as follows: UK – £1.00 per delivery address; overseas surface mail – £2.50 per delivery address; overseas airmail – £3.50 for the first book to each delivery address, plus £1.00 for each additional book by airmail to the same address. If your order is a gift, we will happily enclose your card or message at no extra charge.

**Luath** Press Limited
543/2 Castlehill
The Royal Mile
Edinburgh EH1 2ND
Scotland
Telephone: +44 (0)131 225 4326 (24 hours)
Email: sales@luath.co.uk
Website: www.luath.co.uk